Instructor's Solutions Manual

to accompany

Elementary Statistics
A Brief Version

Fourth Edition

Allan G. Bluman
Professor Emeritus
Community College of Allegheny County

Prepared by
Sally Robinson
South Plains College

Higher Education

Boston   Burr Ridge, IL   Dubuque, IA   New York   San Francisco   St. Louis
Bangkok   Bogotá   Caracas   Kuala Lumpur   Lisbon   London   Madrid   Mexico City
Milan   Montreal   New Delhi   Santiago   Seoul   Singapore   Sydney   Taipei   Toronto

The McGraw·Hill Companies

Instructor's Solutions Manual to accompany
ELEMENTARY STATISTICS: A BRIEF VERSION, FOURTH EDITION
ALLAN G. BLUMAN

Published by McGraw-Hill Higher Education, an imprint of The McGraw-Hill Companies, Inc., 1221 Avenue of the Americas, New York, NY 10020. Copyright © 2008 by The McGraw-Hill Companies, Inc. All rights reserved.

1 2 3 4 5 6 7 8 9 0 BKM/BKM 0 9 8 7 6

ISBN: 978-0-07-328342-5
MHID: 0-07-328342-8

www.mhhe.com

Contents

Solutions to the Exercises

1   The Nature of Probability and Statistics   *1*
2   Frequency Distributions and Graphs   *3*
3   Data Description   *22*
4   Probability and Counting Rules   *57*
5   Discrete Probability Distributions   *75*
6   The Normal Distribution   *86*
7   Confidence Intervals and Sample Size   *115*
8   Hypothesis Testing   *125*
9   Testing the Difference Between Two Means, Two Variances,
         and Two Proportions   *149*
10   Correlation and Regression   *175*
11   Other Chi-Square Tests   *194*

Appendix   *219*

Preface

This manual includes solutions to odd and even exercises in *Elementary Statistics: A Brief Version*, Fourth Edition, by Allan G. Bluman. Solutions are worked out step-by-step where appropriate and generally follow the same procedures used in the examples in the textbook. Answers may be carried to several decimal places to increase accuracy and to facilitate checking. Slight variations may occur in answers due to rounding. Graphs are included with the solutions when appropriate or required. They are intended to convey a general idea and may not be to scale.

Caution: Answers generated using graphing calculators such as the TI-83 may vary from those shown in this manual.

Chapter 1 - The Nature of Probability and Statistics

1. Descriptive statistics describes a set of data. Inferential statistics uses a set of data to make predictions about a population.

2. Probability deals with events that occur by chance. It is used in gambling and insurance.

3. Answers will vary.

4. A population is the totality of all subjects under study. A sample is a subgroup of the population.

5. When the population is large, the researcher saves time and money using samples. Samples are used when the units must be destroyed.

6.
a. Inferential   e. Inferential
b. Descriptive   f. Inferential
c. Descriptive   g. Descriptive
d. Descriptive   h. Inferential

7.
a. Ratio   f. Ordinal
b. Ordinal   g. Ratio
c. Ratio   h. Ratio
d. Interval   i. Nominal
e. Ratio   j. Ratio

8.
a. Quantitative   e. Qualitative
b. Qualitative   f. Quantitative
c. Quantitative   g. Qualitative
d. Quantitative

9.
a. Discrete   e. Discrete
b. Continuous   f. Discrete
c. Continuous   g. Continuous
d. Continuous

10.
a. 42.75 – 42.85 miles   d. 17.5 – 18.5 tons
b. 1.55 – 1.65 milliliters   e. 93.75 – 93.85 ounces
c. 5.355 – 5.365 ounces   f. 39.5 – 40.5 inches

11. Random samples are selected by using chance methods or random numbers.

11. continued
Systematic samples are selected by numbering each subject and selecting every kth number. Stratified samples are selected by dividing the population into groups and selecting from each group. Cluster samples are selected by using intact groups called clusters.

12.
a. Cluster   d. Systematic
b. Systematic   e. Stratified
c. Random

13. Answers will vary.

14. Answers will vary.

15. Answers will vary.

16. Answers will vary.

17.
a. Experimental   c. Observational
b. Observational   d. Experimental

18.
a. Independent variable - type of pill taken
Dependent variable - number of infections
b. Independent variable - color of car
Dependent variable - running red lights
c. Independent variable - level of hostility
Dependent variable - cholesterol level
d. Independent variable - type of diet
Dependent variable - blood pressure

19. Answers will vary. Possible answers include:
(a) overall health of participants, amount of exposure to infected individuals through the workplace or home
(b) gender and/or age of driver, time of day
(c) diet, general health, heredity factors
(d) amount of exercise, heredity factors

20. Only twenty people were used in the study.

21. Claims can be proven only if the entire population is used.

22. The statement is meaningless since there is no definition of "the road less traveled." Also, there is no way to know that for <u>every</u>

22. continued
100 women, 91 would say that they have taken "the road less traveled."

23. Since the results are not typical, the advertisers selected only a few people for whom the product worked extremely well.

24. There is no mention of how this conclusion was obtained.

25. "74% more calories" than what? No comparison group is stated.

26. Since the word "may" is used, there is no guarantee that the product will help fight cancer.

27. What is meant by "24 hours of acid control"?

28. No. There are many other factors that contribute to criminal behavior.

29. Possible reasons for conflicting results: The amount of caffeine in the coffee or tea or the brewing method.

30. Answers will vary.

31. Answers will vary.

32. Answers will vary.

CHAPTER QUIZ
1. True
2. False, it is a data value.
3. False, the highest level is ratio.
4. False, it is stratified sampling.
5. False, it is a quantitative variable.
6. True
7. False, it is 5.5-6.5 inches.
8. c
9. b
10. d
11. a
12. c
13. a
14. Descriptive, inferential
15. Gambling, insurance
16. Population
17. Sample

18.
a. Saves time

18. continued
b. Saves money
c. Use when population is infinite

19.
a. Random   c. Cluster
b. Systematic   d. Stratified

20. Quasi-experimental

21. Random

22.
a. Descriptive   d. Inferential
b. Inferential   e. Inferential
c. Descriptive

23.
a. Nominal   d. Interval
b. Ratio   e. Ratio
c. Ordinal

24.
a. Continuous   d. Continuous
b. Discrete   e. Discrete
c. Continuous

25.
a. $47.5 - 48.5$ seconds   d. $13.65 - 13.75$ p
b. $0.555 - 0.565$ centimeters e. $6.5 - 7.5$ feet
c. $9.05 - 9.15$ quarts

EXERCISE SET 2-2

1. Frequency distributions are used to organize data in a meaningful way, to facilitate computational procedures for statistics, to make it easier to draw charts and graphs, and to make comparisons among different sets of data.

2. Categorical distributions are used with nominal or ordinal data, ungrouped distributions are used with data having a small range, and grouped distributions are used when the range of the data is large.

3.
a. $11.5 - 18.5$, $\frac{12+18}{2} = \frac{30}{2} = 15$, $18.5 - 11.5 = 7$
b. $55.5 - 74.5$, $\frac{56+74}{2} = \frac{130}{2} = 65$, $74.5 - 55.5 = 19$
c. $694.5 - 705.5$, $\frac{695+705}{2} = \frac{1400}{2} = 700$, $705.5 - 694.5 = 11$
d. $13.55 - 14.75$, $\frac{13.6+14.7}{2} = \frac{28.3}{2} = 14.15$, $14.75 - 13.55 = 1.2$
e. $2.145 - 3.935$, $\frac{2.15+3.93}{2} = \frac{6.08}{2} = 3.04$, $3.935 - 2.145 = 1.79$

4. Five to twenty classes. Width should be an odd number so that the midpoint will have the same place value as the data.

5.
a. Class width is not uniform.
b. Class limits overlap, and class width is not uniform.
c. A class has been omitted.
d. Class width is not uniform.

6. An open-ended frequency distribution has either a first class with no lower limit or a last class with no upper limit. They are necessary to accomodate all the data.

7.

Class	Tally	f	Percent
A	IIII	4	10%
M	HI HI HI HI HI III	28	70%
H	HI I	6	15%
S	II	2	5%
		40	100%

8. $H = 36 \quad L = 7$
Range $= 36 - 7 = 29$
Width $= 29 \div 6 = 4.83$ or 5

Limits	Boundaries	f	cf
7 - 11	6.5 - 11.5	2	2
12 - 16	11.5 - 16.5	5	7
17 - 21	16.5 - 21.5	9	16
22 - 26	21.5 - 26.5	2	18
27 - 31	26.5 - 31.5	0	18
32 - 36	31.5 - 36.5	1	19
		19	

9.

Limits	Boundaries	f	cf
19 - 21	18.5 - 21.5	2	2
22 - 24	21.5 - 24.5	13	15
25 - 27	24.5 - 27.5	11	26
28 - 30	27.5 - 30.5	3	29
31 - 33	30.5 - 33.5	1	30
		30	

The average speed is about 24.5 mph.

10. $H = 11{,}588 \quad L = 164$
Range $= 11{,}588 - 164 = 11{,}424$
Width $= 11{,}424 \div 10 = 1142.4$
Width $= 1143$

Limits	Boundaries	f	cf
164 - 1,306	163.5 - 1,306.5	25	25
1,307 - 2,449	1,306.5 - 2,449.5	12	37
2,450 - 3,592	2,449.5 - 3,592.5	5	42
3,593 - 4,735	3,592.5 - 4,735.5	5	47
4,736 - 5,878	4,735.5 - 5,878.5	1	48
5,879 - 7,021	5,878.5 - 7,021.5	0	48
7,022 - 8,164	7,021.5 - 8,164.5	0	48
8,165 - 9,307	8,164.5 - 9,307.5	1	49
9,308 - 10,450	9,307.5 - 10,450.5	0	49
10,451 - 11,593	10,450.5 - 11,593.5	1	50
		50	

The majority of the data is clustered in the first two classes.

11. $H = 780 \quad L = 746$
Range $= 780 - 746 = 34$
Width $= 34 \div 6 = 5.\overline{6}$ or 6; round up to 7

11. continued

Limits	Boundaries	f	cf
745 - 751	744.5 - 751.5	4	4
752 - 758	751.5 - 758.5	5	9
759 - 765	758.5 - 765.5	7	16
766 - 772	765.5 - 772.5	11	27
773 - 779	772.5 - 779.5	2	29
780 - 786	779.5 - 786.5	1	30
		30	

12. $H = 93$ $L = 0$
Range $= 93 - 0 = 93$
Width $= 93 \div 7 \approx 13.29$ or 14
Use $w = 15$ for odd number.

Limits	Boundaries	f	cf
0 - 14	-0.5 - 14.5	14	14
15 - 29	14.5 - 29.5	10	24
30 - 44	29.5 - 44.5	4	28
45 - 59	44.5 - 59.5	1	29
60 - 74	59.5 - 74.5	1	30
75 - 89	74.5 - 89.5	2	32
90 - 104	89.5 - 104.5	1	33
		33	

13. $H = 70$ $L = 27$
Range $= 70 - 27 = 43$
Width $= 43 \div 7 = 6.1$ or 7

Limits	Boundaries	f	cf
27 - 33	26.5 - 33.5	7	7
34 - 40	33.5 - 40.5	14	21
41 - 47	40.5 - 47.5	15	36
48 - 54	47.5 - 54.5	11	47
55 - 61	54.5 - 61.5	3	50
62 - 68	61.5 - 68.5	3	53
69 - 75	68.5 - 75.5	2	55
		55	

14. $H = 4040$ $L = 70$
Range $= 4040 - 70 = 3970$
Width $= 3970 \div 8 = 496.25$ or 497

Limits	Boundaries	f	cf
70 - 566	69.5 - 566.5	14	14
567 - 1063	566.5 - 1063.5	5	19
1064 - 1560	1063.5 - 1560.5	5	24
1561 - 2057	1560.5 - 2057.5	0	24
2058 - 2554	2057.5 - 2554.5	0	24
2555 - 3051	2554.5 - 3051.5	1	25
3052 - 3548	3051.5 - 3548.5	0	25
3549 - 4045	3548.5 - 4045.5	2	27
		27	

15.

Limits	Boundaries	f	cf
31 - 39	30.5 - 39.5	4	4
40 - 48	39.5 - 48.5	5	9
49 - 57	48.5 - 57.5	5	14
58 - 66	57.5 - 66.5	12	26
67 - 75	66.5 - 75.5	13	39
76 - 84	75.5 - 84.5	5	44
85 - 93	84.5 - 93.5	3	47
		47	

16. $H = 775$ $L = 5$
Width $= 775 - 5 = 770$
Range $= 770 \div 8 = 96.25$ or 97

Limits	Boundaries	f	cf
5 - 101	4.5 - 101.5	17	17
102 - 198	101.5 - 198.5	6	23
199 - 295	198.5 - 295.5	6	29
296 - 392	295.5 - 392.5	2	31
393 - 489	392.5 - 489.5	2	33
490 - 586	489.5 - 586.5	3	36
587 - 683	586.5 - 683.5	1	37
684 - 780	683.5 - 780.5	2	39
		39	

17. $H = 11,413$ $L = 150$
Range $= 11,413 - 150 = 11,263$
Width $= 11,263 \div 10 = 1126.3$ or 1127

Limits	Boundaries	f	cf
150 - 1,276	149.5 - 1,276.5	2	2
1,277 - 2,403	1,276.5 - 2,403.5	2	4
2,404 - 3,530	2,403.5 - 3,530.5	5	9
3,531 - 4,657	3,530.5 - 4,657.5	8	17
4,658 - 5,784	4,657.5 - 5,784.5	7	24
5,785 - 6,911	5,784.5 - 6,911.5	3	27
6,912 - 8,038	6,911.5 - 8,038.5	7	34
8,039 - 9,165	8,038.5 - 9,165.5	3	37
9,166 - 10,292	9,165.5 - 10,292.5	3	40
10,293 - 11,419	10,292.5 - 11,419.5	2	42
		42	

18.
$H = 550$ $L = 306$
Range $= 550 - 306 = 244$
Width $= 244 \div 8 = 30.5$ or 31

18. continued

f_M, cf_M = McGwire f_S, cf_S = Sosa

Limits	Boundaries	f_M	cf_M	f_S	cf_S
306 - 336	305.5 - 336.5	1	1	0	0
337 - 367	336.5 - 367.5	6	7	10	10
368 - 398	367.5 - 398.5	19	26	16	26
399 - 429	398.5 - 429.5	15	41	21	47
430 - 460	429.5 - 460.5	18	59	15	62
461 - 491	460.5 - 491.5	6	65	3	65
492 - 522	491.5 - 522.5	3	68	1	66
523 - 553	522.5 - 553.5	2	70	0	66
		70		66	

19. The percents add up to 101%. They should total 100% unless rounding was used.

EXERCISE SET 2-3

1.

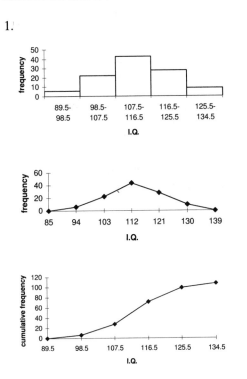

Eighty applicants do not need to enroll in the summer programs.

2.

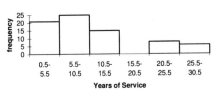

2. continued

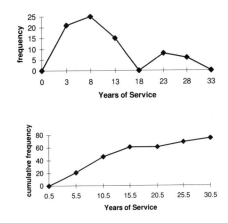

The majority of employees have worked for less than 11 years.

3.

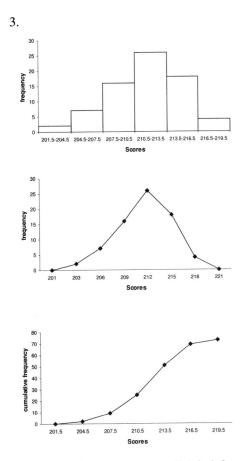

The distribution appears to be slightly left skewed.

4.

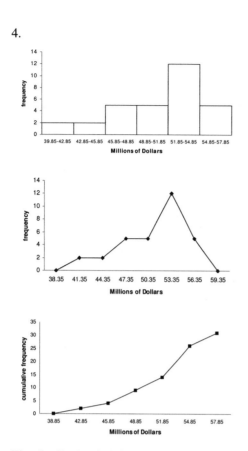

The distribution is left skewed or negatively skewed.

6.

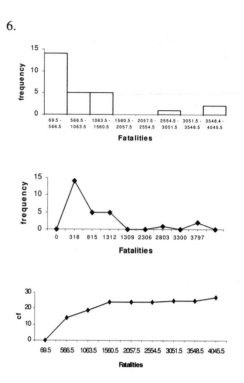

The data are clustered to the left. There are two gaps in the histogram, one between 1560.5 and 2554.5 and the other between 3051.5 and 3548.5. The ogive shows a sharp increase in values at the beginning, followed by a leveling off of values.

5.

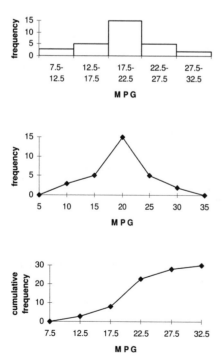

7.

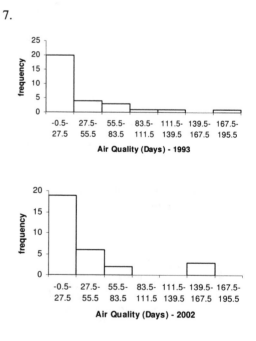

7. continued

Both graphs are similar in that they are positively skewed. Also, it looks as if the air quality has improved somewhat in that there are slightly more smaller values in 2002, which means fewer days with unacceptable levels of pollution.

8.

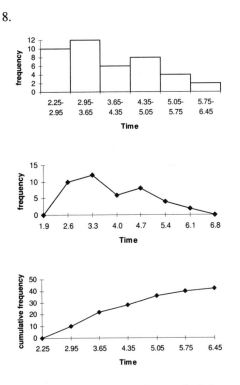

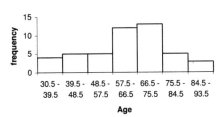

The data values fall somewhat on the left side of the distribution. The histogram is right skewed. There are no gaps in the histogram.

9.

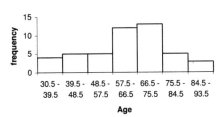

9. continued

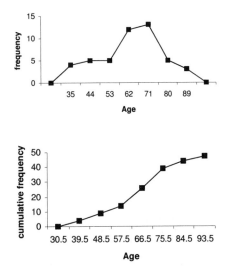

The histogram has a peak at the class of $66.5 - 75.5$ and is somewhat negatively skewed.

10.

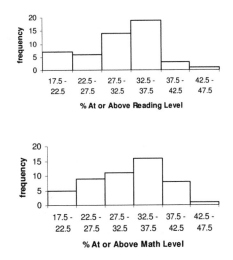

The distribution of math percentages is more bell-shaped than the distribution of reading percentages, and its peak in the class of $32.5 - 37.5$ is not as high as the peak of the reading percentages.

11.

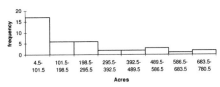

11. continued

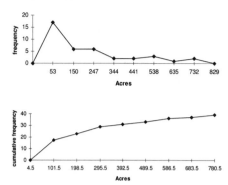

The peak is in the first class, and then the histogram is rather uniform after the first class. Most of the parks have less than 101.5 thousand acres as compared with any other class of values.

12.

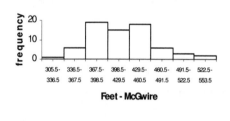

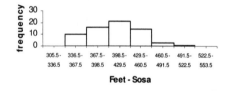

The histograms show that the distances of McGwire's homeruns are more variable (spread out) than Sosa's homerun distances.

13.

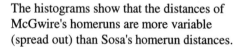

13. continued

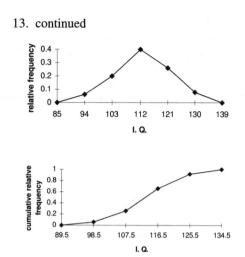

The proportion of applicants who need to enroll in a summer program is 0.26 or 26%.

14.

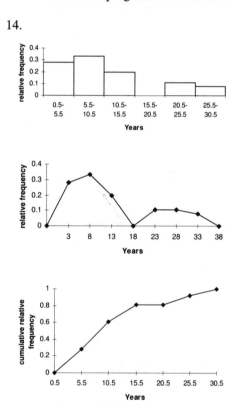

The proportion of employees who have been with the company longer than 20 years is 0.187 or 18.7%.

15. H = 270   L = 80
Range = 270 − 80 = 190
Width = 190 ÷ 7 = 27.1 or 28
Use width = 29 (rule 2)

15. continued

Limits	Boundaries	f	rf	crf
80 - 108	79.5 - 108.5	8	0.17	0.17
109 - 137	108.5 - 137.5	13	0.28	0.45
138 - 166	137.5 - 166.5	2	0.04	0.49
167 - 195	166.5 - 195.5	9	0.20	0.69
196 - 224	195.5 - 224.5	10	0.22	0.91
225 - 253	224.5 - 253.5	2	0.04	0.95
254 - 282	253.5 - 282.5	2	0.04	0.99*
				0.99

*due to rounding

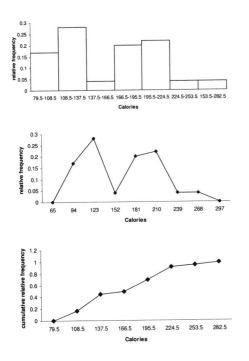

The histogram has two peaks.

16.
H = 57   L = 12
Range = 57 − 12 = 45
Width = 45 ÷ 6 = 7.5 or 8

Limits	Boundaries	f	rf	crf
12 - 19	11.5 - 19.5	7	0.175	0.175
20 - 27	19.5 - 27.5	17	0.425	0.600
28 - 35	27.5 - 35.5	10	0.25	0.850
36 - 43	35.5 - 43.5	4	0.10	0.950
44 - 51	43.5 - 51.5	1	0.025	0.975
52 - 59	51.5 - 59.5	1	0.025	1.000
		40	1.000	

16. continued

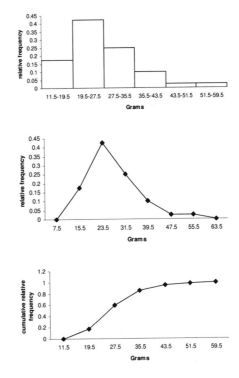

The histogram is positively skewed.

17.

Boundaries	rf	crf
-0.5 - 27.5	0.63	0.63
27.5 - 55.5	0.20	0.83
55.5 - 83.5	0.07	0.90
83.5 - 111.5	0.00	0.90
111.5 - 139.5	0.00	0.90
139.5 - 167.5	0.10	1.00
167.5 - 195.5	0.00	1.00
	100.0	

17. continued

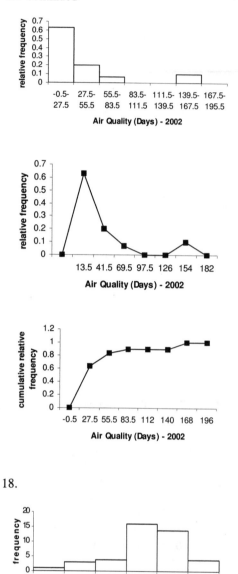

18. continued

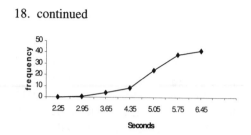

Based on the histograms, the older dogs have longer reaction times. Also, the reaction times for older dogs is more variable.

19.

Limits	Boundaries	X_m	f	cf
22 - 24	21.5 - 24.5	23	1	1
25 - 27	24.5 - 27.5	26	3	4
28 - 30	27.5 - 30.5	29	0	4
31 - 33	30.5 - 33.5	32	6	10
34 - 36	33.5 - 36.5	35	5	15
37 - 39	36.5 - 39.5	38	3	18
40 - 42	39.5 - 42.5	41	<u>2</u>	20
			20	

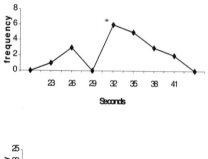

18.

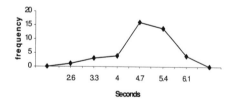

20.
a. 0
b. 14
c. 10
d. 16

10

EXERCISE SET 2-4

1.

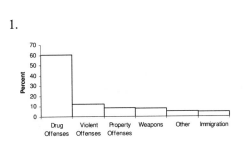

The majority of the money should be spent for drug rehabilitation.

2.

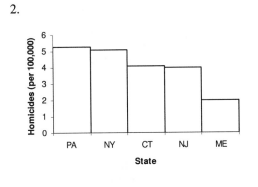

3.

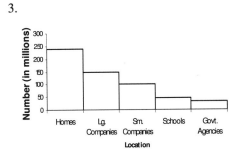

The best place to market products would be to residential users.

4.

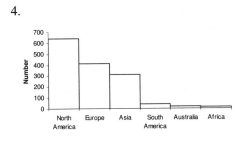

5.

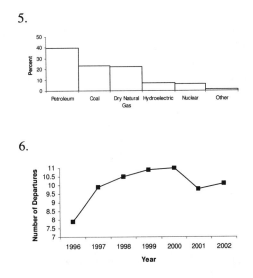

6.

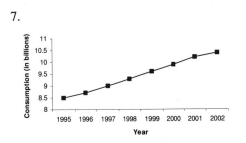

Departures increased until 2000, decreased in 2001, then increased in 2002.

7.

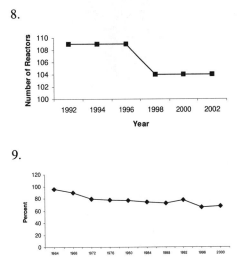

There is a steady increase in consumption of tobacco products.

8.

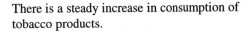

9.

The graph shows a decline in the percentages of registered voters voting in presidential elections.

10.

Personal Business	146	14.6%	52.56°
Visit friends or family	330	33.0%	118.8°
Work-related	225	22.5%	81.0°
Leisure	299	29.9%	107.64°
	1000	100%	360°

About $\frac{1}{3}$ of the travelers visit friends or relatives, with the fewest travelling for personal business.

11.

Principal Residence	7.8%	28.08°
Liquid Assets	5.0%	18.0°
Pension Accounts	6.9%	24.84°
Stocks, Funds, and Trusts	31.6%	113.76°
Business & Real Estate	46.9%	168.84°
Miscellaneous	1.8%	6.48°
	100.0%	360.00°

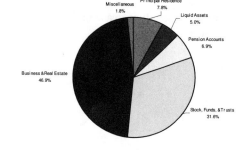

12.

Oxygen	45.6%	164.16°
Silicon	27.3%	98.28°
Aluminum	8.4%	30.24°
Iron	6.2%	22.32°
Calcium	4.7%	16.92°
Other	7.8%	28.08°
	100.0%	360.00°

12. continued

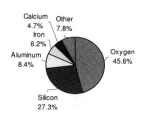

13.

Career change	34%	122.4°
New job	29%	104.4°
Start business	21%	75.6°
Retire	16%	57.6°
	100%	360.0°

Pie chart:

Pareto chart:

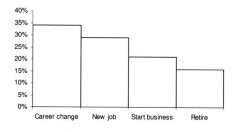

The pie graph better represents the data since we are looking at parts of a whole.

14.
a. Time series graph
b. Pie graph
c. Pareto chart
d. Pie graph
e. Time series graph
f. Pareto chart

15.

```
4 | 2  3
4 | 6  6  7  8  9  9
5 | 0  1  1  1  1  2  2  4  4  4  4  4
5 | 5  5  5  5  6  6  6  7  7  7  7  8
6 | 0  1  1  1  2  4  4
6 | 5  8  9
```

The distribution is somewhat symmetric and unimodal. The majority of the Presidents were in their 50's when inaugurated.

16.

```
3 | 8
4 | 1
5 | 0  0  2  3  3  6  8  9
6 | 6  8  9  9
7 | 0  0  3  4  5  8
8 | 0  1  3  3  4  4  4  5  7  9  9  9
9 | 0  2  4
```

The majority of automobile thefts occurred in the 50's and 80's . The data is grouped towards the higher end of the distribution.

17.

```
           Variety 1                      Variety 2
                       2 | 1 | 3  8
                    3  0 | 2 | 5
              9  8  8  5  2 | 3 | 6  8
                    3  3  1 | 4 | 1  2  5  5
  9  9  8  5  3  3  2  1  0 | 5 | 0  3  5  5  6  7  9
                         | 6 | 2  2
```

The distributions are similar but variety 2 seems to be more variable than variety 1.

18.

```
        Females                        Males
                    5 | 0 | 3
                      | 1 | 5  9
                      | 2 | 2
        7  4  3  2  0 | 3 | 1  1
                    6 | 4 | 1  4  6  6
           9  6  3  0 | 5 | 2  6  6  6  9
                 8  5 | 6 | 0  0  6  6
              7  2  0 | 7 | 7
     8  7  6  6  0  0 | 8 | 7  8
                 4  2 | 9 | 6  8
```

The distribution for unemployed males is more variable than the distribution for unemployed females. There are more unemployed females than males world-wide.

19.

```
1 | 3  4  8  9
2 | 5  8  9
3 | 2  8
4 | 1
```

20.

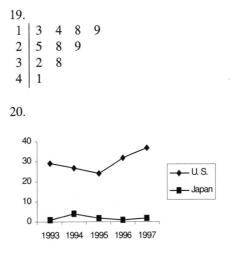

The United States has many more launches than Japan. The number of launches is relatively stable for Japan, while launches varied more for the U. S. The U. S. launches decreased slightly in 1995 and increased after that year.

21.

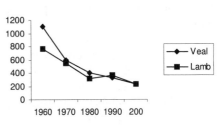

In 1960, veal production was considerably higher than lamb. By 1970, production was approximately the same for both.

22.

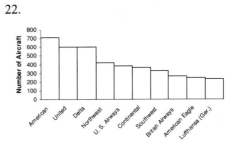

A Pareto chart is most appropriate.

23.

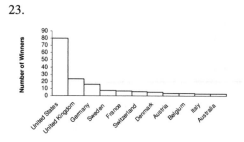

24. The bottle for 2004 is much wider, giving a distorted view of the difference since only the heights of the bottles should be compared.

25. The values on the y axis start at 3.5. Also there are no data values shown for the years 2004 through 2011.

EXERCISE SET 2-5

1. scatter plot or scatter diagram

2. The two variables used are the independent variable, x, and the dependent variable, y.

3. Two variables are positively related when the dependent variable, y, increases as the independent variable, x, increases. The points on the scatter plot fall approximately in an ascending straight line.

4. Two variables are negatively related when the dependent variable, y, decreases as the independent variable, x, increases. The points on the scatter plot fall approximately in a descending straight line.

5.

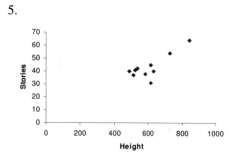

There appears to be a positive linear relationship between the height of a building and the number of stories in the building.

6.

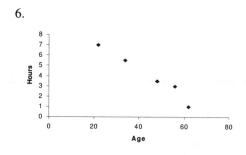

There appears to be a negative linear relationship between age and the number of hours spent jogging per week.

7.

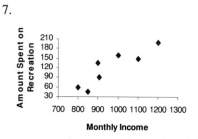

There appears to be a positive linear relationship between monthly income and amount spent on recreation.

8.

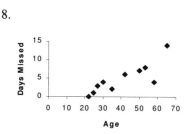

There appears to be a positive linear relationship between an employee's age and number of days missed per year.

9.

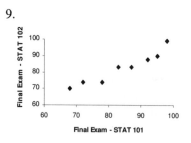

There appears to be a positive linear realationship between a student's final exam score in STAT 101 and STAT 102.

10.

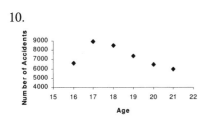

There appears to be a negative linear relationship between the age of a driver and the number of accidents per year.

11.

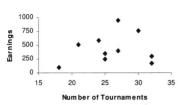

There appears to be neither a positive nor negative linear relationship between the number of tournaments and the earnings of LPGA golfers.

12.

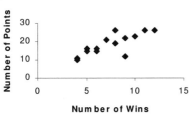

There appears to be a positive linear relationship between number of wins and points scored by NHL teams.

13.

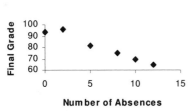

There appears to be a negative linear relationship between the number of absences and at student's final grade in a course.

14.

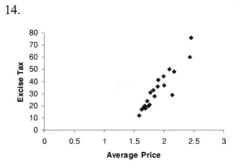

There appears to be a positive linear relationship between average price per pack of cigarettes and state excise tax.

REVIEW EXERCISES - CHAPTER 2

1.

Class	f
Newspaper	10
Television	16
Radio	12
Internet	12
	50

2.

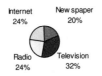

How People Receive News

The graph shows that the percentage of the people who receive their news by television is larger than the percentage who receive their news by other means.

3.

Class	f
baseball	4
golf ball	5
tennis ball	6
soccer ball	5
football	5
	25

4.

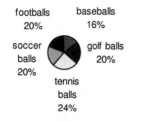

More tennis balls were sold than any other type of ball.

5.

Class	f	cf
11	1	1
12	2	3
13	2	5
14	2	7
15	1	8
16	2	10
17	4	14
18	2	16
19	2	18
20	1	19
21	0	19
22	1	20
	20	

6.

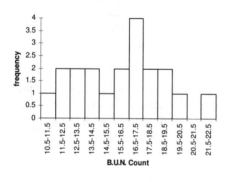

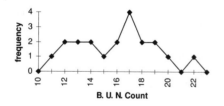

6. continued

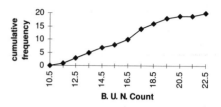

The distribution is somewhat uniform, with a slight peak in the 16.5 - 17.5 class. There is a gap in the 20.5 - 21.5 class.

7.

Limits	Boundaries	f	cf
85 - 105	84.5 - 105.5	4	4
106 - 126	105.5 - 126.5	7	11
127 - 147	126.5 - 147.5	9	20
148 - 168	147.5 - 168.5	10	30
169 - 189	168.5 - 189.5	9	39
190 - 210	189.5 - 210.5	1	40
		40	

8.

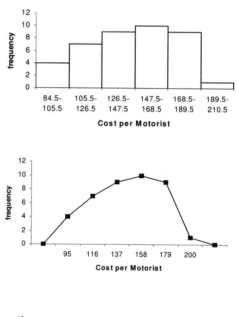

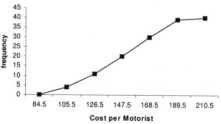

8. continued

The distribution is negatively skewed with most of the data in the two classes 147.5 − 168.5 and 168.5 − 189.5.

9.

Limits	Boundaries	f	cf
170 - 188	169.5 - 188.5	11	11
189 - 207	188.5 - 207.5	9	20
208 - 226	207.5 - 226.5	4	24
227 - 245	226.5 - 245.5	5	29
246 - 264	245.5 - 264.5	0	29
265 - 283	264.5 - 283.5	0	29
284 - 302	283.5 - 302.5	0	29
303 - 321	302.5 - 321.5	1	30
		30	

10.

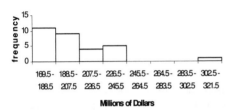

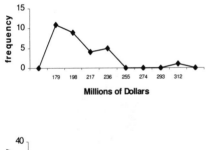

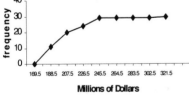

The typical value of the franchises is between $169.5 - $188.5 million. All but one of the franchises are valued between $169.5 and $245.5 million.

11.

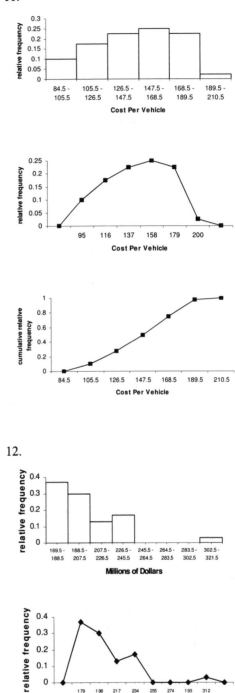

12.

12. continued

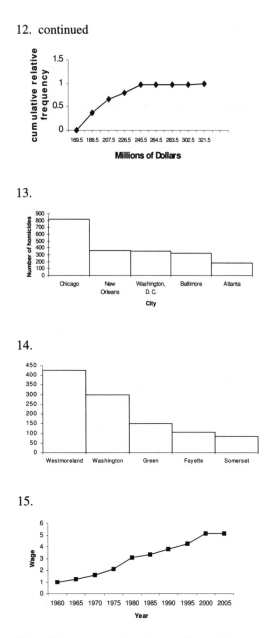

13.

14.

15.

The minimum wage has increased over the years with the largest increase occurring between 1975 and 1980.

16.

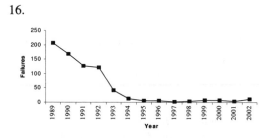

Failures decreased to only one failure in 1997, increased slightly from 1998 to 1999, decreasing through 2001, then increasing in 2002.

17.

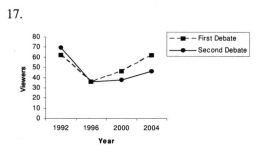

About the same number of people watched the first and second debates in 1992 and 1996. After that more people watched the first debate than watched the second debate.

18.

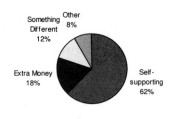

The majority of women worked to support themselves or their families.

19.

The majority of people surveyed would like to spend the rest of their careers with their present employer.

20.

2	9	9				
3	2	4	5	6	8	8
4	1	2	3	7	7	
5	1	3	5	8		
6	2	2	2	3	7	
7	2	3				

21.

1	2	4					
1	6	7	8	8	9		
2	0	2	3	4			
2	5	5	5	6	6	9	9
3	2	3					
3	5	7	8	8	9		

The peak of the distribution is in the range of 25 − 29.

22.

20	0	4	9			
21	0	1	2	7	8	8
22	2	7	7	7	8	
23	0	1	3	7	8	
24	1	2	2	3	7	
25	1	1	3	4	6	
26	0					

The distribution of aptitude scores is fairly uniform.

23.

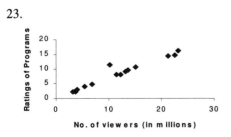

23. continued
There appears to be a positive linear relationship between the number of viewers (in millions) and the ratings of 15 television programs.

24.

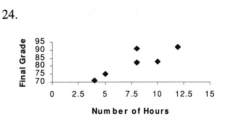

There appears to be a positive linear relationship between the final grade a student receives and the number of hours of tutoring received by the student.

CHAPTER 2 QUIZ

1. False
2. False
3. False
4. True
5. True
6. False
7. False
8. c
9. c
10. b
11. b
12. Categorical, ungrouped, grouped
13. 5, 20
14. Categorical
15. Time series
16. Stem and leaf plot
17. Vertical or y

18.

Class	f	cf
H	6	6
A	5	11
M	6	17
C	8	25
	25	

19.

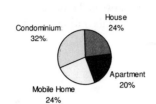

20.

Class	f	cf
0.5 – 1.5	1	1
1.5 – 2.5	5	6
2.5 – 3.5	3	9
3.5 – 4.5	4	13
4.5 – 5.5	2	15
5.5 – 6.5	6	21
6.5 – 7.5	2	23
7.5 – 8.5	3	26
8.5 – 9.5	<u>4</u>	30
	30	

21.

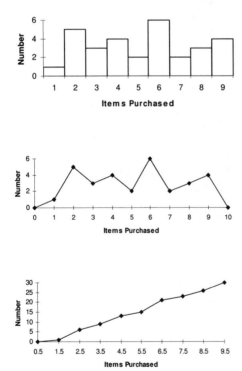

22.

Limits	Boundaries	f	cf
27 - 90	26.5 - 90.5	13	13
91 - 154	90.5 - 154.5	2	15
155 - 218	154.5 - 218.5	0	15
219 - 282	218.5 - 282.5	5	20
283 - 346	282.5 - 346.5	0	20
347 - 410	346.5 - 410.5	2	22
411 - 474	410.5 - 474.5	0	22
475 - 538	474.5 - 538.5	1	23
539 - 602	538.5 - 602.5	<u>2</u>	25
		25	

23.

The distribution is positively skewed with one more than half of the data values in the lowest class.

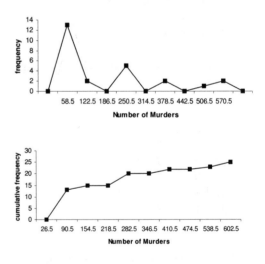

24.

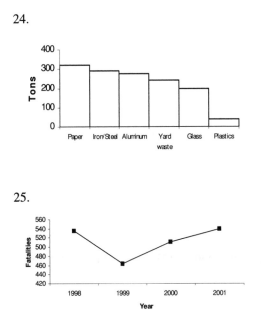

25.

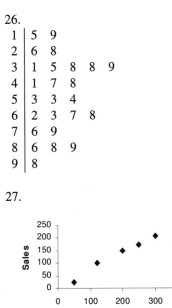

Fatalities decreased in 1999 and then increased the next two years.

26.

1	5	9			
2	6	8			
3	1	5	8	8	9
4	1	7	8		
5	3	3	4		
6	2	3	7	8	
7	6	9			
8	6	8	9		
9	8				

27.

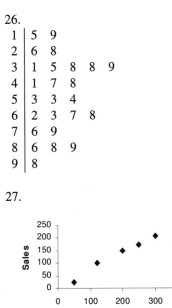

There appears to be a positive linear relationship between the number of miles traveled and the sales (in hundreds of dollars) of a sales representative.

Chapter 3 - Data Description

Note: Answers may vary due to rounding, TI 83's, or computer programs.

EXERCISE SET 3-2

1.
$$\overline{X} = \frac{\Sigma X}{n} = \frac{93.09}{25} = 3.7236 \approx 3.724$$

MD: 3.57, 3.64, 3.64, 3.65, 3.66, 3.67, 3.67, 3.68, 3.7, 3.7, 3.7, 3.73, **3.73**, 3.74, 3.74, 3.74, 3.75, 3.76, 3.77, 3.78, 3.78, 3.8, 3.8, 3.83, 3.86

Mode: 3.70 and 3.74   MR: $\frac{3.57+3.86}{2} = 3.715$

2.
$$\overline{X} = \frac{\Sigma X}{n} = \frac{39,378}{20} = 1968.9$$

MD: 1170, 1182, 1198, 1215, 1388, 1536, 1612, 1650, 1841, **1904, 2000**, 2123, 2151, 2307, 2425, 2499, 2540, 2625, 2800, 3212

$$MD = \frac{1904 + 2000}{2} = 1952$$

Mode: no mode   MR: $\frac{1170 + 3212}{2} = 2191$

3.
$$\overline{X} = \frac{\Sigma X}{n} = \frac{136}{9} = 15.1$$

MD: 1, 2, 3, 3, **7**, 11, 18, 30, 61

Mode = 3   MR $= \frac{1+61}{2} = 31$

For the best measure of average, answers will vary.

4.
For Beaver County:

$\overline{X} = \frac{\Sigma X}{n} = \frac{195}{5} = 39$ MD: 11, 12, **13**, 67, 92   Mode: no mode   MR $= \frac{11+92}{2} = 51.5$

For Butler County:

$\overline{X} = \frac{\Sigma X}{n} = \frac{107}{4} = 26.75$ MD: 12, **18**, **21**, 56   MD $= \frac{18+21}{2} = 19.5$

Mode: no mode   MR $= \frac{12+56}{2} = 34$

Yes, there probably is a difference in the averages.

5.
$$\overline{X} = \frac{\Sigma X}{n} = \frac{3249}{12} = 270.75 \text{ or } 270.8$$

MD: 75, 88, 102, 117, 136, **189**, **229**, 239, 372, 465, 574, 663 MD $= \frac{189 + 229}{2} = 209$

Mode: no mode   MR $= \frac{75 + 663}{2} = 369$

It would seem that the average number of identity thefts is not higher than 300.

6.

For under age 60:

$$\overline{X} = \frac{\Sigma X}{n} = \frac{165.6}{10} = \$16.56 \text{ billion}$$

MD: 5.3, 7.3, 10.4, 12, **12.6, 14**, 18, 18, 20, 48 $MD = \frac{12.6+14}{2} = \$13.3 \text{ billion}$

Mode: $18 billion $MR = \frac{5.3+48}{2} = \$26.65 \text{ billion}$

For age 60 and over:

$$\overline{X} = \frac{\Sigma X}{n} = \frac{206.6}{10} = \$20.66 \text{ billion}$$

MD: 7, 7.6, 10, 11.3, **13.7, 18**, 18, 20, 41, 60 $MD = \frac{13.7+18}{2} = \$15.85 \text{ billion}$

Mode: $18 billion $MR = \frac{7+60}{2} = \$33.5 \text{ billion}$

It can be concluded that those age 60 and over have a slightly higher net worth since the mean, median, and midrange are larger for that age group.

7.
$$\overline{X} = \frac{\Sigma X}{n} = \frac{79.6}{12} = 6.63$$

MD: 5.4, 5.4, 6.2, 6.2, 6.4, **6.4, 6.5**, 7.0, 7.2, 7.2, 7.7, 8.0 $MD = \frac{6.4+6.5}{2} = 6.45$

Mode: no mode $MR = \frac{5.4+8.0}{2} = 6.7$

For the best measure of average, answers will vary.

8.
$$\overline{X} = \frac{\Sigma X}{n} = \frac{1221.1}{50} = \$24.42$$

MD: 16.5, 16.8, 16.9, 16.9, ..., **23.2, 23.7**, ..., 36.8, 37.6, 38.5, 41.7, 41.7 $MD = \frac{23.2+23.7}{2} = \$23.45$

Mode: 16.9, 17.2, 18, 19.1, 24, 25.2, 31.7 $MR = \frac{16.5+47.7}{2} = 32.1$

It appears that the mean and median are good measures of average.

9.
$$\overline{X} = \frac{\Sigma X}{n} = \frac{238,512}{42} = 5678.9$$

MD: 150, 885, ..., **5315, 5370**, ..., 11070, 11413 $MD = \frac{5315+5370}{2} = 5342.5$

Mode: 4450 $MR = \frac{150+11,413}{2} = 5781.5$

The distribution is skewed to the right.

10.
McGwire:
$$\overline{X} = \frac{\Sigma X}{n} = \frac{29,242}{70} = 417.7$$

$$MD = \frac{420+420}{2} = 420$$

10. continued

Mode: 430 $\qquad$ $MR = \frac{306+550}{2} = 428$

Sosa:

$\overline{X} = \frac{\Sigma X}{n} = \frac{26,720}{66} = 404.8$

$MD = 410$ $\qquad$ Mode: 420 $\qquad$ $MR = \frac{340+500}{2} = 420$

The average of the distances of the homeruns hit by McGwire is larger than the average of the homerun distances hit by Sosa.

11.

For Year 1:

$\overline{X} = \frac{\Sigma X}{n} = \frac{24,911}{27} = 922.6 \, MD = 527$

Mode: no mode $\qquad$ $MR = \frac{69+4192}{2} = 2130.5$

For Year 2:

$\overline{X} = \frac{\Sigma X}{n} = \frac{24,615}{2} = 911.7 \, MD = 485$

Mode: 1430 $\qquad$ $MR = \frac{70+4040}{2} = 2055$

The mean, median, and midrange of the traffic fatalities for Year 2 are somewhat less than those for the Year 1 fatalities, indicating that the number of fatalities has decreased.

12.

Class Limits	Boundaries	X_m	f	$f \cdot X_m$	cf
90 - 98	89.5 - 98.5	94	6	564	6
99 - 107	98.5 - 107.5	103	22	2266	28
108 - 116	107.5 - 116.5	112	43	4816	71
117- 125	116.5 - 125.5	121	28	3388	99
126 - 134	125.5 - 134.5	130	9	1170	108
			108	12,204	

a. $\overline{X} = \frac{\Sigma f \cdot X_m}{n} = \frac{12204}{108} = 113$

b. modal class $= 108 - 116$

13.

Class Limits	Boundaries	X_m	f	$f \cdot X_m$
202 - 204	201.5 - 204.5	203	2	406
205 - 207	204.5 - 207.5	206	7	1442
208 - 210	207.5 - 210.5	209	16	3344
211 - 213	210.5 - 213.5	212	26	5512
214 - 216	213.5 - 216.5	215	18	3870
217 - 219	216.5 - 219.5	218	4	872
			73	15,446

a. $\overline{X} = \frac{\Sigma f \cdot X_m}{n} = \frac{15,446}{73} = 211.6$

13. continued
b. modal class: $211 - 213$

14.

Boundaries	X_m	f	$f \cdot X_m$
7.5 - 12.5	10	3	30
12.5 - 17.5	15	5	75
17.5 - 22.5	20	15	300
22.5 - 27.5	25	5	125
27.5 - 32.5	30	2	60
		30	590

a. $\overline{X} = \dfrac{\Sigma f \cdot X_m}{n} = \dfrac{590}{30} = 19.7$

b. modal class: $17.5 - 22.5$

15.

Limits	Boundaries	X_m	f	$f \cdot X_m$
34 - 96	33.5 - 96.5	65	13	845
97 - 159	96.5 - 159.5	128	2	256
160 - 222	159.5 - 222.5	191	0	0
223 - 285	222.5 - 285.5	254	5	1270
286 - 348	285.5 - 348.5	317	1	317
349 - 411	348.5 - 411.5	380	1	380
412 - 474	411.5 - 474.5	443	0	0
475 - 537	474.5 - 537.5	506	1	506
538 - 600	537.5 - 600.5	569	2	1138
			25	4712

a. $\overline{X} = \dfrac{\Sigma f \cdot X_m}{n} = \dfrac{4712}{25} = 188.48$

b. modal class: $34 - 96$

Since most of the data is in the lowest class, the mean is probably not the best measure of average. If the individual data values are available, the median may be a better measure of average. A procedure for finding the approximate median for grouped data is found in Exercise 42 of this section.

16.
Younger Dogs:

Class Limits	Boundaries	X_m	f	$f \cdot X_m$
2.3 - 2.9	2.25 - 2.95	2.6	10	26
3.0 - 3.6	2.95 - 3.65	3.3	12	39.6
3.7 - 4.3	3.65 - 4.35	4.0	6	24
4.4 - 5.0	4.35 - 5.05	4.7	8	37.6
5.1 - 5.7	5.05 - 5.75	5.4	4	21.6
5.8 - 6.4	5.75 - 6.45	6.1	2	12.2
			42	161

a. $\overline{X} = \dfrac{\Sigma f \cdot X_m}{n} = \dfrac{161}{42} = 3.83$

b. modal class: $2.95 - 3.65$

16. continued

Older Dogs:

Class Limits	Boundaries	X_m	f	$f \cdot X_m$
2.3 - 2.9	2.25 - 2.95	2.6	1	2.6
3.0 - 3.6	2.95 - 3.65	3.3	3	9.9
3.7 - 4.3	3.65 - 4.35	4.0	4	16.0
4.4 - 5.0	4.35 - 5.05	4.7	16	75.2
5.1 - 5.7	5.05 - 5.75	5.4	14	75.6
5.8 - 6.4	5.75 - 6.45	6.1	4	24.4
			42	203.7

a. $\overline{X} = \dfrac{\sum f \cdot X_m}{n} = \dfrac{203.7}{42} = 4.85$

b. modal class: $4.35 - 5.05$

No, the older dogs have a longer average reaction time than the younger dogs.

17.

Boundaries	X_m	f	$f \cdot X_m$
52.5 – 63.5	58	6	348
63.5 – 74.5	69	12	828
74.5 – 85.5	80	25	2000
85.5 – 96.5	91	18	1638
96.5 – 107.5	102	14	1428
107.5 – 118.5	113	5	565
		80	6807

a. $\overline{X} = \dfrac{\sum f \cdot X_m}{n} = \dfrac{6807}{80} = 85.1$

b. modal class: $74.5 - 85.5$

18.

Class Limits	Boundaries	X_m	f	$f \cdot X_m$
10 – 20	9.5 – 20.5	15	2	30
21 – 31	20.5 – 31.5	26	8	208
32 – 42	31.5 – 42.5	37	15	555
43 – 53	42.5 – 53.5	48	7	336
54 – 64	53.5 – 64.5	59	10	590
65 – 75	64.5 – 75.5	70	3	210
			45	1929

a. $\overline{X} = \dfrac{\sum f \cdot X_m}{n} = \dfrac{1929}{45} = 42.9$

b. modal class: $32 - 42$

19.

Class Limits	Boundaries	X_m	f	$f \cdot X_m$
13 – 19	12.5 – 19.5	16	2	32
20 – 26	19.5 – 26.5	23	7	161
27 – 33	26.5 – 33.5	30	12	360
34 – 40	33.5 – 40.5	37	5	185
41 – 47	40.5 – 47.5	44	6	264
48 – 54	47.5 – 54.5	51	1	51
55 – 61	54.5 – 61.5	58	0	0
62 – 68	61.5 – 68.5	65	2	130
			35	1183

a. $\overline{X} = \dfrac{\sum f \cdot X_m}{n} = \dfrac{1183}{35} = 33.8$

b. modal class: $27 - 33$

20.

Class Limits	Boundaries	X_m	f	$f \cdot X_m$
150 – 158	149.5 – 158.5	154	5	770
159 – 167	158.5 – 167.5	163	16	2608
168 – 176	167.5 – 176.5	172	20	3440
177 – 185	176.5 – 185.5	181	21	3801
186 – 194	185.5 – 194.5	190	20	3800
195 – 203	194.5 – 203.5	199	15	2985
204 – 212	203.5 – 212.5	208	3	624
			100	18,028

a. $\overline{X} = \dfrac{\sum f \cdot X_m}{n} = \dfrac{18,028}{100} = 180.3$

b. modal class: $177 - 185$

21.

Boundaries	X_m	f	$f \cdot X_m$
15.5 – 18.5	17	14	238
18.5 – 21.5	20	12	240
21.5 – 24.5	23	18	414
24.5 – 27.5	26	10	260
27.5 – 30.5	29	15	435
30.5 – 33.5	32	6	192
		75	1779

a. $\overline{X} = \dfrac{\sum f \cdot X_m}{n} = \dfrac{1779}{75} = 23.7$

b. modal class: $21.5 - 24.5$

22.

Class Limits	Boundaries	X_m	f	$f \cdot X_m$
0.6 − 1.0	0.55 − 1.05	0.8	2	1.6
1.1 − 1.5	1.05 − 1.55	1.3	2	2.6
1.6 − 2.0	1.55 − 2.05	1.8	7	12.6
2.1 − 2.5	2.05 − 2.55	2.3	5	11.5
2.6 − 3.0	2.55 − 3.05	2.8	7	19.5
3.1 − 3.5	3.05 − 3.55	3.3	5	16.5
3.6 − 4.0	3.55 − 4.05	3.8	4	15.2
			32	79.6

$$\overline{X} = \frac{\sum f \cdot X_m}{n} = \frac{79.6}{32} = 2.49$$

modal class: $1.55 − 2.05$ and $2.55 − 3.05$

23.

Limits	Boundaries	X_m	f	$f \cdot X_m$
27 - 33	26.5 - 33.5	30	7	210
34 - 40	33.5 - 40.5	37	14	518
41 - 47	40.5 - 47.5	44	15	660
48 - 54	47.5 - 54.5	51	11	561
55 - 61	54.5 - 61.5	58	3	174
62 - 68	61.5 - 68.5	65	3	195
69 - 75	68.5 - 75.5	72	2	144
			55	2462

$$\overline{X} = \frac{\sum f \cdot X_m}{n} = \frac{2462}{55} = 44.8$$

modal class: $40.5 − 47.5$

24.

Limits	Boundaries	X_m	f	$f \cdot X_m$
70 - 566	69.5 - 566.5	318	14	4452
567 - 1063	566.5 - 1063.5	815	5	4075
1064 - 1560	1063.5 - 1560.5	1312	5	6560
1561 - 2057	1560.5 - 2057.5	1809	0	0
2058 - 2554	2057.5 - 2554.5	2306	0	0
2555 - 3051	2554.5 - 3051.5	2803	1	2803
3052 - 3548	3051.5 - 3548.5	3300	0	0
3549 - 4045	3548.5 - 4045.5	3797	2	7594
			27	25,484

$$\overline{X} = \frac{\sum f \cdot X_m}{n} = \frac{25,484}{27} = 943.9$$

modal class: $69.5 − 566.5$

25.

Limits	Boundaries	X_m	f	$f \cdot X_m$
31 - 39	30.5 - 39.5	35	4	140
40 - 48	39.5 - 48.5	44	5	220
49 - 57	48.5 - 57.5	53	5	265
58 - 66	57.5 - 66.5	62	12	744
67 - 75	66.5 - 75.5	71	13	923
76 - 84	75.5 - 84.5	80	5	400
85 - 93	84.5 - 93.5	89	3	267
			47	2959

$$\overline{X} = \frac{\sum f \cdot X_m}{n} = \frac{2959}{47} = 62.96 \text{ or } 63.0$$

modal class: $66.5 - 75.5$

26.
$$\overline{X} = \frac{\sum w \cdot X}{\sum w} = \frac{8(10,000) + 10(12,000) + 12(8,000)}{8 + 10 + 12} = \frac{296,000}{8 + 10 + 12} = \frac{296,000}{30} = \$ 9866.67$$

27.
$$\overline{X} = \frac{\sum w \cdot X}{\sum w} = \frac{3(3.33) + 3(3.00) + 2(2.5) + 2.5(4.4) + 4(1.75)}{3 + 3 + 2 + 2.5 + 4} = \frac{41.99}{14.5} = 2.896$$

28.
$$\overline{X} = \frac{\sum w \cdot X}{\sum w} = \frac{40(1000) + 30(3000) + 50(800)}{1000 + 3000 + 800} = 35.4\%$$

29.
$$\overline{X} = \frac{\sum w \cdot X}{\sum w} = \frac{9(427000) + 6(365000) + 12(725000)}{9 + 6 + 12} = \frac{14,733,000}{27} = \$545,666.67$$

30.
$$\overline{X} = \frac{\sum w \cdot X}{\sum w} = \frac{20(83) + 30(72) + 50(90)}{100} = 83.2$$

31.
$$\overline{X} = \frac{\sum w \cdot X}{\sum w} = \frac{1(62) + 1(83) + 1(97) + 1(90) + 2(82)}{6} = \frac{496}{6} = 82.7$$

32.
a. Mode
b. Median
c. Median
d. Mode
e. Mean
f. Median

33.
a. Median
b. Mean
c. Mode
d. Mode
e. Mode
f. Mean

34.
Roman letters, $\overline{X}$
Greek letters, μ

35.
Both could be true since one could be using the mean for the average salary, and the other could be using the mode for the average.

36.
$5 \cdot 64 = 320$

37.
$5 \cdot 8.2 = 41$
$6 + 10 + 7 + 12 + x = 41$
$x = 6$

38.
The mean of the original data is 30.
The means will be:
a. 40
b. 20
c. 300
d. 3
e. The results will be the same as adding, subtracting, multiplying, and dividing the mean by 10.

39.
a. $\dfrac{2}{\frac{1}{30} + \frac{1}{45}} = 36$ mph

b. $\dfrac{2}{\frac{1}{40} + \frac{1}{25}} = 30.77$ mph

c. $\dfrac{2}{\frac{1}{50} + \frac{1}{10}} = \$16.67$

40.
a. $\sqrt[3]{(1.35)(1.24)(1.18)} = 1.2547 \approx 1.255$

Average growth rate $1.255 - 1 = 0.255 = 25.5\%$

b. $\sqrt[4]{(1.08)(1.06)(1.04)(1.05)}$

$= 1.057397$

Average growth rate $= 1.057 - 1 = 0.057 = 5.7\%$

c. $\sqrt[5]{(1.10)(1.08)(1.12)(1.09)(1.03)} =$

$\sqrt[5]{1.4938197} = 1.084$

$1.084 - 1 = 0.084$ or 8.4% on average

d. $\sqrt[3]{(1.01)(1.03)(1.055)} = \sqrt[3]{1.0975165} = 1.032$

$1.032 - 1 = 0.032$ or 3.2%

41.

$$\sqrt{\frac{8^2 + 6^2 + 3^2 + 5^2 + 4^2}{5}} = \sqrt{30} = 5.48$$

42. $MD = \frac{\frac{25}{2} - 0}{13}(63) + 33.5 = 94.1$

74 is the median for the individual data values. See Chapter 2 Quiz, Exercise 22 for the individual data values.

EXERCISE SET 3-3

1.
The square root of the variance is equal to the standard deviation.

2.
One extremely high or low data value would influence the range.

3.
σ^2, σ

4.
s^2, s

5.
When the sample size is less than 30, the formula for the true standard deviation of the sample will underestimate the population standard deviation.

6.
a. $s = 4.320$
b. $s = 5.066$
c. $s = 6.00$
Data set A is least variable and data set C is the most variable.

7.
$R = 48 - 0 = 48$

$$s^2 = \frac{\sum X^2 - \frac{(\sum X)^2}{n}}{n-1} = \frac{4061 - \frac{(133)^2}{10}}{10-1} = \frac{2292.1}{9} = 254.68 \approx 254.7$$

$s = \sqrt{254.7} = 15.96 \approx 16$ \qquad The data vary widely.

8.
$R = 70 - 8 = 62$

$$s^2 = \frac{\sum X^2 - \frac{(\sum X)^2}{n}}{n-1} = \frac{30,324 - \frac{(652)^2}{17}}{17-1} = 332.4$$

$s = \sqrt{332.4} = 18.2$

Using the range rule of thumb, $s \approx \frac{70-8}{4} = 15.5$

This is close to the actual standard deviation of 18.2.

9.
For Temperature:
R = 61 − 29 = 32

$$s^2 = \frac{\sum X^2 - \frac{(\sum x)^2}{n}}{n-1} = \frac{20,777 - \frac{441^2}{10}}{10-1} = 147.66$$

$$s = \sqrt{147.66} = 12.15$$

For Precipitation:
R = 5.1 − 1.1 = 4.0

$$s^2 = \frac{\sum X^2 - \frac{(\sum x)^2}{n}}{n-1} = \frac{86.13 - \frac{26.3^2}{10}}{10-1} = 1.88$$

$$s = \sqrt{1.88} = 1.37$$

Temperature is more variable.

10.
Eastern states:
R = 37,741 − 20,966 = 16,775

$$s^2 = \frac{\sum X^2 - \frac{(\sum x)^2}{n}}{n-1} = \frac{5,830,685,308 - \frac{183,684^2}{6}}{6-1} = 41,476,666.4$$

$$s = \sqrt{41,476,666.4} = 6440.2$$

Western states:
R = 101,510 − 54,339 = 47,171

$$s^2 = \frac{\sum X^2 - \frac{(\sum x)^2}{n}}{n-1} = \frac{31,891,035,030 - \frac{428,362^2}{6}}{6-1} = 261,740,238.8$$

$$s = \sqrt{261,740,238.3} = 16,178.4$$

Western states are more variable.

11.
St. Paul, MN:
R = 46 − 16 = 30

$$s^2 = \frac{\sum X^2 - \frac{(\sum x)^2}{n}}{n-1} = \frac{9677 - \frac{313^2}{11}}{11-1} = \frac{770.727}{10} = 77.1$$

$$s = \sqrt{77.1} = 8.8$$

Chicago, IL:
R = 100 − 57 = 43

$$s^2 = \frac{\sum X^2 - \frac{(\sum x)^2}{n}}{n-1} = \frac{59,980 - \frac{796^2}{11}}{11-1} = \frac{2378.545}{10} = 237.85 \approx 237.9$$

$$s = \sqrt{237.9} = 15.4$$

The data for Chicago is more variable since the standard deviation is much larger.

12.
R = 3.80 − 3.20 = \$0.60

$$s^2 = \frac{\sum X^2 - \frac{(\sum X)^2}{n}}{n-1} = \frac{92.573 - \frac{25.42^2}{7}}{7-1} = \$0.04$$

$$s = \sqrt{0.04} = \$0.21$$

No, the sample is very small.

13.
R = 22 − 1 = 21

$$s^2 = \frac{\sum X^2 - \frac{(\sum X)^2}{n}}{n-1} = \frac{1061 - \frac{89^2}{15}}{15-1} = 38.1$$

$$s = \sqrt{38.1} = 6.2$$

Using the range rule of thumb, $s \approx \frac{22-1}{4} = 5.25$. The estimate is close.

14.
McGwire:
R = 550 − 306 = 244

$$s^2 = \frac{\sum X^2 - \frac{(\sum X)^2}{n}}{n-1} = \frac{12,367,642 - \frac{29,242^2}{70}}{70-1} = 2202.98 \text{ or } 2203$$

$$s = \sqrt{2202.98} = 46.9$$

Sosa:
R = 500 − 340 = 160

$$s^2 = \frac{\sum X^2 - \frac{(\sum X)^2}{n}}{n-1} = \frac{10,900,378 - \frac{26,720^2}{66}}{66-1} = 1274.25$$

$$s = \sqrt{1274.25} = 35.7$$

The distances of the homeruns are more variable for McGwire than for Sosa.

15.
For 1995:
R = 4192 − 69 = 4123

$$s^2 = \frac{\sum X^2 - \frac{(\sum X)^2}{n}}{n-1} = \frac{49,784,885 - \frac{24,911^2}{27}}{27-1} = 1,030,817.63$$

$$s = \sqrt{1,030,817.63} = 1015.3$$

For 1996:
R = 4040 − 70 = 3970

$$s^2 = \frac{\sum X^2 - \frac{(\sum X)^2}{n}}{n-1} = \frac{48,956,875 - \frac{24,615^2}{27}}{27-1} = 1,019,853.85$$

$$s = \sqrt{1,019,853.85} = 1009.9$$

The fatalities in 1995 are more variable.

16.
R = 47196 − 734 = 46,462

$$s^2 = \frac{\sum X^2 - \frac{(\sum X)^2}{n}}{n-1} = \frac{4,311,972,653}{50-1} = 87,999,441.9$$

$$s = \sqrt{87,999,441.9} = 9380.8$$

17.
R = 11,413 − 150 = 11,263

$$s^2 = \frac{\sum X^2 - \frac{(\sum X)^2}{n}}{n-1} = \frac{1,659,371,050 - \frac{238,512^2}{42}}{42-1} = \frac{304,895,475.1}{41} = 7,436,475.003$$

$$s = \sqrt{7,436,475.003} = 2726.99 \text{ or } 2727$$

18.

X_m	f	$f \cdot X_m$	$f \cdot X_m^2$
94	6	564	53,016
103	22	2266	233,392
112	43	4816	539,392
121	28	3388	409,948
130	9	1170	152,100
	108	12,204	1,387,854

$$s^2 = \frac{1,387,854 - \frac{12,204^2}{108}}{108-1} = 82.26 \text{ or } 82.3$$

$$s = \sqrt{82.26} = 9.07 \text{ or } 9.1$$

19.

X_m	f	$f \cdot X_m$	$f \cdot X_m^2$
16	2	32	512
23	7	161	3703
30	12	360	10,800
37	5	185	6845
44	6	264	11,616
51	1	51	2601
58	0	0	0
65	2	130	8450
	35	1183	44527

$$s^2 = \frac{\sum f \cdot X_m^2 - \frac{(\sum f \cdot X_m)^2}{n}}{n-1} = \frac{44,527 - \frac{1183^2}{35}}{35-1} = \frac{4541.6}{34} = 133.58 \text{ or } 133.6$$

$$s = \sqrt{133.58} = 11.6$$

20.

X_m	f	$f \cdot X_m$	$f \cdot X_m^2$
10	3	30	300
15	5	75	1125
20	15	300	6000
25	5	125	3125
30	2	60	1800
	30	590	12,350

20. continued

$$s^2 = \frac{12350 - \frac{590^2}{30}}{30-1} = 25.7$$

$$s = \sqrt{25.7} = 5.07 \text{ or } 5.1$$

21.

X_m	f	$f \cdot X_m$	$f \cdot X_m^2$
65	13	845	54,925
128	2	256	32,768
191	0	0	0
254	5	1270	322,580
317	1	317	100,489
380	1	380	144,400
443	0	0	0
506	1	506	256,036
569	2	1138	647,522
		4712	1,558,720

$$s^2 = \frac{\sum f \cdot X_m^2 - \frac{(\sum f \cdot X_m)^2}{n}}{n-1} = \frac{1,558,720 - \frac{4712^2}{25}}{25-1} = \frac{670,602.24}{24} = 27,941.76$$

$$s = \sqrt{27941.76} = 167.16 \text{ or } 167.2$$

22.

X_m	f	$f \cdot X_m$	$f \cdot X_m^2$
2.4	12	28.8	69.12
3.1	13	40.3	124.93
3.8	7	26.6	101.08
4.5	5	22.5	101.25
5.2	2	10.4	54.08
5.9	1	5.9	34.81
	40	134.5	485.27

$$s^2 = \frac{485.27 - \frac{134.5^2}{40}}{40-1} = 0.8465 \text{ or } 0.847$$

$$s = \sqrt{0.8465} = 0.92$$

23.

X_m	f	$f \cdot X_m$	$f \cdot X_m^2$
58	6	348	20,184
69	12	828	57,132
80	25	2000	160,000
91	18	1638	148,058
102	14	1428	145,656
112	5	565	63,845
	80	6807	595,875

$$s^2 = \frac{\sum f \cdot X_m^2 - \frac{(\sum f \cdot X_m)^2}{n}}{n-1} = \frac{59,5875 - \frac{6807^2}{80}}{80-1} = \frac{16,684.39}{79} = 211.2$$

$$s = \sqrt{211.2} = 14.5$$

24.

X_m	f	$f \cdot X_m$	$f \cdot X_m^2$
8	8	64	512
15	5	75	1125
22	7	154	3388
29	1	29	841
36	1	36	1296
43	<u>3</u>	<u>129</u>	<u>5547</u>
	25	487	12709

$$s^2 = \frac{12,709 - \frac{487^2}{25}}{25 - 1} = 134.26 \text{ or } 134.3$$

$$s = \sqrt{134.3} = 11.6$$

25.

X_m	f	$f \cdot X_m$	$f \cdot X_m^2$
68	5	340	23,120
79	14	1106	87,374
90	18	1620	145,800
101	25	2525	255,025
112	12	1344	150,528
123	<u>6</u>	<u>738</u>	<u>90,774</u>
	80	7673	752,621

$$s^2 = \frac{\sum f \cdot X_m^2 - \frac{(\sum f \cdot X_m)^2}{n}}{n - 1} = \frac{752,621 - \frac{7673^2}{80}}{80 - 1} = \frac{16,684.3875}{79} = 211.19 \text{ or } 211.2$$

$$s = \sqrt{211.2} = 14.5$$

No, the variability of the lifetimes of the batteries is quite large.

26.
Younger Dogs:

X_m	f	$f \cdot X_m$	$f \cdot X_m^2$
2.6	10	26	67.6
3.3	12	39.6	130.68
4.0	6	24	96
4.7	8	37.6	176.72
5.4	4	21.6	116.64
6.1	<u>2</u>	<u>12.2</u>	<u>74.42</u>
	42	161	662.06

$$s^2 = \frac{662.06 - \frac{161^2}{42}}{42 - 1} = 1.1$$

$$s = \sqrt{1.1} = 1.0$$

Older Dogs:

26. continued

X_m	f	$f \cdot X_m$	$f \cdot X_m^2$
2.6	1	2.6	6.76
3.3	3	9.9	32.67
4.0	4	16.0	64.0
4.7	16	75.2	353.44
5.4	14	75.6	408.54
6.1	4	24.4	148.84
	42	203.7	1014.25

$$s^2 = \frac{1014.25 - \frac{203.7^2}{42}}{42-1} = 0.6$$

$$s = \sqrt{0.6} = 0.8$$

The reaction times for the younger dogs are more variable than the reaction times for the older dogs.

27.

X_m	f	$f \cdot X_m$	$f \cdot X_m^2$
27	5	135	3645
30	9	270	8100
33	32	1056	34848
36	30	720	25920
39	12	468	18252
62	2	84	3528
	80	2733	94293

$$s^2 = \frac{\sum f \cdot X_m^2 - \frac{(\sum f \cdot X_m)^2}{n}}{n-1} = \frac{94,293 - \frac{2733^2}{80}}{80-1} = \frac{926.89}{79} = 11.7$$

$$s = \sqrt{11.7} = 3.4$$

28.
C. Var = $\frac{s}{\overline{X}} = \frac{5}{110} = 0.045 = 4.5\%$
C. Var = $\frac{s}{\overline{X}} = \frac{4}{106} = 0.038 = 3.8\%$
The first class is more variable.

29.
For East: $\overline{X} = 2660$, s = 991.9; C. Var = $\frac{s}{\overline{X}} = \frac{991.9}{2660} = 0.373$ or 37.3%

For West: $\overline{X} = 2261.2$, s = 1117.9; C. Var = $\frac{s}{\overline{X}} = \frac{1117.9}{2261.2} = 0.494$ or 49.4%
The data for the West is more variable.

30.
C. Var = $\frac{s}{\overline{X}} = \frac{5}{85} = 0.059 = 5.9\%$

C. Var = $\frac{s}{\overline{X}} = \frac{8}{110} = 0.073 = 7.3\%$
The history class is more variable.

31.
C. Var = $\frac{s}{\overline{X}} = \frac{6}{26} = 0.231 = 23.1\%$

C. Var = $\frac{s}{\overline{X}} = \frac{4000}{31,000} = 0.129 = 12.9\%$
The age is more variable.

32.

a. $1 - \frac{1}{2^2} = \frac{3}{4}$ or 75%

b. $1 - \frac{1}{1.5^2} = 0.56$ or 56%

33.

a. $1 - \frac{1}{5^2} = 0.96$ or 96%

b. $1 - \frac{1}{4^2} = 0.9375$ or 93.75%

34.

a. $1 - \frac{1}{4^2} = 0.9375$

0.9375 (200) = 187.5

b. $1 - \frac{1}{2^2} = \frac{3}{4}$ or 0.75

0.75 (200) = 150

200 − 150 = 50

35.

$\overline{X} = 5.02$ s = 0.09

At least 75% of the data values will fall withing two standard deviations of the mean; hence, 2($0.09) = $0.18 and $5.02 − $0.18 = $4.84 and $5.02 + $0.18 = $5.20. Hence at least 75% of the data values will fall between $4.84 and $5.20.

36.

$\overline{X} = \$2.60$ s = $0.15

$2.60 − 3($0.15) = $2.15; $2.60 + 3($0.15) = $3.05

At least 88.89% of the data values will fall between $2.15 and $3.05.

37.

$\overline{X} = 95$ s = 2

At least 88.89% of the data values will fall within 3 standard deviations of the mean, hence 95 − 3(2) = 89 and 95 + 3(2) = 101. Therefore at least 88.89% of the data values will fall between 89 mg and 101 mg.

38.

$\overline{X} = 53$ x = 6

53 − 2 (6) = 41 and 53 + 2 (6) = 65. At least 75% of the scores will fall between 41 and 65.

39.

$\overline{X} = 12$ s = 3

20 − 12 = 8 and 8 ÷ 3 = 2.67

Hence, $1 - \frac{1}{k^2} = 1 - \frac{1}{2.67^2} = 1 - 0.14 = 0.86 = 86\%$

At least 86% of the data values will fall between 4 and 20.

40.

$\overline{X} = 4$ s = 0.10

4.18 − 4 = 0.18 and $k = \frac{0.18}{0.10} = 1.8$

$1 - \frac{1}{k^2} = 1 - \frac{1}{1.8^2} = 0.69$ or 69%

41.
$26.8 + 1(4.2) = 31$
By the Empirical Rule, 68% of consumption is within 1 standard deviation of the mean. Then $\frac{1}{2}$ of 32%, or 16%, of consumption would be more than 31 pounds of citrus fruit per year.

42.
(a) $53 + 4.2K = 58.6$
$4.2K = 5.6$
$K = 2$
By Chebyshev's Theorem, $1 - \frac{1}{2^2} = .75$ or 75% of hours worked are within 2 standard deviations of the mean. Then $\frac{1}{2}$ of 25%, or 12.5%, work more than 58.6 hours per week.

(b) By the Empirical Rule, $K = 2$ standard deviations of the mean is 95% of hours worked. Then $\frac{1}{2}$ of 5%, or 2.5%, worked more than 58.6 hours per week.

43.
$n = 30$ $\overline{X} = 214.97$ $s = 20.76$ At least 75% of the data values will fall between $\overline{X} \pm 2s$.
$\overline{X} - 2(20.76) = 214.97 - 41.52 = 173.45$ and $\overline{X} + 2(20.76) = 214.97 + 41.52 = 256.49$
In this case all 30 values fall within this range; hence Chebyshev's Theorem is correct for this example.

44.
$n = 30$ $\overline{X} = 34.47$ $s = 13.32$
$\overline{X} - 2s = 34.47 - 2(13.32) = 7.83$ and $\overline{X} + 2s = 34.47 + 2(13.32) = 61.11$
In this case 28 out of 30 data values fall withing the range of 7.83 to 61.11. This is 93.3% which is consistent with Chebyshev's Theorem.

45.
For $k = 1.5$, $1 - \frac{1}{1.5^2} = 1 - 0.44 = 0.56$ or 56%
For $k = 2$, $1 - \frac{1}{2^2} = 1 - 0.25 = 0.75$ or 75%
For $k = 2.5$, $1 - \frac{1}{2.5^2} = 1 - 0.16 = 0.84$ or 84%
For $k = 3$, $1 - \frac{1}{3^2} = 1 - 0.1111 = .8889$ or 88.89%
For $k = 3.5$, $1 - \frac{1}{3.5^2} = 1 - 0.08 = 0.92$ or 92%

46.
a. $s = 15.81$
b. $s = 15.81$
c. $s = 15.81$
d. $s = 79.06$
e. $s = 3.16$
f. The standard deviation is unchanged by adding or subtracting a specific number to each data value. If each data value is multiplied by a number the standard deviation increases by the number times the original standard deviation. For division the standard deviation is divided by the number.
g. When adding or subtracting the same number to each data value the mean will increase or decrease by that number, but the standard deviation will remain unchanged. When multiplying each data value by the same number the mean or standard deviation will be equal to that number times the original mean or standard deviation. When dividing each data value by the same number the mean or standard deviation will be equal to the original mean or standard deviation divided by that number.

47.

$\overline{X} = 13.3$

Mean Dev $= \frac{|5-13.3|+|9-13.3|+|10-13.3|+|11-13.3|+|11-13.3|}{10}$

$+ \frac{|12-13.3|+|15-13.3|+|18-13.3|+|20-13.3|+|22-13.3|}{10} = 4.36$

48.

a. $Sk = \frac{3(10-8)}{3} = 2$ positively skewed

b. $Sk = \frac{3(42-45)}{4} = -2.25$ negatively skewed

c. $Sk = \frac{3(18.6-18.6)}{1.5} = 0$ symmetric

d. $Sk = \frac{3(98-97.6)}{4} = 0.3$ positively skewed

49.

For $n = 25$, $\overline{X} = 50$, and $s = 3$:

$$s\sqrt{n-1} = 3\sqrt{25-1} = 14.7 \qquad \overline{X} + s\sqrt{n-1} = 50 + 14.7 = 64.7$$

67 must be an incorrect data value, since is beyond the range using the formula $s\sqrt{n-1}$.

EXERCISE SET 3-4

1.

A z score tells how many standard deviations the data value is above or below the mean.

2.

A percentile rank indicates the percent of data values that fall below the specific rank.

3.

A percentile is a relative measure while a percent is an absolute measure of the part to the total.

4.

A quartile is a relative measure of position obtained by dividing the data set into quarters.

5.

$Q_1 = P_{25}$, $Q_2 = P_{50}$, $Q_3 = P_{75}$

6.

A decile is a relative measure of position obtained by dividing the data set into tenths.

7.

$D_1 = P_{10}$, $D_2 = P_{20}$, $D_3 = P_{30}$, etc

8.

P_{50}, Q_2, D_5

9.

a. $z = \frac{X - \overline{X}}{s} = \frac{136 - 127}{9} = 1$

b. $z = \frac{109 - 127}{9} = -2$

9. continued

c. $z = \frac{104.5 - 127}{9} = -2.5$

d. $z = \frac{113.5 - 127}{9} = -1.5$

e. $z = \frac{133 - 127}{9} = 0.67$

10.

a. $z = \frac{X - \overline{X}}{s} = \frac{2.7 - 2.5}{0.3} = 0.67$

b. $z = \frac{3.9 - 2.5}{0.3} = 4.67$

c. $z = \frac{2.8 - 2.5}{0.3} = 1$

d. $z = \frac{3.1 - 2.5}{0.3} = 2$

e. $z = \frac{2.2 - 2.5}{0.3} = -1$

11.

a. $z = \frac{X - \overline{X}}{s} = \frac{87 - 84}{4} = 0.75$

b. $z = \frac{79 - 84}{4} = -1.25$

c. $z = \frac{93 - 84}{4} = 2.25$

d. $z = \frac{76 - 84}{4} = -2$

e. $z = \frac{82 - 84}{4} = -0.5$

12.

a. $z = \frac{X - \overline{X}}{s} = \frac{200 - 220}{10} = -2$

b. $z = \frac{232 - 220}{10} = 1.2$

c. $z = \frac{218 - 220}{10} = -0.2$

d. $z = \frac{212 - 220}{10} = -0.8$

e. $z = \frac{225 - 220}{10} = 0.5$

13.

a. $z = \frac{42 - 39}{4} = 0.75$

b. $z = \frac{76 - 71}{3} = 1.67$

The score for part b is has a higher relative position.

14.

For mathematics: $z = \frac{60 - 54}{3} = 2.0$ For history: $z = \frac{80 - 75}{2} = 2.5$

The student did better in history.

15.

a. $z = \frac{3.2-4.6}{1.5} = -0.93$ b. $z = \frac{630-800}{200} = -0.85$ c. $z = \frac{43-50}{5} = -1.4$

The score in part b is the highest.

16.

a. 58   b. 62.8   c. 64.5   d. 67.1

17.

a. 21st   b. 58th   c. 77th   d. 33rd

18.

a. 7   b. 25   c. 64   d. 76   e. 93

19.

a. a. 235   b. 255   c. 261   d. 275   e. 283

20.

a. 376   b. 389   c. 432   d. 473   e. 498

21.

a. 17th   b. 39th   c. 53rd   d. 79th   e. 91st

22.

Percentile $= \frac{\text{number of values below} + 0.5}{\text{total number of values}} \cdot 100\%$ Data: 78, 82, 86, 88, 92, 97

For 78, $\frac{0+.5}{6} \cdot 100\% = 8$th percentile   For 82, $\frac{1+.5}{6} \cdot 100\% = 25$th percentile

For 86, $\frac{2+.5}{6} \cdot 100\% = 42$nd percentile   For 88, $\frac{3+.5}{6} \cdot 100\% = 58$th percentile

For 92, $\frac{4+.5}{6} \cdot 100\% = 75$th percentile   For 97, $\frac{5+.5}{6} \cdot 100\% = 92$nd percentile

23.

$c = \frac{6(30)}{100} = 1.8$ or 2   82

24.

For 12, $\frac{0+.5}{7} \cdot 100\% = 7$th percentile   For 28, $\frac{1+.5}{7} \cdot 100\% = 21$st percentile

For 35, $\frac{2+.5}{7} \cdot 100\% = 36$th percentile   For 42, $\frac{3+.5}{7} \cdot 100\% = 50$th percentile

For 47, $\frac{4+.5}{7} \cdot 100\% = 64$th percentile   For 49, $\frac{5+.5}{7} \cdot 100\% = 79$th percentile

For 50, $\frac{6+.5}{7} \cdot 100\% = 93$rd percentile

25.

$c = \frac{n \cdot p}{100} = \frac{7(60)}{100} = 4.2$ or 5   Hence, 47 is the closest value to the 60th percentile.

26.

Percentile $= \frac{\text{number of values below} + 0.5}{\text{total number of values}} \cdot 100\%$ Data: 1.1, 1.7, 1.9, 2.1, 2.2, 2.5, 3.3, 6.2, 6.8, 20.3

For 1.1, $\frac{0+.5}{10} \cdot 100\% = 5$th percentile   For 1.7, $\frac{1+.5}{10} \cdot 100\% = 15$th percentile

For 1.9, $\frac{2+.5}{10} \cdot 100\% = 25$th percentile   For 2.1, $\frac{3+.5}{10} \cdot 100\% = 35$th percentile

26. continued

For 2.2, $\frac{4+.5}{10} \cdot 100\% = 45^{\text{th}}$ percentile   For 2.5, $\frac{5+.5}{10} \cdot 100\% = 55^{\text{nd}}$ percentile

For 3.3, $\frac{6+.5}{10} \cdot 100\% = 65^{\text{th}}$ percentile   For 6.2, $\frac{7+.5}{10} \cdot 100\% = 75^{\text{th}}$ percentile

For 6.8, $\frac{8+.5}{10} \cdot 100\% = 85^{\text{th}}$ percentile   For 20.3, $\frac{9+.5}{10} \cdot 100\% = 95^{\text{th}}$ percentile

27.

$c = \frac{10(40)}{100} = 4$ average the 4th and 5th values: $P_{40} = \frac{2.1+2.2}{2} = 2.15$

28.

Percentile $= \frac{\text{number of values below} + 0.5}{\text{total number of values}} \cdot 100\%$ Data: 5, 12, 15, 16, 20, 21

For 5, $\frac{0+.5}{6} \cdot 100\% = 8^{\text{th}}$ percentile   For 12, $\frac{1+.5}{6} \cdot 100\% = 25^{\text{th}}$ percentile

For 15, $\frac{3+.5}{6} \cdot 100\% = 42^{\text{nd}}$ percentile   For 16, $\frac{4+.5}{6} \cdot 100\% = 58^{\text{th}}$ percentile

For 20, $\frac{5+.5}{6} \cdot 100\% = 75^{\text{th}}$ percentile   For 21, $\frac{5+.5}{6} \cdot 100\% = 92^{\text{nd}}$ percentile

29.

$c = \frac{6(33)}{100} = 1.98$ or 2   5, 12, 15, 16, 20, 21

$\uparrow P_{33}$

The second data value is 12.

30.

a. 3 16 17 18 19 20 21 22

     $\uparrow$ $\uparrow$ $\uparrow$

    Q_1 MD Q_3

$MD = \frac{18+19}{2} = 18.5$

For Q_1: $Q_1 = \frac{16+17}{2} = 16.5$ For Q_3: $Q_3 = \frac{20+21}{2} = 20.5$

$Q_3 - Q_1 = 20.5 - 16.5 = 4$ and $4(1.5) = 6$. $16.5 - 6 = 10.5$ and $20.5 + 6 = 26.5$.

Only the value 3 lies outside the range of 10.5 to 26.5 and is a suspected outlier.

b. 14 16 17 18 19 20 24 31 32 54

      $\uparrow$ $\uparrow$ $\uparrow$

     Q_1 MD Q_3

$MD = \frac{19+20}{2} = 19.5$

For Q_1: $Q_1 = 17$, the median of 14, 16, 17, 18, and 19.

For Q_3: $Q_3 = 31$, the median of 20, 24, 31, 32, and 54.

$Q_3 - Q_1$: $31 - 17 = 14$ and $14(1.5) = 21$. $17 - 21 = -4$ and $31 + 21 = 52$. Only the value 54 lies outside the range of -4 to 52 and is a suspected outlier.

30. continued

c. 200 321 327 343 350
     ↑   ↑   ↑
     Q_1 MD Q_3

MD = 327

For Q_1: $Q_1 = \frac{200 + 321}{2} = 260.5$ For Q_3: $Q_3 = \frac{343 + 350}{2} = 346.5$

$Q_3 - Q_1$: $346.5 - 260.5 = 86$ and $86(1.5) = 129$. $260.5 - 129 = 131.5$ and $260.5 + 129 = 475.5$.

Since all the values fall within the range of 131.5 to 475.5, there are no outliers.

d. 72 84 85 86 88 97 100
       ↑   ↑   ↑
       Q_1 MD Q_3

MD = 86

For Q_1: $Q_1 = 84$ For Q_3: $Q_3 = 97$.

$Q_3 - Q_1$: $97 - 84 = 13$ and $13(1.5) = 19.5$. $84 - 19.5 = 64.5$ and $97 + 19.5 = 116.5$.

Since all values fall within the range of 64.5 to 116.5, there are no outliers.

e. 116 118 119 122 125 145
        ↑   ↑   ↑
        Q_1 MD Q_3

$MD = \frac{119 + 122}{2} = 120.5$

For Q_1: $Q_1 = 118$.   For Q_3: $Q_3 = 125$.

$Q_3 - Q_1$: $125 - 118 = 7$ and $7(1.5) = 10.5$. $118 - 10.5 = 107.5$ and $125 + 10.5 = 125.5$.

Only the value 145 is outside the range of 107.5 to 135.5 and is a suspected outlier.

f. 13 14 15 16 18 19 20 27 36
         ↑   ↑   ↑
         Q_1 MD Q_3

MD = 18

For Q_1: $Q_1 = \frac{14 + 15}{2} = 14.5$ For Q_3: $Q_3 = \frac{20 + 27}{2} = 23.5$

$Q_3 - Q_1$: $23.5 - 14.5 = 9$ and $9(1.5) = 13.5$. $14.5 - 13.5 = 1$ and $23.5 + 13.5 = 37$.

Since all values fall within the range of 1 to 37, there are no outliers.

31.
a. 5, 12, 16, 25, 32, 38 $Q_1 = 12$, $Q_2 = 20.5$, $Q_3 = 32$

Midquartile = $\frac{12 + 32}{2} = 22$ Interquartile range: $32 - 12 = 20$

31. continued

b. 53, 62, 78, 94, 96, 99, 103 $Q_1 = 62$, $Q_2 = 94$, $Q_3 = 99$

Midquartile = $\frac{62 + 99}{2} = 80.5$ Interquartile range: $99 - 62 = 37$

EXERCISE SET 3-5

1. Data arranged in order: 6, 8, 12, 19, 27, 32, 54

Minimum: 6
Q_1: 8
Median: 19
Q_3: 32
Maximum: 54
Interquartile Range: $32 - 8 = 24$

2. Data arranged in order: 7, 16, 19, 22, 48

Minimum: 7
Q_1: $\frac{7 + 16}{2} = 11.5$
Median: 19
Q_3: $\frac{22 + 48}{2} = 35$
Maximum: 48
Interquartile Range: $35 - 11.5 = 23.5$

3. Data arranged in order: 188, 192, 316, 362, 437, 589

Minimum: 188
Q_1: 192
Median: $\frac{316 + 362}{2} = 339$
Q_3: 437
Maximum: 589
Interquartile Range: $437 - 192 = 245$

4. Data arranged in order: 147, 156, 243, 303, 543, 632

Minimum: 147
Q_1: 156
Median: $\frac{243 + 303}{2} = 273$
Q_3: 543
Maximum: 632
Interquartile Range: $543 - 156 = 387$

5. Data arranged in order: 14.6, 15.5, 16.3, 18.2, 19.8

Minimum: 14.6
Q_1: $\frac{14.6 + 15.5}{2} = 15.05$
Median: 16.3
Q_3: $\frac{18.2 + 19.8}{2} = 19.0$
Maximum: 19.8
Interquartile Range: $19.0 - 15.05 = 3.95$

6. Data arranged in order: 2.2, 3.7, 3.8, 4.6, 6.2, 9.4, 9.7

Minimum: 2.2
Q_1: 3.7
Median: 4.6
Q_3: 9.4
Maximum: 9.7
Interquartile Range: $9.4 - 3.7 = 5.7$

7. Minimum: 3
Q_1: 5
Median: 8
Q_3: 9
Maximum: 11
Interquartile Range: $9 - 5 = 4$

8. Minimum: 200
Q_1: 225
Median: 275
Q_3: 300
Maximum: 325
Interquartile Range: $300 - 225 = 75$

9. Minimum: 55
Q_1: 65
Median: 70
Q_3: 90
Maximum: 95
Interquartile Range: $90 - 65 = 25$

10. Minimum: 2000
Q_1: 3000
Median: 4000
Q_3: 5000
Maximum: 6000
Interquartile Range: $5000 - 3000 = 2000$

11.
$MD = \frac{3.9+4.7}{2} = 4.3$
$Q_1 = 2.0 \quad Q_3 = 7.6$

The distribution is positively skewed.

12.
$MD = 198$
$Q_1 = 144.5 \qquad Q_3 = 243$

46

12. continued

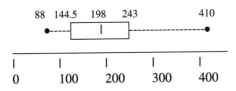

88   144.5   198   243   410

| | | | |
0   100   200   300   400

The distribution is positively skewed.

13. Data arranged in order: 13, 25, 25, 26, 28, 34, 35, 37, 42
Minimum: 13   Maximum: 42
MD = 28
$Q_1 = \frac{25+25}{2} = 25$ $Q_3 = \frac{35+37}{2} = 36$

13   25 28   36   42

| | | | |
10   20   30   40   50

14. Data arranged in order: 28, 29, 30, 33, 34, 35, 37, 37, 37, 38, 39
Minimum: 28   Maximum: 39
MD: 35
Q_1: 30 Q_3: 37

28   30   35 37   39

| | | | |
25   30   35   40   45

The distribution is negatively skewed.

15. Data arranged in order: 3.2, 3.9, 4.4, 8.0, 9.8, 11.7, 13.9, 15.9, 17.6, 21.7, 24.8, 34.1
Minimum: 3.2   Maximum: 34.1

MD: $\frac{11.7+13.9}{2} = 12.8$

Q_1: $\frac{4.4+8.0}{2} = 6.2$ Q_3: $\frac{17.6+21.7}{2} = 19.65$

3.2   6.2   12.8   19.65   34.1

| | | | | | | |
0   5   10   15   20   25   30   35

The distribution is positively skewed.

16.
For USA: min = 50,000; max = 125,628; MD = 72,100; Q_1 = 57,642.5; and Q_3 = 85,004

16. continued

For South America: min = 46,563; max = 311,539; MD = 103,979; Q_1 = 56,242; and Q_3 = 274,026

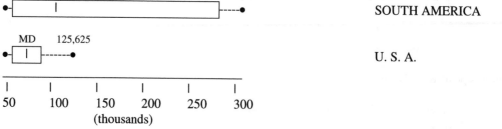

The range and variation of the capacity of the dams in South America is considerably larger than those of the United States.

17.

(a)

For April: $\overline{X} = 149.3$
For May: $\overline{X} = 264.3$
For June: $\overline{X} = 224.0$
For July: $\overline{X} = 123.3$

The month with the highest mean number of tornadoes is May.

(b)

For 2001: $\overline{X} = 186.0$
For 2000: $\overline{X} = 165.0$
For 1999: $\overline{X} = 219.75$

The year with the highest mean number of tornadoes is 1999.

(c) The 5-number summaries for each year are:

For 2001: 120, 127.5, 188, 244.5, 248
For 2000: 135, 135.5, 142, 194.5, 241
For 1999: 102, 139.5, 233, 300, 311

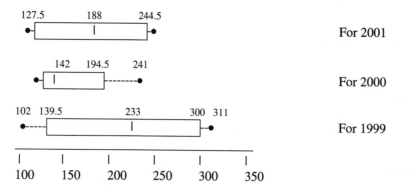

The data for 2001 is approximately symmetric while the data for 2000 and 1999 are skewed. The data for 2000 is positively skewed and the data for 1999 is negatively skewed. The data for the year 2000 is the least variable and has the smallest median.

18. Data arranged in order: 39, 39, 42, 43, 43, 53, 54, 66, 91, 97

Minimum: 39
Q_1: 42
Median: $\frac{43+53}{2} = 48$
Q_3: 66
Maximum: 97
Interquartile Range: $66 - 42 = 24$
$1.5(24) = 36$ for mild outliers; $3(24) = 72$ for extreme outliers
There are no outliers.

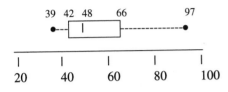

REVIEW EXERCISES - CHAPTER 3

1.

a. $\overline{X} = \dfrac{\sum X}{n} = \dfrac{1649}{15} = 109.9$

b.   60, 68, 70, 75, 89, 93, 95, **97**, 112, 114, 114, 122, 128, 182, 229

MD = 97

c. Mode = 114

d. MR = $\dfrac{60+229}{2} = 144.5$

e. Range = $229 - 60 = 169$

f. $s^2 = \dfrac{\sum X^2 - \frac{(\sum x)^2}{n}}{n-1} = \dfrac{209379 - \frac{1649^2}{15}}{15-1} = 2007.1$

g. $s = \sqrt{2007.1} = 44.8$

2.
Caribbean Sea:

a. $\overline{X} = \dfrac{108+75+\cdots+59+134}{19} = 4873.2$

b. 59, 75, 100, 108, 116, 134, 166, 171, 290, **436**, 687, 926, 1864, 2300, 3339, 4244, 5382, 29389, 42804

MD = 436

c. no mode

d. MR = $\dfrac{59+42,804}{2} = 21,431.5$

e. Range = $42,804 - 59 = 42,745$

f. $s^2 = \dfrac{2,764,509,234 - \frac{92,590^2}{19}}{19-1} = 128,516,863.6$

2. continued

g. $s = \sqrt{128,516,863.6} = 11,336.5$

Mediterranean Sea:

a. $\overline{X} = \frac{1927+229+\cdots+9301+9926}{10} = 3027.6$

b. 86, 95, 229, 540, **1411, 1927**, 3189, 3572, 9301, 9926

$MD = \frac{1411+1927}{2} = 1669$

c. no mode

d. $MR = \frac{86+9926}{2} = 5006$

e. Range $= 9926 - 86 = 9840$

f. $s^2 = \frac{214,027,694+\frac{30,276^2}{10}}{10-1} = 13,596,008.5$

g. $s = \sqrt{13,596,008.5} = 3687.3$

The Mediterranean islands are smaller and less variable than the Caribbean islands.

3.

Class	X_m	f	$f \cdot X_m$	$f \cdot X_m^2$	cf
1 - 3	2	1	2	4	1
4 - 6	5	4	20	100	5
7 - 9	8	5	40	320	10
10 - 12	11	1	11	121	11
13 - 15	14	1	14	196	12
		12	87	741	

a. $\overline{X} = \frac{\sum f \cdot X_m}{n} = \frac{87}{12} = 7.3$

b. Modal Class $= 7 - 9$ or $6.5 - 9.5$

c. $s^2 = \frac{741 - \frac{87^2}{12}}{11} = \frac{110.25}{11} = 10.0$

f. $s = \sqrt{10.0} = 3.2$

4.

X_m	f	$f \cdot X_m$	$f \cdot X_m^2$
36	4	144	5184
41	6	246	10086
46	3	138	6348
51	4	204	10404
56	3	168	9408
	20	900	41430

a. $\overline{X} = \frac{\sum f \cdot X_m}{n} = \frac{900}{20} = 45$

4. continued

b. Modal Class $= 39 - 43$

c. $s^2 = \frac{41430 - \frac{900^2}{20}}{19} = 48.9$

d. $s = \sqrt{48.9} = 6.99$ or 7

5.

Class Boundaries	X_m	f	$f \cdot X_m$	$f \cdot X_m^2$	cf
12.5 - 27.5	20	6	120	2400	6
27.5 - 42.5	35	3	105	3675	9
42.5 - 57.5	50	5	250	12,500	14
57.5 - 72.5	65	8	520	33,800	22
72.5 - 87.5	80	6	480	38,400	28
87.5 - 102.5	95	2	190	18,050	30
		30	1665	108,825	

a. $\overline{X} = \frac{\sum f \cdot X_m}{n} = \frac{1665}{30} = 55.5$

b. Modal class $= 57.5 - 72.5$

c. $s^2 = \frac{\sum f \cdot X_m^2 - \frac{(\sum f \cdot X_m)^2}{n}}{n-1} = \frac{108825 - \frac{1665^2}{30}}{30 - 1} = \frac{16417.5}{29} = 566.1$

d. $s = \sqrt{566.1} = 23.8$

6.

Class	X_m	f	$f \cdot X_m$	$f \cdot X_m^2$	cf
10 - 12	11	6	66	726	6
13 - 15	14	4	56	784	10
16 - 18	17	14	238	4046	24
19 - 21	20	15	300	6000	39
22 - 24	23	8	184	4232	47
25 - 27	26	2	52	1352	49
28 - 30	29	1	29	841	50
		50	925	17981	

a. $\overline{X} = \frac{925}{50} = 18.5$

b. Modal Class $= 19 - 21$ or $18.5 - 21.5$

c. $s^2 = \frac{17981 - \frac{925^2}{50}}{50 - 1} = \frac{868.5}{49} = 17.7$

d. $s = \sqrt{17.7} = 4.2$

7.

$\overline{X} = \frac{\sum w \cdot X}{\sum w} = \frac{12 \cdot 0 + 8 \cdot 1 + 5 \cdot 2 + 5 \cdot 3}{12 + 8 + 5 + 5} = \frac{33}{30} = 1.1$

8.

$\overline{X} = \frac{0.3(10,000) + 0.5(3000) + 0.2(1000)}{0.3 + 0.5 + 0.2} = \$4,700$

9.

$$\overline{X} = \frac{\sum w \cdot X}{\sum w} = \frac{8 \cdot 3 + 1 \cdot 6 + 1 \cdot 30}{8 + 1 + 1} = \frac{60}{10} = 6$$

10.

C. Var $= \frac{5}{16} = 0.3125$

C. Var $= \frac{8}{43} = 0.186$

The number of books is more variable.

11.

Magazines: C. Var $= \frac{s}{\overline{X}} = \frac{12}{56} = 0.214$

Year: C. Var $= \frac{s}{\overline{X}} = \frac{2.5}{6} = 0.417$

The number of years is more variable.

12.

Percentile $= \frac{\text{number of values below} + 0.5}{\text{total number of values}} \cdot 100\%$

a. For 2, $\frac{0 + 0.5}{6} \cdot 100\% = 8^{\text{th}}$ percentile

For 4, $\frac{1 + 0.5}{6} \cdot 100\% = 25^{\text{th}}$ percentile

For 5, $\frac{2 + 0.5}{6} \cdot 100\% = 42^{\text{nd}}$ percentile

For 6, $\frac{3 + 0.5}{6} \cdot 100\% = 58^{\text{th}}$ percentile

For 8, $\frac{4 + 0.5}{6} \cdot 100\% = 75^{\text{th}}$ percentile

For 9, $\frac{5 + 0.5}{6} \cdot 100\% = 92^{\text{nd}}$ percentile

b. c $= \frac{np}{100} = \frac{6(30)}{100} = \frac{180}{100} = 1.8$ round up to 2

Hence, 4 is closest to the 30th percentile

c. 2 4 5 6 8 9

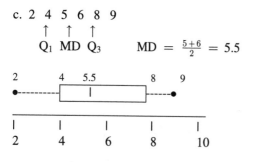

MD $= \frac{5 + 6}{2} = 5.5$

slightly negatively skewed

13.

a.

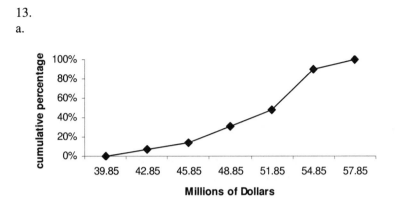

b. $P_{35} = 49$; $P_{65} = 52$; $P_{85} = 53$ (answers are approximate)

c. $44 = 15^{th}$ percentile; $48 = 33^{rd}$ percentile; $54 = 91^{nd}$ percentile (answers are approximate)

14.

a. 400 506 511 514 517 521

         ↑   ↑

       Q_1 Q_3

For Q_1: $c = \frac{np}{100} = \frac{6(25)}{100} = 1.5$ round up to 2 $Q_1 = 506$

For Q_3: $c = \frac{np}{100} = \frac{6(75)}{100} = 4.5$ round up to 5 $Q_3 = 517$

$Q_3 - Q_1 = 517 - 506 = 11$; $11(1.5) = 16.5$; $506 - 16.5 = 489.5$ and $517 + 16.5 = 533.5$
Therefore, only the value 400 lies outside the range of 489.5 to 533.5 and is a suspected outlier.

b. 3 6 7 8 9 10 12 14 16 20

        ↑   ↑

      Q_1 Q_3

For Q_1: $c = \frac{np}{100} = \frac{10(25)}{100} = 2.5$ round up to 3 $Q_1 = 7$

For Q_3: $c = \frac{np}{100} = \frac{10(75)}{100} = 7.5$ round up to 8 $Q_3 = 14$

$Q_3 - Q_1 = 14 - 7 = 7$; $7(1.5) = 10.5$; $7 - 10.5 = -3.5$ and $14 + 10.5 = 24.5$
Since all values fall within the range of -3.5 to 24.5, there are no outliers.

c. 5 13 14 18 19 25 26 27

     ↑   ↑

   $Q_1 = 13.5$ $Q_3 = 25.5$

For Q_1: $c = \frac{np}{100} = \frac{8(25)}{100} = 2.0$ Use the value between the 2nd and 3rd position: $Q_1 = \frac{13+14}{2} = 13.5$

For Q_3: $c = \frac{np}{100} = \frac{8(75)}{100} = 6.0$ Use the value between the 6th and 7th position: $Q_3 = \frac{25+26}{2} = 25.5$

$Q_3 - Q_1 = 25.5 - 13.5 = 12$; $12(1.5) = 18$: $13.5 - 18 = -4.5$ and $25.5 + 18 = 43.5$
Since all values fall within the range of -4.5 to 43.5, there are no outliers.

14. continued

d. 112 116 129 131 153 157 192

   $\qquad$ $\uparrow$ $\qquad\qquad\qquad\qquad$ $\uparrow$

   $\qquad$ Q_1 $\qquad\qquad\qquad\qquad$ Q_3

For Q_1: $c = \frac{np}{100} = \frac{7(25)}{100} = 1.75$ Round up to 2. $Q_1 = 116$

For Q_3: $c = \frac{np}{100} = \frac{7(75)}{100} = 5.25$ Round up to 6. $Q_3 = 157$

$Q_3 - Q_1 = 157 - 116 = 41$; $41(1.5) = 61.5$: $116 - 61.5 = 54.5$ and $157 + 61.5 = 218.5$
Since all values fall within the range of 54.5 to 218.5, there are no outliers.

15.
$\overline{X} = 0.32$ $s = 0.03$ $k = 2$
$0.32 - 2(0.03) = 0.26$ and $0.32 + 2(0.03) = 0.38$
At least 75% of the values will fall between \$0.26 and \$0.38.

16.
$\overline{X} = 42$ $s = 3$ $k = 3$
$42 - 3(3) = 33$ and $42 + 3(3) = 51$
At least 88.89% of the data values will fall between \$33 and \$51.

17.
$\overline{X} = 54$ $s = 4$ $60 - 54 = 6$ $k = \frac{6}{4} = 1.5$ $1 - \frac{1}{1.5^2} = 1 - 0.44 = 0.56$ or 56%

18.
$\overline{X} = 231$ $s = 5$ $243 - 231 = 12$ $k = \frac{12}{5} = 2.4$ $1 - \frac{1}{2.4^2} = 0.83$ or 83%

19.
$\overline{X} = 32$ $s = 4$ $44 - 32 = 12$ $k = \frac{12}{4} = 3$ $1 - \frac{1}{3^2} = 0.8889 = 88.89\%$

20.
a. $z = \frac{82 - 85}{6} = -0.5$ b. $z = \frac{56 - 60}{5} = -0.8$ Exam A has a better relative position.

21.
Before Christmas:
$MD = 30$ $Q_1 = 21$ $Q_3 = 33.5$

After Christmas:
$MD = 18$ $Q_1 = 14.5$ $Q_3 = 23$

The employees worked more hours before Christmas than after Christmas. Also, the range and variability of the distribution of hours worked before Christmas is greater than that of hours worked after Christmas.

22. By the Empirical Rule, 68% of the scores will be within 1 standard deviation of the mean.
$29.7 + 1(6) = 35.7$
$29.7 - 1(6) = 23.7$
Then 68% of commuters will get to work between 23.7 and 35.7 minutes.

CHAPTER 3 QUIZ

1. True
2. True
3. False
4. False
5. False
6. False
7. False
8. False
9. False
10. c
11. c
12. a and b
13. b
14. d
15. b
16. Statistic
17. Parameters, statistics
18. Standard deviation
19. σ
20. Midrange
21. Positively
22. Outlier
23. a. 15.3   b. 15.5   c. 15, 16, 17   d. 15   e. 6   f. 3.61   g. 1.9
24. a. 6.4   b. $6 - 8$ c. 11.6   d. 3.4
25. a. 51.4   b. $35.5 - 50.5$ c. 451.5   d. 21.2
26. a. 8.2   b. $7 - 9$ c. 21.6   d. 4.6
27. 1.6
28. 4.46 or 4.5
29. 0.33; 0.162; newspapers
30. 0.3125; 0.229; brands
31. $-0.75; -1.67$; science
32. a. 0.5   b. 1.6   c. 15, c is higher
33. a. 56.25; 43.75; 81.25; 31.25; 93.75; 18.75; 6.25; 68.75   b. 0.9
    c.

34.

a.

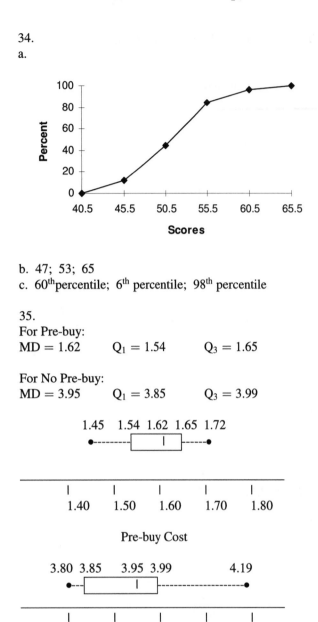

b. 47; 53; 65

c. 60th percentile; 6th percentile; 98th percentile

35.

For Pre-buy:

MD = 1.62 $Q_1 = 1.54$ $Q_3 = 1.65$

For No Pre-buy:

MD = 3.95 $Q_1 = 3.85$ $Q_3 = 3.99$

The cost of pre-buy gas is much less than to return the car without filling it with gas. The variability of the return without filling with gas is larger than the variability of the pre-buy gas.

36.

For above 1129: 16%

For above 799: 97.5%

Note: Answers may vary due to rounding, TI-83's or computer programs.

EXERCISE SET 4-2

1.
A probability experiment is a chance process which leads to well-defined outcomes.

2.
The set of all possible outcomes of a probability experiment is called a sample space.

3.
An outcome is the result of a single trial of a probability experiment, whereas an event can consist of one or more outcomes.

4.
Equally likely events have the same probability of occurring.

5.
The range of values is $0 \le P(E) \le 1$.

6.
1

7.
0

8.
1

9.
$1 - 0.20 = 0.80$
Since the probability that it won't rain is 80%, you could leave your umbrella at home and be fairly safe.

10.
b, d, f, i

11.
a. Empirical   e. Empirical
b. Classical   f. Empirical
c. Empirical   g. Subjective
d. Classical

12.
a. $\frac{1}{6}$ d. 1
b. $\frac{1}{2}$ e. 1
c. $\frac{1}{3}$ f. $\frac{5}{6}$

12. continued
g. $\frac{1}{6}$

13.
There are 6^2 or 36 outcomes.
a. There are 5 ways to get a sum of 6. They are (1,5), (2,4), (3,3), (4,2), and (5,1). The probability then is $\frac{5}{36}$.

b. There are six ways to get doubles. They are (1,1), (2,2), (3,3), (4,4), (5,5), and (6,6). The probability then is $\frac{6}{36} = \frac{1}{6}$.

c. There are six ways to get a sum of 7. They are (1,6), (2,5), (3,4), (4,3), (5,2), and (6,1). There are two ways to get a sum of 11. They are (5,6) and (6,5). Hence, the total number of ways to get a 7 or 11 is eight. The probability then is $\frac{8}{36} = \frac{2}{9}$.

d. To get a sum greater than nine, one must roll a 10, 11, or 12. There are six ways to get a 10, 11, or 12. They are (4,6), (5,5), (6,4), (5,6), (6,5), and (6,6). The probability then is $\frac{6}{36} = \frac{1}{6}$.

e. To get a sum less than or equal to four, one must roll a 4, 3, or 2. There are six ways to do this. They are (3,1), (2,2), (1,3), (2,1), (1,2), and (1,1). The probability is $\frac{6}{36} = \frac{1}{6}$.

14.
a. $\frac{1}{13}$ f. $\frac{4}{13}$

b. $\frac{1}{4}$ g. $\frac{1}{2}$

c. $\frac{1}{52}$ h. $\frac{1}{26}$

d. $\frac{2}{13}$ i. $\frac{7}{13}$

e. $\frac{4}{13}$ j. $\frac{1}{26}$

15.
There are 24 possible outcomes.

a. P(winning $10) = P(rolling a 1)
P(rolling a 1) $= \frac{4}{24} = \frac{1}{6}$

b. P(winning $5 or $10) = P(rolling either a 1 or 2)
P(1 or 2) $= \frac{12}{24} = \frac{1}{2}$

15. continued
c. P(winning a coupon) = P(rolling either a 3 or 4)
P(3 or 4) = $\frac{12}{24} = \frac{1}{2}$

16.
a. P(begins with M) = $\frac{8}{50} = \frac{4}{25}$

b. P(begins with a vowel) = $\frac{12}{50} = \frac{6}{25}$
P(not a vowel) = $1 - \frac{6}{25} = \frac{19}{25}$

17.
a. P(graduate school) = $\frac{110}{250} = \frac{11}{25}$ or 0.44

b. P(medical school) = $\frac{10}{250} = \frac{1}{25}$ or 0.04

c. P(not going to graduate school) = $1 - \frac{110}{250} = \frac{140}{250}$ or 0.56

18.
P(doesn't believe in gun licensing) = $1 - 0.69 = 0.31$

19.
a. P(2 or 3 children) = $0.19 + 0.07 = 0.26$ or 26%

b. P(more than 1 child) = $0.19 + 0.07 + 0.03 = 0.29$ or 29%

c. P(less than 3 children) = $0.51 + 0.20 + 0.19 = 0.90$ or 90%

d. The event in part c is most likely.

20.
a. P(education) = $\frac{106,000}{1,184,000} \approx 0.0895$

b. P(not business) = $1 - \frac{233,000}{1,184,000}$
P(not business) = $\frac{951,000}{1,184,000} \approx 0.8032$

21.
The sample space is BBB, BBG, BGB, GBB, GGB, GBG, BGG, and GGG.

a. All boys is the outcome BBB; hence P(all boys) = $\frac{1}{8}$.

b. All girls or all boys would be BBB and GGG; hence, P(all girls or all boys) = $\frac{1}{4}$.

c. Exactly two boys or two girls would be BBG, BGB, GBB, BBG, GBG, or BGG. The probability then is $\frac{6}{8} = \frac{3}{4}$.

d. At least one child of each gender means at least one boy or at least one girl. The outcomes are the same as those of part c, hence the probability is the same, $\frac{3}{4}$.

22.
There are 6 ways to get a 7 and 2 ways to get 11; hence, P(7 or 11) = $\frac{8}{36} = \frac{2}{9}$.

23.
The outcomes for 2, 3, or 12 are (1,1), (1,2), (2,1), and (6,6); hence P(2, 3, or 12) = $\frac{1+2+1}{36} = \frac{4}{36} = \frac{1}{9}$.

24.
P(Houston, Chicago, or Los Angeles) = $\frac{118}{2541}$ or 0.0464

P(some other city) = $1 - \frac{118}{2541} = \frac{2423}{2541}$ or 0.9536

25.
a. There are 18 odd numbers; hence, P(odd) = $\frac{18}{36} = \frac{9}{19}$.

b. There are 9 numbers greater than 27 (28 through 36) hence, the probability is $\frac{9}{38}$.

c. There are 5 numbers containing the digit 0 hence the probability is $\frac{5}{38}$.

d. The event in part a is most likely to occur since it has the highest probability of occurring.

26.
$\frac{39}{50} = 0.78$

27.
P(right amount or too little) = $0.35 + 0.19$
P(right amount or too little) = 0.54

28.
$1 - 0.16 = 0.84$ or 84%

29.

a.

	1	2	3	4	5	6
1	1	2	3	4	5	6
2	2	4	6	8	10	12
3	3	6	9	12	15	18
4	4	8	12	16	20	24
5	5	10	15	20	25	30
6	6	12	18	24	30	36

b. P(multiple of 6) $= \frac{15}{36} = \frac{5}{12}$

c. P(less than 10) $= \frac{17}{36}$

30.

P(individual or corporate taxes) $= 0.60$

31.

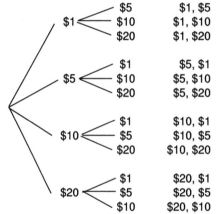

32.

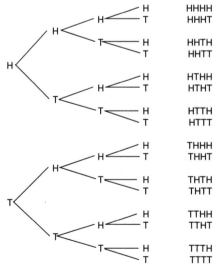

33.

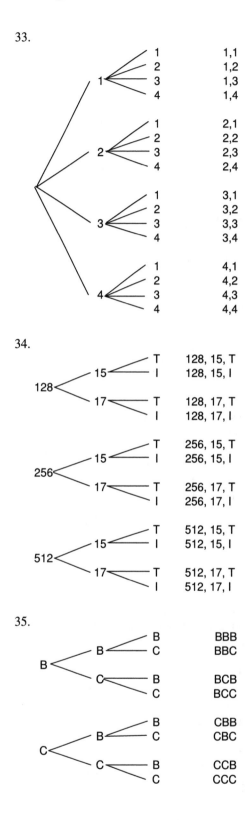

34.

35.

36.

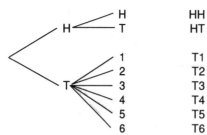

37.
a. 0.08
b. 0.01
c. $0.08 + 0.27 = 0.35$
d. $0.01 + 0.24 + 0.11 = 0.36$

38.
Probably.

39.
The statement is probably not based on empirical probability and probably not true.

40.
The outcomes will be:

0,0	0,1	0,2	0,3	0,4
1,0	1,1	1,2	1,3	1,4
2,0	2,1	2,2	2,3	2,4
3,0	3,1	3,2	3,3	3,4
4,0	4,1	4,2	4,3	4,4

a. $\frac{6}{25}$ b. $\frac{10}{25} = \frac{2}{5}$ c. $\frac{9}{25}$

d. $\frac{12}{25}$ e. $\frac{5}{25} = \frac{1}{5}$

41.
Actual outcomes will vary, however each number should occur approximately $\frac{1}{6}$ of the time.

42.
Actual outcomes will differ; however, the probabilities of 0, 1, and 2 heads will be approximately $\frac{1}{4}$, $\frac{1}{2}$, and $\frac{1}{4}$ respectively.

43.
a. 1:5, 5:1   e. 1:12, 12:1
b. 1:1, 1:1   f. 1:3, 3:1
c. 1:3, 3:1   g. 1:1, 1:1
d. 1:1, 1:1

EXERCISE SET 4-3

1.
Two events are mutually exclusive if they cannot occur at the same time. Examples will vary.

2.
a. No   e. No
b. No   f. Yes
c. Yes g. Yes
d. No

3.
Using months: P(September or October) $= \frac{2}{12} = \frac{1}{6}$

Using days: P(September or October) $= \frac{61}{365}$

Using days makes the probability slightly larger than using months.

4.
$\frac{8}{15} + \frac{2}{15} = \frac{10}{15}$ or $\frac{2}{3}$

5.
$\frac{4}{19} + \frac{7}{19} = \frac{11}{19}$

6.
$\frac{310}{980} + \frac{150}{980} = \frac{460}{980}$ or $\frac{23}{49}$

The probability of the event is slightly less than 0.5 which makes it about equally likely to occur or not to occur.

7.
a. $\frac{56}{200} = \frac{7}{25}$ or 0.28
b. $\frac{75}{200} = \frac{3}{8}$ or 0.375
c. $\frac{34}{200} = \frac{17}{100}$ or 0.17
d. Event b has the highest probability so it is most likely to occur.

8.
P(car or computer) $=$
$0.65 + 0.82 - 0.55 = 0.92$
P(neither) $= 1 - 0.92 = 0.08$

9.
P(football or basketball) $=$
$\frac{58 + 40 - 8}{200} = \frac{90}{200}$ or 0.45

P(neither) $= 1 - \frac{90}{200} = \frac{11}{20}$ or 0.55

10.

a. There are four 4's and 13 diamonds, but the 4 of diamonds is counted twice; hence, P(4 or diamond) = P(4) + P(diamonds) − P(4 of diamonds) = $\frac{4}{52} + \frac{13}{52} - \frac{1}{52}$ = $\frac{16}{52} = \frac{4}{13}$.

b. P(club or diamond) = $\frac{13}{52} + \frac{13}{52} = \frac{26}{52}$ or $\frac{1}{2}$

c. P(jack or black) = $\frac{4}{52} + \frac{26}{52} - \frac{2}{52}$ = $\frac{28}{52}$ or $\frac{7}{13}$

11.

	Junior	Senior	Total
Female	6	6	12
Male	12	4	16
Total	18	10	28

a. $\frac{18}{28} + \frac{12}{28} - \frac{6}{28} = \frac{24}{28} = \frac{6}{7}$

b. $\frac{10}{28} + \frac{12}{28} - \frac{6}{28} = \frac{16}{28} = \frac{4}{7}$

c. $\frac{18}{28} + \frac{10}{28} = \frac{28}{28} = 1$

12.

	Fiction	Non-Fiction	Total
Adult	30	70	100
Children	100	60	160
Total	130	130	260

a. P(fiction) = $\frac{130}{260} = \frac{1}{2}$ or 0.5

b. P(children's nonfiction) = $\frac{60}{260} = \frac{3}{13}$
P(not a children's nonfiction) = $1 - \frac{3}{13} = \frac{10}{13}$ or 0.7692

c. P(adult book or children's nonfiction) = $\frac{100}{260} + \frac{60}{260} = \frac{160}{260}$ or $\frac{8}{13}$ or 0.6154

13.

	SUV	Compact	Mid-sized	Total
Foreign	20	50	20	90
Domestic	65	100	45	210
Total	85	150	65	300

a. P(domestic) = $\frac{210}{300} = \frac{7}{10}$ or 0.7

b. P(foreign and mid-sized) = $\frac{20}{300} = \frac{1}{15} = 0.0667$

c. P(domestic or SUV) = $\frac{210}{300} + \frac{85}{300} - \frac{65}{300}$ = $\frac{230}{300} = \frac{23}{30}$ or 0.7667

14.

	Mammals	Birds	Reptiles	Amphibians	Total
U. S.	63	78	14	10	165
Foreign	251	175	64	8	498
Total	314	253	78	18	663

a. P(found in U. S. and is a bird) = $\frac{78}{663} = \frac{2}{17}$ or 0.1176

b. P(foreign or a mammal) = $\frac{498}{663} + \frac{314}{663} - \frac{251}{663} = \frac{561}{663}$ or 0.846

c. P(warm-blooded) = $\frac{314}{663} + \frac{253}{663} = \frac{567}{663}$ or 0.8552

15.

	Cashier	Clerk	Deli	Total
Married	8	12	3	23
Not Married	5	15	2	22
Total	13	27	5	45

a. P(stock clerk or married) = P(clerk) + P(married) − P(married stock clerk) = $\frac{27}{45} + \frac{23}{45} - \frac{12}{45} = \frac{38}{45}$

b. P(not married) = $\frac{22}{45}$

c. P(cashier or not married) = P(cashier) + P(not married) − P(unmarried cashier) = $\frac{13}{45} + \frac{22}{45} - \frac{5}{45} = \frac{30}{45} = \frac{2}{3}$

16.

Comics	Morning	Evening	Weekly	Total
Yes	2	3	1	6
No	3	4	2	9
Total	5	7	3	15

a. P(weekly) = $\frac{3}{15}$ or $\frac{1}{5}$

b. P(morning or has comics) = P(morning) + P(has comics) − P(morning with comics) = $\frac{5}{15} + \frac{6}{15} - \frac{2}{15} = \frac{9}{15} = \frac{3}{5}$

c. P(weekly or no comics) = P(weekly) + P(no comics) − P(weekly with no comics) = $\frac{3}{15} + \frac{9}{15} - \frac{2}{15} = \frac{10}{15} = \frac{2}{3}$

17.

	Ch. 6	Ch. 8	Ch. 10	Total
Quiz	5	2	1	8
Comedy	3	2	8	13
Drama	4	4	2	10
Total	12	8	11	31

17. continued

a. P(quiz show or channel 8) = P(quiz) + P(channel 8) − P(quiz show on ch. 8) = $\frac{8}{31} + \frac{8}{31} - \frac{2}{31} = \frac{14}{31}$

b. P(drama or comedy) = P(drama) + P(comedy) = $\frac{13}{31} + \frac{10}{31} = \frac{23}{31}$

c. P(channel 10 or drama) = P(ch. 10) + P(drama) − P(drama on channel 10) = $\frac{11}{31} + \frac{10}{31} - \frac{2}{31} = \frac{19}{31}$

18.

	1st Class	Ad	Magazine	Total
Home	325	406	203	934
Business	732	1021	97	1850
Total	1057	1427	300	2784

a. P(home) = $\frac{934}{2784} = \frac{467}{1392}$

b. P(advertisement or business) = P(ad) + P(business) − P(business and ad) = $\frac{1427}{2784} + \frac{1850}{2784} - \frac{1021}{2784} = \frac{2256}{2784} = \frac{47}{58}$

c. P(1st class or home) = P(1st class) + P(home) − P(1st class and home) = $\frac{1057}{2784} + \frac{934}{2784} - \frac{325}{2784} = \frac{1666}{2784} = \frac{833}{1392}$

19.

The total of the frequencies is 30.

a. $\frac{2}{30} = \frac{1}{15}$

b. $\frac{2+3+5}{30} = \frac{10}{30} = \frac{1}{3}$

c. $\frac{12+8+2+3}{30} = \frac{25}{30} = \frac{5}{6}$

d. $\frac{12+8+2+3}{30} = \frac{25}{30} = \frac{5}{6}$

e. $\frac{8+2}{30} = \frac{10}{30} = \frac{1}{3}$

20.

The total of the frequencies is 40.

a. $\frac{2}{40} = \frac{1}{20}$

b. $\frac{15+2}{40} = \frac{17}{40}$

c. $\frac{9}{40}$

d. $\frac{2+15+8}{40} = \frac{25}{40} = \frac{5}{8}$

21.

The total of the frequencies is 24.

a. $\frac{10}{24} = \frac{5}{12}$

21. continued

b. $\frac{2+1}{24} = \frac{3}{24} = \frac{1}{8}$

c. $\frac{10+3+2+1}{24} = \frac{16}{24} = \frac{2}{3}$

d. $\frac{8+10+3+2}{24} = \frac{23}{24}$

22.

	High Chol.	Normal Chol.	Total
Alcoholic	87	13	100
Non-Alcoholic	43	157	200
Total	56	244	300

a. P(alcoholic with elevated cholesterol) = $\frac{87}{300} = \frac{29}{100}$

b. P(non-alcoholic) = $\frac{200}{300} = \frac{2}{3}$

c. P(non-alcoholic with normal cholesterol) = $\frac{157}{300}$

23.

a. There are 4 kings, 4 queens, and 4 jacks; hence P(king or queen or jack) = $\frac{12}{52} = \frac{3}{13}$

b. There are 13 clubs, 13 hearts, and 13 spades; hence, P(club or heart or spade) = $\frac{13+13+13}{52} = \frac{39}{52} = \frac{3}{4}$

c. There are 4 kings, 4 queens, and 13 diamonds but the king and queen of diamonds were counted twice, hence; P(king or queen or diamond) = P(king) + P(queen) + P(diamond) − P(king and queen of diamonds) = $\frac{4}{52} + \frac{4}{52} + \frac{13}{52} - \frac{2}{52} = \frac{19}{52}$

d. There are 4 aces, 13 diamonds, and 13 hearts. There is one ace of diamonds and one ace of hearts; hence, P(ace or diamond or heart) = P(ace) + P(diamond) + P(heart) − P(ace of hearts and ace of diamonds) = $\frac{4}{52} + \frac{13}{52} + \frac{13}{52} - \frac{2}{52} = \frac{28}{52} = \frac{7}{13}$

e. There are 4 nines, 4 tens, 13 spades, and 13 clubs. There is one nine of spades, one ten of spades, one nine of clubs and one ten of clubs. Hence, P(9 or 10 or spade or club) = P(9) + P(10) + P(spade) + P(club) − P(9 and 10 of clubs and spades) = $\frac{4}{52} + \frac{4}{52} + \frac{13}{52} + \frac{13}{52} - \frac{4}{52} = \frac{30}{52} = \frac{15}{26}$

24.

a. $\frac{4}{36} + \frac{5}{36} + \frac{6}{36} = \frac{15}{36} = \frac{5}{12}$ or 0.42

24. continued

b. $\frac{6}{36} + \frac{10}{36} - \frac{2}{36} = \frac{14}{36} = \frac{7}{18}$ or 0.39

c. $\frac{10}{36} + \frac{1}{36} = \frac{11}{36}$ or 0.31

d. The event in part a is most likely to occur since it has the highest probability.

25.
P(red or white ball) $= \frac{7}{10}$

26.
There are $6^3 = 216$ possible outcomes.
a. $\frac{6}{216} = \frac{1}{36}$ since there are 6 triples, (1,1,1), (2,2,2), . . . , (6,6,6).

b. $\frac{6}{216} = \frac{1}{36}$ since there are six possible outcomes summing to 5. (1,2,2), (2,1,2), (2,2,1), (1,1,3), (1,3,1), and (3,1,1).

27.
P(mushrooms or pepperoni) =
     P(mushrooms) + P(pepperoni) −
     P(mushrooms and pepperoni)

Let X = P(mushrooms and pepperoni)
Then $0.55 = 0.32 + 0.17 - X$
$X = 0.06$

28.
P(one or two car garage) =
$0.20 + 0.70 = 0.90$
Hence, P(no garage) $= 1 - 0.90 = 0.10$

29.
P(not a two-car garage) $= 1 - 0.70 = 0.30$

30.
No. $P(A \cap B) \neq 0$

EXERCISE SET 4-4

1.
a. Independent e. Independent
b. Dependent   f. Dependent
c. Dependent   g. Dependent
d. Dependent   h. Independent

2.
P(all 5 exercise
regularly) $= (0.37)^5 = 0.007$ or 0.7%
The event is unlikely to occur since its
probability is very small.

3.
P(both are women) $= (.84)^2 = 0.706$ or 70.6%
The event is likely to occur since the probability is greater than 0.5.

4.
P(all 4 used a seat belt) $= (.52)^4 = 7.3\%$

5.
P(male graduate) $= 1 - 0.28 = 0.72$
P(all 3 are male) $= (0.72)^3 = 0.373$ or 37.3%
The event is unlikely to occur since the probability is less than 0.5.

6.
P(two inmates are not citizens) $= (0.25)^2$
    $= 0.0625$ or 6.3%

7.
a. P(no computer) $= 1 - 0.543 = 0.457$
P(none of three has a computer) =
$(0.457)^3 = 0.0954$

b. P(at least one has a computer) =
$1 - $ P(none of three has a computer) $=$
$1 - 0.0954 = 0.9046$

c. P(all three have computers) =
$(0.543)^3 = 0.1601$

8.
a. P(both are spades) $= \frac{13}{52} \cdot \frac{12}{51} = \frac{1}{17}$

b. P(both are the same suit) =
$\frac{4}{4} \cdot \frac{12}{51} = \frac{4}{17}$

c. P(both are kings) $= \frac{4}{52} \cdot \frac{3}{51} = \frac{1}{221}$

9.
P(all are citizens) $= (0.801)^3 = 0.5139$

10.
P(three agree to government's
responsibility) $= (\frac{1}{2})^3 = \frac{1}{8}$

11.
P(all three have NFL apparel) =
$(0.31)^3 = 0.0298$

12.
P(both are defective) $= \frac{2}{6} \cdot \frac{1}{5} = \frac{1}{15}$

13.
$P(\text{no insurance}) = 0.12$
$P(\text{none are covered}) = (0.12)^4 = 0.0002$

14.
$P(\text{three murders with no}$
$\text{weapon}) = (.06)^3 = 0.0002 \text{ or } 0.02\%$

15.
$P(5 \text{ buy at least } 1) = (\frac{90}{120})^5 = \frac{243}{1024}$

16.
a. $\frac{4}{52} \cdot \frac{3}{51} \cdot \frac{2}{50} = \frac{1}{5525}$

b. $\frac{13}{52} \cdot \frac{12}{51} \cdot \frac{11}{50} = \frac{11}{850}$

c. $\frac{26}{52} \cdot \frac{25}{51} \cdot \frac{24}{50} = \frac{2}{17}$

17.
$\frac{5}{8} \cdot \frac{4}{7} \cdot \frac{3}{6} = \frac{5}{28}$

18.
$\frac{3}{8} \cdot \frac{2}{7} \cdot \frac{1}{6} = \frac{1}{56}$

19.
$\frac{23}{38} \cdot \frac{22}{37} \cdot \frac{21}{36} = \frac{1771}{8436}$ or 0.210
The event is unlikely to occur since the
probability is less than 0.5.

20.
$\frac{15}{38} \cdot \frac{14}{37} \cdot \frac{13}{36} = \frac{455}{8436}$ or 0.054

21.

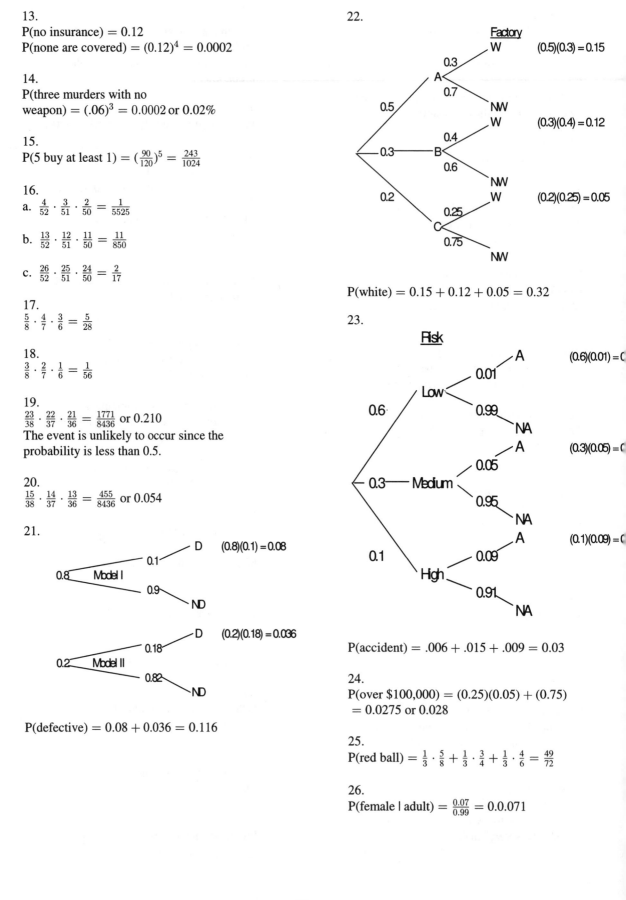

$P(\text{defective}) = 0.08 + 0.036 = 0.116$

22.

$P(\text{white}) = 0.15 + 0.12 + 0.05 = 0.32$

23.

$P(\text{accident}) = .006 + .015 + .009 = 0.03$

24.
$P(\text{over } \$100{,}000) = (0.25)(0.05) + (0.75)$
$= 0.0275 \text{ or } 0.028$

25.
$P(\text{red ball}) = \frac{1}{3} \cdot \frac{5}{8} + \frac{1}{3} \cdot \frac{3}{4} + \frac{1}{3} \cdot \frac{4}{6} = \frac{49}{72}$

26.
$P(\text{female} \mid \text{adult}) = \frac{0.07}{0.99} = 0.0.071$

27.
P(auto will be found within one week | it's
been stolen) $= \frac{P(\text{stolen and found within 1 week})}{P(\text{stolen})}$
$= \frac{0.0009}{0.0015} = 0.6$

28.
P(2nd defective | 1st defective) $=$

$\frac{P(\text{1st and 2nd defective})}{P(\text{1st defective})} = \frac{\frac{2}{8} \cdot \frac{1}{7}}{\frac{2}{8}} = \frac{1}{7}$

29.
P(swim | bridge) $= \frac{P(\text{play bridge and swim})}{P(\text{play bridge})}$

$= \frac{0.73}{0.82} = 0.89$ or 89%

30.
P(calculus | dean's list) $= \frac{0.042}{0.21} = 0.2$

31.
P(garage | deck) $= \frac{0.42}{0.60} = 0.7$ or 70%

32.
P(salad | pizza) $= \frac{0.65}{0.95} = 0.684$ or 68.4%

33.
P(champagne | bridge) $= \frac{0.68}{0.83} = 0.82$ or
82%

34.

Class	Favor	Oppose	No Opinion	Total
Fr	15	27	8	50
Soph	23	5	2	30
Total	38	32	10	80

a. $\frac{27}{80} \div \frac{50}{80} = \frac{27}{50}$

b. $\frac{23}{80} \div \frac{38}{80} = \frac{23}{38}$

35.
a. P(foreign patent | corporation) $=$

$\frac{P(\text{corporation and foreign patent})}{P(\text{corporation})} =$

$\frac{\frac{63,182}{147,497}}{\frac{134,076}{147,497}} = \frac{63,182}{134,076} = 0.4712$

b. P(individual | U. S.) $= \frac{P(\text{U. S. \& individual})}{P(\text{U. S.})}$

$\frac{\frac{6129}{147,497}}{\frac{77,944}{147,497}} = \frac{6129}{77,944} = 0.0786$

36.
a. P(gold | U. S.) $= \frac{P(\text{U. S. and gold})}{P(\text{U. S.})}$

$\frac{\frac{39}{928}}{\frac{97}{928}} = \frac{39}{97} = 0.4021$

b. P(U. S. | gold) $= \frac{P(\text{gold and U. S.})}{P(\text{gold})}$

$\frac{\frac{39}{928}}{\frac{301}{928}} = \frac{39}{301} = 0.1296$

c. No, because P(gold | U. S.) $\neq$ P(gold).

37.
a. P(none have been
married) $= (0.703)^5 = 0.1717$

b. P(at least one has been married) $=$
$1 - $ P(none have been married)
$= 1 - 0.1717$
$= 0.8283$

38.
a. P(all three caused by driver
error) $= (0.54)^3 = 0.157$

b. P(none caused by driver
error) $= (0.46)^3 = 0.097$

c. P(at least one caused by driver
error) $= 1 - $ P(none by driver error)
$= 1 - 0.0973 = 0.9027$

39.
P(at least one not immunized) $= 1 - $ P(none
of the six are not immunized)
$= 1 - $ P(all six are immunized)
$= 1 - (0.76)^6 = 0.8073$

40.
P(at least one defective) $=$
$1 - $ P(none defective) $= 1 - \frac{15}{18} \cdot \frac{14}{17} = \frac{16}{51}$

41.
If P(read to) $= 0.58$, then
P(not being read to) $= 1 - 0.58 = 0.42$

P(at least one is read to) $= 1 - $ P(none are
read to)
$= 1 - $ P(all five are not read to)
$= 1 - (0.42)^5 = 0.9869$

42.
a. P(all three have
assistantships) $= (0.6)^3 = 0.216$

42. continued

b. P (none have
assistantships) $= (0.4)^3 = 0.064$

c. P(at least one has an
assistantship) $= 1 - $ (none have
assistantships)
$= 1 - 0.064 = 0.936$

43.
P(at least one club) $= 1 - $ P(no clubs)
$1 - \frac{39}{52} \cdot \frac{38}{51} \cdot \frac{37}{50} \cdot \frac{36}{49} = 1 - \frac{6327}{20,825}$
$= \frac{14,498}{20,825}$

44.
P(at least one child) $= 1 - $ P(no children)
$1 - \frac{13}{16} \cdot \frac{12}{15} \cdot \frac{11}{14} = 1 - \frac{143}{280} = \frac{137}{280}$

45.
P(at least one defective) $= 1 - $ P(no
defective) $= 1 - (.94)^5 = 0.266$ or 26.6%

46.
P(at least one will not improve) $= 1 - $
P(all will improve) $= 1 - (0.75)^{12}$
$= 0.968$ or 96.8%

47.
P(at least one tail) $= 1 - $ P(no tails)
$1 - \left(\frac{1}{2}\right)^5 = 1 - \frac{1}{32} = \frac{31}{32}$

48.
P(at least one X) $= 1 - $ P(no X's)
$1 - \left(\frac{25}{26}\right)^3 = 1 - \frac{15,625}{17,576} = \frac{1951}{17,576}$ or 0.111
The event is unlikely to occur since the
probability is only about 11%.

49.
P(at least one 3) $= 1 - $ P(no 3's)
$1 - \left(\frac{5}{6}\right)^7 = 1 - \frac{78,125}{279,936} = \frac{201,811}{279,936}$ or 0.721
The event is likely to occur since the
probability is about 72%.

50.
P(at least one science) $= 1 - $ P(no science)
$1 - \frac{7}{12} \cdot \frac{6}{11} \cdot \frac{5}{10} \cdot \frac{4}{9} = 1 - \frac{7}{99} = \frac{92}{99}$

51.
P(at least one even) $= 1 - $ P(no evens)
$1 - \left(\frac{1}{2}\right)^3 = 1 - \frac{1}{8} = \frac{7}{8}$

52.
P(at least one rose) $= 1 - $ P(no roses)

52. continued
$1 - \frac{26}{34} \cdot \frac{25}{33} \cdot \frac{24}{32} \cdot \frac{23}{31} = 1 - \frac{7475}{23,188} = \frac{15,713}{23,188}$ or
0.678 Yes. The event is likely to occur.

53.
No, because P(A $\cap$ B) $= 0$ therefore
P(A $\cap$ B) $\neq$ P(A) $\cdot$ P(B)

54.
If independent, then P(compact |
domestic) $= $ P(compact)

P(compact) $= \frac{150}{300} = \frac{1}{2}$
P(compact | domestic) $= \frac{\text{P(domestic and compact)}}{\text{P(domestic)}}$
$= \frac{\frac{100}{300}}{\frac{210}{300}} = \frac{100}{210}$ or $\frac{10}{21}$

Thus, P(compact | domestic) $\neq$ P(compact)
since $\frac{1}{2} \neq \frac{10}{21}$.

55.
Yes.

P(enroll) $= 0.55$

P(enroll | DW) $>$ P(enroll) which indicates
that DW has a positive effect on enrollment.

P(enroll | LP) $= $ P(enroll) which indicates
that LP has no effect on enrollment.

P(enroll | MH) $<$ P(enroll) which indicates
that MH has a low effect on enrollment.

Thus, all students should meet with DW.

56.
P(buy) $= 0.35$

a. If P(buy | ad) $= 0.20$, then the
commercial adversely effects the probability
of buying since the events are dependent and
the probability that a person buys the
product is less than 0.35. The events are
dependent.

b. If P(buy | ad) $= 0.35$, then the
commercial has no effect on buying the
product. The events are independent.

c. If P(buy | ad) $= 0.55$, then the
commercial has an effect on buying the
product. The events are dependent.

EXERCISE SET 4-5

1.
$10^5 = 100,000$
$10 \cdot 9 \cdot 8 \cdot 7 \cdot 6 = 30,240$

2.
$9! = 9 \cdot 8 \cdot 7 \cdot 6 \cdot 5 \cdot 4 \cdot 3 \cdot 2 \cdot 1 = 362,880$

3.
$7! = 7 \cdot 6 \cdot 5 \cdot 4 \cdot 3 \cdot 2 \cdot 1 = 5040$

4.
$6! = 6 \cdot 5 \cdot 4 \cdot 3 \cdot 2 \cdot 1 = 720$

5.
$8! = 8 \cdot 7 \cdot 6 \cdot 5 \cdot 4 \cdot 3 \cdot 2 \cdot 1 = 40,320$

6.
$8 \cdot 6 \cdot 3 = 144$

7.
$5! = 5 \cdot 4 \cdot 3 \cdot 2 \cdot 1 = 120$

8.
$2 \cdot 25 \cdot 24 \cdot 23 = 27,600$
$2 \cdot 26 \cdot 26 \cdot 26 = 35,152$

9.
$10 \cdot 10 \cdot 10 = 1000$
$1 \cdot 9 \cdot 8 = 72$

10.
$9! = 9 \cdot 8 \cdot 7 \cdot 6 \cdot 5 \cdot 4 \cdot 3 \cdot 2 \cdot 1 = 362,880$

11.
$5 \cdot 2 = 10$

12.
$2 \cdot 4 = 8$

13.
a. $8! = 8 \cdot 7 \cdot 6 \cdot 5 \cdot 4 \cdot 3 \cdot 2 \cdot 1 = 40,320$

b. $10! = 10 \cdot 9 \cdot 8 \cdot 7 \cdot 6 \cdot 5 \cdot 4 \cdot 3 \cdot 2 \cdot 1$
$10! = 3,628,800$

c. $0! = 1$

d. $1! = 1$

e. $_7P_5 = \frac{7!}{(7-5)!}$

$= \frac{7 \cdot 6 \cdot 5 \cdot 4 \cdot 3 \cdot 2 \cdot 1}{2 \cdot 1} = 2520$

13. continued

f. $_{12}P_4 = \frac{12!}{(12-4)!}$

$= \frac{12 \cdot 11 \cdot 10 \cdot 9 \cdot 8 \cdot 7 \cdot 6 \cdot 5 \cdot 4 \cdot 3 \cdot 2 \cdot 1}{8 \cdot 7 \cdot 6 \cdot 5 \cdot 4 \cdot 3 \cdot 2 \cdot 1} = 11,880$

g. $_5P_3 = \frac{5!}{(5-3)!}$

$= \frac{5 \cdot 4 \cdot 3 \cdot 2 \cdot 1}{2 \cdot 1} = 60$

h. $_6P_0 = \frac{6!}{(6-0)!}$

$= \frac{6 \cdot 5 \cdot 4 \cdot 3 \cdot 2 \cdot 1}{6 \cdot 5 \cdot 4 \cdot 3 \cdot 2 \cdot 1} = 1$

i. $_5P_5 = \frac{5!}{(5-5)!}$

$= \frac{5 \cdot 4 \cdot 3 \cdot 2 \cdot 1}{0!} = 120$

j. $_6P_2 = \frac{6!}{(6-2)!}$

$= \frac{6 \cdot 5 \cdot 4 \cdot 3 \cdot 2 \cdot 1}{4 \cdot 3 \cdot 2 \cdot 1} = 30$

14.
$_8P_8 = \frac{8!}{(8-8)!} = \frac{8!}{0!} = 40,320$

15.
$_4P_4 = \frac{4!}{(4-4)!} = \frac{4 \cdot 3 \cdot 2 \cdot 1}{0!} = 24$

16.
$_7P_3 = \frac{7!}{(7-3)!} = \frac{7 \cdot 6 \cdot 5 \cdot 4!}{4!} = 210$

17.
$_6P_3 = \frac{6!}{(6-3)!} = \frac{6!}{3!} = 120$

18.
$_{10}P_5 = \frac{10!}{(10-5)!} = \frac{10!}{5!} = 30,240$

19.
$_7P_4 = \frac{7!}{(7-4)!} = \frac{7 \cdot 6 \cdot 5 \cdot 4 \cdot 3 \cdot 2 \cdot 1}{3 \cdot 2 \cdot 1} = 840$

20.
$_8P_3 = \frac{8!}{(8-3)!} = \frac{8 \cdot 7 \cdot 6 \cdot 5 \cdot 4 \cdot 3 \cdot 2 \cdot 1}{5 \cdot 4 \cdot 3 \cdot 2 \cdot 1} = 336$

21.
$_{10}P_6 = \frac{10!}{(10-6)!} = \frac{10 \cdot 9 \cdot 8 \cdot 7 \cdot 6 \cdot 5 \cdot 4 \cdot 3 \cdot 2 \cdot 1}{4 \cdot 3 \cdot 2 \cdot 1} = 151,200$

22.
$_5P_5 = \frac{5!}{(5-5)!} = \frac{5!}{0!} = 120$

23.
$_{50}P_4 = \frac{50!}{(50-4)!} = \frac{50!}{46!} = 5,527,200$

24.
$$_{20}P_5 = \frac{20!}{(20-5)!} = \frac{20!}{15!}$$

$$= \frac{20 \cdot 19 \cdot 18 \cdot 17 \cdot 16 \cdot 15!}{15!} = 1,860,480$$

25.
$$_5P_3 + {}_5P_4 + {}_5P_5 = \frac{5!}{2!} + \frac{5!}{1!} + \frac{5!}{0!}$$

$$= 60 + 120 + 120 = 300$$

26.
$$_7P_5 = \frac{7!}{(7-5)!} = \frac{7!}{2!} = \frac{7 \cdot 6 \cdot 5 \cdot 4 \cdot 3 \cdot 2!}{2!} = 2520$$

27.
a. $\frac{5!}{3! \, 2!} = 10$ f. $\frac{3!}{3! \, 0!} = 1$

b. $\frac{8!}{5! \, 3!} = 56$ g. $\frac{3!}{0! \, 3!} = 1$

c. $\frac{7!}{3! \, 4!} = 35$ h. $\frac{9!}{2! \, 7!} = 36$

d. $\frac{6!}{4! \, 2!} = 15$ i. $\frac{12!}{10! \, 2!} = 66$

e. $\frac{6!}{2! \, 4!} = 15$ j. $\frac{4!}{1! \, 3!} = 4$

28.
$$_{52}C_3 = \frac{52!}{49! \, 3!} = \frac{52 \cdot 51 \cdot 50 \cdot 49!}{49! \cdot 3 \cdot 2 \cdot 1} = 22,100$$

29.
$$_{10}C_3 = \frac{10!}{7! \, 3!} = \frac{10 \cdot 9 \cdot 8 \cdot 7!}{7! \cdot 3 \cdot 2 \cdot 1} = 120$$

30.
$$_{12}C_4 \cdot {}_9C_3 = \frac{12!}{8! \, 4!} \cdot \frac{9!}{6! \, 3!}$$

$$= \frac{12 \cdot 11 \cdot 10 \cdot 9 \cdot 8!}{8! \cdot 4 \cdot 3 \cdot 2 \cdot 1} \cdot \frac{9 \cdot 8 \cdot 7 \cdot 6!}{6! \cdot 3 \cdot 2 \cdot 1} = 41,580$$

31.
$$_{10}C_4 = \frac{10!}{6! \, 4!} = 210$$

32.
$$_{10}C_3 = \frac{10!}{7! \, 3!} = \frac{10 \cdot 9 \cdot 8 \cdot 7!}{7! \, 3 \cdot 2 \cdot 1} = 120$$

33.
$$_{20}C_5 = \frac{20!}{15! \, 5!} = 15,504$$

34.
$$_{11}C_6 = \frac{11!}{5! \, 6!} = \frac{11 \cdot 10 \cdot 9 \cdot 8 \cdot 7 \cdot 6!}{6! \cdot 5 \cdot 4 \cdot 3 \cdot 2 \cdot 1} = 462$$

35.
$$_{11}C_2 \cdot {}_8C_3 = 55 \cdot 56 = 3080$$

36.
$$_4C_2 \cdot {}_{12}C_5 \cdot {}_7C_3 = \frac{4!}{2! \, 2!} \cdot \frac{12!}{7! \, 5!} \cdot \frac{7!}{4! \, 3!}$$

$$= \frac{4 \cdot 3 \cdot 2!}{2! \cdot 2 \cdot 1} \cdot \frac{12 \cdot 11 \cdot 10 \cdot 9 \cdot 8 \cdot 7!}{7! \cdot 5 \cdot 4 \cdot 3 \cdot 2 \cdot 1} \cdot \frac{7 \cdot 6 \cdot 5 \cdot 4!}{4! \cdot 3 \cdot 2 \cdot 1}$$

$$= 6 \cdot 792 \cdot 35 = 166,320$$

37.
$$_{12}C_4 = 495$$
$$_7C_2 \cdot {}_5C_2 = 21 \cdot 10 = 210$$
$$_7C_2 \cdot {}_5C_2 + {}_7C_3 \cdot {}_5C_1 + {}_7C_4 =$$
$$21 \cdot 10 + 35 \cdot 5 + 35 =$$
$$210 + 175 + 35 = 420$$

38.
$$_{10}C_3 \cdot {}_{10}C_3 = \frac{10!}{7! \, 3!} \cdot \frac{10!}{7! \, 3!}$$
$$= \frac{10 \cdot 9 \cdot 8 \cdot 7!}{7! \cdot 3 \cdot 2 \cdot 1} \cdot \frac{10 \cdot 9 \cdot 8 \cdot 7!}{7! \cdot 3 \cdot 2 \cdot 1} = 120 \cdot 120 = 14,400$$

39.
$$_6C_3 \cdot {}_5C_2 = \frac{6!}{3! \, 3!} \cdot \frac{5!}{3! \, 2!}$$
$$= \frac{6 \cdot 5 \cdot 4 \cdot 3!}{3! \cdot 3 \cdot 2 \cdot 1} \cdot \frac{5 \cdot 4 \cdot 3!}{3! \cdot 2 \cdot 1} = 200$$

40.
$$_{12}C_6 \cdot {}_{10}C_6 = \frac{12!}{6! \, 6!} \cdot \frac{10!}{4! \, 6!}$$

$$= \frac{12 \cdot 11 \cdot 10 \cdot 9 \cdot 8 \cdot 7 \cdot 6!}{6! \cdot 6 \cdot 5 \cdot 4 \cdot 3 \cdot 2 \cdot 1} \cdot \frac{10 \cdot 9 \cdot 8 \cdot 7 \cdot 6!}{6! \cdot 4 \cdot 3 \cdot 2 \cdot 1}$$

$$= 924 \cdot 210 = 194,040$$

41.
$$_{10}C_2 \cdot {}_{12}C_2 = \frac{10!}{8! \, 2!} \cdot \frac{12!}{10! \, 2!}$$
$$= 45 \cdot 66 = 2,970$$

42.
$$_{25}C_5 = \frac{25!}{20! \, 5!} = \frac{25 \cdot 24 \cdot 23 \cdot 22 \cdot 21 \cdot 20!}{20! \cdot 5 \cdot 4 \cdot 3 \cdot 2 \cdot 1}$$
$$= 53,130$$

43.
$$_{17}C_2 = \frac{17!}{15! \, 2!} = 136$$

44.
$$_9C_5 = \frac{9!}{4! \, 5!} = \frac{9 \cdot 8 \cdot 7 \cdot 6 \cdot 5!}{5! \cdot 4 \cdot 3 \cdot 2 \cdot 1} = 126$$

45.
$$_{11}C_7 = \frac{11!}{4! \, 7!} = \frac{11 \cdot 10 \cdot 9 \cdot 8 \cdot 7!}{7! \cdot 4 \cdot 3 \cdot 2 \cdot 1} = 330$$

46.
$$_{10}C_8 = \frac{10!}{2! \, 8!} = \frac{10 \cdot 9 \cdot 8!}{8! \cdot 2 \cdot 1} = 45$$

47.
$$_{20}C_8 = \frac{20!}{12! \, 8!} = \frac{20 \cdot 19 \cdot 18 \cdot 17 \cdot 16 \cdot 15 \cdot 14 \cdot 13 \cdot 12!}{12! \cdot 8 \cdot 7 \cdot 6 \cdot 5 \cdot 4 \cdot 3 \cdot 2 \cdot 1}$$
$$= 125,970$$

48.
$_{17}C_8 = \frac{17!}{9!\,8!} = \frac{17\cdot16\cdot15\cdot14\cdot13\cdot12\cdot11\cdot10\cdot9!}{9!\cdot8\cdot7\cdot6\cdot5\cdot4\cdot3\cdot2\cdot1}$
$= 24{,}310$

49.
Selecting 1 coin there are 4 ways. Selecting 2 coins there are 6 ways. Selecting 3 coins there are 4 ways. Selecting 4 coins there is 1 way. Hence the total is $4 + 6 + 4 + 1 = 15$ ways. (List all possibilities.)

50.
X = number of chickens
$2X$ = number of chicken legs
$15 - X$ = number of cows
$4(15 - X)$ = number of cow legs
$2X + 4(15 - X) = 46$
$2X + 60 - 4X = 46$
$-2X = -14$
$X = 7$
There are 7 chickens and 8 cows.

51.
a. $2\cdot4\cdot3\cdot2\cdot1 = 48$
b. $4\cdot6 + 3\cdot6 + 2\cdot6 + 1\cdot6 = 60$
c. 72

52.
a. 4
b. $_4C_1 \cdot _9C_1 \cdot 1 \cdot 1 \cdot 1 \cdot 1 = 36$
c. $48 \cdot 13 = 624$
d. $13 \cdot 12 \cdot _4C_3 \cdot _4C_2 = 3744$

EXERCISE SET 4-6

1.
P(2 face cards) $= \frac{12}{52} \cdot \frac{11}{51} = \frac{11}{221}$

2.
a. $\frac{_5C_4}{_{25}C_4} = \frac{\frac{5\cdot4!}{4!\,1}}{\frac{25\cdot24\cdot23\cdot22\cdot21!}{21!\cdot4\cdot3\cdot2\cdot1}} = \frac{1}{2530}$

b. $\frac{_5C_2\cdot_{20}C_2}{_{25}C_4} = \frac{\frac{5\cdot4\cdot3!}{3!\cdot2\cdot1}\cdot\frac{20\cdot19\cdot18!}{18!\cdot2\cdot1}}{25\cdot23\cdot22} = \frac{38}{253}$

c. $\frac{_{20}C_4}{_{25}C_4} = \frac{\frac{20\cdot19\cdot18\cdot17\cdot16!}{16!\cdot4\cdot3\cdot2\cdot1}}{25\cdot23\cdot22} = \frac{969}{2530}$

d. $\frac{_5C_1\cdot_{20}C_3}{_{25}C_4} = \frac{\frac{5\cdot4!}{4!\cdot1}\cdot\frac{20\cdot19\cdot18\cdot17!}{17!\cdot3\cdot2\cdot1}}{25\cdot23\cdot22} = \frac{114}{253}$

3.
a. There are $_4C_3$ ways of selecting 3 women and $_7C_3$ total ways to select 3 people; hence, P(all women) $= \frac{_4C_3}{_7C_3} = \frac{4}{35}$.

3. continued
b. There are $_3C_3$ ways of selecting 3 men; hence, P(all men) $= \frac{_3C_3}{_7C_3} = \frac{1}{35}$.

c. There are $_3C_2$ ways of selecting 2 men and $_4C_1$ ways of selecting one woman; hence, P(2 men and 1 woman) $= \frac{_3C_2\cdot_4C_1}{_7C_3}$
$= \frac{12}{35}$.

d. There are $_3C_1$ ways to select one man and $_4C_2$ ways of selecting two women; hence, P(1 man and 2 women) $= \frac{_3C_1\cdot_4C_2}{_7C_3} = \frac{18}{35}$.

4. There are $_{49}C_3$ ways to select 3 Republicans; hence, P(3 Republicans) $=$
$\frac{_{49}C_3}{_{100}C_3} = \frac{18{,}424}{161{,}700} = 0.1139$

There are $_{50}C_3$ ways to select 3 Democrats; hence P(3 Democrats) $= \frac{_{50}C_3}{_{100}C_3}$
P(3 Democrats) $= \frac{19{,}600}{161{,}700} = 0.1212$

There are $_{49}C_1$ ways to select one Republican, $_1C_1$ ways to select one Independent, and $_{50}C_1$ ways to select one Democrat; hence P(one from each party) $= \frac{_{49}C_1\cdot_1C_1\cdot_{50}C_1}{_{100}C_3} = \frac{2450}{161{,}700} = 0.0152$

5.
a. There are $_9C_4$ ways to select four from Pennsylvania; hence P(all four are from Pennsylvania) $= \frac{_9C_4}{_{56}C_4} = \frac{126}{367{,}290} = 0.0003$

b. There are $_9C_2$ ways to select two from Pennsylvania and $_7C_2$ ways to select two from Virginia; hence P(two from Pennsylvania and two from Virginia) $= \frac{_9C_2\cdot_7C_2}{_{56}C_4} = \frac{756}{367{,}290} = 0.0021$

6.
a. $\frac{_9C_4}{_{12}C_4} = \frac{126}{495} = \frac{14}{55}$

b. $\frac{_3C_1\cdot_9C_3}{_{12}C_4} = \frac{252}{495} = \frac{28}{55}$

c. $\frac{_3C_3\cdot_9C_1}{_{12}C_4} = \frac{1}{55}$

7.
$\frac{2}{50} \cdot \frac{1}{49} = \frac{1}{1225}$

8.

There are $_4C_3$ ways of getting 3 of a kind for one denomination and there are 13 denominations. There are $_4C_2$ ways of getting two of a kind and 12 denominations left. There are $_{52}C_5$ ways to get five cards; hence,

P(full house) $= \frac{13 \cdot _4C_3 \cdot 12 \cdot _4C_2}{_{52}C_5} = \frac{6}{4165}$

9.

a. $\frac{_8C_4}{_{14}C_4} = \frac{70}{1001} = \frac{10}{143}$

b. $\frac{_6C_2 \cdot _8C_2}{_{14}C_4} = \frac{420}{1001} = \frac{60}{143}$

c. $\frac{_6C_4}{_{14}C_4} = \frac{15}{1001}$

d. $\frac{_6C_3 \cdot _8C_1}{_{14}C_4} = \frac{160}{1001}$

e. $\frac{_6C_1 \cdot _8C_3}{_{14}C_4} = \frac{336}{1001} = \frac{48}{143}$

10.

a. $\frac{_8C_3}{_{15}C_3} = \frac{56}{455} = \frac{8}{65}$

b. $\frac{_2C_2 \cdot _{13}C_1}{_{15}C_3} = \frac{13}{455} = \frac{1}{35}$

c. $\frac{_5C_3}{_{15}C_3} = \frac{10}{455} = \frac{2}{91}$

d. $\frac{_8C_1 \cdot _5C_1 \cdot _2C_1}{_{15}C_3} = \frac{80}{455} = \frac{16}{91}$

e. $\frac{_8C_2 \cdot _5C_1}{_{15}C_3} = \frac{140}{455} = \frac{4}{13}$

11.

a. $\frac{_{11}C_2}{_{19}C_2} = \frac{55}{171} = 0.3216$

b. $\frac{_8C_2}{_{19}C_2} = \frac{28}{171} = 0.1637$

c. $\frac{_{11}C_1 \cdot _8C_1}{_{19}C_2} = \frac{88}{171} = 0.5146$

d. It probably got lost in the wash!

12.

$\frac{_8C_3 \cdot _9C_4}{_{17}C_7} = \frac{56 \cdot 126}{19,448} = \frac{7056}{19,448} = \frac{882}{2431}$

13.

There are $6^3 = 216$ ways of tossing three dice, and there are 15 ways of getting a sum of 7; i.e., (1, 1, 5), (1, 5, 1), (5, 1, 1), (1, 2, 4), etc. Hence the probability of rolling a sum of 7 is $\frac{15}{216} = \frac{5}{72}$.

14.

$\frac{_4C_2 \cdot _8C_3}{_{12}C_5} = \frac{336}{792} = \frac{14}{33}$

15.

There are $5! = 120$ ways to arrange 5 washers in a row and 2 ways to have them in correct order, small to large or large to small; hence, the probability is $\frac{2}{120} = \frac{1}{60}$.

16.

There are $_{52}C_5 = \frac{52!}{47! \, 5!} = 2,598,960$ possible hands.

a. $\frac{4}{2,598,960}$ b. $\frac{36}{2,598,960}$

c. $\frac{624}{2,598,960}$

REVIEW EXERCISES - CHAPTER 4

1.

a. $\frac{1}{6}$ b. $\frac{1}{6}$ c. $\frac{4}{6} = \frac{2}{3}$

2.

a. $\frac{13}{52} = \frac{1}{4}$ d. $\frac{4}{52} = \frac{1}{13}$

b. $\frac{11}{26}$ e. $\frac{26}{52} = \frac{1}{2}$

c. $\frac{1}{52}$

3.

$\frac{16}{45}$

4.

a. $\frac{1}{6}$ b. $\frac{3}{6} = \frac{1}{2}$ c. $\frac{2}{6} = \frac{1}{3}$

5.

$\frac{850}{1500} = \frac{17}{30}$

6.

a. $\frac{9}{35}$

b. $\frac{7}{35} + \frac{16}{35} = \frac{23}{35}$

c. $\frac{3}{35} + \frac{7}{35} + \frac{9}{35} = \frac{19}{35}$

d. $1 - \frac{16}{35} = \frac{19}{35}$

7.

a. $\frac{3}{30} = \frac{1}{10}$ c. $\frac{16+7+3}{30} = \frac{26}{30} = \frac{13}{15}$

b. $\frac{7+4}{30} = \frac{11}{30}$ d. $1 - \frac{4}{30} = \frac{26}{30} = \frac{13}{15}$

8.

Refer to the sample space for tossing two dice.

a. There are 4 ways to roll a 5 and 5 ways to roll a 6; hence, $P(5 \text{ or } 6) = \frac{4}{36} + \frac{5}{36} = \frac{1}{4}$

b. There are 3 ways to get a 10, 2 ways to get an 11 and 1 way to get a 12; hence, $P(\text{sum greater than } 9) = \frac{3}{36} + \frac{2}{26} + \frac{1}{36} = \frac{1}{6}$

c. A sum less than 4 means 3 or 2, and greater than 9 means 10, 11, 12; hence, the probability is $\frac{2+1+3+2+1}{36} = \frac{9}{36} = \frac{1}{4}$.

d. Four, 8, and 12 are divisible by 4; hence, the probability of rolling a 4, 8, or 12 is $\frac{3+5+1}{36} = \frac{9}{36} = \frac{1}{4}$.

e. Since this is impossible, the answer is 0.

f. Since this is the entire sample space, the probability is $\frac{36}{36} = 1$.

9.
$0.80 + 0.30 - 0.12 = 0.98$

10.
P(John or Mary) =
P(John) + P(Mary) $-$ P(John and Mary) =
$0.39 + 0.73 - 0.36 = 0.76$
The probability that neither purchases a new car is $1 - 0.76 = 0.24$.

11.
$(0.78)^5 = 0.289$ or 28.9%

12.
P(five borrowed books) $= (0.67)^5 = 0.1350$

P(none borrowed
books) $= (0.33)^5 = 0.0039$

13.
a. $\frac{26}{52} \cdot \frac{25}{51} \cdot \frac{24}{50} = \frac{2}{17}$

b. $\frac{13}{52} \cdot \frac{12}{51} \cdot \frac{11}{50} = \frac{33}{2550} = \frac{11}{850}$

c. $\frac{4}{52} \cdot \frac{3}{51} \cdot \frac{2}{50} = \frac{1}{5525}$

14.
a. $\frac{1}{2} \cdot \frac{4}{52} = \frac{1}{26}$

14. continued
b. $\frac{1}{2} \cdot \frac{26}{52} = \frac{1}{4}$

c. $\frac{1}{2} \cdot \frac{13}{52} = \frac{1}{8}$

15.
$P(C \text{ or } PP) = P(C) + P(PP) = \frac{2+3}{13} = \frac{5}{13}$

16.

	X	Y	Z	Total
TV	18	32	15	65
Stereo	6	20	13	39
Total	24	52	28	104

a. $\frac{24}{104} + \frac{39}{104} - \frac{6}{104} = \frac{57}{104}$

b. $\frac{52}{104} + \frac{28}{104} = \frac{80}{104} = \frac{10}{13}$

c. $\frac{65}{104} + \frac{28}{104} - \frac{15}{104} = \frac{78}{104} = \frac{3}{4}$

17.

$P(\text{disease}) = 0.025 + 0.375 = 0.4$

18.

$P(\text{stereo}) = 0.012 + 0.028 + 0.018 = 0.058$
or 5.8%

19.
$P(NC \mid C) = \frac{P(NC \text{ and } C)}{P(C)} = \frac{0.37}{0.73} = 0.51$

20.
$P(\text{warranty} \mid TV) = \frac{P(\text{warranty and TV})}{P(TV)}$

$= \frac{0.03}{0.11} = 0.273$

21.
$\frac{0.43}{0.75} = 0.573$ or 57.3%

22.
$P(\text{bus late} \mid \text{bad weather}) =$
$\frac{P(\text{bus late and bad weather})}{P(\text{bad weather})} = \frac{0.023}{0.40} = 0.058$

23.

	<4 yrs HS	HS	College	Total
Smoker	6	14	19	39
Non-Smoker	18	7	25	50
Total	24	21	44	89

a. There are 44 college graduates and 19 of them smoke; hence, the probability is $\frac{19}{44}$.

b. There are 24 people who did not graduate from high school, 6 of whom do not smoke; hence, the probability is
$\frac{6}{24} = \frac{1}{4}$.

24.
P(at least one does not wear a helmet) =
$1 - P(\text{none do not wear a helmet})$
$= 1 - P(\text{all 4 wear a helmet})$
$= 1 - (0.23)^4 = 0.997$ or 99.7%

25.
P(at least one tail) $= 1 - P(\text{all heads})$
$1 - (\frac{1}{2})^5 = 1 - \frac{1}{32} = \frac{31}{32}$

26.
P(at least one has chronic sinusitis) =
$1 - P(\text{none has chronic sinusitis})$
$1 - (0.85)^5 = 0.556$ or 55.6%

27.
If repetitions are allowed:
$26 \cdot 26 \cdot 26 \cdot 10 \cdot 10 \cdot 10 = 175,760,000$

If repetitions are not allowed:
$_{26}P_3 \cdot _{10}P_4 = \frac{26 \cdot 25 \cdot 24 \cdot 23!}{23!} \cdot \frac{10 \cdot 9 \cdot 8 \cdot 7 \cdot 6!}{6!}$
$= 78,624,000$

27. continued
If repetitions are allowed in the letters but not in the digits:
$26 \cdot 26 \cdot 26 \cdot _{10}P_4 = 88,583,040$

28.
$_5P_5 = \frac{5!}{(5-5)!} = \frac{5!}{0!} = 120$

29.
$_5C_3 \cdot _7C_4 = \frac{5!}{2!\,3!} \cdot \frac{7!}{3!\,4!} = 10 \cdot 35 = 350$

30.
$8! = _8P_8 = \frac{8!}{(8-8)!} = \frac{8!}{0!} = 40,320$

31.
$_{10}C_2 = \frac{10!}{8!\,2!} = 45$

32.
$_6C_3 \cdot _5C_2 \cdot _4C_1 = \frac{6!}{3!\,3!} \cdot \frac{5!}{3!\,2!} \cdot \frac{4!}{3!\,1!}$

$= 20 \cdot 10 \cdot 4 = 800$

33.
$26 \cdot 10 \cdot 10 \cdot 10 = 26,000$

34.
$5 \cdot 3 \cdot 2 = 30$

35.
$_{12}C_4 = \frac{12!}{8!\,4!} = \frac{12 \cdot 11 \cdot 10 \cdot 9 \cdot 8!}{4 \cdot 3 \cdot 2 \cdot 1 \cdot 8!} = 495$

36.
$_{13}C_3 = \frac{13!}{10!\,3!} = \frac{13 \cdot 12 \cdot 11 \cdot 10!}{10! \cdot 3 \cdot 2 \cdot 1} = 286$

37.
$_{20}C_5 = \frac{20!}{15!\,5!} = \frac{20 \cdot 19 \cdot 18 \cdot 17 \cdot 16 \cdot 15!}{15! \cdot 5 \cdot 4 \cdot 3 \cdot 2 \cdot 1} = 15,504$

38.
$3 \cdot 5 \cdot 4 = 60$

39.
Total number of outcomes:
$26 \cdot 26 \cdot 26 \cdot 10 \cdot 10 \cdot 10 \cdot 10 = 175,760,000$

Total number of ways for USA followed by a number divisible by 5:
$1 \cdot 1 \cdot 1 \cdot 10 \cdot 10 \cdot 10 \cdot 2 = 2000$

Hence $P = \frac{2000}{175,760,000} = 0.0000114$

40.
There are $_3C_2$ ways of attending two plays and $_5C_1$ ways of attending one movie, and a

40. continued

total of $_{10}C_3$ of attending 3 events; hence, the probability is:

$$\frac{_3C_2 \cdot _5C_1}{_{10}C_3} = \frac{15}{120} = \frac{1}{8}$$

41.

$$\frac{_3C_1 \cdot _4C_1 \cdot _2C_1}{_9C_3} = \frac{2}{7}$$

42.

CHAPTER 4 QUIZ

1. False, subjective probability can be used when other types of probabilities cannot be found.
2. False, empirical probability uses frequency distributions.
3. True
4. False, $P(A \text{ or } B) = P(A) + P(B) - P(A \text{ and } B)$
5. False, the probabilities can be different.
6. False, complementary events cannot occur at the same time.
7. True
8. False, order does not matter in combinations.
9. b
10. b and d
11. d
12. b
13. c
14. b
15. d
16. b
17. b
18. Sample space
19. Zero and one
20. Zero
21. One
22. Mutually exclusive
23. a. $\frac{4}{52} = \frac{1}{13}$ c. $\frac{16}{52} = \frac{4}{13}$

    b. $\frac{4}{52} = \frac{1}{13}$

24. a. $\frac{13}{52} = \frac{1}{4}$ d. $\frac{4}{52} = \frac{1}{13}$

    b. $\frac{4+13-1}{52} = \frac{4}{13}$ e. $\frac{26}{52} = \frac{1}{2}$

    c. $\frac{1}{52}$

25. a. $\frac{12}{31}$ c. $\frac{27}{31}$

    b. $\frac{12}{31}$ d. $\frac{24}{31}$

26. a. $\frac{11}{36}$ d. $\frac{1}{3}$

    b. $\frac{5}{18}$ e. 0

    c. $\frac{11}{36}$ f. $\frac{11}{12}$

27. $(0.75 - 0.16) + (0.25 - 0.16) = 0.68$

28. $(0.3)^5 = 0.002$

29. a. $\frac{26}{52} \cdot \frac{25}{51} \cdot \frac{24}{50} \cdot \frac{23}{49} \cdot \frac{22}{48} = \frac{253}{9996}$

    b. $\frac{13}{52} \cdot \frac{12}{51} \cdot \frac{11}{50} \cdot \frac{10}{49} \cdot \frac{9}{48} = \frac{33}{66,640}$

    c. 0

30. $\frac{0.35}{0.65} = 0.54$

31. $\frac{0.16}{0.3} = 0.53$

32. $\frac{0.57}{0.7} = 0.81$

33. $\frac{0.028}{0.5} = 0.056$

34. a. $\frac{1}{2}$ b. $\frac{3}{7}$

35. $1 - (0.45)^6 = 0.99$

36. $1 - \left(\frac{5}{6}\right)^4 = 0.518$

37. $1 - (0.15)^6 = 0.9999886$

38. 2,646

39. 40,320

40. 1,365

41. 1,188,137,600; 710,424,000

42. 720

43. 33,554,432

44. 56

45. $\frac{1}{4}$

46. $\frac{3}{14}$

47. $\frac{12}{55}$

48.

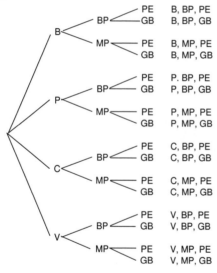

Note: Answers may vary due to rounding, TI-83's or computer programs.

EXERCISE SET 5-2

1.
A random variable is a variable whose values are determined by chance. Examples will vary.

2.
If the values a random variable can assume are countable, then the variable is called discrete; otherwise, it is called a continuous variable.

3.
The number of commercials a radio station plays during each hour.
The number of times a student uses his or her calculator during a mathematics exam.
The number of leaves on a specific type of tree.

4.
The weights of strawberries grown in a specific plot.
The heights of all seniors at a specific college.
The times it takes students to complete a mathematics exam.

5.
A probability distribution is a distribution which consists of the values a random variable can assume along with the corresponding probabilities of these values.

6.
No; the sum of the probabilities is greater than one.

7.
No; probabilities cannot be negative and the sum of the probabilities is not one.

8.
No, probability values cannot be negative.

9.
Yes

10.
No, probability values cannot be greater than 1.

11.
No, probability values cannot be greater than 1.

12.
Continuous

13.
Discrete

14.
Discrete

15.
Continuous

16.
Continuous

17.
Discrete

18.
Continuous

19.

X	0	1	2	3
P(X)	$\frac{6}{15}$	$\frac{5}{15}$	$\frac{3}{15}$	$\frac{1}{15}$

20.

X	$1000	$2000	$3000
P(X)	$\frac{1}{2}$	$\frac{1}{4}$	$\frac{1}{4}$

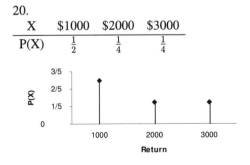

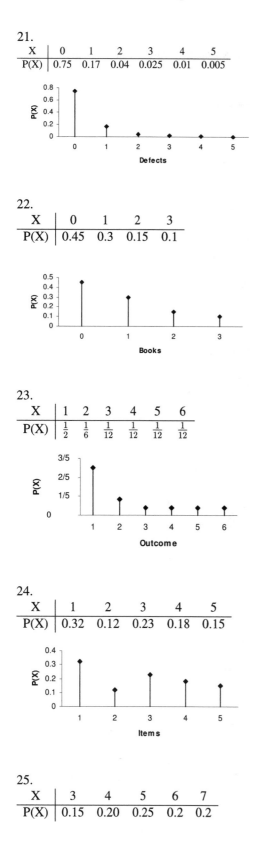

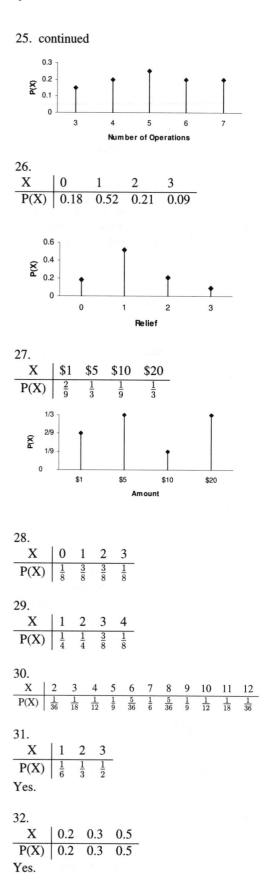

21.

X	0	1	2	3	4	5
P(X)	0.75	0.17	0.04	0.025	0.01	0.005

22.

X	0	1	2	3
P(X)	0.45	0.3	0.15	0.1

23.

X	1	2	3	4	5	6
P(X)	$\frac{1}{2}$	$\frac{1}{6}$	$\frac{1}{12}$	$\frac{1}{12}$	$\frac{1}{12}$	$\frac{1}{12}$

24.

X	1	2	3	4	5
P(X)	0.32	0.12	0.23	0.18	0.15

25.

X	3	4	5	6	7
P(X)	0.15	0.20	0.25	0.2	0.2

25. continued

26.

X	0	1	2	3
P(X)	0.18	0.52	0.21	0.09

27.

X	$1	$5	$10	$20
P(X)	$\frac{2}{9}$	$\frac{1}{3}$	$\frac{1}{9}$	$\frac{1}{3}$

28.

X	0	1	2	3
P(X)	$\frac{1}{8}$	$\frac{3}{8}$	$\frac{3}{8}$	$\frac{1}{8}$

29.

X	1	2	3	4
P(X)	$\frac{1}{4}$	$\frac{1}{4}$	$\frac{3}{8}$	$\frac{1}{8}$

30.

X	2	3	4	5	6	7	8	9	10	11	12
P(X)	$\frac{1}{36}$	$\frac{1}{18}$	$\frac{1}{12}$	$\frac{1}{9}$	$\frac{5}{36}$	$\frac{1}{6}$	$\frac{5}{36}$	$\frac{1}{9}$	$\frac{1}{12}$	$\frac{1}{18}$	$\frac{1}{36}$

31.

X	1	2	3
P(X)	$\frac{1}{6}$	$\frac{1}{3}$	$\frac{1}{2}$

Yes.

32.

X	0.2	0.3	0.5
P(X)	0.2	0.3	0.5

Yes.

33.

X	3	4	7
P(X)	$\frac{3}{6}$	$\frac{4}{6}$	$\frac{7}{6}$

No, the sum of the probabilities is greater than one and $P(7) = \frac{7}{6}$ which is also greater than one.

34.

X	0.1	0.02	0.04
P(X)	0.2	0.12	0.14

No, the sum of the probabilities is less than one.

35.

X	1	2	4
P(X)	$\frac{1}{7}$	$\frac{2}{7}$	$\frac{4}{7}$

Yes.

36.

X	0	1	2
P(X)	0	$\frac{1}{3}$	$\frac{1}{2}$

No, the sum of the probabilities is less than one.

EXERCISE SET 5-3

1.

X	0	1	2	3
P(X)	0.92	0.03	0.03	0.02

$\mu = \sum X \cdot P(X) = 0(0.92) + 1(0.03) +$

$2(0.03) + 3(0.02) = 0.15$ or 0.2

$\sigma^2 = \sum X^2 \cdot P(X) - \mu^2 = [0^2(0.92) + 1^2(0.03) + 2^2(0.03) + 3^2(0.02)] - 0.15^2 = 0.3075$

$\sigma = \sqrt{0.3075} = 0.55$ or 0.6

The company would need $0.2(10) = 2$ extra transistors on hand each day.

X	P(X)	X · P(X)	$X^2 \cdot P(X)$
0	0.92	0	0
1	0.03	0.03	0.03
2	0.03	0.06	0.12
3	0.02	0.06	0.18
		$\mu = 0.15$	0.33

2.

$\mu = 19(0.2) + 20(0.2) + 21(0.3) + 22(0.2) + 23(0.1) = 20.8$

2. continued

$\sigma^2 = [19^2(0.2) + 20^2(0.2) + 21^2(0.3) + 22^2(0.2) + 23^2(0.1)] - 20.8^2 = 1.56$ or 1.6

$\sigma = \sqrt{1.56} = 1.25$ or 1.3

The manager would need to purchase $20.8(5) = 104$ suits.

X	P(X)	X · P(X)	$X^2 \cdot P(X)$
8	0.1	0.8	6.4
9	0.2	1.8	16.2
10	0.2	2.0	20.0
11	0.3	3.3	36.3
12	0.2	2.4	28.8
		$\mu = 10.3$	107.7

3.

$\mu = \sum X \cdot P(X) = 0(0.18) + 1(0.44) + 2(0.27) + 3(0.08) + 4(0.03) = 1.34$ or 1.3

$\sigma^2 = \sum X^2 \cdot P(X) - \mu^2 = [0^2(0.18) + 1^2(0.44) + 2^2(0.27) + 3^2(0.08) + 4^2(0.03)] - 1.34^2 = 0.92$ or 0.9

$\sigma = \sqrt{0.92} = 0.96$ or 1

No, on average each person has about one credit card.

X	P(X)	X · P(X)	$X^2 \cdot P(X)$
0	0.18	0	0
1	0.44	0.44	0.44
2	0.27	0.54	1.08
3	0.08	0.24	0.72
4	0.03	0.12	0.48
		$\mu = 1.34$	2.72

4.

$\mu = \sum X \cdot P(X) = 0(0.10) + 1(0.20) + 2(0.30) + 3(0.20) + 4(0.20) = 2.2$

$\sigma^2 = \sum X^2 \cdot P(X) - \mu^2 = [0^2(0.10) + 1^2(0.20) + 2^2(0.30) + 3^2(0.20) + 4^2(0.20)] - 2.2^2 = 1.56$ or 1.6

$\sigma = \sqrt{1.6} = 1.3$

4. continued

X	P(X)	X · P(X)	X² · P(X)
0	0.10	0.00	0.00
1	0.20	0.20	0.20
2	0.30	0.60	1.20
3	0.20	0.60	1.80
4	0.20	0.80	3.20
		$\mu = 2.2$	6.4

5.

$\mu = \sum X \cdot P(X) = 0(0.06) + 1(0.42) +$
$2(0.22) + 3(0.12) + 4(0.15) + 5(0.03)$
$= 1.97$ or 2.0

$\sigma^2 = \sum X^2 \cdot P(X) - \mu^2 = [0^2(0.06) +$
$1^2(0.42) + 2^2(0.22) + 3^2(0.12) + 4^2(0.15)$
$+ 5^2(0.03)] - 1.97^2 = 1.649$ or 1.6

$\sigma = \sqrt{1.649} = 1.28$ or 1.3

X	P(X)	X · P(X)	X² · P(X)
0	0.06	0.00	0.00
1	0.42	0.42	0.42
2	0.22	0.44	0.88
3	0.12	0.36	1.08
4	0.15	0.60	2.40
5	0.03	0.15	0.75
		$\mu = 1.97$	5.53

She would average $200 per week.

6.

$\mu = \sum X \cdot P(X) = 2(0.3) + 3(0.4) + 4(0.2)$
$+ 5(0.1) = 3.1$

$\sigma^2 = \sum X^2 \cdot P(X) - \mu^2 = [2^2(0.3) +$
$3^2(0.4) + 4^2(0.2) + 5^2(0.1)] - 3.1^2 = 0.89$
or 0.9

$\sigma = \sqrt{0.89} = 0.9$

X	P(X)	X · P(X)	X² · P(X)
2	0.3	0.6	1.2
3	0.4	1.2	3.6
4	0.2	0.8	3.2
5	0.1	0.5	2.5
		$\mu = 3.1$	10.5

7.

$\mu = \sum X \cdot P(X) = 5(0.2) + 6(0.25) +$
$7(0.38) + 8(0.10) + 9(0.07) = 6.59$ or 6.6

7. continued

$\sigma^2 = \sum X^2 \cdot P(X) - \mu^2 = [5^2(0.2) +$
$6^2(0.25) + 7^2(0.38) + 8^2(0.10) +$
$9^2(0.07) - 6.59^2 = 1.2619$ or 1.3

$\sigma = \sqrt{1.2619} = `1.123$ or 1.1

X	P(X)	X · P(X)	X² · P(X)
5	0.20	1.00	5.00
6	0.25	1.50	9.00
7	0.38	2.66	18.62
8	0.10	0.80	6.40
9	0.07	0.63	5.67
		$\mu = 6.59$	44.69

8.

$\mu = \sum X \cdot P(X) = 1(0.32) + 2(0.51) +$

$3(0.12) + 4(0.05) = 1.9$

$\sigma^2 = \sum X^2 \cdot P(X) - \mu^2 = [1^2(0.32) +$
$2^2(0.51) + 3^2(0.12) + 4^2(0.05)] -$
$1.9^2 = 0.63$ or 0.6

$\sigma = \sqrt{0.63} = 0.794$ or 0.8
Send 2 diaries to each household.

X	P(X)	X · P(X)	X² · P(X)
1	0.32	0.32	0.32
2	0.51	1.02	2.04
3	0.12	0.36	1.08
4	0.05	0.20	0.80
		$\mu = 1.90$	4.24

9.

$\mu = \sum X \cdot P(X) = 12(0.15) + 13(0.20) +$
$14(0.38) + 15(0.18) + 16(0.09) = 13.86$ or
13.9

$\sigma^2 = \sum X^2 \cdot P(X) - \mu^2 = [12^2(0.15) +$
$13^2(0.20) + 14^2(0.38) + 15^2(0.18) +$
$16^2(0.09)] - 13.86^2 = 1.3204$ or 1.3

$\sigma = \sqrt{1.3204} = 1.1491$ or 1.1

X	P(X)	X · P(X)	X² · P(X)
12	0.15	1.80	21.60
13	0.20	2.60	33.80
14	0.38	5.32	74.48
15	0.18	2.70	40.50
16	0.09	1.44	23.04
		$\mu = 13.86$	193.42

10.
$\mu = \sum X \cdot P(X) = 35(0.1) + 36(0.2) +$
$37(0.3) + 38(0.3) + 37(0.1) = 37.1$

$\sigma^2 = \sum X^2 \cdot P(X) - \mu^2 = [35^2(0.1) +$
$36^2(0.2) + 37^2(0.3) + 38^2(0.3) + 39^2(0.1)]$
$- 37.1^2 = 1.29$ or 1.3

$\sigma = \sqrt{1.39} = 1.136$ or 1.1

X	P(X)	$X \cdot P(X)$	$X^2 \cdot P(X)$
35	0.1	3.5	122.5
36	0.2	7.2	259.2
37	0.3	11.1	410.7
38	0.3	11.4	433.2
39	0.1	3.9	152.1
		$\mu = 37.1$	1377.7

It could happen (perhaps on a Super Bowl Sunday), but it is highly unlikely.

11.
$E(X) = \sum X \cdot P(X) = \$300(0.998) -$
$\$19,700(0.002) = \$260$

12.
$\mu = 1(0.2) + 2(0.3) + 3(0.4) + 4(0.1) = 2.4$

Expected Profit $= 2.4(\$3000) = \$7200$

13.
$E(X) = \sum X \cdot P(X) = \$5.00(\frac{1}{6}) = \$0.83$
He should pay about $0.83.

14.
$E(X) = \$20.00(\frac{2}{36}) + \$5.00(\frac{6}{36}) - \$3.00$
$= 1.94 - \$3.00 = -\$1.06$

Alternate Solution:
$E(X) = 17.00(\frac{2}{36}) + 2.00(\frac{6}{36}) - 3.00(\frac{28}{36})$
$= -\$1.06$

15.
$E(X) = \sum X \cdot P(X) = \$1000(\frac{1}{1000}) +$
$\$500(\frac{1}{1000}) + \$100(\frac{5}{1000}) - \$3.00$
$= -\$1.00$

Alternate Solution:
$E(X) = 997(\frac{1}{1000}) + 497(\frac{1}{1000}) + 97(\frac{5}{1000})$
$- 3(\frac{993}{1000}) = -\$1.00$

16.
$E(X) = 2(-1.00) = -\$2.00$

17.
$E(X) = \sum X \cdot P(X) = \$500(\frac{1}{1000}) - \$1.00$
$= -\$0.50$

Alternate Solution:
$E(X) = \$499(\frac{1}{1000}) - 1(\frac{999}{1000}) = -\$0.50$

There are 6 possibilities when a number with all different digits is boxed, $(3 \cdot 2 \cdot 1 = 6)$. Hence,
$\$80.00 \cdot \frac{6}{1000} - \$1.00 = \$0.48 - \$1.00$
$= -\$0.52$

Alternate Solution:
$E(X) = 79(\frac{6}{1000}) - 1(\frac{994}{1000}) = -\$0.52$

18.
$E(X) = \$360(0.999057) -$
$\$99,640(0.000943) = \$265.70$

19.
$E(X) = \sum X \cdot P(X) = \$80,000(0.2) +$
$\$40,000(0.7) - \$50,000(0.1) = \$39,000$
Yes.

20.

X	2	3	4	5	6	7	8	9	10	11	12
P(X)	$\frac{1}{36}$	$\frac{2}{36}$	$\frac{3}{36}$	$\frac{4}{36}$	$\frac{5}{36}$	$\frac{6}{36}$	$\frac{5}{36}$	$\frac{4}{36}$	$\frac{3}{36}$	$\frac{2}{36}$	$\frac{1}{36}$

$\mu = \sum X \cdot P(X) = 2(\frac{1}{36}) + 3(\frac{2}{36}) + 4(\frac{3}{36}) +$
$5(\frac{4}{36}) + 6(\frac{5}{36}) + 7(\frac{6}{36}) + 8(\frac{5}{36}) + 9(\frac{4}{36}) +$
$10(\frac{3}{36}) + 11(\frac{2}{36}) + 12(\frac{1}{36}) = 7$

$\sigma^2 = \sum X^2 \cdot P(X) - \mu^2 = [2^2(\frac{1}{36}) + 3^2(\frac{2}{36})$
$+ 4^2(\frac{3}{36}) + 5^2(\frac{4}{36}) + 6^2(\frac{5}{36}) + 7^2(\frac{6}{36}) +$
$8^2(\frac{5}{36}) + 9^2(\frac{4}{36}) + 10^2(\frac{3}{36}) + 11^2(\frac{2}{36}) +$
$12^2(\frac{1}{36})] - 7^2 = 5.83$ or 5.8

$\sigma = \sqrt{5.83} = 2.4$

21.
The expected value for a single die is 3.5, and since 3 die are rolled, the expected value is $3(3.5) = 10.5$

22.
$\sigma^2 = \sum(X - \mu)^2 \cdot P(X)$
$\sigma^2 = \sum(X^2 - 2\mu X + \mu^2)P(X)$
$\sigma^2 = \sum[X^2 P(X) - 2\mu X P(X) + \mu^2 P(X)]$
$\sigma^2 = \sum x^2 P(X) - 2\mu \sum X P(X) + \mu^2 \sum P(X)$
$\sigma^2 = \sum X^2 \cdot P(X) - 2\mu \cdot \mu + \mu^2(1)$
$\sigma^2 = \sum X^2 \cdot P(X) - 2\mu^2 + \mu^2$
$\sigma^2 = \sum X^2 \cdot P(X) - \mu^2$

23.
Answers will vary.

24.
Answers will vary.

25.
Answers will vary.

26.
$E(X) = [\$100,000 \cdot \frac{1}{1,000,000} + 10,000 \cdot \frac{2}{50,000}$
$+ 1000 \cdot \frac{5}{10,000} + 100 \cdot \frac{10}{1000}] - \$0.30 =$
$\$0.10 + \$0.40 + \$0.50 + \$1.00 - \$0.37 =$
$\$1.63$ when the cost of a stamp $= \$0.37$

EXERCISE SET 5-4

1.
a. Yes
b. Yes
c. Yes
d. No, there are more than two outcomes.
e. No, there are more than two outcomes.
f. Yes
g. Yes
h. Yes
i. No, there are more than two outcomes.
j. Yes

2.
a. 0.420
b. 0.346
c. 0.590
d. 0.251
e. 0.000
f. 0.250
g. 0.418
h. 0.176
i. 0.246

3.
a. $P(X) = \frac{n!}{(n-X)!\,X!} \cdot p^X \cdot q^{n-X}$

$P(X) = \frac{6!}{3!\cdot 3!} \cdot (0.03)^3 (0.97)^3 = 0.0005$

b. $P(X) = \frac{4!}{2!\cdot 2!} \cdot (0.18)^2 \cdot (0.82)^2 = 0.131$

c. $P(X) = \frac{5!}{2!\cdot 3!} = (0.63)^3 \cdot (0.37)^2 = 0.342$

d. $P(X) = \frac{9!}{9!\cdot 0!} \cdot (0.42)^0 \cdot (0.58)^9 = 0.007$

e. $P(X) = \frac{10!}{5!\cdot 5!} \cdot (0.37)^5 \cdot (0.63)^5 = 0.173$

4.
a. $n = 6, p = 0.05, X = 3$
$P(X) = 0.002$
b. $n = 6, p = 0.05, X = 0, 1$
$P(X) = 0.735 + 0.232 = 0.967$
c. $n = 6, p = 0.05, X = 0$
$P(X) = 0.735$
d. The answers are reasonable because the probability any component will fail is very small (0.05).

5.
$n = 20, p = 0.5, X \geq 15$
$P(X) = 0.015 + 0.005 + 0.001 = 0.021$
No, it's only about a 2% chance.

6.
$n = 10, p = 0.2, X \geq 15$
$P(X) = 0$
The event is unlikely to occur because the probability is extremely small (≈ 0).

7.
$n = 9, p = 0.30, X = 3$
$P(X) = 0.267$

8.
$n = 15, p = 0.90, X = 9, 10, 11, ..., 15$
$P(X) = 1.00$

9.
$n = 7, p = 0.75, X = 0, 1, 2, 3$

$P(X) = \frac{7!}{7!\,0!}(0.75)^0(0.25)^7 +$

$\frac{7!}{6!\,1!}(0.75)^1(0.25)^6 + \frac{7!}{5!\,2!}(0.75)^2(0.25)^5 +$

$\frac{7!}{4!\,3!}(0.75)^3(0.25)^4 = 0.071$

10.
$n = 10, p = 0.6, X = 3$
$P(X) = 0.042$

11.
$n = 5, p = 0.40$
a. $X = 2, P(X) = 0.346$
b. $X = 0, 1, 2,$ or 3 people
$P(X) = 0.078 + 0.259 + 0.346 + 0.230$
$= 0.913$
c. $X = 2, 3, 4,$ or 5 people
$P(X) = 0.346 + 0.230 + 0.077 + 0.01$
$= 0.663$
d. $X = 0, 1,$ or 2 people
$P(X) = 0.683$

12.
a. $n = 20$, $p = 0.7$, $X \geq 14$
$P(X) = 0.192 + 0.179 + 0.130 + 0.072 +$
$0.028 + 0.007 + 0.001 = 0.609$
(TI83 answer $= 0.608$)
b. $n = 20$, $p = 0.7$, $X = 9$
$P(X) = 0.012$
c. $n = 20$, $p = 0.7$, $X = 18, 19, 20$
$P(X) = 0.028 + 0.007 + 0.001 = 0.036$
d. Event a is most likely to occur since it has the highest probability.

13.
a. $n = 10$, $p = 0.8$, $X = 0, 1, 2, 3, 4, 5, 6$
$P(X) = 0.001 + 0.006 + 0.026 + 0.088 =$
0.121
b. $n = 10$, $p = 0.8$, $X = 6$, $P(X) = 0.088$
c. $n = 10$, $p = 0.8$, $X = 6, 7, 8, 9, 10$
$P(X) = 0.088 + 0.201 + 0.302 + 0.268 +$
$0.107 = 0.966$ (TI83 answer $= 0.967$)
d. Event c is most likely to occur since it has the highest probability.

14.
a. $\mu = 100(0.75) = 75$
$\sigma^2 = 100(0.75)(0.25) = 18.75$ or 18.8
$\sigma = \sqrt{18.75} = 4.33$ or 4.3
b. $\mu = 300(0.3) = 90$
$\sigma^2 = 300(0.3)(0.7) = 63$
$\sigma = \sqrt{63} = 7.94$ or 7.9
c. $\mu = 20(0.5) = 10$
$\sigma^2 = 20(0.5)(0.5) = 5$
$\sigma = \sqrt{5} = 2.236$ or 2.2
d. $\mu = 10(0.8) = 8$
$\sigma^2 = 10(0.8)(0.2) = 1.6$
$\sigma = \sqrt{1.6} = 1.265$ or 1.3
e. $\mu = 1000(0.1) = 100$
$\sigma^2 = 1000(0.1)(0.9) = 90$
$\sigma = \sqrt{90} = 9.49$ or 9.5
f. $\mu = 500(0.25) = 125$
$\sigma^2 = 500(0.25)(0.75) = 93.75$ or 93.8
$\sigma = \sqrt{93.75} = 9.68$ or 9.7
g. $\mu = 50(\frac{2}{5}) = 20$
$\sigma^2 = 50(\frac{2}{5})(\frac{3}{5}) = 12$
$\sigma = \sqrt{12} = 3.464$ or 3.5
h. $\mu = 36(\frac{1}{6}) = 6$
$\sigma^2 = 36(\frac{1}{6})(\frac{5}{6}) = 5$
$\sigma = \sqrt{5} = 2.236$ or 2.2

15.
$n = 800$, $p = 0.01$
$\mu = 800(0.01) = 8$
$\sigma^2 = 800(0.01)(0.99) = 7.9$

15. continued
$\sigma = \sqrt{7.92} = 2.8$

16.
$n = 20$, $p = \frac{1}{2}$ or 0.5
$\mu = 20(0.5) = 10$
$\sigma^2 = 20(0.5)(0.5) = 5$
$\sigma = \sqrt{5} = 2.24$

17.
$n = 300$, $p = 0.03$
$\mu = 300(0.03) = 9$
$\sigma^2 = 300(0.03)(0.97) = 8.73$
$\sigma = \sqrt{8.73} = 2.95$

18.
$n = 200$, $p = 0.83$
$\mu = 200(0.83) = 166$
$\sigma^2 = 200(0.83)(0.17) = 28.2$
$\sigma = \sqrt{28.2} = 5.3$

19.
$n = 1000$, $p = 0.21$
$\mu = 1000(0.21) = 210$
$\sigma^2 = 1000(0.21)(0.79) = 165.9$
$\sigma = \sqrt{165.9} = 12.9$

20.
$n = 80$, $p = 0.42$
$\mu = 80(0.42) = 33.6$
$\sigma^2 = 80(0.42)(0.58) = 19.5$
$\sigma = \sqrt{19.5} = 4.4$

Using the mean as a guide, there should be about 34 seats.

21.
$n = 18$, $p = 0.25$, $X = 5$
$P(X) = \frac{18!}{13! \, 5!}(0.25)^5(0.75)^{13} = 0.199$

22.
$n = 14$, $p = 0.63$, $X = 9$
$P(X) = \frac{14!}{5! \, 9!}(0.63)^9(0.37)^5 = 0.217$

23.
$n = 10$, $p = \frac{1}{3}$, $X = 0, 1, 2, 3$
$P(X) = \frac{10!}{10! \, 0!}(\frac{1}{3})^0(\frac{2}{3})^{10} + \frac{10!}{9! \, 1!}(\frac{1}{3})^1(\frac{2}{3})^9$
$+ \frac{10!}{8! \, 2!}(\frac{1}{3})^2(\frac{2}{3})^8 + \frac{10!}{7! \, 3!}(\frac{1}{3})^3(\frac{2}{3})^7 = 0.559$

24.
$n = 20$, $p = 0.58$, $X = 12$
$P(X) = \frac{20!}{8! \, 12!}(0.58)^{12}(0.42)^8 = 0.177$

25.

$n = 5$, $p = 0.13$, $X = 3, 4, 5$

$P(X) = \frac{5!}{2!\,3!}(0.13)^3(0.87)^2 +$
$\frac{5!}{1!\,4!}(0.13)^4(0.87)^1 + \frac{5!}{0!\,5!}(0.13)^5(0.87)^0$
$= 0.018$

26.

$n = 7$, $p = 0.14$, $X = 2$ or 3

$P(X) = \frac{7!}{5!\,2!}(0.14)^2(0.86)^5 +$
$\frac{7!}{4!\,3!}(0.14)^3(0.86)^4 = 0.246$

27.

$n = 12$, $p = 0.86$, $X = 10, 11, 12$

$P(X) = \frac{12!}{2!\,10!}(0.86)^{10}(0.14)^2 +$
$\frac{12!}{1!\,11!}(0.86)^{11}(0.14)^1 + \frac{12!}{0!\,12!}(0.86)^{12}(0.14)^0$
$= 0.7697$ or 0.770

Yes. The probability is high, 77%.

28.

X	0	1	2	3
P(X)	0.125	0.375	0.375	0.125

29.

$n = 4$, $p = 0.3$, $X = 0, 1, 2, 3, 4$

X	0	1	2	3	4
P(X)	0.240	0.412	0.265	0.076	0.008

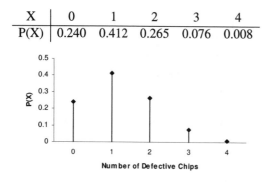

REVIEW EXERCISES - CHAPTER 5

1.
Yes.

2.
No, the sum of the probabilities is less than one.

3.
No, the sum of the probabilities is greater than one.

4.

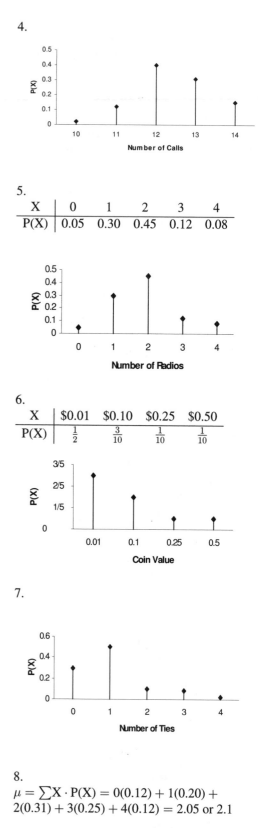

5.

X	0	1	2	3	4
P(X)	0.05	0.30	0.45	0.12	0.08

6.

X	$0.01	$0.10	$0.25	$0.50
P(X)	$\frac{1}{2}$	$\frac{3}{10}$	$\frac{1}{10}$	$\frac{1}{10}$

7.

8.

$\mu = \sum X \cdot P(X) = 0(0.12) + 1(0.20) +$
$2(0.31) + 3(0.25) + 4(0.12) = 2.05$ or 2.1

$\sigma^2 = \sum X^2 \cdot P(X) - \mu^2 = [0^2(0.12) +$
$1^2(0.2) + 2^2(0.31) + 3^2(0.25) + 4^2(0.12)]$
$- 2.05^2 = 1.4075$ or 1.4

8. continued

$\sigma = \sqrt{1.4075} = 1.186$ or 1.2

X	P(X)	X·P(X)	X²·P(X)
0	0.12	0.00	0.00
1	0.20	0.20	0.20
2	0.31	0.62	1.24
3	0.25	0.75	2.25
4	0.12	0.48	1.92
	μ =	2.05	5.61

9.

$\mu = \sum X \cdot P(X) = 13(0.12) + 14(0.15) + 15(0.29) + 16(0.25) + 17(0.19) = 15.24$ or 15.2

$\sigma^2 = \sum X^2 \cdot P(X) - \mu^2 = [13^2(0.12) + 14^2(0.15) + 15^2(0.29) + 16^2(0.25) + 17^2(0.19)] - 15.24^2 = 1.5824$ or 1.6

$\sigma = \sqrt{1.5824} = 1.26$ or 1.3

X	P(X)	X·P(X)	X²·P(X)
13	0.12	1.56	20.28
14	0.15	2.1	29.4
15	0.29	4.35	65.25
16	0.25	4	64
17	0.19	3.23	54.91
		μ = 15.24	233.84

10.

$\mu = \sum X \cdot P(X) = 1(0.42) + 2(0.27) + 3(0.15) + 4(0.1) + 5(0.06) = 2.11$ or 2.1

$\sigma^2 = \sum X^2 \cdot P(X) - \mu^2 = [1^2(0.42) + 2^2(0.27) + 3^2(0.15) + 4^2(0.1) + 5^2(0.06)] - 2.11^2 = 1.4979$ or 1.5

$\sigma = \sqrt{1.4979} = 1.22$ or 1.2

X	P(X)	X·P(X)	X²·P(X)
1	0.42	0.42	0.42
2	0.27	0.54	1.08
3	0.15	0.45	1.35
4	0.10	0.40	1.60
5	0.06	0.30	1.50
	μ =	2.11	5.95

11.

$\mu = \sum X \cdot P(X) = 22(0.08) + 23(0.19) + 24(0.36) + 25(0.25) + 26(0.07) + 27(0.05) = 24.19$ or 24.2

11. continued

$\sigma^2 = \sum X^2 \cdot P(X) - \mu^2 = [22^2(0.08) + 23^2(0.19) + 24^2(0.36) + 25^2(0.25) + 26^2(0.07) + 27^2(0.05)] - 24.19^2 = 1.4539$ or 1.5

$\sigma = \sqrt{1.4539} = 1.206$ or 1.2

X	P(X)	X·P(X)	X²·P(X)
22	0.08	1.76	38.72
23	0.19	4.37	100.51
24	0.36	8.64	207.36
25	0.25	6.25	156.25
26	0.07	1.82	47.32
27	0.05	1.35	36.45
	μ =	24.19	586.61

12.

$\mu = \$15,000(0.7) - \$8000(0.3) = \$8100$

13.

$\mu = \sum X \cdot P(X) = \frac{1}{2}(\$1.00) + \frac{18}{52}(\$5.00) + \frac{6}{52}(\$10.00) + \frac{2}{52}(\$100.00) = \$7.23$

To break even, a person should bet $7.23.

14.

n = 10, p = 0.3, X = 5
P(X) = 0.103

15.

a. 0.122
b. $1 - 0.002 + 0.009 = 0.989$
c. $0.002 + 0.009 + 0.032 = 0.043$

16.

a. In this case, it is easier to compute the probabilities for X = 0 and X = 1 and subtract the result from one.
n = 15, p = 0.10, X > 2
P(X) = 1 − (0.206 + 0.343) = 0.451
b. n = 15, p = 0.10, X = 3
P(X) = 0.129
c. n = 15, p = 0.10, X < 4
P(X) = 0.206 + 0.343 + 0.267 + 0.129 + 0.043 = 0.988

17.

$\mu = n \cdot p = 180(0.75) = 135$
$\sigma^2 = n \cdot p \cdot q = 180(0.75)(0.25) = 33.75$ or 33.8
$\sigma = \sqrt{33.75} = 5.809$ or 5.8

18.

$n = 225, p = 0.7$

$\mu = n \cdot p = 225(0.7) = 157.5$

$\sigma^2 = n \cdot p \cdot q = 225(0.7)(0.3) = 47.25$ or 47.3

$\sigma = \sqrt{47.25} = 6.87$ or 6.9

19.

$n = 8, p = 0.25$

$P(X \leq 3) = \frac{8!}{8!\,0!}(0.25)^0(0.75)^8 +$

$\frac{8!}{7!\,1!}(0.25)^1(0.75)^7 + \frac{8!}{6!\,2!}(0.25)^2(0.75)^6 +$

$\frac{8!}{5!\,3!}(0.25)^3(0.75)^5 = 0.8862$ or 0.886

20.

$N = 500, p = 0.27$

$\mu = 500(0.27) = 135$

$\sigma^2 = 500(0.27)(0.73) = 98.55$ or 98.6

$\sigma = \sqrt{98.55} = 9.9$

21.

$n = 20, p = 0.75, X = 16$

P(16 have eaten pizza for breakfast) =

$\frac{20!}{4!\,16!}(0.75)^{16}(0.25)^4 = 0.1897$ or 0.190

22.

$n = 10, p = 0.25, X = 0, 1, 2, 3$

P(at most 3 have pizza for breakfast) =

$\frac{10!}{10!\,0!}(0.25)^0(0.75)^{10} + \frac{10!}{9!\,1!}(0.25)^1(0.75)^9 +$

$\frac{10!}{8!\,2!}(0.25)^2(0.75)^8 + \frac{10!}{7!\,3!}(0.25)^3(0.75)^7 =$

$= 0.776$

CHAPTER 5 QUIZ

1. True
2. False, it is a discrete random variable.
3. False, the outcomes must be independent.
4. True
5. chance
6. $\mu = n \cdot p$
7. one
8. c
9. c
10. d
11. No, the sum of the probabilities is greater than one.
12. Yes
13. Yes
14. Yes

15.

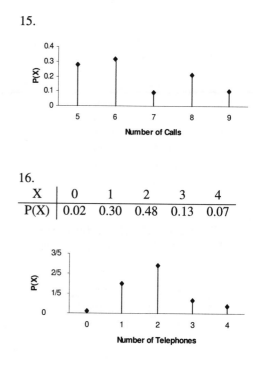

16.

X	0	1	2	3	4
P(X)	0.02	0.30	0.48	0.13	0.07

17.

$\mu = 0(0.10) + 1(0.23) + 2(0.31) + 3(0.27)$

$+ 4(0.09) = 2.02$ or 2

$\sigma^2 = [0^2(0.10) + 1^2(0.23) + 2^2(0.31) +$

$3^2(0.27) + 4^2(0.09)] - 2.02^2 = 1.3$

$\sigma = \sqrt{1.3} = 1.1$

18.

$\mu = 30(0.05) + 31(0.21) + 32(0.38) +$

$33(0.25) + 34(0.11) = 32.16$ or 32.2

$\sigma^2 = [30^2(0.05) + 31^2(0.21) + 32^2(0.38) +$

$33^2(0.25) + 34^2(0.11)] - 32.16^2 = 1.07$ or 1.1

$\sigma = \sqrt{1.07} = 1.0$

19.

$\mu = 4(\frac{1}{6}) + 5(\frac{1}{6}) + 2(\frac{1}{6}) + 10(\frac{1}{6}) + 3(\frac{1}{6})$

$+ 7(\frac{1}{6}) = 5.17$ or 5.2

20.

$\mu = \$2(\frac{1}{2}) + \$10(\frac{5}{26}) + \$25(\frac{3}{26}) +$

$\$100(\frac{1}{26}) = \$9.65$

21.

$n = 20, p = 0.40, X = 5$

$P(5) = 0.124$

22.

$n = 20, p = 0.60$

a. $P(15) = 0.075$

22. continued
b. $P(10, 11, ..., 20) = 0.872$
c. $P(0, 1, 2, 3, 4, 5) = 0.125$

23.
$n = 300, p = 0.80$
$\mu = 300(0.80) = 240$
$\sigma^2 = 300(0.80)(0.20) = 48$
$\sigma = \sqrt{48} = 6.9$

24.
$n = 75, p = 0.12$
$\mu = 75(0.12) = 9$
$\sigma^2 = 75(0.12)(0.88) = 7.9$
$\sigma = \sqrt{7.9} = 2.8$

Note to instructors: Graphs are not to scale and are intended to convey a general idea.

Answers are generated using Table E. Answers generated using the TI-83 will vary slightly.

EXERCISE SET 6-3

1.
The characteristics of the normal distribution are:
1. It is bell-shaped.
2. It is symmetric about the mean.
3. The mean, median, and mode are equal.
4. It is continuous.
5. It never touches the X-axis.
6. The area under the curve is equal to one.
7. It is unimodal.

2.
Many variables are normally distributed, and the distribution can be used to describe these variables.

3.
One or 100%.

4.
50% of the area lies below the mean, and 50% lies above the mean.

5.
68%, 95%, 99.7%

6.
The area is found by looking up $z = 1.66$ in Table E as shown in Block 1 of Procedure Table 6. Area $= 0.4515$

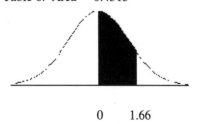

0   1.66

7.
The area is found by looking up $z = 0.75$ in Table E as shown in Block 1 of Procedure Table 6. Area $= 0.2734$

7. continued

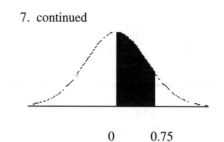

0   0.75

8.
The area is found by looking up $z = 0.35$ in Table E as shown in Block 1 of Procedure Table 6. Area $= 0.1368$

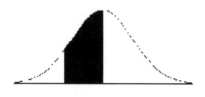

$- 0.35$ 0

9.
The area is found by looking up $z = 2.07$ in Table E as shown in Block 1 of Procedure Table 6. Area $= 0.4808$

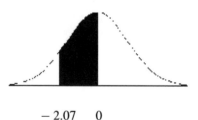

$- 2.07$ 0

10.
The area is found by looking up $z = 1.10$ in Table E and subtracting the value from 0.5. $0.5 - 0.3643 = 0.1357$

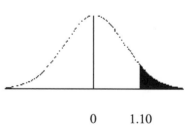

0   1.10

11.
The area is found by looking up $z = 0.23$ in Table E and subtracting it from 0.5 as shown in Block 2 of Procedure Table 6.

11. continued

$0.5 - 0.0910 = 0.4090$

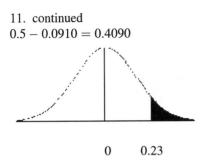

0 0.23

12.

The area is found by looking up $z = 0.48$ in Table E and subtracting the area from 0.5.

$0.5 - 0.1844 = 0.3156$

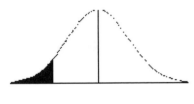

-0.48 0

13.

The area is found by looking up $z = 1.43$ in Table E and subtracting it from 0.5 as shown in Block 2 of Procedure Table 6.

$0.5 - 0.4236 = 0.0764$

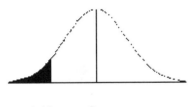

-1.43 0

14.

The area is found by looking up the values 1.23 and 1.90 in Table E and subtracting the areas. $0.4713 - 0.3907 = 0.0806$

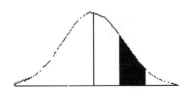

0 1.23 1.90

15.

The area is found by looking up the values 0.79 and 1.28 in Table E and subtracting the areas as shown in Block 3 of Procedure Table 6. $0.3997 - 0.2852 = 0.1145$

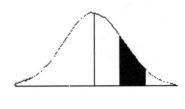

0 0.79 1.28

16.

The area is found by looking up the values 0.96 and 0.36 in Table E and subtracting the areas. $0.3315 - 0.1406 = 0.1909$

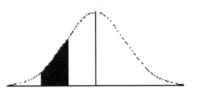

-0.96 -0.36 0

17.

The area is found by looking up the values 1.56 and 1.83 in Table E and subtracting the areas as shown in Block 3 of Procedure Table 6. $0.4664 - 0.4406 = 0.0258$

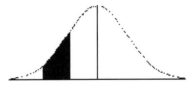

-1.83 -1.56 0

18.

$0.3686 + 0.0948 = 0.4634$

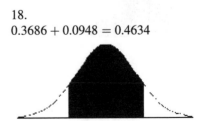

-1.12 0 0.24

19.
The area is found by looking up the values 2.47 and 1.03 in Table E and adding them together as shown in Block 4 of Procedure Table 6. $0.3485 + 0.4932 = 0.8417$

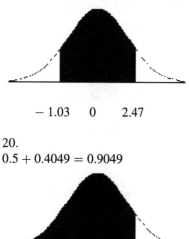

$-1.03 \quad 0 \quad 2.47$

20.
$0.5 + 0.4049 = 0.9049$

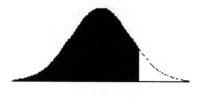

$0 \quad 1.31$

21.
The area is found by looking up $z = 2.11$ in Table E, then adding the area to 0.5 as shown in Block 5 of Procedure Table 6.
$0.5 + 0.4826 = 0.9826$

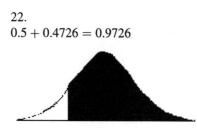

$0 \quad 2.11$

22.
$0.5 + 0.4726 = 0.9726$

$-1.92 \quad 0$

23.
The area is found by looking up $z = 0.15$ in Table E and adding it to 0.5 as shown in Block 6 of Procedure Table 6.
$0.5 + 0.0596 = 0..5596$

23. continued

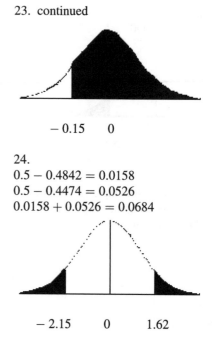

$-0.15 \quad 0$

24.
$0.5 - 0.4842 = 0.0158$
$0.5 - 0.4474 = 0.0526$
$0.0158 + 0.0526 = 0.0684$

$-2.15 \quad 0 \quad 1.62$

25.
The area is found by looking up the values 1.92 and 0.44 in Table E, subtracting both areas from 0.5, and adding them together as shown in Block 7 of Procedure Table 6.
$0.5 - 0.4726 = 0.0274$
$0.5 - 0.1700 = 0.3300$
$0.0274 + 0.3300 = 0.3574$

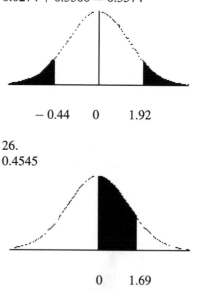

$-0.44 \quad 0 \quad 1.92$

26.
0.4545

$0 \quad 1.69$

27.
The area is found by looking up $z = 0.67$ in Table E as shown in Block 1 of Procedure Table 6. Area $= 0.2486$

27. continued

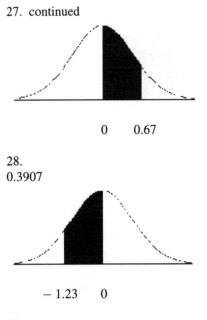

0   0.67

28.
0.3907

-1.23 0

29.
The area is found by looking up z = 1.57 in
Table E as shown in Block 1 of Procedure
Table 6. Area = 0.4418

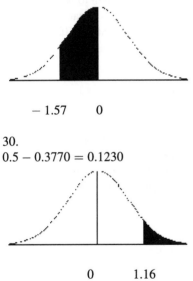

-1.57 0

30.
$0.5 - 0.3770 = 0.1230$

0   1.16

31.
The area is found by looking up z = 2.83
in Table E then subtracting the area from 0.5
as shown in Block 2 of Procedure Table 6.
$0.5 - 0.4977 = 0.0023$

31. continued

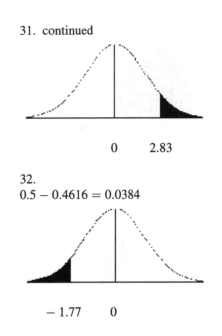

0   2.83

32.
$0.5 - 0.4616 = 0.0384$

-1.77 0

33.
The area is found by looking up z = 1.21 in
Table E then subtracting the area from 0.5 as
shown in Block 2 of Procedure Table 6.
$0.5 - 0.3869 = 0.1131$

-1.21 0

34.
$0.0199 + 0.3643 = 0.3842$

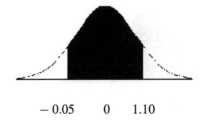

-0.05 0   1.10

35.
The area is found by looking the values 2.46
and 1.74 in Table E and adding the areas
together as shown in Block 4 of Procedure
Table 6. $0.4931 + 0.4591 = 0.9522$

35. continued

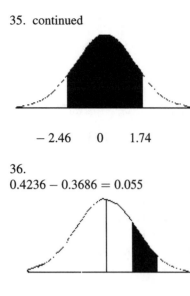

$-2.46 \quad 0 \quad 1.74$

36.
$0.4236 - 0.3686 = 0.055$

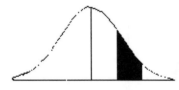

$0 \quad 1.12 \; 1.43$

37.
The area is found by looking up the values
1.46 and 2.97 in Table E and subtracting the
areas as shown in Block 3 of Procedure
Table 6. $0.4985 - 0.4279 = 0.0706$

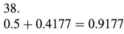

$0 \quad 1.46 \quad 2.97$

38.
$0.5 + 0.4177 = 0.9177$

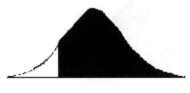

$-1.39 \quad 0$

39.
The area is found by looking up $z = 1.42$ in
Table E and adding 0.5 to it as shown in
Block 5 of Procedure Table 6.
$0.5 + 0.4222 = 0.9222$

39. continued

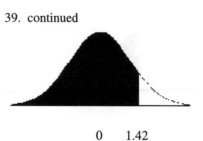

$0 \quad 1.42$

40.
$+1.32$

41.
$z = -1.94$, found by looking up the area
0.4738 in Table E to get 1.94; it is negative
because the z value is on the left side of 0.

42.
$0.5 - 0.0239 = 0.4761$
$z = +1.98$

43.
$z = -2.13$, found by subtracting 0.0166
from 0.5 to get 0.4834 then looking up the
area to get $z = 2.13$; it is negative because
the z value is on the left side of 0.

44.
$0.9671 - 0.5 = 0.4671$
$z = +1.84$

45.
$z = -1.26$, found by subtracting 0.5 from
0.8962 to get 0.3962, then looking up the
area in Table E to get $z = 1.26$; it is
negative because the z value is on the left
side of 0.

46.
a. $0.5398 - 0.5 = 0.0398$
$z = 0.10$

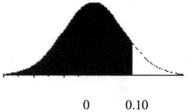
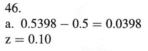

$0 \quad 0.10$

b. $0.7190 - 0.5 = 0.2190$
$z = 0.58$

46b. continued

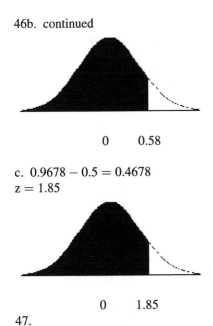

0   0.58

c. $0.9678 - 0.5 = 0.4678$
$z = 1.85$

0   1.85

47.
a. $z = -2.28$, found by subtracting 0.5 from 0.9886 to get 0.4886. Find the area in Table E, then find z. It is negative since the z value falls to the left of 0.

-2.28 0

b. $z = -0.92$, found by subtracting 0.5 from 0.8212 to get 0.3212. Find the area in Table E, then find z. It is negative since the z value falls to the left of 0.

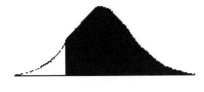

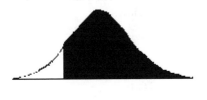

-0.92 0

c. $z = -0.27$, found by subtracting 0.5 from 0.6064 to get 0.1064. Find the area in Table E, then find z. It is negative since the z value falls to the left of 0.

47c. continued

-0.27 0

48.
$z = \pm 0.58$, approximately.

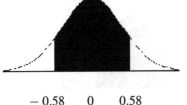

-0.58 0   0.58

49.
a. $z = \pm 1.96$, found by:
$0.05 \div 2 = 0.025$ is the area in each tail.
$0.5 - 0.025 = 0.4750$ is the area needed to determine z.

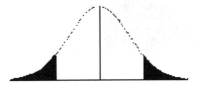

-1.96 0   1.96

b. $z = \pm 1.65$, found by:
$0.10 \div 2 = 0.05$ is the area in each tail.
$0.5 - 0.05 = 0.4500$ is the area needed to determine z.

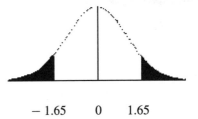

-1.65 0   1.65

c. $z = \pm 2.58$, found by:
$0.01 \div 2 = 0.005$ is the area in each tail.
$0.5 - 0.005 = 0.4950$ is the area needed to determine z.

49c. continued

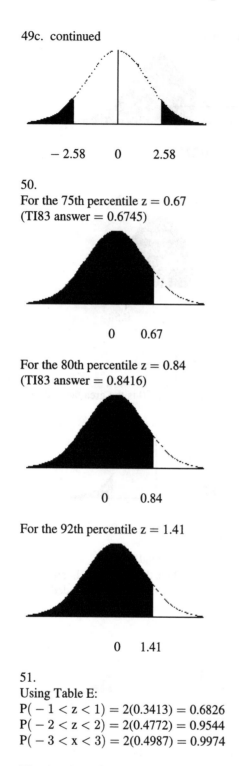

−2.58   0   2.58

50.

For the 75th percentile z = 0.67
(TI83 answer = 0.6745)

0   0.67

For the 80th percentile z = 0.84
(TI83 answer = 0.8416)

0   0.84

For the 92th percentile z = 1.41

0   1.41

51.

Using Table E:
$P(-1 < z < 1) = 2(0.3413) = 0.6826$
$P(-2 < z < 2) = 2(0.4772) = 0.9544$
$P(-3 < x < 3) = 2(0.4987) = 0.9974$

They are very close.

52.

$0.5 - 0.1234 = 0.3766$
For area = 0.3766, $z_0 = 1.16$
Thus, $P(z > 1.16) = 0.1234$

53.

For z = −1.2, area = 0.3849
$0.8671 - 0.3849 = 0.4822$
For area = 0.4822, z = 2.10
Thus, $P(-1.2 < z < 2.10) = 0.8671$

54.

For z = 2.5, area = 0.4938
$0.7672 - 0.4938 = 0.2734$
For area = 0.2734, z = 0.75
Thus, $P(-0.75 < z < 2.5) = 0.7672$

55.

For z = −0.5, area = 0.1915
$0.2345 - 0.1915 = 0.043$
For area = 0.043, z = 0.11
Thus, $P(-0.5 < z < 0.11) = 0.2345$

For z = −0.5, area = 0.1915
$0.2345 + 0.1915 = 0.4260$
For area = 0.426, z = −1.45
Thus, $P(-1.45 < z < -0.5) = 0.2345$

56.

$0.86 \div 2 = 0.43$
For area = 0.43, z = ±1.48
Thus, $P(-1.48 < z < 1.48) = 0.86$

57.

$$y = \frac{e^{\frac{-(X-0)^2}{2(1)^2}}}{1\sqrt{2\pi}} = \frac{e^{\frac{-X^2}{2}}}{\sqrt{2\pi}}$$

58.

Each x value (−2, −1.5, etc.) is
substituted in the formula $y = \frac{e^{\frac{-X^2}{2}}}{\sqrt{2\pi}}$ to get the
corresponding y value. The pairs are then
plotted as shown below.

For x = −2, $y = \frac{e^{\frac{-(-2)^2}{2}}}{\sqrt{2\pi}} = \frac{e^{-2}}{\sqrt{6.28}}$
$= \frac{0.1353}{\sqrt{6.28}} = 0.05$

X	Y
-2.0	0.05
-1.5	0.13
-1.0	0.24
-0.5	0.35
0	0.40
0.5	0.35
1.0	0.24
1.5	0.13
2.0	0.05

58. continued

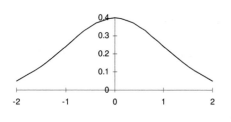

EXERCISE SET 6-4

1.
$z = \frac{\$3.00-\$5.39}{\$0.79} = -3.03$
area $= 0.4988$
$P(z < -3.03) = 0.5 - 0.4988 = 0.0012$ or
0.12%

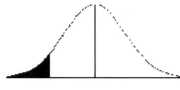

$-3.03 \qquad 0$

2.
a. $z = \frac{20,000-27,989}{3250} = -2.46$
area $= 0.4931$

$z = \frac{30,000-27,989}{3250} = 0.62$
area $= 0.2324$

$P(-2.46 < z < 0.62) = 0.4931 + 0.2324$
$P = 0.7255$ or 72.55%

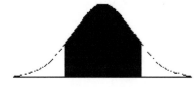

$-2.46 \qquad\qquad 0.62$

b. $z = -2.46$
area $= 0.4931$

$P(z < -2.46) = 0.5 - 0.4931 = 0.0069$
or 0.007

2b. continued

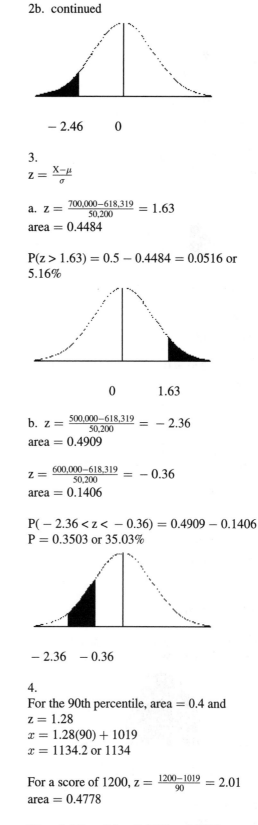

$-2.46 \qquad 0$

3.
$z = \frac{X-\mu}{\sigma}$

a. $z = \frac{700,000-618,319}{50,200} = 1.63$
area $= 0.4484$

$P(z > 1.63) = 0.5 - 0.4484 = 0.0516$ or
5.16%

$0 \qquad 1.63$

b. $z = \frac{500,000-618,319}{50,200} = -2.36$
area $= 0.4909$

$z = \frac{600,000-618,319}{50,200} = -0.36$
area $= 0.1406$

$P(-2.36 < z < -0.36) = 0.4909 - 0.1406$
$P = 0.3503$ or 35.03%

$-2.36 \quad -0.36$

4.
For the 90th percentile, area $= 0.4$ and
$z = 1.28$
$x = 1.28(90) + 1019$
$x = 1134.2$ or 1134

For a score of 1200, $z = \frac{1200-1019}{90} = 2.01$
area $= 0.4778$

$P(z > 2.01) = 0.5 - 0.4778 = 0.0222$ or
2.22%

5.

$$z = \frac{X-\mu}{\sigma}$$

a. $z = \frac{200-225}{10} = -2.5$
area = 0.4938

$z = \frac{220-225}{10} = -0.5$
area = 0.1915

$P(-2.5 < z < -0.5) =$
$0.4938 - 0.1915 = 0.3023$ or 30.23%

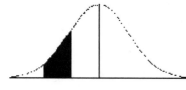

$-2.5 \quad -0.5$

b. $z = -2.5$
area = 0.4938

$P(z < -2.5) = 0.5 - 0.4938 = 0.0062$ or
0.62%

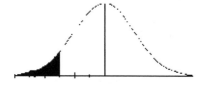

-2.5

6.

a. $z = \frac{53-56}{4} = -0.75$
area = 0.2734

$z = \frac{59-56}{4} = 0.75$
area = 0.2734

$P(-0.75 < z < 0.75) = 0.2734 + 0.2734$
$= 0.5468$ or 54.68%

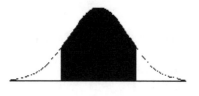

$-0.75 \quad 0 \quad 0.75$

b. $z = \frac{58-56}{4} = 0.5$
area = 0.1915

6b. continued

$z = \frac{63-56}{4} = 1.75$
area = 0.4599

$P(0.5 < z < 1.75) = 0.4599 - 0.1915$
$= 0.2684$ or 26.84%

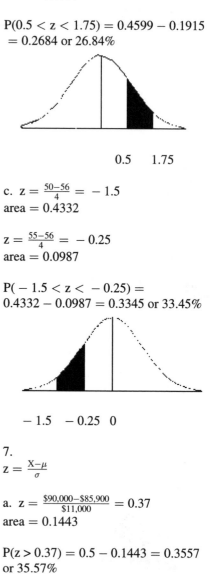

$0.5 \quad 1.75$

c. $z = \frac{50-56}{4} = -1.5$
area = 0.4332

$z = \frac{55-56}{4} = -0.25$
area = 0.0987

$P(-1.5 < z < -0.25) =$
$0.4332 - 0.0987 = 0.3345$ or 33.45%

$-1.5 \quad -0.25 \quad 0$

7.

$$z = \frac{X-\mu}{\sigma}$$

a. $z = \frac{\$90,000-\$85,900}{\$11,000} = 0.37$
area = 0.1443

$P(z > 0.37) = 0.5 - 0.1443 = 0.3557$
or 35.57%

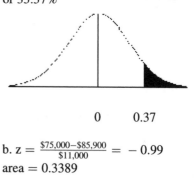

$0 \quad 0.37$

b. $z = \frac{\$75,000-\$85,900}{\$11,000} = -0.99$
area = 0.3389

$P(z > -0.99) = 0.5 + 0.3389$
$= 0.8389$ or 83.89%

7b. continued

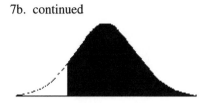

-0.99

8.

a. $z = \frac{15,000-12,837}{1500} = 1.44$

area $= 0.4251$

$P(z > 1.44) = 0.5 - 0.4251 = 0.0749$ or 7.49%

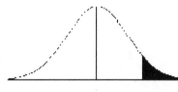

0   1.44

b. $z = \frac{13,000-12,837}{1500} = 0.11$

area $= 0.0438$

$z = \frac{14,000-12,837}{1500} = 0.78$

area $= 0.2823$

$P(0.11 < z < 0.78) =$

$0.2823 - 0.0438 = 0.2385$ or 23.85%

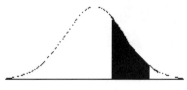

0.11   0.78

9.

$z = \frac{X-\mu}{\sigma}$

a. $z = \frac{1.5-3.2}{0.56} = -3.04$ area $= 0.4988$

$P(z < -3.04) = 0.5 - 0.4988 = 0.0012$

-3.04 0

9. continued

b. $z = \frac{2-3.2}{0.56} = -2.14$ area $= 0.4838$

$z = \frac{3-3.2}{0.56} = -0.36$ area $= 0.1406$

$P(-2.14 < z < -0.36) =$
$0.4838 - 0.1406 = 0.3432$

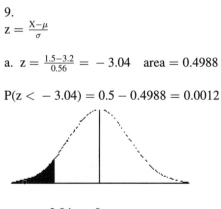

-2.14 -0.36

c. $z = \frac{3.2-3.2}{0.56} = 0$ area $= 0.5$

$P(z > 0) = 0.5$

0

d. For an 18 month (1.5 year) warranty,
$z = -3.04$.
$P(z < -3.04) = .5 - 0.4988 = 0.0012$
Hence, 0.12% of the ovens would be replaced.

10.
$z = \frac{30-25.5}{6.1} = 0.74$
area $= 0.2704$

$P(z > 0.74) = 0.5 - 0.2704 = 0.2296$ or
22.96% (TI83 answer $= 0.2303$)

11.
$z = \frac{X-\mu}{\sigma}$

a. $z = \frac{1000-3262}{1100} = -2.06$
area $= 0.4803$

$P(z \geq -2.06) = 0.5 + 0.4803 = 0.9803$
or 98.03%

11a. continued

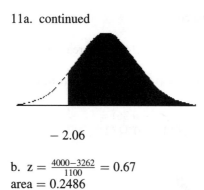

$$-2.06$$

b. $z = \frac{4000-3262}{1100} = 0.67$
area $= 0.2486$

P(z > 0.67) = 0.5 − 0.2486 = 0.2514 or
25.14%

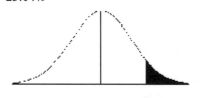

$$0 \qquad 0.67$$

c. $z = \frac{3000-3262}{1100} = -0.24$
area $= 0.0948$

P(−0.24 < z < 0.67) =
0.0948 + 0.2486 = 0.3434 or 34.34%

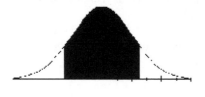

$$-0.24 \qquad\qquad 0.67$$

12.
a. $z = \frac{120-96}{17} = 1.41$ \qquad area $= 0.4207$

P(z ≥ 1.41) = 0.5 − 0.4207 = 0.0793

$$0 \qquad 1.41$$

b. $z = \frac{80-96}{17} = -0.94$ \qquad area $= 0.3264$

P(z ≤ −0.94) = 0.5 − 0.3264 = 0.1736

12b. continued

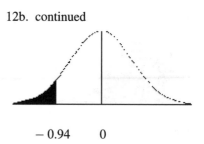

$$-0.94 \qquad 0$$

c. The bus should make a trip about every
130 minutes, or $\mu + 2\sigma$.

13.
a. $z = \frac{350-380}{16} = -1.88$
area $= 0.4699$

P(z ≥ −1.88) = 0.5 + 0.4699 = 0.9699

$$-1.88 \qquad 0$$

b. $z = \frac{395-380}{16} = 0.94$
area $= 0.3264$

P(z ≤ 0.94) = 0.5 + 0.3264 = 0.8264

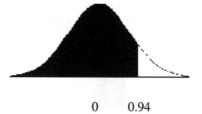

$$0 \qquad 0.94$$

c. Use the range rule of thumb:
If $\frac{\text{Range}}{4} = 16$, then the range is about
$16 \cdot 4 = 64$.

14.
a. $z = \frac{54-53.2}{2.3} = 0.35$ \qquad area $= 0.1368$

P(z > 0.35) = 0.5 − 0.1368 = 0.3632

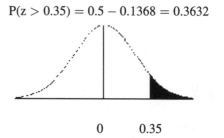

$$0 \qquad 0.35$$

14. continued

b. $z = \frac{60-53.2}{2.3} = 2.96$ area = 0.4985

$P(z < 2.96) = 0.5 + 0.4985 = 0.9985$

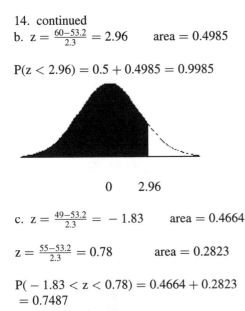

0   2.96

c. $z = \frac{49-53.2}{2.3} = -1.83$ area = 0.4664

$z = \frac{55-53.2}{2.3} = 0.78$ area = 0.2823

$P(-1.83 < z < 0.78) = 0.4664 + 0.2823$
$= 0.7487$

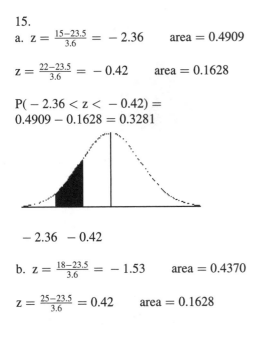

-1.83   0   0.78

d. For 60°, z = 2.96 (see part b)
$P(z > 2.96) = 0.5 - 0.4985 = 0.0015$
Since the probability is very small, a
temperature above 60° is very warm.

15.
a. $z = \frac{15-23.5}{3.6} = -2.36$ area = 0.4909

$z = \frac{22-23.5}{3.6} = -0.42$ area = 0.1628

$P(-2.36 < z < -0.42) =$
$0.4909 - 0.1628 = 0.3281$

-2.36   -0.42

b. $z = \frac{18-23.5}{3.6} = -1.53$ area = 0.4370

$z = \frac{25-23.5}{3.6} = 0.42$ area = 0.1628

15b. continued
$P(z < -1.53 \text{ or } z > 0.42) =$
$(0.5 - 0.4370) + (0.5 - 0.1628) =$
$0.063 + 0.3372 = 0.4002$

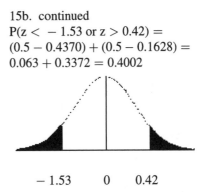

-1.53   0   0.42

c. For 15 minutes, z = -2.36.
$P(z < -2.36) = 0.5 - 0.4909 = 0.0091$
Since the probability is small, it is not likely
that a person would be seated in less than 15
minutes.

16.
The top 25% (area) is in the left tail of the
normal curve, since the top scores in a race
would be scores that are below the mean.
The corresponding z score is found using
area = 0.5 - 0.25 = 0.25 so z = -0.67.
Thus $x = -0.67(3.6) + 45.8 = 43.39$
seconds.

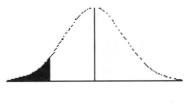

43.39   45.8

17.
The middle 66% means that 33% of the area
will be on either side of the mean. Thus,
area = 0.33 and z = ±0.95.
$x = -0.95(1025) + 6492 = \$5518.25$
$x = 0.95(1025) + 6492 = \$7465.75$

The prices are between \$5518.25 and
\$7465.75.

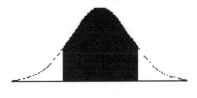

\$5518.25   \$7465.75

17. continued
Yes, a boat priced at $5550 would be sold in this store.

18.
The middle 50% means that 25% of the area will be on either side of the mean. Thus, area = 0.25 and z = ±0.67.
$x = 0.67(103) + 792 = 861.01$
$x = -0.67(103) + 792 = 722.99$

The contributions are between 723 and 861.

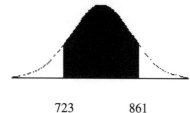

723   861

19.
The middle 80% means that 40% of the area will be on either side of the mean. The corresponding z scores will be ±1.28.
$x = -1.28(92) + 1810 = 1692.24$ sq. ft.
$x = 1.28(92) + 1810 = 1927.76$ sq. ft.

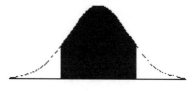

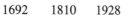
1692   1810   1928

20.
$z = ±1.28$
$x = -1.28(1500) + 145,500 = \$143,580$
$x = 1.28(1500) + 145,500 = \$147,420$

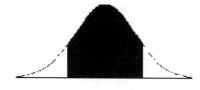

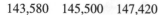
143,580   145,500   147,420

21.
$z = \frac{1200-949}{100} = 2.51$
area = 0.4940

$P(z > 2.51) = 0.5 - 0.4940 = 0.006$ or 0.6%

21. continued

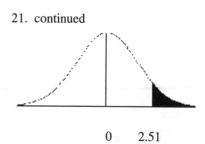

0   2.51

For the least expensive 10%, the area is 0.4 on the left side of the curve. Thus, z = −1.28.
$x = -1.28(100) + 949 = \$821$

22.
The bottom 5% (area) is in the left tail of the normal curve. The corresponding z score is found using area = 0.5 − 0.05 = 0.45. Thus z = −1.65.
$x = -1.65(18) + 122.6 = 92.9$ or 93

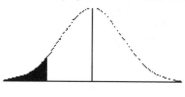

92.9   122.6

23.
The middle 60% means that 30% of the area will be on either side of the mean. The corresponding z scores will be ±0.84.
$x = -0.84(1150) + 8256 = \$7290$
$x = 0.84(1150) + 8256 = \$9222$

$7290 $8256 $9222

24.
For the oldest 20%, the area is 0.3 on the right side of the curve. Thus, z = 0.84.
$22.8 = 0.84\sigma + 19.4$
$s = 4.048$ or 4.05 years

25.
For the fewest 15%, the area is 0.35 on the left side of the curve. Thus, z = −1.04.
$x = -1.04(1.7) + 5.9$
$x = 4.132$ days

98

25. continued
For the longest 25%, the area is 0.25 on the right side of the curve. Thus, z = 0.67.
$x = 0.67(1.7) + 5.9$
$x = 7.039$ days or 7.04 days

26.
a. For the top 3%, the area is 0.47 on the right side of the curve. Thus, z = 1.88.
$x = 1.88(100) + 400$
$x = 588$ minimum score to receive the award.

b. For the bottom 1.5%, the area is 0.485 on the left side of the curve. Thus, z = −2.17.
$x = -2.17(100) + 400$
$x = 183$ minimum score to avoid summer school.

27.
The bottom 18% means that 32% of the area is between 0 and −z. The corresponding z score will be −0.92.
$x = -0.92(6256) + 24,596 = \$18,840.48$

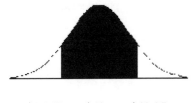

$\$18,840.48 \qquad \$24,596$

28.
The middle 50% means that 25% of the area is on either side of the mean. The corresponding z scores will be ±0.67.
$x = -0.67(5) + 40 = \$36.65$
$x = 0.67(5) + 40 = \$43.35$

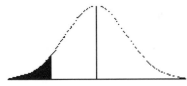

$\$36.65 \qquad \$40 \qquad \$43.35$

29.
The 10% to be exchanged would be at the left, or bottom, of the curve; therefore, 40% of the area is between 0 and −z. The corresponding z score will be −1.28.
$x = -1.28(5) + 25 = 18.6$ months.

29. continued

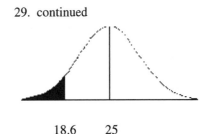

$18.6 \qquad 25$

30.
The top 15% means that 35% of the area is between 0 and z. The corresponding z score is 1.04.
$x = 1.04(8) + 62 = 70.32 \approx 70$

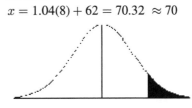

$62 \qquad 70.32$

31.
a. $\mu = 120 \qquad \sigma = 20$
b. $\mu = 15 \qquad \sigma = 2.5$
c. $\mu = 30 \qquad \sigma = 5$

32.
No. Any subgroup would not be a perfect representation of the seniors; therefore, the mean and standard deviation would be different.

33.
There are several mathematical tests that can be used including drawing a histogram and calculating Pearson's index of skewness.

34.
No. The shape of the distributions would be the same, since z scores are raw scores scaled by the standard deviation.

35.
2.87% area in the right tail of the curve means that 47.13% of the area is between 0 and z, corresponding to a z score of 1.90.
$z = \frac{X - \mu}{\sigma}$
$1.90 = \frac{112 - 110}{\sigma}$
$1.90\sigma = 2$
$\sigma = 1.05$

36.
3.75% area in the left tail means that 46.25% of the area is between 0 and $-z$, corresponding to a z score of -1.78.
$-1.78 = \frac{85-\mu}{6}$
$-1.78(6) = 85 - \mu$
$\mu = 95.68$

37.
1.25% of the area in each tail means that 48.75% of the area is between 0 and $\pm z$. The corresponding z scores are ± 2.24.
Then $\mu = \frac{42+48}{2} = 45$ and $X = \mu + z\sigma$.
$48 = 45 + 2.24\sigma$
$\sigma = 1.34$

38.
The cutoff for the A's and F's would be:
$x = \mu + z\sigma$
$x = 60 + 1.65(10)$
$x = 76.5$ for the A's
$x = 60 + (-1.65)(10)$
$x = 43.5$ for the F's

For the B's and D's:
$x = 60 + (0.84)(10)$
$x = 68.4$ for the B's
$x = 60 + (-0.84)(10)$
$x = 51.6$ for the D's

The grading scale would be:

77 and up	A
68 − 76	B
52 − 67	C
44 − 51	D
0 − 43	F

39.
Histogram:

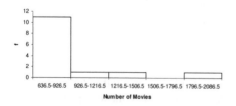

The histogram shows a positive skew.

$PI = \frac{3(970.2-853.5)}{376.5} = 0.93$

$IQR = Q_3 - Q_1 = 910 - 815 = 95$
$1.5(IQR) = 1.5(95) = 142.5$
$Q_1 - 142.5 = 672.5$

39. continued
$Q_3 + 142.5 = 1052.5$
There are several outliers.

Conclusion: The distribution is not normal.

40.
Histogram:

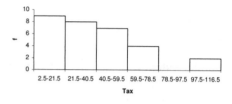

The histogram shows a positive skew.

$PI = \frac{3(39.9-33.5)}{27.18} = 0.71$

$IQR = Q_3 - Q_1 = 58 - 20 = 38$
$1.5(IQR) = 1.5(38) = 57$
$Q_1 - 57 = -37$
$Q_3 + 57 = 115$
There are no outliers.

Conclusion: The distribution is not normal.

41.
Histogram:

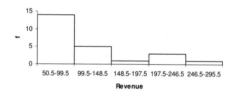

The histogram shows a positive skew.

$PI = \frac{3(115.3-92.5)}{66.32} = 1.03$

$IQR = Q_3 - Q_1 = 154.5 - 67 = 87.5$
$1.5(IQR) = 1.5(87.5) = 131.25$
$Q_1 - 131.25 = -64.25$
$Q_3 + 131.25 = 285.75$
There is one outlier.

Conclusion: The distribution is not normal.

42.

Histogram:

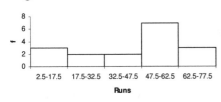

Runs

The histogram shows a negative skew.

$$PI = \frac{3(45.2-52)}{20.58} = -0.99$$

$IQR = Q_3 - Q_1 = 60.5 - 29.5 = 31$
$1.5(IQR) = 1.5(31) = 46.5$
$Q_1 - 46.5 = -17$
$Q_3 + 46.5 = 107$
There are no outliers.

Conclusion: The distribution is not normal.

EXERCISE SET 6-5

1.
The distribution is called the sampling distribution of sample means.

2.
The sample is not a perfect representation of the population. The difference is due to what is called sampling error.

3.
The mean of the sample means is equal to the population mean.

4.
The standard deviation of the sample means is called the standard error of the mean.
$$\sigma_X = \frac{\sigma}{\sqrt{n}}$$

5.
The distribution will be approximately normal when sample size is large.

6.
$$z = \frac{X-\mu}{\sigma}$$

7.
$$z = \frac{\overline{X}-\mu}{\sigma/\sqrt{n}}$$

8.
$$z = \frac{\overline{X}-\mu}{\frac{\sigma}{\sqrt{n}}} = \frac{17-17.2}{\frac{2.5}{\sqrt{55}}} = -0.59$$

8. continued
area = 0.2224

$$z = \frac{18-17.2}{\frac{2.5}{\sqrt{55}}} = 2.37 \qquad area = 0.4911$$
$$P(-0.59 < z < 2.37) = 0.2224 + 0.4911$$
$$= 0.7135 \text{ or } 71.35\%$$

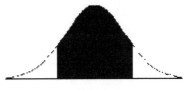

17   17.2   18

9.
$$z = \frac{\overline{X}-\mu}{\frac{\sigma}{\sqrt{n}}} = \frac{\$175-\$186.80}{\frac{\$32}{\sqrt{50}}} = -2.61$$
area = 0.4955
$$P(z < -2.61) = 0.5 - 0.4955 = 0.0045 \text{ or } 0.45\%$$

$175 $186.8

10.
a. $$z = \frac{\$50,000-\$52,174}{\frac{\$7500}{}} = -0.29$$
area = 0.1141
$$P(z < -0.29) = 0.5 - 0.1141 = 0.3859 \text{ or } 38.6\%$$

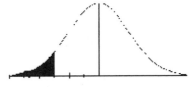

$50,000 $52,174

b. $$z = \frac{\$50,000-\$52,174}{\frac{\$7500}{\sqrt{100}}} = -2.90$$
area = 0.4981
$$P(z < -2.90) = 0.5 - 0.4981 = 0.0019 \text{ or } 0.19\%$$

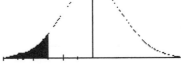

$50,000 $52,174

11.

$$z = \frac{\overline{X}-\mu}{\frac{\sigma}{\sqrt{n}}} = \frac{144.5-142}{\frac{12.3}{\sqrt{36}}} = 1.22$$

area = 0.3888

P(z > 1.22) = 0.5 − 0.3888 = 0.1112 or 11.12%

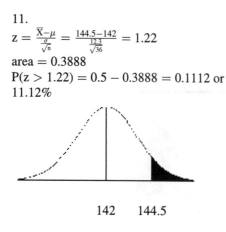

142   144.5

12.

a. $z = \frac{\$40,000-\$29,863}{\$5100} = 1.99$

area = 0.4767

P(z > 1.99) = 0.5 − 0.4767 = 0.0233 or 2.33%

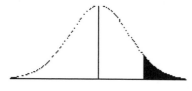

$29,863 $40,000

b. $z = \frac{\$30,000-\$29,863}{\frac{\$5100}{\sqrt{80}}} = 0.24$

area = 0.0948

P(z > 0.24) = 0.5 − 0.0948 = 0.4052 or 40.52%

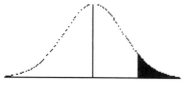

$29,863 $30,000

13.

$$z = \frac{\overline{X}-\mu}{\frac{\sigma}{\sqrt{n}}} = \frac{\$2.00-\$2.02}{\frac{\$0.08}{\sqrt{40}}} = -1.58$$

area = 0.4429

P(z < − 1.58) = 0.5 − 0.4429 = 0.0571 or 5.71%

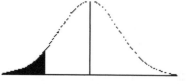

$2.00 $2.02

14.

$$z = \frac{1050-1019}{\frac{100}{\sqrt{200}}} = 4.38$$

area = 0.4999

P(z ≥ 4.38) = 0.5 − 0.4999 = 0.0001 or 0.01%

(Note: Using the TI-83 Plus the answer is 0.000006)

Hence, we would be surprised to get a sample mean of 1050 since the probability is very small.

15.

a. $z = \frac{\overline{X}-\mu}{\sigma} = \frac{670-660}{35} = 0.29$

area = 0.1141

P(z > 0.29) = 0.5 − 0.1141 = 0.3859

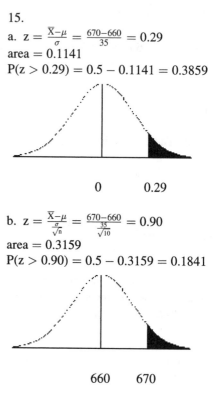

0   0.29

b. $z = \frac{\overline{X}-\mu}{\frac{\sigma}{\sqrt{n}}} = \frac{670-660}{\frac{35}{\sqrt{10}}} = 0.90$

area = 0.3159

P(z > 0.90) = 0.5 − 0.3159 = 0.1841

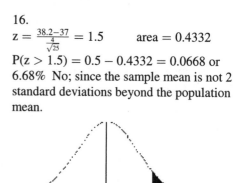

660   670

c. Individual values are more variable than means.

16.

$z = \frac{38.2-37}{\frac{4}{\sqrt{25}}} = 1.5$ area = 0.4332

P(z > 1.5) = 0.5 − 0.4332 = 0.0668 or 6.68% No; since the sample mean is not 2 standard deviations beyond the population mean.

37   38.2

17.

$$z = \frac{\overline{X}-\mu}{\frac{\sigma}{\sqrt{n}}} = \frac{120-123}{\frac{21}{\sqrt{15}}} = -0.55$$

area = 0.2088

$$z = \frac{\overline{X}-\mu}{\frac{\sigma}{\sqrt{n}}} = \frac{126-123}{\frac{21}{\sqrt{15}}} = 0.55$$

area = 0.2088

$P(-0.55 < z < 0.55) = 2(0.2088)$

$\quad = 0.4176$ or 41.76%

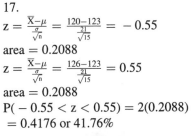

120	123	126

18.

$$z = \frac{450-458}{\frac{97}{\sqrt{36}}} = -0.49 \qquad \text{area} = 0.1879$$

$$z = \frac{465-458}{\frac{97}{\sqrt{36}}} = 0.43 \qquad \text{area} = 0.1664$$

$P(-0.49 < z < 0.43) = 0.1879 + 0.1664$

$\quad = 0.3543$ or 35.43%

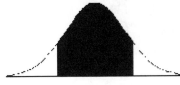

450	458	465

19.

$$z = \frac{\overline{X}-\mu}{\frac{\sigma}{\sqrt{n}}} = \frac{1980-2000}{\frac{187.5}{\sqrt{50}}} = -0.75$$

area = 0.2734

$$z = \frac{\overline{X}-\mu}{\frac{\sigma}{\sqrt{n}}} = \frac{1990-2000}{\frac{187.5}{\sqrt{50}}} = -0.38$$

area = 0.1480

$P(-0.75 < z < -0.38) = 0.2734 -$

$0.1480 = 0.1254$ or 12.54%

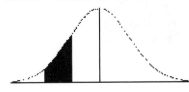

1980 1990 2000

20.

a. $z = \frac{X-\mu}{\sigma} = \frac{26,000-24,393}{4362} = 0.37$

area = 0.1443

$P(z < 0.37) = 0.5 + 0.1443 = 0.6443$ or

64.43%

20. continued

26,000

b. $z = \frac{26,000-24,393}{\frac{4362}{\sqrt{25}}} = 1.84$

area = 0.4671

$P(z < 1.84) = 0.5 + 0.4671 = 0.9671$ or

96.71%

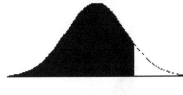

$26,000

c. Sample means are less variable than individual data.

21.

a. $z = \frac{X-\mu}{\sigma} = \frac{43-46.2}{8} = -0.4$

area = 0.1554

$P(z < -0.4) = 0.5 - 0.1554 = 0.3446$ or

34.46%

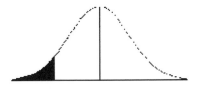

43	46.2

b. $z = \frac{43-46.2}{\frac{8}{\sqrt{50}}} = -2.83 \qquad \text{area} = 0.4977$

$P(z < -2.83) = 0.5 - 0.4977 = 0.0023$ or

0.23%

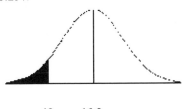

43	46.2

c. Yes, since it is within one standard deviation of the mean.

21. continued
d. Very unlikely, since the probability would be less than 1%.

22.
a. $z = \frac{121.8-120}{5.6} = 0.32$
$P(0 < z < 0.32) = 0.1255$ or 12.55%

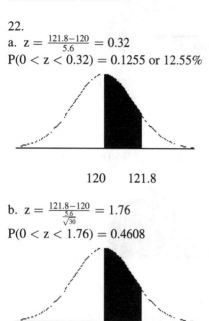

120   121.8

b. $z = \frac{121.8-120}{\frac{5.6}{\sqrt{30}}} = 1.76$
$P(0 < z < 1.76) = 0.4608$

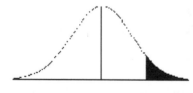

120   121.8

c. Sample means are less variable than individual data.

23.
a. $z = \frac{220-215}{15} = 0.33$ area $= 0.1293$
$P(z > 0.33) = 0.5 - 0.1293 = 0.3707$ or 37.07%

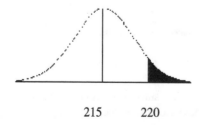

215   220

b. $z = \frac{220-215}{\frac{15}{\sqrt{25}}} = 1.67$ area $= 0.4525$
$P(z > 1.67) = 0.5 - 0.4525 = 0.0475$ or 4.75%

215   220

24.
a. $z_1 = \frac{36-36.2}{3.7} = -0.05$ area $= 0.0199$

$z_2 = \frac{37.5-36.2}{3.7} = 0.35$ area $= 0.1368$

$P(-0.05 < z < 0.35) = 0.0199 + 0.1368$
$= 0.1567$ or 15.67%

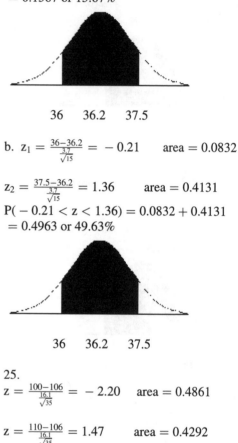

36   36.2   37.5

b. $z_1 = \frac{36-36.2}{\frac{3.7}{\sqrt{15}}} = -0.21$ area $= 0.0832$

$z_2 = \frac{37.5-36.2}{\frac{3.7}{\sqrt{15}}} = 1.36$ area $= 0.4131$
$P(-0.21 < z < 1.36) = 0.0832 + 0.4131$
$= 0.4963$ or 49.63%

36   36.2   37.5

25.
$z = \frac{100-106}{\frac{16.1}{\sqrt{35}}} = -2.20$ area $= 0.4861$

$z = \frac{110-106}{\frac{16.1}{\sqrt{35}}} = 1.47$ area $= 0.4292$

$P(-2.20 < z < 1.47) = 0.4861 + 0.4292$
$= 0.9153$ or 91.53%

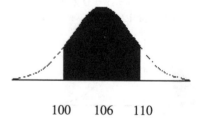

100   106   110

26.
Since $50 > 0.05(500)$ or 25, the correction factor must be used.
It is $\sqrt{\frac{500-50}{500-1}} = 0.950$

$z = \frac{\overline{X}-\mu}{\frac{\sigma}{\sqrt{n}} \cdot \sqrt{\frac{N-n}{n-1}}} = \frac{70-72}{\frac{5.3}{\sqrt{50}} \cdot (0.95)} = -2.81$

26. continued
area $= 0.5 - 0.4975 = 0.0025$

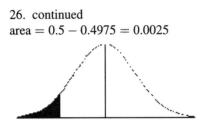

70   72

27.
Since $50 > 0.05(800)$ or 40, the correction factor is necessary.

It is $\sqrt{\frac{800-50}{800-1}} = 0.969$

$z = \frac{\overline{X}-\mu}{\frac{\sigma}{\sqrt{n}} \cdot \sqrt{\frac{N-n}{n-1}}} = \frac{83,500-82,000}{\frac{5000}{\sqrt{50}}(0.969)} = 2.19$

area $= 0.4857$
$P(z > 2.19) = 0.5 - 0.4857 = 0.0143$ or 1.43%

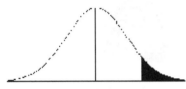

82,000   83,500

28.
The upper 95% is the same as 5% in the left tail; therefore, 45% of the area is between 0 and $-z$. The corresponding z score is -1.65.

$-1.65 = \frac{\overline{X}-2000}{\frac{100}{\sqrt{20}}}$

$-1.65(\frac{100}{\sqrt{20}}) + 2000 = \overline{X}$

$\overline{X} = 1963.10$

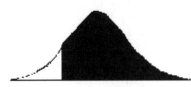

1963.10 2000

29.
$\sigma_x = \frac{\sigma}{\sqrt{n}} = \frac{15}{\sqrt{100}} = 1.5$

$2(1.5) = \frac{15}{\sqrt{n}}$

$3 \cdot \sqrt{n} = 15$

$\sqrt{n} = 5$

29. continued
$n = 25$, the sample size necessary to double the standard error.

30.
$\frac{1.5}{2} = \frac{15}{\sqrt{n}}$

$0.75 \cdot \sqrt{n} = 15$

$\sqrt{n} = \frac{15}{0.75} = 20$

$n = 400$, the sample size necessary to cut the standard error in half.

EXERCISE SET 6-6

1.
When p is approximately 0.5 and as n increases, the shape of the binomial distribution becomes similar to the normal distribution. The normal approximation should be used only when $n \cdot p$ and $n \cdot q$ are both greater than or equal to 5. The correction for continuity is necessary because the normal distribution is continuous and the binomial is discrete.

2.
For each problem use the following formulas:

$\mu = np \quad \sigma = \sqrt{npq} \quad z = \frac{\overline{X}-\mu}{\sigma}$

Be sure to correct each X for continuity.

a. $\mu = 0.5(30) = 15$
$\sigma = \sqrt{(0.5)(0.5)(30)} = 2.74$

$z = \frac{17.5-15}{2.74} = 0.91 \qquad$ area $= 0.3186$

$z = \frac{18.5-15}{2.74} = 1.28 \qquad$ area $= 0.3997$

$P(17.5 < X < 18.5) = 0.3997 - 0.3186$
$= 0.0811 = 8.11\%$

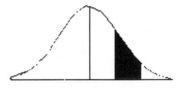

15   17.5 18.5

b. $\mu = 0.8(50) = 40$
$\sigma = \sqrt{(50)(0.8)(0.2)} = 2.83$

2b. continued

$z = \frac{43.5-40}{2.83} = 1.24$ area = 0.3925

$z = \frac{44.5-40}{2.83} = 1.59$ area = 0.4441

$P(43.5 < X < 44.5) = 0.4441 - 0.3925$
$= 0.0516$ or 5.16%

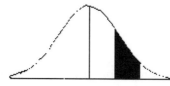

40   43.5 44.5

c. $\mu = 0.1(100) = 10$
$\sigma = \sqrt{(0.1)(0.9)(100)} = 3$

$z = \frac{11.5-10}{3} = 0.50$ area = 0.1915

$z = \frac{12.5-10}{3} = 0.83$ area = 0.2967

$P(11.5 < X < 12.5) = 0.2967 - 0.1915$
$= 0.1052$ or 10.52%

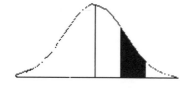

10   11.5 12.5

d. $\mu = 10(0.5) = 5$
$\sigma = \sqrt{(0.5)(0.5)(10)} = 1.58$

$z = \frac{6.5-5}{1.58} = 0.95$ area = 0.3289

$P(X \geq 6.5) = 0.5 - 0.3289 = 0.1711$ or
17.11%

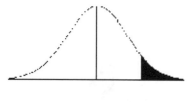

5   6.5

e. $\mu = 20(0.7) = 14$
$\sigma = \sqrt{(20)(0.7)(0.3)} = 2.05$

$z = \frac{12.5-14}{2.05} = -0.73$ area = 0.2673

2e. continued

$P(X \leq 12.5) = 0.5 - 0.2673 = 0.2327$ or
23.27%

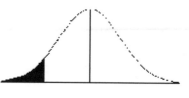

12.5   14

f. $\mu = 50(0.6) = 30$
$\sigma = \sqrt{(50)(0.6)(0.4)} = 3.46$

$z = \frac{40.5-30}{3.46} = 3.03$ area = 0.4988

$P(X \leq 40.5) = 0.5 + 0.4988 = 0.9988$ or
99.88%

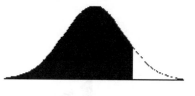

30   40.5

3.
a. $np = 20(0.50) = 10 \geq 5$ Yes
   $nq = 20(0.50) = 10 \geq 5$
b. $np = 10(0.60) = 6 \geq 5$ No
   $nq = 10(0.40) = 4 < 5$
c. $np = 40(0.90) = 36 \geq 5$ No
   $nq = 40(0.10) = 4 < 5$
d. $np = 50(0.20) = 10 \geq 5$ Yes
   $nq = 50(0.80) = 40 \geq 5$
e. $np = 30(0.80) = 24 \geq 5$ Yes
   $nq = 30(0.20) = 6 \geq 5$
f. $np = 20(0.85) = 17 \geq 5$ No
   $nq = 20(0.15) = 3 > 5$

4.
$\mu = 500(0.56) = 280$
$\sigma = \sqrt{(500)(0.56)(0.44)} = 11.1$

$z = \frac{249.5-280}{11.1} = -2.75$ area = 0.4970

$P(X > 249.5) = 0.5 + 0.4970 = 0.9970$ or
99.7%

4. continued

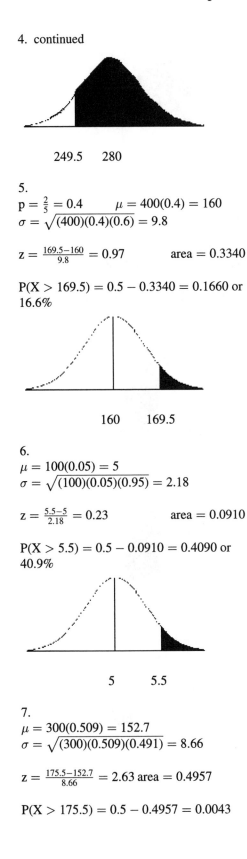

249.5   280

5.
$p = \frac{2}{5} = 0.4$ $\mu = 400(0.4) = 160$
$\sigma = \sqrt{(400)(0.4)(0.6)} = 9.8$

$z = \frac{169.5-160}{9.8} = 0.97$ area $= 0.3340$

$P(X > 169.5) = 0.5 - 0.3340 = 0.1660$ or 16.6%

160   169.5

6.
$\mu = 100(0.05) = 5$
$\sigma = \sqrt{(100)(0.05)(0.95)} = 2.18$

$z = \frac{5.5-5}{2.18} = 0.23$ area $= 0.0910$

$P(X > 5.5) = 0.5 - 0.0910 = 0.4090$ or 40.9%

5   5.5

7.
$\mu = 300(0.509) = 152.7$
$\sigma = \sqrt{(300)(0.509)(0.491)} = 8.66$

$z = \frac{175.5-152.7}{8.66} = 2.63$ area $= 0.4957$

$P(X > 175.5) = 0.5 - 0.4957 = 0.0043$

7. continued

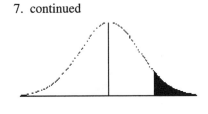

152.7   175.5

8.
$\mu = 175(0.53) = 92.75$
$\sigma = \sqrt{(175)(0.53)(0.47)} = 6.60$

$z = \frac{75.5-92.75}{6.60} = -2.61$ area $= 0.4955$

$z = \frac{109.5-92.75}{6.60} = 2.54$ area $= 0.4945$

$P(75.5 < X < 109.5) = 0.4955 + 0.4945$
$P(75.5 < X < 109.5) = 0.99$

75.5   92.75   109.5

9.
$\mu = 180(0.236) = 42.48$
$\sigma = \sqrt{(180)(0.236)(0.764)} = 5.70$

$z = \frac{50.5-42.48}{5.70} = 1.41$ area $= 0.4207$

$P(X > 50.5) = 0.5 - 0.4207 = 0.0793$

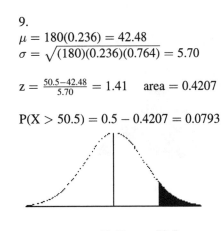

42.48   50.5

10.
$\mu = 400(0.24) = 96$
$\sigma = \sqrt{(400)(0.24)(0.76)} = 8.54$

$z = \frac{120.5-96}{8.54} = 2.87$ area $= 0.4979$

$P(X > 120.5) = 0.5 - 0.4979 = 0.0021$

10. continued

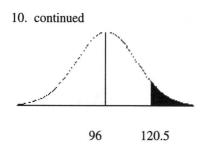

96   120.5

11.

$\mu = 300(0.167) = 50.1$

$\sigma = \sqrt{(300)(0.167)(0.833)} = 6.46$

$z = \frac{50.5 - 50.1}{6.46} = 0.06$ area $= 0.0239$

$P(X > 50.5) = 0.5 - 0.0239 = 0.4761$

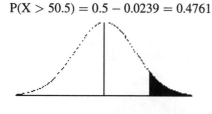

50.1   50.5

12.

$\mu = 290(0.23) = 66.7$

$\sigma = \sqrt{(290)(0.23)(0.77)} = 7.17$

$z = \frac{50.5 - 66.7}{7.17} = -2.26$ area $= 0.4881$

$P(X > 50.5) = 0.5 + 0.4881 = 0.9881$

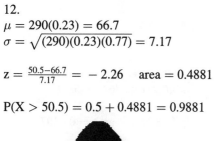

50.5   66.7

13.

$\mu = 350(0.35) = 122.5$

$\sigma = \sqrt{(350)(0.35)(0.65)} = 8.92$

$z = \frac{99.5 - 122.5}{8.92} = -2.58$

$P(X > 99.5) = 0.5 + 0.4951 = 0.9951$ or
99.51% Yes.

13. continued

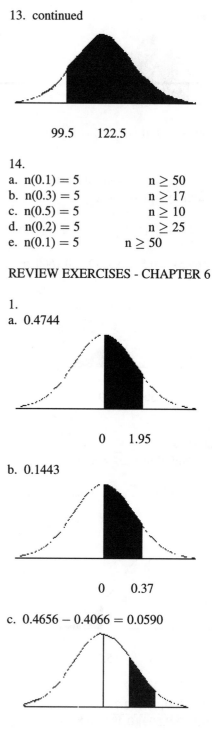

99.5   122.5

14.

a. $n(0.1) = 5$ $n \geq 50$
b. $n(0.3) = 5$ $n \geq 17$
c. $n(0.5) = 5$ $n \geq 10$
d. $n(0.2) = 5$ $n \geq 25$
e. $n(0.1) = 5$ $n \geq 50$

REVIEW EXERCISES - CHAPTER 6

1.
a. 0.4744

0   1.95

b. 0.1443

0   0.37

c. $0.4656 - 0.4066 = 0.0590$

0   1.32 1.82

1. continued
d. $0.3531 + 0.4798 = 0.8329$

1. continued
i. $0.5 - 0.4817 = 0.0183$

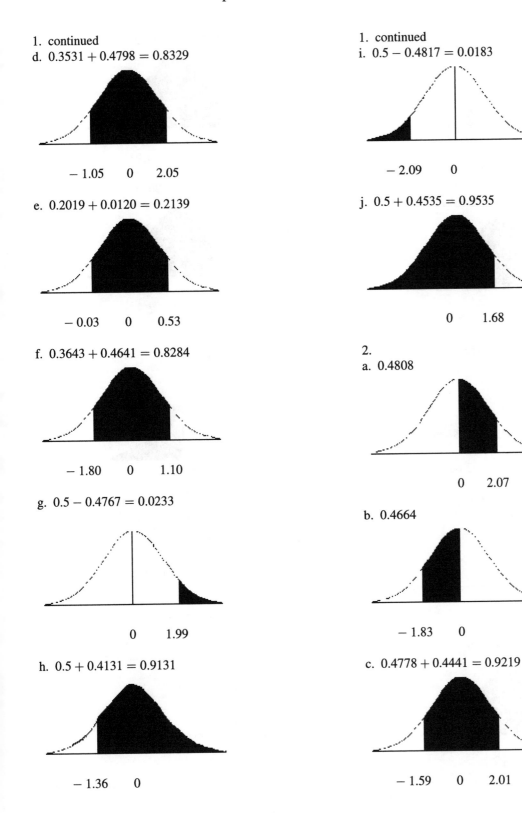

$-1.05 \quad 0 \quad 2.05$

$-2.09 \quad 0$

e. $0.2019 + 0.0120 = 0.2139$

j. $0.5 + 0.4535 = 0.9535$

$-0.03 \quad 0 \quad 0.53$

$0 \quad 1.68$

f. $0.3643 + 0.4641 = 0.8284$

2.
a. 0.4808

$-1.80 \quad 0 \quad 1.10$

$0 \quad 2.07$

g. $0.5 - 0.4767 = 0.0233$

b. 0.4664

$0 \quad 1.99$

$-1.83 \quad 0$

h. $0.5 + 0.4131 = 0.9131$

c. $0.4778 + 0.4441 = 0.9219$

$-1.36 \quad 0$

$-1.59 \quad 0 \quad 2.01$

2. continued

d. $0.4699 - 0.4082 = 0.0617$

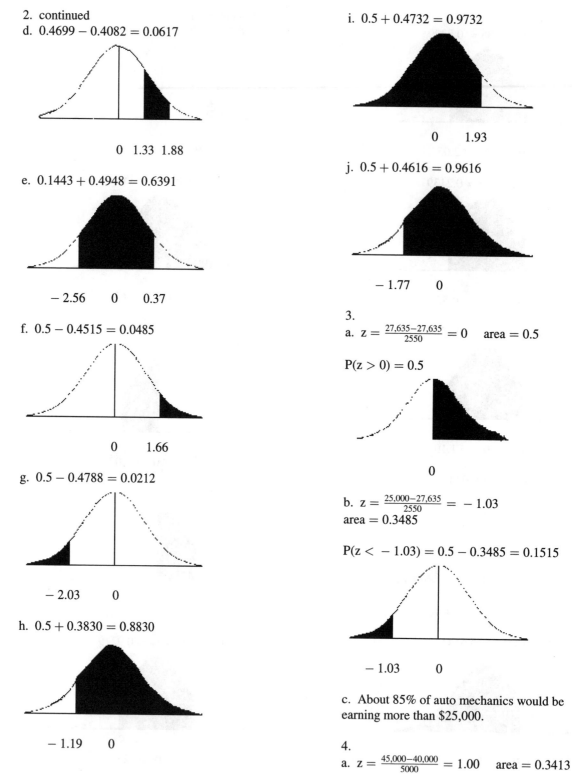

0   1.33 1.88

e. $0.1443 + 0.4948 = 0.6391$

-2.56 0   0.37

f. $0.5 - 0.4515 = 0.0485$

0   1.66

g. $0.5 - 0.4788 = 0.0212$

-2.03 0

h. $0.5 + 0.3830 = 0.8830$

-1.19 0

i. $0.5 + 0.4732 = 0.9732$

0   1.93

j. $0.5 + 0.4616 = 0.9616$

-1.77 0

3.

a. $z = \frac{27,635 - 27,635}{2550} = 0$ area $= 0.5$

$P(z > 0) = 0.5$

0

b. $z = \frac{25,000 - 27,635}{2550} = -1.03$
area $= 0.3485$

$P(z < -1.03) = 0.5 - 0.3485 = 0.1515$

-1.03 0

c. About 85% of auto mechanics would be earning more than $25,000.

4.

a. $z = \frac{45,000 - 40,000}{5000} = 1.00$ area $= 0.3413$

$P(z > 1.00) = 0.5 - 0.3413 = 0.1587$

4a. continued

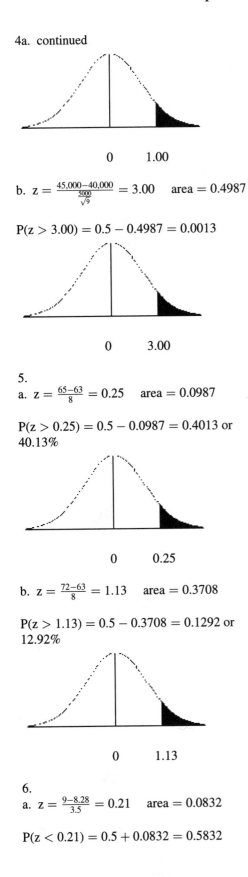

b. $z = \frac{45,000 - 40,000}{\frac{5000}{\sqrt{9}}} = 3.00$ area $= 0.4987$

$P(z > 3.00) = 0.5 - 0.4987 = 0.0013$

5.
a. $z = \frac{65 - 63}{8} = 0.25$ area $= 0.0987$

$P(z > 0.25) = 0.5 - 0.0987 = 0.4013$ or 40.13%

b. $z = \frac{72 - 63}{8} = 1.13$ area $= 0.3708$

$P(z > 1.13) = 0.5 - 0.3708 = 0.1292$ or 12.92%

6.
a. $z = \frac{9 - 8.28}{3.5} = 0.21$ area $= 0.0832$

$P(z < 0.21) = 0.5 + 0.0832 = 0.5832$

6a. continued

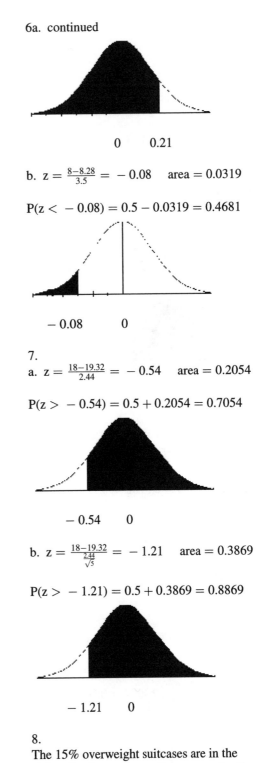

b. $z = \frac{8 - 8.28}{3.5} = -0.08$ area $= 0.0319$

$P(z < -0.08) = 0.5 - 0.0319 = 0.4681$

7.
a. $z = \frac{18 - 19.32}{2.44} = -0.54$ area $= 0.2054$

$P(z > -0.54) = 0.5 + 0.2054 = 0.7054$

b. $z = \frac{18 - 19.32}{\frac{2.44}{\sqrt{5}}} = -1.21$ area $= 0.3869$

$P(z > -1.21) = 0.5 + 0.3869 = 0.8869$

8.
The 15% overweight suitcases are in the right tail; the corresponding z score for the area is 1.04.
$X = \mu + z\sigma$
$X = 45 + (1.04)(2)$
$X = 47.08$ lbs

8. continued

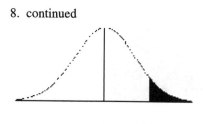

45   47.08

9.
The middle 40% means that 20% of the area is on either side of the mean. The corresponding z scores are ± 0.52.
$X_1 = 100 + (0.52)(15) = 107.8$
$X_2 = 100 + (-0.52)(15) = 92.2$
The scores should be between 92.2 and 107.8.

92.2   100   107.8

10.
$z = \frac{X-\mu}{\frac{\sigma}{\sqrt{n}}} = \frac{70-73}{\frac{8}{\sqrt{9}}} = -1.13$
area = 0.3708
$P(\overline{X} < 70) = 0.5 - 0.3708 = 0.1292$ or 12.92%

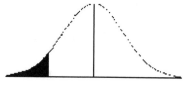

70   73

11.
$z = \frac{3.4-3.7}{\frac{0.6}{\sqrt{32}}} = -2.83$ area = 0.4977
$P(\overline{X} < 3.4) = 0.5 - 0.4977 = 0.0023$ or 0.23%

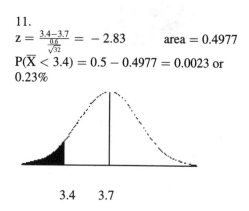

3.4   3.7

Yes, since the probability is less than 1%.

12.
$\mu = np = 500(0.05) = 25$
$\sigma = \sqrt{npq} = \sqrt{(500)(0.05)(0.95)} = 4.87$
$z = \frac{30.5-25}{4.87} = 1.13$ area = 0.3708

$z = \frac{29.5-25}{4.87} = 0.92$ area = 0.3212

$P(0.92 < z < 1.13) = 0.3708 - 0.3212$
= 0.0496 or 4.96%

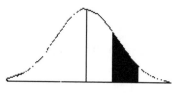

25 29.5 30.5

13.
$\mu = 200(0.18) = 36$
$\sigma = \sqrt{(200)(0.18)(0.82)} = 5.43$

$z = \frac{40.5-36}{5.43} = 0.83$ area = 0.2967

$P(X > 40.5) = 0.5 - 0.2967 = 0.2033$ or 20.33%

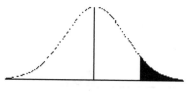

36   40.5

14.
$\mu = 800(0.30) = 240$
$\sigma = \sqrt{(800)(0.3)(0.7)} = 12.96$

$z = \frac{259.5-240}{12.96} = 1.50$ area = 0.4332

$P(X \geq 259.5) = 0.5 - 0.4332 = 0.0668$ or 6.68%

240   259.5

15.
$\mu = 200(0.2) = 40$
$\sigma = \sqrt{(200)(0.2)(0.8)} = 5.66$

15. continued

$$z = \frac{49.5-40}{5.66} = 1.68 \qquad \text{area} = 0.4535$$

$P(X \geq 49.5) = 0.5 - 0.4535 = 0.0465$ or 4.65%

40   49.5

16.
Histogram:

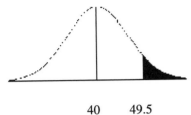

The histogram shows a positive skew.

$$PI = \frac{3(6972.2-5931.5)}{3458.85} = 0.90$$

$IQR = Q_3 - Q_1$
$IQR = 9348 - 5135 = 4213$
$1.5(IQR) = 1.5(4213) = 6319.5$
$Q_1 - 6319.5 = -1184.5$
$Q_3 + 6319.5 = 15,667.5$

There are no outliers.

Conclusion: The distribution is not normal.

17.
Histogram:

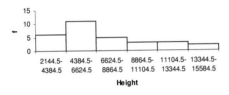

The histogram shows a positive skew.

$$PI = \frac{3(2136.1-1755)}{1171.7} = 0.98$$

$IQR = Q_3 - Q_1$
$IQR = 2827 - 1320 = 1507$

17. continued
$1.5(IQR) = 1.5(1507) = 2260.5$
$Q_1 - 2260.5 = -940.5$
$Q_3 + 2260.5 = 5087.5$

There are no outliers.

Conclusion: The distribution is not normal.

CHAPTER 6 QUIZ

1. False, the total area is equal to one.
2. True
3. True
4. True
5. False, the area is positive.
6. False, it applies to means taken from the same population.
7. a
8. a
9. b
10. b
11. c
12. 0.5
13. Sampling error
14. The population mean
15. Standard error of the mean
16. 5
17. 5%
18. the areas are:
a. 0.4332   f. 0.8284
b. 0.3944   g. 0.0401
c. 0.0344   h. 0..8997
d. 0.1029   i. 0.017
e. 0.2912   j. 0.9131
19. the probabilities are:
a. 0.4846   f. 0.0384
b. 0.4693   g. 0.0089
c. 0.9334   h. 0.9582
d. 0.0188   i. 0.9788
e. 0.7461   j. 0.8461
20. the probabilities are:
a. 0.7734
b. 0.0516
c. 0.3837
d. Any rainfall above 65 inches could be considered an extremely wet year since this value is two standard deviations above the mean.
21. the probabilities are:
a. 0.0668   c. 0.4649
b. 0.0228   d. 0.0934
22. the probabilities are:
a. 0.4525   c. 0.3707
b. 0.3707   d. 0.019

23. the probabilities are:
a. 0.0013   c. 0.0081
b. 0.5   d. 0.5511
24. the probabilities are:
a. 0.0037   c. 0.5
b. 0.0228   d. 0.3232
25. 8.804 cm
26. The lowest acceptable score is 121.24.
27. 0.015
28. 0.9738
29. 0.0495; no
30. 0.0630
31. 0.8577
32. 0.0495
33. The distribution is not normal.
34. The distribution is approximately
normal.

Note: Answers may vary due to rounding.

EXERCISE SET 7-2

1.
A point estimate of a parameter specifies a specific value such as $\mu = 87$, whereas an interval estimate specifies a range of values for the parameter such as $84 < \mu < 90$. The advantage of an interval estimate is that a specific confidence level (say 95%) can be selected, and one can be 95% confident that the parameter being estimated lies in the interval.

2.
The standard deviation of the population must be known or it must be estimated or specified in terms of E. Sample size must be specified, and the degree of confidence must be selected.

3.
The maximum error of estimate is the likely range of values to the right or left of the statistic which may contain the parameter.

4.
A 95% confidence interval means that one can be 95% confident that the parameter being estimated will be contained within the limits of the interval.

5.
A good estimator should be unbiased, consistent, and relatively efficient.

6.
$\overline{X}$

7.
To determine sample size, the maximum error of estimate and the degree of confidence must be specified and the population standard deviation must be known.

8.
No, as long as it is much larger than the sample size needed.

9.
a. 2.58   d. 1.65
b. 2.33   e. 1.88
c. 1.96

10.
$\overline{X} = 46{,}970.9 \quad s = 14{,}358.2$
$46{,}970.9 - 1.96(\frac{14{,}358.2}{\sqrt{30}}) < \mu < 46{,}970.9$
$\qquad + 1.96(\frac{14{,}358.2}{\sqrt{30}})$
$41{,}832.9 < \mu < 52{,}108.9$

11.
a. $\overline{X} = 82$ is the point estimate for μ.

b. $\overline{X} - z_{\frac{\alpha}{2}}(\frac{s}{\sqrt{n}}) < \mu < \overline{X} + z_{\frac{\alpha}{2}}(\frac{s}{\sqrt{n}})$
$82 - (1.96)(\frac{15}{\sqrt{35}}) < \mu < 82 + (1.96)(\frac{15}{\sqrt{35}})$
$82 - 4.97 < \mu < 82 + 4.97$
$77 < \mu < 87$

c. $82 - (2.58)(\frac{15}{\sqrt{35}}) < \mu < 82 + (2.58)(\frac{15}{\sqrt{35}})$
$82 - 6.54 < \mu < 82 + 6.54$
$75 < \mu < 89$

d. The 99% confidence interval is larger because the confidence level is larger.

12.
$\overline{X} = \$196.0 \quad s = \$617.3$
$196.0 - 1.65(\frac{617.3}{\sqrt{50}}) < \mu <$
$\qquad 196.0 + 1.65(\frac{617.3}{\sqrt{50}})$
$196.0 - 144.0 < \mu < 196.0 + 144.0$
$52.0 < \mu < 340.0$

13.
a. $\overline{X} = 12.6$ is the point estimate for μ.

b. $\overline{X} - z_{\frac{\alpha}{2}}(\frac{\sigma}{\sqrt{n}}) < \mu < \overline{X} + z_{\frac{\alpha}{2}}(\frac{\sigma}{\sqrt{n}})$
$12.6 - 1.65(\frac{2.5}{\sqrt{40}}) < \mu < 12.6 + 1.65(\frac{2.5}{\sqrt{40}})$
$12.6 - 0.652 < \mu < 12.6 + 0.652$
$11.9 < \mu < 13.3$

c. It would be highly unlikely since this is far larger than 13.3 minutes.

14.
a. $\overline{X} = 92$ is the point estimate for μ.

b. $92 - 1.96(\frac{5}{\sqrt{35}}) < \mu < 92 + 1.96(\frac{5}{\sqrt{35}})$
$92 - 1.66 < \mu < 92 + 1.66$
$90.3 < \mu < 93.7$ or $90 < \mu < 94$

c.
$92 - 1.96(\frac{5}{\sqrt{60}}) < \mu < 92 + 1.96(\frac{5}{\sqrt{60}})$
$92 - 1.27 < \mu < 92 + 1.27$
$90.7 < \mu < 93.3$ or $91 < \mu < 93$

14. continued
d. The interval found in part c is smaller because a larger sample size was used.

15.
$$\overline{X} - z_{\frac{\alpha}{2}}\left(\frac{s}{\sqrt{n}}\right) < \mu < \overline{X} + z_{\frac{\alpha}{2}}\left(\frac{s}{\sqrt{n}}\right)$$
$$\$150,000 - 1.96\left(\frac{15,000}{\sqrt{35}}\right) < \mu <$$
$$\$150,000 + 1.96\left(\frac{15,000}{\sqrt{35}}\right)$$
$$\$150,000 - 4969.51 < \mu <$$
$$\$150,000 + 4969.51$$

$$\$145,030 < \mu < \$154,970$$

16.
$\overline{X} = 43.45 \quad s = 31.27$

$$43.45 - 1.65\left(\frac{31.27}{\sqrt{31}}\right) < \mu <$$
$$43.45 + 1.65\left(\frac{31.27}{\sqrt{31}}\right)$$
$43.45 - 9.27 < \mu < 43.45 + 9.27$
$34.19 < \mu < 52.72$ or $34.2 < \mu < 52.7$

17.
$\overline{X} = 5000 \quad s = 900$
$$5000 - 1.96\left(\frac{900}{\sqrt{415}}\right) < \mu < 5000 +$$
$$1.96\left(\frac{900}{\sqrt{415}}\right)$$
$4913 < \mu < 5087$

4000 hours does not seem reasonable since it is outside this interval.

18.
$$3648 - 1.65\left(\frac{630}{\sqrt{50}}\right) < \mu < 3648 +$$
$$1.65\left(\frac{630}{\sqrt{50}}\right)$$
$3501 < \mu < 3795$

$3500 would be a reasonable amount to charge for tuition.

19.
$$\overline{X} - z_{\frac{\alpha}{2}}\left(\frac{s}{\sqrt{n}}\right) < \mu < \overline{X} + z_{\frac{\alpha}{2}}\left(\frac{s}{\sqrt{n}}\right)$$
$$61.2 - 1.96\left(\frac{7.9}{\sqrt{84}}\right) < \mu < 61.2 + 1.96\left(\frac{7.9}{\sqrt{84}}\right)$$
$61.2 - 1.69 < \mu < 61.2 + 1.69$
$59.5 < \mu < 62.9$

20.
$$190.7 - 1.96\left(\frac{54.2}{\sqrt{35}}\right) < \mu <$$
$$190.7 + 1.96\left(\frac{54.2}{\sqrt{35}}\right)$$
$190.7 - 17.96 < \mu < 190.7 + 17.96$
$172.74 < \mu < 208.66$

21.
$$n = \left[\frac{z_{\frac{\alpha}{2}}\sigma}{E}\right]^2 = \left[\frac{(2.58)(6.2)}{1.5}\right]^2$$
$$= (10.664)^2 = 113.7 \text{ or } 114$$

22.
$$58.0 - 1.65\left(\frac{4.8}{\sqrt{171}}\right) < \mu < 58.0 + 1.65\left(\frac{4.8}{\sqrt{171}}\right)$$

$$58.0 - 0.61 < \mu < 58.0 + 0.61$$

$$57.4 < \mu < 58.6$$

23.
$$n = \left[\frac{z_{\frac{\alpha}{2}}\sigma}{E}\right]^2 = \left[\frac{(1.96)(2.5)}{1}\right]^2$$

$$= (4.9)^2 = 24.01 \text{ or } 25$$

24.
$$n = \left[\frac{z_{\frac{\alpha}{2}}\sigma}{E}\right]^2 = \left[\frac{(1.96)(0.26)}{0.15}\right]^2$$

$$= (3.397)^2 = 11.5 \text{ or } 12$$

25.
$$n = \left[\frac{z_{\frac{\alpha}{2}}\sigma}{E}\right]^2 = \left[\frac{(1.65)(1100)}{150}\right]^2$$

$$= (12.1)^2 = 146.4 \text{ or } 147$$

EXERCISE SET 7-3

1.
The characteristics of the t-distribution are: It is bell-shaped, symmetrical about the mean, and never touches the x-axis. The mean, median, and mode are equal to 0 and are located at the center of the distribution. The variance is greater than 1. The t-distribution is a family of curves based on degrees of freedom. As sample size increases the t-distribution approaches the normal distribution.

2.
The degrees of freedom are the number of values free to vary after a sample statistic has been computed.

3.
The t-distribution should be used when σ is unknown and $n < 30$.

4.
a. 2.898 where d. f. $= 17$

4. continued

b. 2.074 where d. f. $= 22$

c. 2.624 where d. f. $= 14$

d. 1.833 where d. f. $= 9$

e. 2.093 where d. f. $= 19$

5.

$\overline{X} - t_{\frac{\alpha}{2}}(\frac{s}{\sqrt{n}}) < \mu < \overline{X} + t_{\frac{\alpha}{2}}(\frac{s}{\sqrt{n}})$

$16 - (2.861)(\frac{2}{\sqrt{20}}) < \mu < 16 + (2.861)(\frac{2}{\sqrt{20}})$

$16 - 1.28 < \mu < 16 + 1.28$

$15 < \mu < 17$

6.

$\overline{X} = 91.06 \quad s = 38.37$

$\overline{X} - t_{\frac{\alpha}{2}}(\frac{s}{\sqrt{n}}) < \mu < \overline{X} + t_{\frac{\alpha}{2}}(\frac{s}{\sqrt{n}})$

$91.06 - 2.583(\frac{38.37}{\sqrt{17}}) < \mu <$

$\qquad 91.06 + 2.583(\frac{38.37}{\sqrt{17}})$

$91.06 - 24.04 < \mu < 91.06 + 24.04$

$67.0 < \mu < 115.1$

7.

$\overline{X} = 33.4 \quad s = 28.7$

$\overline{X} - t_{\frac{\alpha}{2}}(\frac{s}{\sqrt{n}}) < \mu < \overline{X} + t_{\frac{\alpha}{2}}(\frac{s}{\sqrt{n}})$

$33.4 - 1.746(\frac{28.7}{\sqrt{17}}) < \mu < 33.4 + 1.746(\frac{28.7}{\sqrt{17}})$

$33.4 - 12.2 < \mu < 33.4 + 12.2$

$21.2 < \mu < 45.6$

The point estimate is 33.4 and is close to the actual population mean of 32, which is within the 90% confidence interval. The mean may not be the best estimate since the data value 132 is large and possibly an outlier.

8.

$\overline{X} = 4.1125 \quad s = 2.2025$

$\overline{X} - t_{\frac{\alpha}{2}}(\frac{s}{\sqrt{n}}) < \mu < \overline{X} + t_{\frac{\alpha}{2}}(\frac{s}{\sqrt{n}})$

$4.1125 - 2.365\left(\frac{2.2025}{\sqrt{8}}\right) < \mu <$

$\qquad 4.1125 + 2.365\left(\frac{2.2025}{\sqrt{8}}\right)$

$2.271 < \mu < 5.954$

9.

$\overline{X} - t_{\frac{\alpha}{2}}(\frac{s}{\sqrt{n}}) < \mu < \overline{X} + t_{\frac{\alpha}{2}}(\frac{s}{\sqrt{n}})$

$276 - 2.015(\frac{12}{\sqrt{6}}) < \mu <$

$\qquad 276 + 2.015(\frac{12}{\sqrt{6}})$

$276 - 9.9 < \mu < 276 + 9.9$

$266.1 < \mu < 285.9$ or $266 < \mu < 286$

The coach's claim is highly unlikely.

10.

$\overline{X} = 58.9 \quad s = 5.1$

$\overline{X} - t_{\frac{\alpha}{2}}(\frac{s}{\sqrt{n}}) < \mu < \overline{X} + t_{\frac{\alpha}{2}}(\frac{s}{\sqrt{n}})$

$58.9 - 1.895(\frac{5.1}{\sqrt{8}}) < \mu <$

$\qquad 58.9 + 1.895(\frac{5.1}{\sqrt{8}})$

$58.9 - 3.4 < \mu < 58.9 + 3.4$

$55.5 < \mu < 62.3$

11.

$\overline{X} - t_{\frac{\alpha}{2}}(\frac{s}{\sqrt{n}}) < \mu < \overline{X} + t_{\frac{\alpha}{2}}(\frac{s}{\sqrt{n}})$

$14.3 - 2.052(\frac{2}{\sqrt{28}}) < \mu < 14.3 + 2.052(\frac{2}{\sqrt{28}})$

$14.3 - 0.8 < \mu < 14.3 + 0.8$

$13.5 < \mu < 15.1$

The employees should allow about 30 minutes.

12.

$\overline{X} - t_{\frac{\alpha}{2}}(\frac{s}{\sqrt{n}}) < \mu < \overline{X} + t_{\frac{\alpha}{2}}(\frac{s}{\sqrt{n}})$

$15 - 3.055(\frac{1.7}{\sqrt{13}}) < \mu < 15 + 3.055(\frac{1.7}{\sqrt{13}})$

$15 - 1.4 < \mu < 15 + 1.4$

$13.6 < \mu < 16.4$

The highest speed would be 16.4 mph.

13.

$\overline{X} - t_{\frac{\alpha}{2}}(\frac{s}{\sqrt{n}}) < \mu < \overline{X} + t_{\frac{\alpha}{2}}(\frac{s}{\sqrt{n}})$

$18.53 - 2.064(\frac{3}{\sqrt{25}}) < \mu <$

$\qquad 18.53 + 2.064(\frac{3}{\sqrt{25}})$

$18.53 - 1.238 < \mu < 18.53 + 1.238$

$\$17.29 < \mu < \$19.77$

14.

$\overline{X} - t_{\frac{\alpha}{2}}(\frac{s}{\sqrt{n}}) < \mu < \overline{X} + t_{\frac{\alpha}{2}}(\frac{s}{\sqrt{n}})$

$126 - 2.262(\frac{4}{\sqrt{10}}) < \mu < 126 + 2.262(\frac{4}{\sqrt{10}})$

$126 - 2.861 < \mu < 126 + 2.861$

$123 < \mu < 129$

15.

$\overline{X} - t_{\frac{\alpha}{2}}(\frac{s}{\sqrt{n}}) < \mu < \overline{X} + t_{\frac{\alpha}{2}}(\frac{s}{\sqrt{n}})$

$115 - 2.571(\frac{6}{\sqrt{6}}) < \mu < 115 + 2.571(\frac{6}{\sqrt{6}})$

$115 - 6.298 < \mu < 115 + 6.298$

$109 < \mu < 121$

16.

$\overline{X} - t_{\frac{\alpha}{2}}(\frac{s}{\sqrt{n}}) < \mu < \overline{X} + t_{\frac{\alpha}{2}}(\frac{s}{\sqrt{n}})$

$41.6 - 2.069(\frac{7.5}{\sqrt{24}}) < \mu <$

$\qquad 41.6 + 2.069(\frac{7.5}{\sqrt{24}})$

$41.6 - 3.17 < \mu < 41.6 + 3.17$

$38.4 < \mu < 44.8$

17.
$\overline{X} = 41.6 \quad x = 5.995$

$\overline{X} - t_{\frac{\alpha}{2}}(\frac{s}{\sqrt{n}}) < \mu < \overline{X} + t_{\frac{\alpha}{2}}(\frac{s}{\sqrt{n}})$

$41.6 - 2.093(\frac{5.995}{\sqrt{20}}) < \mu <$

$\qquad 41.6 + 2.093(\frac{5.995}{\sqrt{20}})$

$41.6 - 2.806 < \mu < 41.6 + 2.806$

$38.8 < \mu < 44.4$

18.
$\overline{X} - t_{\frac{\alpha}{2}}(\frac{s}{\sqrt{n}}) < \mu < \overline{X} + t_{\frac{\alpha}{2}}(\frac{s}{\sqrt{n}})$

$86 - 1.721(\frac{5}{\sqrt{22}}) < \mu < 86 + 1.721(\frac{5}{\sqrt{22}})$

$86 - 1.8 < \mu < 86 + 1.8$

$84.2 < \mu < 87.8$ or $84 < \mu < 88$

He should use a maximum pulse rate of 88.

19.
$\overline{X} - t_{\frac{\alpha}{2}}(\frac{s}{\sqrt{n}}) < \mu < \overline{X} + t_{\frac{\alpha}{2}}(\frac{s}{\sqrt{n}})$

$\$56{,}718 - 2.052(\frac{650}{\sqrt{28}}) < \mu <$

$\qquad \$56{,}718 + 2.052(\frac{650}{\sqrt{28}})$

$\$56{,}466 < \mu < \$56{,}970$

He should use $56,466.

20.
$\overline{X} = 33.5 \quad s = 27.678$

$\overline{X} - t_{\frac{\alpha}{2}}(\frac{s}{\sqrt{n}}) < \mu < \overline{X} + t_{\frac{\alpha}{2}}(\frac{s}{\sqrt{n}})$

$33.5 - 2.821(\frac{27.678}{\sqrt{10}}) < \mu <$

$\qquad 33.5 + 2.821(\frac{27.678}{\sqrt{10}})$

$33.5 - 24.691 < \mu < 33.5 + 24.691$

$8.8 < \mu < 58.2$

21.
$\overline{X} = 2.175 \quad s = 0.585$

For $\mu > \overline{X} - t_{\frac{\alpha}{2}}(\frac{s}{\sqrt{n}})$:

$\mu > 2.175 - 1.729(\frac{0.585}{\sqrt{20}})$

$\mu > 2.175 - 0.226$

Thus, $\mu > \$1.95$ means that one can be 95% confident that the mean revenue is greater than $1.95.

For $\mu < \overline{X} + t_{\frac{\alpha}{2}}(\frac{s}{\sqrt{n}})$:

$\mu < 2.175 + 1.729(\frac{0.585}{\sqrt{20}})$

$\mu < 2.175 + 0.226$

Thus, $\mu < \$2.40$ means that one can be 95% confident that the mean revenue is less than $2.40.

EXERCISE SET 7-4

1.
a. $\hat{p} = \frac{40}{80} = 0.5 \qquad\qquad \hat{q} = \frac{40}{80} = 0.5$

b. $\hat{p} = \frac{90}{200} = 0.45 \qquad \hat{q} = \frac{110}{200} = 0.55$

c. $\hat{p} = \frac{60}{130} = 0.46 \qquad \hat{q} = \frac{70}{130} = 0.54$

d. $\hat{p} = \frac{35}{60} = 0.58 \qquad \hat{q} = \frac{25}{60} = 0.42$

e. $\hat{p} = \frac{43}{95} = 0.45 \qquad \hat{q} = \frac{52}{95} = 0.55$

2.
For each part, change the percent to a decimal by dividing by 100, and find $\hat{q}$ using $\hat{q} = 1 - \hat{p}$.

a. $\hat{p} = 0.15 \qquad \hat{q} = 1 - 0.15 = 0.85$

b. $\hat{p} = 0.37 \qquad \hat{q} = 1 - 0.37 = 0.63$

c. $\hat{p} = 0.71 \qquad \hat{q} = 1 - 0.71 = 0.29$

d. $\hat{p} = 0.51 \qquad \hat{q} = 1 - 0.51 = 0.49$

e. $\hat{p} = 0.79 \qquad \hat{q} = 1 - 0.79 = 0.21$

3.
$\hat{p} = 0.39 \qquad\qquad\qquad \hat{q} = 0.61$

$\hat{p} - (z_{\frac{\alpha}{2}})\sqrt{\frac{\hat{p}\hat{q}}{n}} < p < \hat{p} + (z_{\frac{\alpha}{2}})\sqrt{\frac{\hat{p}\hat{q}}{n}}$

$0.39 - (1.96)\sqrt{\frac{(0.39)(0.61)}{1500}} < p <$

$\qquad 0.39 + (1.96)\sqrt{\frac{(0.39)(0.61)}{1500}}$

$0.39 - 0.025 < p < 0.39 + 0.025$

$0.365 < p < 0.415$

4.
$\hat{p} = \frac{X}{n} = \frac{27}{100} = 0.27$

$\hat{q} = 1 - 0.27 = 0.73$

$\hat{p} - (z_{\frac{\alpha}{2}})\sqrt{\frac{\hat{p}\hat{q}}{n}} < p < \hat{p} + (z_{\frac{\alpha}{2}})\sqrt{\frac{\hat{p}\hat{q}}{n}}$

$0.27 - 1.65\sqrt{\frac{(0.27)(0.73)}{100}} < p <$

$\qquad 0.27 + 1.65\sqrt{\frac{(0.27)(0.73)}{100}}$

$0.27 - 0.073 < p < 0.27 + 0.073$

$0.197 < p < 0.343$

5.
$\hat{p} = \frac{X}{n} = \frac{55}{450} = 0.12$

$\hat{q} = 1 - 0.12 = 0.88$

$\hat{p} - (z_{\frac{\alpha}{2}})\sqrt{\frac{\hat{p}\hat{q}}{n}} < p < \hat{p} + (z_{\frac{\alpha}{2}})\sqrt{\frac{\hat{p}\hat{q}}{n}}$

$0.12 - 1.96\sqrt{\frac{(0.12)(0.88)}{450}} < p < 0.12 + 1.96\sqrt{\frac{(0.12)(0.88)}{450}}$

$0.12 - 0.03 < p < 0.12 + 0.03$

5. continued
0.09 or 9% $< p <$ 0.15 or 15%
(Note: TI-83 answer is $0.092 < p < 0.153$)
11% is contained in the confidence interval.

6.
$\hat{p} = 0.27 \quad \hat{q} = 0.73$
$n = (0.27)(0.73)\left(\frac{1.96}{0.025}\right)^2 = 1211.5$
The sample size should be 1212.

7.
$\hat{p} = 0.84 \qquad\qquad \hat{q} = 0.16$
$\hat{p} - (z_{\frac{\alpha}{2}})\sqrt{\frac{\hat{p}\hat{q}}{n}} < p < \hat{p} + (z_{\frac{\alpha}{2}})\sqrt{\frac{\hat{p}\hat{q}}{n}}$
$0.84 - 1.65\sqrt{\frac{(0.84)(0.16)}{200}} < p <$
$\qquad 0.84 + 1.65\sqrt{\frac{(0.84)(0.16)}{200}}$
$0.84 - 0.043 < p < 0.84 + 0.043$
$0.797 < p < 0.883$

8.
$\hat{p} = \frac{X}{n} = \frac{329}{763} = 0.4312$
$\hat{q} = 1 - 0.431 = 0.5688$
$\hat{p} - (z_{\frac{\alpha}{2}})\sqrt{\frac{\hat{p}\hat{q}}{n}} < p < \hat{p} + (z_{\frac{\alpha}{2}})\sqrt{\frac{\hat{p}\hat{q}}{n}}$
$0.4312 - 1.75\sqrt{\frac{(0.4312)(0.5688)}{763}} < p <$
$\qquad 0.4312 + 1.75\sqrt{\frac{(0.4312)(0.5688)}{763}}$
$0.4312 - 0.0314 < p < 0.4312 + 0.0314$
$0.3998 < p < 0.4625$ or $0.400 < p < 0.463$

9.
$\hat{p} = 0.23 \qquad\qquad \hat{q} = 0.77$
$\hat{p} - (z_{\frac{\alpha}{2}})\sqrt{\frac{\hat{p}\hat{q}}{n}} < p < \hat{p} + (z_{\frac{\alpha}{2}})\sqrt{\frac{\hat{p}\hat{q}}{n}}$
$0.23 - 2.58\sqrt{\frac{(0.23)(0.77)}{200}} < p <$
$\qquad 0.23 + 2.58\sqrt{\frac{(0.23)(0.77)}{200}}$
$0.23 - 0.077 < p < 0.23 + 0.077$
$0.153 < p < 0.307$
The statement that one in five or 20% of 13
to 14 year olds is a sometime smoker is
within the interval.

10.
$\hat{p} = \frac{X}{n} = \frac{23}{50} = 0.46$
$\hat{q} = 1 - 0.46 = 0.54$
$\hat{p} - (z_{\frac{\alpha}{2}})\sqrt{\frac{\hat{p}\hat{q}}{n}} < p < \hat{p} + (z_{\frac{\alpha}{2}})\sqrt{\frac{\hat{p}\hat{q}}{n}}$
$0.46 - 1.65\sqrt{\frac{(0.46)(0.54)}{50}} < p <$
$\qquad 0.46 + 1.65\sqrt{\frac{(0.46)(0.54)}{50}}$
$0.46 - 0.116 < p < 0.46 + 0.116$

10. continued
$0.344 < p < 0.576$ or $34.4\% < p < 57.6\%$
The should print enough brochures to
distribute to 34.4% of first time canoers.

11.
$\hat{p} = \frac{36}{85} = 0.424 \quad \hat{q} = \frac{49}{85} = 0.576$
$\hat{p} - (z_{\frac{\alpha}{2}})\sqrt{\frac{\hat{p}\hat{q}}{n}} < p < \hat{p} + (z_{\frac{\alpha}{2}})\sqrt{\frac{\hat{p}\hat{q}}{n}}$
$0.424 - 2.58\sqrt{\frac{(0.424)(0.576)}{85}} < p <$
$\qquad 0.424 + 2.58\sqrt{\frac{(0.424)(0.576)}{85}}$
$0.424 - 0.138 < p < 0.424 + 0.138$
$0.286 < p < 0.562$
It would not be considered larger since 0.52
is in the interval.

12.
$\hat{p} = \frac{X}{n} = 0.28$
$\hat{q} = 1 - 0.28 = 0.72$
$\hat{p} - (z_{\frac{\alpha}{2}})\sqrt{\frac{\hat{p}\hat{q}}{n}} < p < \hat{p} + (z_{\frac{\alpha}{2}})\sqrt{\frac{\hat{p}\hat{q}}{n}}$
$0.28 - 1.96\sqrt{\frac{(0.28)(0.72)}{350}} < p <$
$\qquad 0.28 + 1.96\sqrt{\frac{(0.28)(0.72)}{350}}$
$0.28 - 0.047 < p < 0.28 + 0.047$
$0.233 < p < 0.327$
The cafeteria manager should make lunches
for about 33% of the students.

13.
$\hat{p} = 0.44975 \qquad \hat{q} = 0.55025$
$\hat{p} - (z_{\frac{\alpha}{2}})\sqrt{\frac{\hat{p}\hat{q}}{n}} < p < \hat{p} + (z_{\frac{\alpha}{2}})\sqrt{\frac{\hat{p}\hat{q}}{n}}$
$0.44975 - 1.96\sqrt{\frac{(0.44975)(0.55025)}{1005}} < p <$
$\qquad 0.44975 + 1.96\sqrt{\frac{(0.44975)(0.55025)}{1005}}$
$0.44975 - 0.03076 < p <$
$\qquad\qquad 0.44975 + 0.03076$
$0.419 < p < 0.481$

14.
$\hat{p} = \frac{560}{1000} = 0.56 \quad \hat{q} = \frac{440}{1000} = 0.44$
$\hat{p} - (z_{\frac{\alpha}{2}})\sqrt{\frac{\hat{p}\hat{q}}{n}} < p < \hat{p} + (z_{\frac{\alpha}{2}})\sqrt{\frac{\hat{p}\hat{q}}{n}}$
$0.56 - 1.96\sqrt{\frac{(0.56)(0.44)}{1000}} < p <$
$\qquad 0.56 + 1.96\sqrt{\frac{(0.56)(0.44)}{1000}}$
$0.56 - 0.030766 < p < 0.56 + 0.030766$
$0.529 < p < 0.591$

15.
a. $\hat{p} = 0.25 \qquad \hat{q} = 0.75$
$n = \hat{p}\,\hat{q}\left[\frac{z_{\frac{\alpha}{2}}}{E}\right]^2 = (0.25)(0.75)\left[\frac{2.58}{0.02}\right]^2$

15. continued
n = 3120.1875 or 3121

b. $\hat{p} = 0.5$ $\hat{q} = 0.5$

$n = \hat{p}\,\hat{q}\left[\dfrac{z_{\frac{\alpha}{2}}}{E}\right]^2 = (0.5)(0.5)\left[\dfrac{2.58}{0.02}\right]^2$

n = 4160.25 or 4161

16.
a. $\hat{p} = 0.29$ $\hat{q} = 0.71$

$n = \hat{p}\,\hat{q}\left[\dfrac{z_{\frac{\alpha}{2}}}{E}\right]^2 = (0.29)(0.71)\left[\dfrac{1.65}{0.05}\right]^2$

$= 224.2251$ or 225

b. $\hat{p} = 0.5$ $\hat{q} = 0.5$

$n = \hat{p}\,\hat{q}\left[\dfrac{z_{\frac{\alpha}{2}}}{E}\right]^2 = (0.5)(0.5)\left[\dfrac{1.65}{0.05}\right]^2$

n = 272.25 or 273

17.
a. $\hat{p} = \dfrac{30}{300} = 0.1$ $\hat{q} = \dfrac{270}{300} = 0.9$

$n = \hat{p}\,\hat{q}\left[\dfrac{z_{\frac{\alpha}{2}}}{E}\right]^2 = (0.1)(0.9)\left[\dfrac{1.65}{0.05}\right]^2$

$= 98.01$ or 99

b. $\hat{p} = 0.5$ $\hat{q} = 0.5$

$n = \hat{p}\,\hat{q}\left[\dfrac{z_{\frac{\alpha}{2}}}{E}\right]^2 = (0.5)(0.5)\left[\dfrac{1.65}{0.05}\right]^2$

n = 272.25 or 273

18.
a. $\hat{p} = 0.5$ $\hat{q} = 0.5$

$n = \hat{p}\,\hat{q}\left[\dfrac{z_{\frac{\alpha}{2}}}{E}\right]^2 = (0.5)(0.5)\left[\dfrac{1.96}{0.055}\right]^2$

n = 317.48 or 318

19.
$\hat{p} = 0.5$ $\hat{q} = 0.5$

$n = \hat{p}\,\hat{q}\left[\dfrac{z_{\frac{\alpha}{2}}}{E}\right]^2$

$n = (0.5)(0.5)\left[\dfrac{1.96}{0.03}\right]^2$

n = 1067.11 or 1068

20.
$n = \hat{p}\,\hat{q}\left[\dfrac{z_{\frac{\alpha}{2}}}{E}\right]^2$

$n = (0.27)(0.73)\left[\dfrac{1.96}{0.02}\right]^2$

n = 1892.9 or 1893

21.

$600 = (0.5)(0.5)\left[\dfrac{z}{0.04}\right]^2$

$600 = 156.25z^2$

$3.84 = z^2$

$\sqrt{3.84} = 1.96 = z$

1.96 corresponds to a 95% degree of confidence.

22.

$1015 = (0.68)(0.32)\left[\dfrac{z}{0.03}\right]^2$

$1015 = 241.78z^2$

$4.198 = z^2$

$\sqrt{4.198} = 2.05 = z$

For z = 2.05, the area under the normal curve is 0.4798. Since $0.5 - 0.4798 = 0.0202$, $\frac{\alpha}{2} = 0.0202$. Then $\alpha = 0.0404$ or 4%, and $100\% - 4\% = 96\%$. Thus, 2.05 corresponds to a 96% degree of confidence.

EXERCISE SET 7-5

1.
χ^2

2.
The variable must be normally distributed.

3.

	χ^2_{left}	χ^2_{right}
a.	3.816	21.920
b.	10.117	30.144
c.	13.844	41.923
d.	0.412	16.750
e.	26.509	55.758

4.
$\dfrac{(n-1)s^2}{\chi^2_{\text{right}}} < \sigma^2 < \dfrac{(n-1)s^2}{\chi^2_{\text{left}}}$

$\dfrac{15(2.1)^2}{24.996} < \sigma^2 < \dfrac{15(2.1)^2}{7.261}$

$2.65 < \sigma^2 < 9.11$
$1.63 < \sigma < 3.02$

Yes. The lifetimes deviate between 1.5 and 3 months.

5.
$\dfrac{(n-1)s^2}{\chi^2_{\text{right}}} < \sigma^2 < \dfrac{(n-1)s^2}{\chi^2_{\text{left}}}$

$\dfrac{22(3.8)^2}{36.781} < \sigma^2 < \dfrac{22(3.8)^2}{10.982}$

5. continued

$8.64 < \sigma^2 < 28.93$

$2.94 < \sigma < 5.38$

Yes. The times deviate between 3 and 5 minutes.

6.

$\frac{(n-1)s^2}{\chi^2_{right}} < \sigma^2 < \frac{(n-1)s^2}{\chi^2_{left}}$

$\frac{13(3.2)}{29.819} < \sigma^2 < \frac{13(3.2)}{3.565}$

$1.4 < \sigma^2 < 11.7$

$1.2 < \sigma < 3.4$

7.

$s^2 = 0.80997$ or 0.81

$\frac{(n-1)s^2}{\chi^2_{right}} < \sigma^2 < \frac{(n-1)s^2}{\chi^2_{left}}$

$\frac{19(0.81)}{38.582} < \sigma^2 < \frac{19(0.81)}{6.844}$

$0.40 < \sigma^2 < 2.25$

$0.63 < \sigma < 1.50$

8.

$\frac{(n-1)s^2}{\chi^2_{right}} < \sigma^2 < \frac{(n-1)s^2}{\chi^2_{left}}$

$\frac{23(2.3)^2}{35.172} < \sigma^2 < \frac{23(2.3)^2}{13.091}$

$3.5 < \sigma^2 < 9.3$

$1.9 < \sigma < 3$

9.

$\frac{(n-1)s^2}{\chi^2_{right}} < \sigma^2 < \frac{(n-1)s^2}{\chi^2_{left}}$

$\frac{19(19.1913)^2}{30.144} < \sigma^2 < \frac{19(19.1913)^2}{10.117}$

$232.1 < \sigma^2 < 691.6$

$15.2 < \sigma < 26.3$

10.

$s^2 = 411.455$

$\frac{(n-1)s^2}{\chi^2_{right}} < \sigma^2 < \frac{(n-1)s^2}{\chi^2_{left}}$

$\frac{19(411.455)}{30.144} < \sigma^2 < \frac{19(411.455)}{10.117}$

$259.343 < \sigma^2 < 772.724$

$16.104 < \sigma < 27.798$

11.

$\frac{(n-1)s^2}{\chi^2_{right}} < \sigma^2 < \frac{(n-1)s^2}{\chi^2_{left}}$

$\frac{27(5.2)^2}{43.194} < \sigma^2 < \frac{27(5.2)^2}{14.573}$

$16.9 < \sigma^2 < 50.1$

$4.1 < \sigma < 7.1$

12.

$s^2 = \frac{\sum X^2 - \frac{(\sum X)^2}{n}}{n-1} = \frac{1155.3752 - \frac{96.14^2}{8}}{8-1}$

$s^2 = 0.0018$

$s = \sqrt{0.0018} = 0.043$

$\frac{(n-1)s^2}{\chi^2_{right}} < \sigma^2 < \frac{(n-1)s^2}{\chi^2_{left}}$

$\frac{7(0.043)^2}{16.013} < \sigma^2 < \frac{7(0.043)^2}{1.690}$

$0.001 < \sigma^2 < 0.008$

$0.032 < \sigma < 0.089$

13.

$s - z_{\frac{\alpha}{2}}\left(\frac{s}{\sqrt{2n}}\right) < \sigma < s + z_{\frac{\alpha}{2}}\left(\frac{s}{\sqrt{2n}}\right)$

$18 - 1.96\left(\frac{18}{\sqrt{400}}\right) < \sigma < 18 + 1.96\left(\frac{18}{\sqrt{400}}\right)$

$16.2 < \sigma < 19.8$

REVIEW EXERCISES - CHAPTER 7

1.

$\overline{X} = 7.8$ is the point estimate of μ.

$\overline{X} - z_{\frac{\alpha}{2}}\left(\frac{s}{\sqrt{n}}\right) < \mu < \overline{X} + z_{\frac{\alpha}{2}}\left(\frac{s}{\sqrt{n}}\right)$

$7.8 - 1.65\left(\frac{0.6}{\sqrt{36}}\right) < \mu < 7.8 + 1.65\left(\frac{0.6}{\sqrt{36}}\right)$

$7.64 < \mu < 7.97$

The minimum speed should be about 7.64 miles per hour.

2.

$\hat{p} - (z_{\frac{\alpha}{2}})\sqrt{\frac{\hat{p}\hat{q}}{n}} < p < \hat{p} + (z_{\frac{\alpha}{2}})\sqrt{\frac{\hat{p}\hat{q}}{n}}$

$0.44 - 1.96\sqrt{\frac{(0.44)(0.56)}{1004}} < P <$

$\qquad 0.44 + 1.96\sqrt{\frac{(0.44)(0.56)}{1004}}$

$0.44 - 0.0307 < p < 0.44 + 0.0307$

$0.409 < p < 0.471$

3.

$\overline{X} = 7.5$ is the point estimate of μ.

$$\overline{X} - z_{\frac{\alpha}{2}}\left(\frac{s}{\sqrt{n}}\right) < \mu < \overline{X} + z_{\frac{\alpha}{2}}\left(\frac{s}{\sqrt{n}}\right)$$

$$7.5 - 1.96\left(\frac{0.8}{\sqrt{1500}}\right) < \mu < 7.5 + 1.96\left(\frac{0.8}{\sqrt{1500}}\right)$$

$$7.46 < \mu < 7.54$$

4.

$\overline{X} = 1151$ is the point estimate of μ.

$$\overline{X} - t_{\frac{\alpha}{2}}\left(\frac{s}{\sqrt{n}}\right) < \mu < \overline{X} + t_{\frac{\alpha}{2}}\left(\frac{s}{\sqrt{n}}\right)$$

$$\$1151 - 2.201\left(\frac{281.97227}{\sqrt{12}}\right) < \mu <$$
$$\$1151 + 2.201\left(\frac{281.97227}{\sqrt{12}}\right)$$

$$\$1151 - 179.2 < \mu < \$1151 + 179.2$$
$$\$971.8 < \mu < \$1330.2$$

5.

$$\overline{X} - t_{\frac{\alpha}{2}}\left(\frac{s}{\sqrt{n}}\right) < \mu < \overline{X} + t_{\frac{\alpha}{2}}\left(\frac{s}{\sqrt{n}}\right)$$

$$28 - 2.132\left(\frac{3}{\sqrt{5}}\right) < \mu < 28 + 2.132\left(\frac{3}{\sqrt{5}}\right)$$

$$25 < \mu < 31$$

6.

$$n = \left[\frac{z_{\frac{\alpha}{2}}\,\sigma}{E}\right]^2 = \left[\frac{1.96(1050)}{200}\right]^2$$

$$= 105.88 \text{ or } 106$$

7.

$$n = \left[\frac{z_{\frac{\alpha}{2}}\,\sigma}{E}\right]^2 = \left[\frac{1.65(80)}{25}\right]^2$$

$$= (5.28)^2 = 27.88 \text{ or } 28$$

8.

$\hat{p} = 0.42 \qquad \hat{q} = 0.58$

$$\hat{p} - (z_{\frac{\alpha}{2}})\sqrt{\frac{\hat{p}\hat{q}}{n}} < p < \hat{p} + (z_{\frac{\alpha}{2}})\sqrt{\frac{\hat{p}\hat{q}}{n}}$$

$$0.42 - 1.96\sqrt{\frac{(0.42)(0.58)}{1500}} < p <$$
$$0.42 + 1.96\sqrt{\frac{(0.42)(0.58)}{1500}}$$

$$0.42 - 1.96(0.013) < p < 0.42 + 1.96(0.013)$$

$$0.395 < p < 0.445$$

9.

$\hat{p} = 0.547 \qquad \hat{q} = 0.453$

$$\hat{p} - (z_{\frac{\alpha}{2}})\sqrt{\frac{\hat{p}\hat{q}}{n}} < p < \hat{p} + (z_{\frac{\alpha}{2}})\sqrt{\frac{\hat{p}\hat{q}}{n}}$$

$$0.547 - 1.96\sqrt{\frac{(0.547)(0.453)}{75}} < p <$$
$$0.547 + 1.96\sqrt{\frac{(0.547)(0.453)}{75}}$$

$$0.547 - 0.113 < p < 0.547 + 0.113$$
$$0.434 < p < 0.660$$

Yes; it seems that as many as 66% were dissatisfied.

10.

$\hat{p} = 0.85 \qquad \hat{q} = 0.15$

$$\hat{p} - (z_{\frac{\alpha}{2}})\sqrt{\frac{\hat{p}\hat{q}}{n}} < p < \hat{p} + (z_{\frac{\alpha}{2}})\sqrt{\frac{\hat{p}\hat{q}}{n}}$$

$$0.85 - 1.65\sqrt{\frac{(0.85)(0.15)}{100}} < p <$$
$$0.85 + 1.65\sqrt{\frac{(0.85)(0.15)}{100}}$$

$$0.85 - 0.059 < p < 0.85 + 0.059$$
$$0.791 < p < 0.909$$

11.

$\hat{p} = 0.88 \qquad \hat{q} = 0.12$

$$n = \hat{p}\,\hat{q}\left[\frac{z_{\frac{\alpha}{2}}}{E}\right]^2 = (0.88)(0.12)\left[\frac{1.65}{0.025}\right]^2$$

$$n = 459.99 \text{ or } 460$$

12.

$\hat{p} = 0.80 \qquad \hat{q} = 0.20$

$$n = \hat{p}\,\hat{q}\left[\frac{z_{\frac{\alpha}{2}}}{E}\right]^2 = (0.80)(0.20)\left[\frac{2.33}{0.03}\right]^2$$

$$n = 965.1 \text{ or } 966$$

13.

$$\frac{(n-1)s^2}{\chi^2_{right}} < \sigma^2 < \frac{(n-1)s^2}{\chi^2_{left}}$$

$$\frac{(18-1)(0.29)^2}{30.191} < \sigma^2 < \frac{(18-1)(0.29)^2}{7.564}$$

$$0.0474 < \sigma^2 < 0.1890$$
$$0.218 < \sigma < 0.435$$

Yes; it seems that there is a large standard deviation.

14.

$$\frac{(n-1)s^2}{\chi^2_{\text{right}}} < \sigma^2 < \frac{(n-1)s^2}{\chi^2_{\text{left}}}$$

$$\frac{(22-1)(2.6)}{35.479} < \sigma^2 < \frac{(22-1)(2.6)}{10.283}$$

$$1.5 < \sigma^2 < 5.3$$

15.

$$\frac{(n-1)s^2}{\chi^2_{\text{right}}} < \sigma^2 < \frac{(n-1)s^2}{\chi^2_{\text{left}}}$$

$$\frac{(15-1)(8.6)}{23.685} < \sigma^2 < \frac{(15-1)(8.6)}{6.571}$$

$$5.1 < \sigma^2 < 18.3$$

16.

$$\frac{(n-1)s^2}{\chi^2_{\text{right}}} < \sigma^2 < \frac{(n-1)s^2}{\chi^2_{\text{left}}}$$

$$\frac{(28-1)(1.83)^2}{43.194} < \sigma^2 < \frac{(28-1)(1.83)^2}{14.573}$$

$$2.093 < \sigma^2 < 6.205$$
$$1.447 < \sigma < 2.491$$

CHAPTER 7 QUIZ

1. True
2. True
3. False, it is consistent if, as sample size increases, the estimator approaches the parameter being estimated.
4. True
5. b
6. a
7. b
8. Unbiased, consistent, relatively efficient
9. Maximum error of estimate
10. Point
11. 90, 95, 99

12.
$\overline{X} = \$23.45$ is the point estimate for μ.
$$\overline{X} - z_{\frac{\alpha}{2}}\left(\tfrac{s}{\sqrt{n}}\right) < \mu < \overline{X} + z_{\frac{\alpha}{2}}\left(\tfrac{s}{\sqrt{n}}\right)$$

$$\$23.45 - 1.65\left(\tfrac{2.80}{\sqrt{49}}\right) < \mu <$$
$$\$23.45 + 1.65\left(\tfrac{2.80}{\sqrt{49}}\right)$$

$$\$22.79 < \mu < \$24.11$$

13.
$\overline{X} = \$44.80$ is the point estimate for μ.

$$\overline{X} - t_{\frac{\alpha}{2}}\left(\tfrac{s}{\sqrt{n}}\right) < \mu < \overline{X} + t_{\frac{\alpha}{2}}\left(\tfrac{s}{\sqrt{n}}\right)$$

13. continued
$$\$44.80 - 2.093\left(\tfrac{3.53}{\sqrt{20}}\right) < \mu <$$
$$\$44.80 + 2.093\left(\tfrac{3.53}{\sqrt{20}}\right)$$

$$\$43.15 < \mu < \$46.45$$

14.
$\overline{X} = 4150$ is the point estimate for μ.

$$\overline{X} - z_{\frac{\alpha}{2}}\left(\tfrac{s}{\sqrt{n}}\right) < \mu < \overline{X} + z_{\frac{\alpha}{2}}\left(\tfrac{s}{\sqrt{n}}\right)$$

$$\$4150 - 2.58\left(\tfrac{480}{\sqrt{40}}\right) < \mu <$$
$$\$4150 + 2.58\left(\tfrac{480}{\sqrt{40}}\right)$$

$$\$3954 < \mu < \$4346$$

15.
$$\overline{X} - t_{\frac{\alpha}{2}}\left(\tfrac{s}{\sqrt{n}}\right) < \mu < \overline{X} + t_{\frac{\alpha}{2}}\left(\tfrac{s}{\sqrt{n}}\right)$$

$$48.6 - 2.262\left(\tfrac{4.1}{\sqrt{10}}\right) < \mu < 48.6 + 2.262\left(\tfrac{4.1}{\sqrt{10}}\right)$$

$$45.7 < \mu < 51.5$$

16.
$$\overline{X} - t_{\frac{\alpha}{2}}\left(\tfrac{s}{\sqrt{n}}\right) < \mu < \overline{X} + t_{\frac{\alpha}{2}}\left(\tfrac{s}{\sqrt{n}}\right)$$

$$438 - 3.499\left(\tfrac{16}{\sqrt{8}}\right) < \mu < 438 + 3.499\left(\tfrac{16}{\sqrt{8}}\right)$$

$$418 < \mu < 458$$

17.
$$\overline{X} - t_{\frac{\alpha}{2}}\left(\tfrac{s}{\sqrt{n}}\right) < \mu < \overline{X} + t_{\frac{\alpha}{2}}\left(\tfrac{s}{\sqrt{n}}\right)$$

$$31 - 2.353\left(\tfrac{4}{\sqrt{4}}\right) < \mu < 31 + 2.353\left(\tfrac{4}{\sqrt{4}}\right)$$

$$26 < \mu < 36$$

18.
$$n = \left[\frac{z_{\frac{\alpha}{2}}\,\sigma}{E}\right]^2 = \left[\frac{2.58(2.6)}{0.5}\right]^2$$

$$= 179.98 \text{ or } 180$$

19.
$$n = \left[\frac{z_{\frac{\alpha}{2}}\,\sigma}{E}\right]^2 = \left[\frac{1.65(900)}{300}\right]^2$$

$$= 24.5 \text{ or } 25$$

20.
$$\hat{p} - \left(z_{\frac{\alpha}{2}}\right)\sqrt{\tfrac{\hat{p}\hat{q}}{n}} < p < \hat{p} + \left(z_{\frac{\alpha}{2}}\right)\sqrt{\tfrac{\hat{p}\hat{q}}{n}}$$

20. continued

$$\hat{p} = \frac{53}{75} = 0.707 \quad \hat{q} = \frac{22}{75} = 0.293$$

$$0.71 - 1.96\sqrt{\frac{(0.707)(0.293)}{75}} < p <$$
$$0.71 + 1.96\sqrt{\frac{(0.707)(0.293)}{75}}$$

$$0.604 < p < 0.810$$

21.

$$\hat{p} - (z_{\frac{\alpha}{2}})\sqrt{\frac{\hat{p}\hat{q}}{n}} < p < \hat{p} + (z_{\frac{\alpha}{2}})\sqrt{\frac{\hat{p}\hat{q}}{n}}$$

$$0.36 - 1.65\sqrt{\frac{(0.36)(0.64)}{150}} < p <$$
$$0.36 + 1.65\sqrt{\frac{(0.36)(0.64)}{150}}$$

$$0.295 < p < 0.425$$

22.

$$\hat{p} - (z_{\frac{\alpha}{2}})\sqrt{\frac{\hat{p}\hat{q}}{n}} < p < \hat{p} + (z_{\frac{\alpha}{2}})\sqrt{\frac{\hat{p}\hat{q}}{n}}$$

$$0.4444 - 1.96\sqrt{\frac{(0.4444)(0.5556)}{90}} < p <$$
$$0.4444 + 1.96\sqrt{\frac{(0.4444)(0.5556)}{90}}$$

$$0.342 < p < 0.547$$

23.

$$n = \hat{p}\,\hat{q}\left[\frac{z_{\frac{\alpha}{2}}}{E}\right]^2$$

$$= (0.15)(0.85)\left[\frac{1.96}{0.03}\right]^2$$

$$= 544.22 \text{ or } 545$$

24.

$$\frac{(n-1)s^2}{\chi^2_{right}} < \sigma^2 < \frac{(n-1)s^2}{\chi^2_{left}}$$

$$\frac{24(9)^2}{39.364} < \sigma^2 < \frac{24(9)^2}{12.401}$$

$$49.4 < \sigma^2 < 156.8$$
$$7 < \sigma < 13$$

25.

$$\frac{(n-1)s^2}{\chi^2_{right}} < \sigma^2 < \frac{(n-1)s^2}{\chi^2_{left}}$$

$$\frac{26(6.8)^2}{38.885} < \sigma^2 < \frac{26(6.8)^2}{15.379}$$

$$30.9 < \sigma^2 < 78.2$$
$$5.6 < \sigma < 8.8$$

26.

$$\frac{(n-1)s^2}{\chi^2_{right}} < \sigma^2 < \frac{(n-1)s^2}{\chi^2_{left}}$$

$$\frac{19(2.3)^2}{30.144} < \sigma^2 < \frac{19(2.3)^2}{10.177}$$

$$3.33 < \sigma^2 < 10$$
$$1.8 < \sigma < 3.2$$

Note: Graphs are not to scale and are intended to convey a general idea. Answers may vary due to rounding.

EXERCISE SET 8-2

1.
The null hypothesis is a statistical hypothesis that states there is no difference between a parameter and a specific value or there is no difference between two parameters. The alternative hypothesis specifies a specific difference between a parameter and a specific value, or that there is a difference between two parameters. Examples will vary.

2.
Type I error occurs by rejecting the null hypothesis when it is true. Type II error occurs when the null hypothesis is not rejected and it is false. They are related in that decreasing the probability of one type of error increases the probability of the other type of error.

3.
A statistical test uses the data obtained from a sample to make a decision as to whether or not the null hypothesis should be rejected.

4.
A one-tailed test indicates the null hypothesis should be rejected when the test statistic value is in the critical region on one side of the mean. A two-tailed test indicates the null hypothesis should be rejected when the test statistic value is in either critical region on both sides of the mean.

5.
The critical region is the region of values of the test-statistic that indicates a significant difference and the null hypothesis should be rejected. The non-critical region is the region of values of the test-statistic that indicates the difference was probably due to chance, and the null hypothesis should not be rejected.

6.
"H_0" represents the null hypothesis. "H_1" represents the alternative hypothesis.

7.
Type I is represented by α, type II is represented by β.

8.
When the difference between the sample mean and the hypothesized mean is large, then the difference is said to be significant and probably not due to chance.

9.
A one-tailed test should be used when a specific direction, such as greater than or less than, is being hypothesized, whereas when no direction is specified, a two-tailed test should be used.

10.
The steps in hypothesis testing are:
1. State the hypotheses.
2. Find the critical value(s).
3. Compute the test statistic value.
4. Make the decision.
5. Summarize the results.

11.
Hypotheses can only be proved true when the entire population is used to compute the test statistic. In most cases, this is impossible.

12.
a. ± 1.96

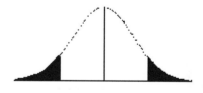

$-1.96 \quad 0 \quad +1.96$

b. -2.33

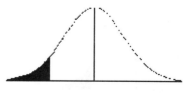

$-2.33 \quad 0$

12. continued

c. $+2.58$

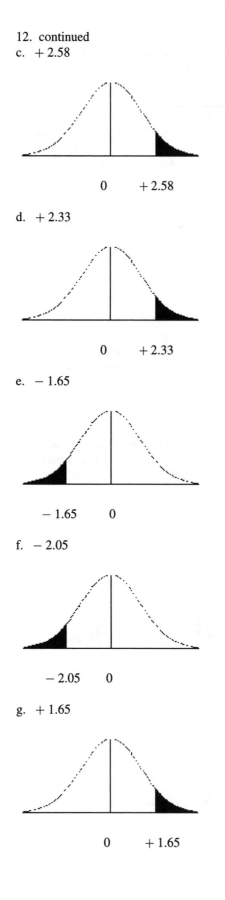

d. $+2.33$

0    $+2.33$

e. -1.65

-1.65 0

f. -2.05

-2.05 0

g. $+1.65$

0    $+1.65$

12. continued

h. ± 2.58

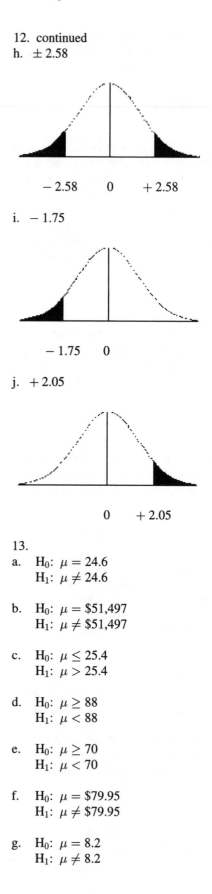

-2.58 0 $+2.58$

i. -1.75

-1.75 0

j. $+2.05$

0    $+2.05$

13.

a. H_0: $\mu = 24.6$
   H_1: $\mu \neq 24.6$

b. H_0: $\mu = \$51,497$
   H_1: $\mu \neq \$51,497$

c. H_0: $\mu \leq 25.4$
   H_1: $\mu > 25.4$

d. H_0: $\mu \geq 88$
   H_1: $\mu < 88$

e. H_0: $\mu \geq 70$
   H_1: $\mu < 70$

f. H_0: $\mu = \$79.95$
   H_1: $\mu \neq \$79.95$

g. H_0: $\mu = 8.2$
   H_1: $\mu \neq 8.2$

EXERCISE SET 8-3

1.
H_0: $\mu = \$69.21$ (claim)
H_1: $\mu \neq \$69.21$

C. V. $= \pm 1.96$
$z = \dfrac{\overline{X} - \mu}{\frac{\sigma}{\sqrt{n}}} = \dfrac{\$68.43 - \$69.21}{\frac{3.72}{\sqrt{30}}} = -1.15$

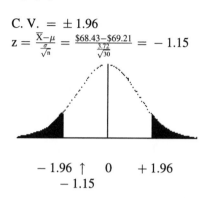

$-1.96 \uparrow \quad 0 \quad +1.96$
$\quad -1.15$

Do not reject the null hypothesis. There is not enough evidence to reject the claim that the average cost of a hotel stay in Atlanta is $69.21.

2.
H_0: $\mu \geq \$3262$
H_1: $\mu < \$3262$ (claim)

C. V. $= -1.65$
$z = \dfrac{\overline{X} - \mu}{\frac{\sigma}{\sqrt{n}}} = \dfrac{2995 - 3262}{\frac{1100}{\sqrt{50}}} = -1.72$

$\uparrow -1.65 \quad 0$
-1.72

Reject the null hypothesis. There is enough evidence to support the claim that the average debt is less than $3262.

3.
H_0: $\mu \leq \$24$ billion
$H1$: $\mu > \$24$ billion   (claim)

C. V. $= +1.65$ $\overline{X} = \$31.5$ $s = \$28.7$
$z = \dfrac{\overline{X} - \mu}{\frac{\sigma}{\sqrt{n}}} = \dfrac{31.5 - 24}{\frac{28.7}{\sqrt{50}}} = 1.85$

3. continued

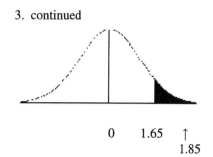

$0 \quad 1.65 \quad \uparrow$
$\quad\quad\quad 1.85$

Reject the null hypothesis. There is enough evidence to support the claim that the average revenue exceeds $24 billion.

4.
H_0: $\mu \leq \$12,837$
H_1: $\mu > \$12,837$ (claim)

C. V. $= 1.65$
$z = \dfrac{\overline{X} - \mu}{\frac{\sigma}{\sqrt{n}}} = \dfrac{14,445 - 12,837}{\frac{1500}{\sqrt{44}}} = 7.11$

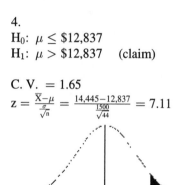

$0 \quad 1.65 \quad \uparrow$
$\quad\quad\quad 7.11$

Reject the null hypothesis. There is enough evidence to support the claim that the average salary is more than $12,837.

5.
H_0: $\mu \geq 14$
H_1: $\mu < 14$ (claim)

C. V. $= -2.33$
$z = \dfrac{\overline{X} - \mu}{\frac{s}{\sqrt{n}}} = \dfrac{11.8 - 14}{\frac{2.7}{\sqrt{36}}} = -4.89$

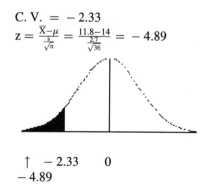

$\uparrow \quad -2.33 \quad 0$
-4.89

Reject the null hypothesis. There is enough evidence to support the claim that the average age of the planes in the executive's airline is less than the national average.

6.

H_0: $\mu \leq 3000$

H_1: $\mu > 3000$ (claim)

C. V. $= 1.65$

$z = \frac{\overline{X} - \mu}{\frac{\sigma}{\sqrt{n}}} = \frac{3120 - 3000}{\frac{578}{\sqrt{60}}} = 1.61$

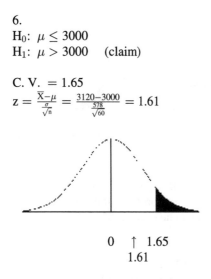

0   ↑ 1.65
    1.61

Do not reject the null hypothesis. There is not enough evidence to support the claim that the average production has increased.

7.

H_0: $\mu = 29$

H_1: $\mu \neq 29$ (claim)

C. V. $= \pm 1.96$ $\overline{X} = 29.45$ $s = 2.61$

$z = \frac{\overline{X} - \mu}{\frac{\sigma}{\sqrt{n}}} = \frac{29.45 - 29}{\frac{2.61}{\sqrt{30}}} = 0.944$

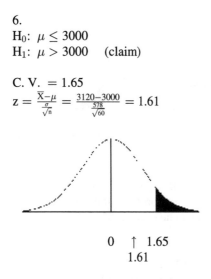

1.96   0   ↑ 1.96
           0.944

Do not reject the null hypothesis. There is enough evidence to reject the claim that the average height differs from 29 inches.

8.

H_0: $\mu \leq \$91,600$

H_1: $\mu > \$91,600$ (claim)

C. V. $= 1.65$

8. continued

$z = \frac{\overline{X} - \mu}{\frac{s}{\sqrt{n}}} = \frac{\$96,321 - \$91,600}{\frac{\$9555}{\sqrt{100}}} = 4.94$

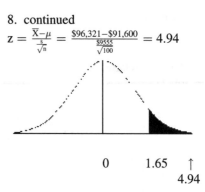

0   1.65   ↑
               4.94

Reject the null hypothesis. There is enough evidence to support the claim that the average income is greater than $91,600.

9.

H_0: $\mu \leq \$19,410$

H_1: $\mu > \$19,410$ (claim)

C. V. $= 2.33$

$z = \frac{\overline{X} - \mu}{\frac{\sigma}{\sqrt{n}}} = \frac{\$22,098 - \$19,410}{\frac{6050}{\sqrt{40}}} = 2.81$

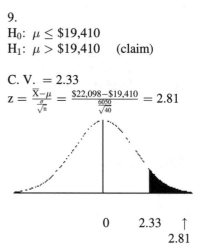

0   2.33   ↑
               2.81

Reject the null hypothesis. There is enough evidence to support the claim that the average tuition cost has increased.

10.

H_0: $\mu = \$60,000$ (claim)

H_1: $\mu \neq \$60,000$

C. V. $= \pm 1.96$ $\overline{X} = \$82,496$

$s = \$76,025$

$z = \frac{\overline{X} - \mu}{\frac{\sigma}{\sqrt{n}}} = \frac{82496 - 60,000}{\frac{76,025}{\sqrt{36}}} = 1.78$

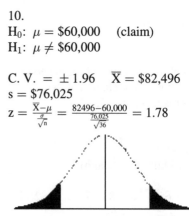

-1.96 0   ↑ 1.96
              1.78

10. continued
Do not reject the null hypothesis. There is not enough evidence to reject the claim that the average price of a home is $60,000.

11.
H_0: $\mu = 125$
H_1: $\mu \neq 125$ (claim)

C. V. $= \pm 2.58$
$z = \frac{\overline{X}-\mu}{\frac{\sigma}{\sqrt{n}}} = \frac{110-125}{\frac{30}{\sqrt{35}}} = -2.96$

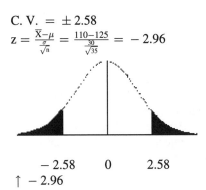

$-2.58 \quad 0 \quad 2.58$
$\uparrow -2.96$

Reject the null hypothesis. There is enough evidence to support the claim that the average number of guests differs from 125.

12.
H_0: $\mu = \$39,385$
H_1: $\mu \neq \$39,385$ (claim)

C. V. $= \pm 1.96$
$z = \frac{\overline{X}-\mu}{\frac{\sigma}{\sqrt{n}}} = \frac{\$41,680-\$39,385}{\frac{5975}{\sqrt{50}}} = 2.72$

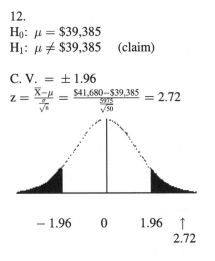

$-1.96 \quad 0 \quad 1.96 \quad \uparrow$
$\qquad\qquad\qquad 2.72$

Reject the null hypothesis. There is enough evidence to support the claim that the mean salary differs from $39,385.

13.
H_0: $\mu = \$24.44$
H_1: $\mu \neq \$24.44$ (claim)

C. V. $= \pm 2.33$
$z = \frac{\overline{X}-\mu}{\frac{s}{\sqrt{n}}} = \frac{22.97-24.44}{\frac{3.70}{\sqrt{33}}} = -2.28$

13. continued

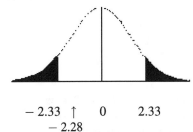

$-2.33 \uparrow \quad 0 \quad 2.33$
$\quad -2.28$

Do not reject the null hypothesis. There is not enough evidence to support the claim that the amount spent at a local mall is not equal to the national average of $24.44.

14.
The P value is the actual probability of getting the sample mean if the null hypothesis is true.

15.
a. Do not reject.
b. Reject.
c. Do not reject.
d. Reject
e. Reject

16.
H_0: $\mu = 52$ (claim)
H_1: $\mu \neq 52$
$z = \frac{\overline{X}-\mu}{\frac{s}{\sqrt{n}}} = \frac{56.3-52}{\frac{3.5}{\sqrt{50}}} = 8.69$

The area corresponding to $z = 8.69$ is $+0.4999$. Then P-value < 0.01. Hence, the null hypothesis should be rejected. There is enough evidence to reject the claim that the mean is 52. The researcher's claim is not valid.

17.
H_0: $\mu \geq 264$
H_1: $\mu < 264$ (claim)
$z = \frac{\overline{X}-\mu}{\frac{\sigma}{\sqrt{n}}} = \frac{262.3-264}{\frac{3}{\sqrt{20}}} = -2.53$

The area corresponding to $z = 2.53$ is 0.4943. The P-value is $0.5 - 0.4943 = 0.0057$. The decision is to reject the null hypothesis since $0.0057 < 0.01$. There is enough evidence to support the claim that the average stopping distance is less than 264 feet.

18.

H_0: $\mu \geq 40$

H_1: $\mu < 40$ (claim)

$\overline{X} = 29.3$ $s = 30.9$

$z = \frac{\overline{X} - \mu}{\frac{\sigma}{\sqrt{n}}} = \frac{29.3 - 40}{\frac{30.9}{\sqrt{50}}} = -2.45$

The area corresponding to z = 2.45 is 0.4929. The P-value is $0.5 - 0.4929 = 0.0071$. The decision is reject the null hypothesis since $0.0071 < 0.01$. There is enough evidence to support the claim that the average number of copies is less than 40.

19.

H_0: $\mu \geq 546$

H_1: $\mu < 546$ (claim)

$z = \frac{\overline{X} - \mu}{\frac{\sigma}{\sqrt{n}}} = \frac{544.8 - 546}{\frac{3}{\sqrt{36}}} = -2.4$

The area corresponding to z = -2.4 is 0.4918. The P-value is $0.5 - 0.4918 = 0.0082$. The decision is to reject the null hypothesis since $0.0082 < 0.01$. There is enough evidence to support the claim that the number of calories burned is less than 546.

20.

H_0: $\mu = 800$ (claim)

H_1: $\mu \neq 800$

$z = \frac{\overline{X} - \mu}{\frac{\sigma}{\sqrt{n}}} = \frac{793 - 800}{\frac{12}{\sqrt{200}}} = -2.61$

The area corresponding to z = 2.61 is 0.4955. The P-value is found by subtracting the area from 0.5 then multiplying by 2 since this is a two-tailed test. Hence, $2(0.5 - 0.4955) = 2(0.0045) = 0.0090$. The decision is to reject the null hypothesis since $0.009 < 0.01$. There is enough evidence to reject the null hypothesis that the breaking strength is 800 pounds.

21.

H_0: $\mu \geq 47.1$

H_1: $\mu < 47.1$ (claim)

$z = \frac{\overline{X} - \mu}{\frac{\sigma}{\sqrt{n}}} = \frac{43.2 - 47.1}{\frac{8.6}{\sqrt{50}}} = -3.21$

The area corresponding to z = 3.21 is $+0.4999$. To get the P-value, subtract 0.4999 from 0.5 and then multiply by 2 since this is a two-tailed test.

$2(0.5 - 0.4999) = 2(0.0001) = 0.0002$. thus the P-value is less than 0.0002.

21. continued

The decision is to reject the null hypothesis since P-value < 0.01. There is enough evidence to support the claim that the mean is less than 47.1 acres.

22.

H_0: $\mu = 65$ (claim)

H_1: $\mu \neq 65$

$z = \frac{\overline{X} - \mu}{\frac{\sigma}{\sqrt{n}}} = \frac{63.2 - 65}{\frac{7}{\sqrt{22}}} = -1.21$

The area corresponding to z = -1.21 is 0.3869. The P-value is $2(0.5 - 0.3869) = 2(0.1131) = 0.2262$. The decision is do not reject the null hypothesis since $0.2262 > 0.10$. Hence, there is not enough evidence to reject the claim that the average is 65 acres.

23.

H_0: $\mu = 30,000$ (claim)

H_1: $\mu \neq 30,000$

$z = \frac{\overline{X} - \mu}{\frac{s}{\sqrt{n}}} = \frac{30,456 - 30,000}{\frac{1684}{\sqrt{40}}} = 1.71$

The area corresponding to z = 1.71 is 0.4564. The P-value is $2(0.5 - 0.4564) = 2(0.0436) = 0.0872$. The decision is to reject the null hypothesis at $\alpha = 0.10$ since $0.0872 < 0.10$. The conclusion is that there is enough evidence to reject the claim that customers are adhering to the recommendation. A 0.10 significance level is probably appropriate since there is little consequence of a Type I error. The dealer would be advised to increase efforts to make its customers aware of the service recommendation.

24.

H_0: $\mu = 60$ (claim)

H_1: $\mu \neq 60$

$\overline{X} = 59.93$ $s = 13.42$

$z = \frac{\overline{X} - \mu}{\frac{s}{\sqrt{n}}} = \frac{59.93 - 60}{\frac{13.42}{\sqrt{30}}} = -0.03$

The area corresponding to 0.03 is 0.0120. The P-value is $2(0.5 - 0.0120) = 0.976$. Since $0.976 > 0.05$, the decision is do not reject the null hypothesis. There is not enough evidence to reject the claim that the average number of speeding tickets is 60.

25.

H_0: $\mu \geq 10$

H_1: $\mu < 10$ (claim)

$\overline{X} = 5.025$ $s = 3.63$

$z = \dfrac{\overline{X} - \mu}{\frac{s}{\sqrt{n}}} = \dfrac{5.025 - 10}{\frac{3.63}{\sqrt{40}}} = -8.67$

The area corresponding to 8.67 is greater than 0.4999. The P-value is $0.5 - 0.4999 < 0.0001$. Since $0.0001 < 0.05$, the decision is to reject the null hypothesis. There is enough evidence to support the claim that the average number of days missed per year is less than 10.

26.

Reject the claim at $\alpha = 0.05$ but not at $\alpha = 0.01$. There is no contradiction since the value of α should be chosen before the test is conducted.

27.

The mean and standard deviation are found as follows:

	f	X_m	$f \cdot X_m$	$f \cdot X_m^2$
8.35 - 8.43	2	8.39	16.78	140.7842
8.44 - 8.52	6	8.48	50.88	431.4624
8.53 - 8.61	12	8.57	102.84	881.3388
8.62 - 8.70	18	8.66	155.88	1349.9208
8.71 - 8.79	10	8.75	87.5	765.625
8.80 - 8.88	2	8.84	17.68	156.2912
	50		431.56	3725.4224

$\overline{X} = \dfrac{\sum f \cdot X_m}{n} = \dfrac{431.56}{50} = 8.63$

$s = \sqrt{\dfrac{\sum f \cdot X_m^2 - \frac{\sum (f \cdot X_m)^2}{n}}{n-1}} = \sqrt{\dfrac{3725.4224 - \frac{(431.56)^2}{50}}{49}}$

$= 0.105$

H_0: $\mu = 8.65$ (claim)

H_1: $\mu \neq 8.65$

C. V. $= \pm 1.96$

$z = \dfrac{\overline{X} - \mu}{\frac{s}{\sqrt{n}}} = \dfrac{8.63 - 8.65}{\frac{0.105}{\sqrt{50}}} = -1.35$

Do not reject the null hypothesis. There is not enough evidence to reject the claim that the average hourly wage of the employees is $8.65.

EXERCISE SET 8-4

1.

It is bell-shaped, symmetric about the mean, and it never touches the x axis. The mean, median, and mode are all equal to 0 and they are located at the center of the distribution. The t distribution differs from the standard normal distribution in that it is a family of curves, the variance is greater than one, and as the degrees of freedom increase the t distribution approaches the standard normal distribution.

2.

The degrees of freedom are the number of values that are free to vary after a sample statistic has been computed. They tell the researcher which specific curve to use when a distribution consists of a family of curves.

3.

a. d. f. = 9   C. V. = + 1.833

b. d. f. = 17   C. V. = ± 1.740

c. d. f. = 5   C. V. = − 3.365

d. d. f. = 8   C. V. = + 2.306

e. d. f. = 14   C. V. = ± 2.145

f. d. f. = 22   C. V. = − 2.819

g. d. f. = 27   C. V. = ± 2.771

h. d. f. = 16   C. V. = ± 2.583

4.

a. 0.01 < P-value < 0.025 (0.018)

b. 0.05 < P-value < 0.10 (0.062)

c. 0.10 < P-value < 0.25 (0.123)

d. 0.10 < P-value < 0.20 (0.138)

e. P-value < 0.005   (0.003)

f. 0.10 < P-value < 0.25 (0.158)

g. P-value = 0.05   (0.05)

h. P-value > 0.25   (0.261)

5.

H_0: $\mu \geq 11.52$

H_1: $\mu < 11.52$ (claim)

C. V. $= -1.833$ d. f. = 9

$t = \dfrac{\overline{X} - \mu}{\frac{s}{\sqrt{n}}} = \dfrac{7.42 - 11.52}{\frac{1.3}{\sqrt{10}}} = -9.97$

5. continued

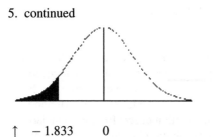

↑ − 1.833   0
− 9.97

Reject the null hypothesis. There is enough evidence to support the claim that the rainfall is below average.

6.
H_0: $\mu \geq 2000$
H_1: $\mu < 2000$ (claim)

C. V. = − 3.747   d. f. = 4
$\overline{X} = 1885.8$ s = 2456.3
$t = \frac{\overline{X}-\mu}{\frac{s}{\sqrt{n}}} = \frac{1885.8-2000}{\frac{2456.3}{\sqrt{5}}} = -0.104$

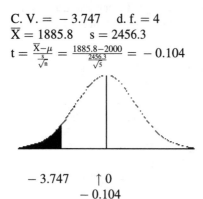

− 3.747   ↑ 0
          − 0.104

Do not reject the null hypothesis. There is not enough evidence to support the claim that the average acreage is less than 2000.

7.
H_0: $\mu = \$40,000$
H_1: $\mu \neq \$40,000$ (claim)

C. V. = ± 2.093   d. f. = 19
$t = \frac{\overline{X}-\mu}{\frac{s}{\sqrt{n}}} = \frac{43,228-40,000}{\frac{4000}{\sqrt{20}}} = 3.61$

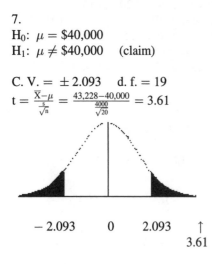

− 2.093   0   2.093   ↑
                    3.61

Reject the null hypothesis. There is enough evidence to support the claim that the average salary is not $40,000.

8.
H_0: $\mu \geq 25.4$
H_1: $\mu < 25.4$ (claim)

C. V. = − 1.318   d. f. = 24
$t = \frac{\overline{X}-\mu}{\frac{s}{\sqrt{n}}} = \frac{22.1-25.4}{\frac{5.3}{\sqrt{25}}} = -3.11$

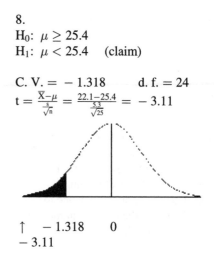

↑   − 1.318   0
− 3.11

Reject the null hypothesis. There is enough evidence to support the claim that the commute time is less than 25.4 minutes.

9.
H_0: $\mu \geq 700$ (claim)
H_1: $\mu < 700$
$\overline{X} = 606.5$ s = 109.1

C. V. = − 2.262   d. f. = 9
$t = \frac{\overline{X}-\mu}{\frac{s}{\sqrt{n}}} = \frac{606.5-700}{\frac{109.1}{\sqrt{10}}} = -2.71$

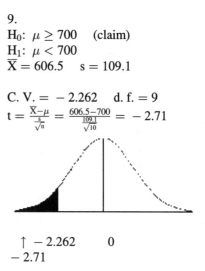

↑ − 2.262   0
− 2.71

Reject the null hypothesis. There is enough evidence to reject the claim that the average height of the buildings is at least 700 feet.

10.
H_0: $\mu = \$17.63$ (claim)
H_1: $\mu \neq \$17.63$

C. V. = ± 2.145   d. f. = 14
$t = \frac{\overline{X}-\mu}{\frac{s}{\sqrt{n}}} = \frac{18.72-17.63}{\frac{3.64}{\sqrt{15}}} = 1.16$

10. continued

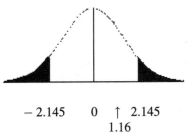

$$-2.145 \quad 0 \quad \uparrow \quad 2.145$$
$$1.16$$

Do not reject the null hypothesis. There is not enough evidence to reject the claim that there is no difference in the rates.

11.
H_0: $\mu \leq \$13,252$
H_1: $\mu > \$13,252$ (claim)

C. V. = 2.539   d. f. = 19
$t = \frac{\overline{X}-\mu}{\frac{s}{\sqrt{n}}} = \frac{\$15,560-\$13,252}{\frac{\$3500}{\sqrt{20}}} = 2.949$

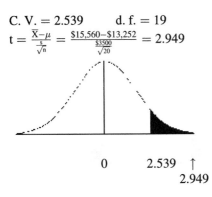

$$0 \quad 2.539 \quad \uparrow$$
$$2.949$$

Reject the null hypothesis. There is enough evidence to support the claim that the average tuition cost has increased.

12.
H_0: $\mu = \$91,600$
H_1: $\mu \neq \$91,600$ (claim)

C. V. = ± 1.703   d. f. = 27
$t = \frac{\overline{X}-\mu}{\frac{s}{\sqrt{n}}} = \frac{\$88,500-\$91,600}{\frac{\$10,000}{\sqrt{28}}} = -1.64$

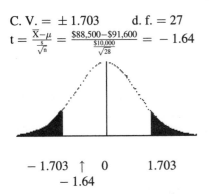

$$-1.703 \quad \uparrow \quad 0 \quad \quad 1.703$$
$$-1.64$$

Do not reject the null hypothesis. There is not enough evidence to support the claim that the average income differs from $91,600.

13.
H_0: $\mu \leq \$54.8$
H_1: $\mu > \$54.8$ (claim)

C. V. = 1.761   d. f. = 14
$t = \frac{\overline{X}-\mu}{\frac{s}{\sqrt{n}}} = \frac{\$62.3-\$54.8}{\frac{\$9.5}{\sqrt{15}}} = 3.058$

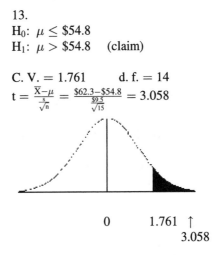

$$0 \quad \quad 1.761 \quad \uparrow$$
$$3.058$$

Reject the null hypothesis. There is enough evidence to support the claim that the cost to produce an action movie is more than $54.8 million.

14.
H_0: $\mu \leq 110$
H_1: $\mu > 110$ (claim)

$\overline{X} = 137.333$ s = 24.11777
C. V. = 2.624   d. f. = 14
$t = \frac{\overline{X}-\mu}{\frac{s}{\sqrt{n}}} = \frac{137.333-110}{\frac{24.11777}{\sqrt{15}}} = 4.389$

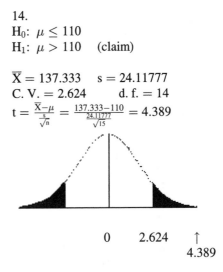

$$0 \quad \quad 2.624 \quad \quad \uparrow$$
$$4.389$$

Reject the null hypothesis. There is enough evidence to support the claim that the average calorie content is greater than 110.

15.
H_0: $\mu = 132$ min.   (claim)
H_1: $\mu \neq 132$ min.

C. V. = ± 2.365   d. f. = 7
$t = \frac{\overline{X}-\mu}{\frac{s}{\sqrt{n}}} = \frac{125-132}{\frac{11}{\sqrt{8}}} = -1.7999$

Do not reject the null hypothesis. There is enough evidence to support the claim that the average show time is 132 minutes, or 2 hours and 12 minutes.

16.
H_0: $\mu = 123$
H_1: $\mu \neq 123$ (claim)
d. f. = 15
P-value < 0.01   (0.0086)
$t = \frac{\overline{X}-\mu}{\frac{s}{\sqrt{n}}} = \frac{119-123}{\frac{5.3}{\sqrt{16}}} = -3.02$

Reject the null hypothesis. There is enough evidence to support the claim that the mean is not 123 gallons. The *Old Farmer's Almanac* figure may have changed.

17.
H_0: $\mu = 5.8$
H_1: $\mu \neq 5.8$ (claim)
$\overline{X} = 3.85$ s = 2.52
d. f. = 19 $\alpha = 0.05$
P-value < 0.01   (0.0026)
$t = \frac{\overline{X}-\mu}{\frac{s}{\sqrt{n}}} = \frac{3.85-5.8}{\frac{2.52}{\sqrt{20}}} = -3.46$

Since P-value < 0.01, reject the null hypothesis. There is enough evidence to support the claim that the mean has changed.

18.
H_0: $\mu = 9.2$ (claim)
H_1: $\mu \neq 9.2$
$\overline{X} = 8.25$ s = 5.06
d. f. = 7
P-value > 0.50   (0.6121)
$t = \frac{\overline{X}-\mu}{\frac{s}{\sqrt{n}}} = \frac{8.25-9.2}{\frac{5.06}{\sqrt{8}}} = -0.531$

Since P-value > 0.50, do not reject the null hypothesis. There is enough evidence to support the claim that the mean number of jobs is 9.2. One reason why a person may not give the exact number of jobs is that he or she may have forgotten about a particular job.

19.
H_0: $\mu = \$15,000$
H_1: $\mu \neq \$15,000$ (claim)

$\overline{X} = \$14,347.17$ s = \$2048.54
d. f. = 11   C. V. = ± 2.201

$t = \frac{\overline{X}-\mu}{\frac{s}{\sqrt{n}}} = \frac{\$14,347.17-\$15,000}{\frac{\$2048.54}{\sqrt{12}}} = -1.10$

19. continued

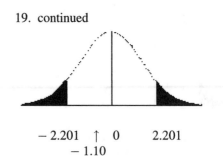

−2.201   ↑ 0   2.201
         −1.10

Do not reject the null hypothesis. There is not enough evidence to say that the average stipend differs from \$15,000.

20.
H_0: $\mu = 3.18$
H_1: $\mu \neq 3.18$ (claim)

$\overline{X} = 3.833$ s = 1.434563
d. f. = 23   C. V. = ± 2.069

$t = \frac{\overline{X}-\mu}{\frac{s}{\sqrt{n}}} = \frac{3.833-3.18}{\frac{1.434563}{\sqrt{24}}} = 2.23$

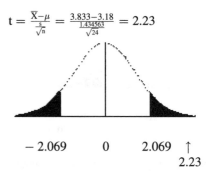

−2.069   0   2.069 ↑
                          2.23

Reject the null hypothesis. There is enough evidence to support the claim that the average family size differs from the national average.

EXERCISE SET 8-5

1.
Answers will vary.

2.
The proportion of A items can be considered a success whereas the proportion of items that are not included in A can be considered a failure.

3.
$np \geq 5$ and $nq \geq 5$

4.
$\mu = np$ $\sigma = \sqrt{npq}$

5.

H_0: $p = 0.647$

H_1: $p \neq 0.647$ (claim)

$\hat{p} = \frac{92}{150} = 0.613$ $p = 0.647$ $q = 0.353$

C. V. $= \pm 2.58$

$z = \frac{\hat{p}-p}{\sqrt{\frac{pq}{n}}} = \frac{0.613-0.647}{\sqrt{\frac{(0.647)(0.353)}{150}}} = -0.86$

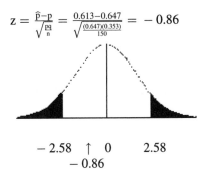

-2.58 ↑ 0   2.58
   -0.86

Do not reject the null hypothesis. There is not enough evidence to support the claim that the proportion of homeowners is different from 0.647.

6.

H_0: $p = 0.488$

H_1: $p \neq 0.488$ (claim)

$\hat{p} = \frac{142}{250} = 0.568$ $p = 0.488$ $q = 0.512$

$z = \frac{\hat{p}-p}{\sqrt{\frac{pq}{n}}} = \frac{0.568-0.488}{\sqrt{\frac{(0.488)(0.512)}{250}}} = 2.53$

Since the p-value $= 0.0114$, it can be concluded that the null hypothesis would be rejected for any $\alpha \leq 0.0114$.

7.

H_0: $p = 0.40$

H_1: $p \neq 0.40$ (claim)

$\hat{p} = \frac{65}{180} = 0.361$ $p = 0.40$ $q = 0.60$

C. V. $= \pm 2.58$

$z = \frac{\hat{p}-p}{\sqrt{\frac{pq}{n}}} = \frac{0.361-0.40}{\sqrt{\frac{(0.40)(0.60)}{180}}} = -1.07$

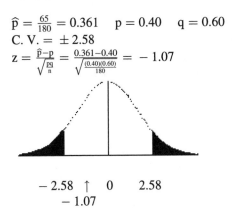

-2.58 ↑ 0   2.58
   -1.07

7. continued

Do not reject the null hypothesis. There is not enough evidence to conclude that the proportion differs from 0.40.

8.

H_0: $p \leq 0.279$

H_1: $p > 0.279$ (claim)

$\hat{p} = \frac{45}{120} = 0.375$ $p = 0.279$ $q = 0.721$

C. V. $= 1.65$

$z = \frac{\hat{p}-p}{\sqrt{\frac{pq}{n}}} = \frac{0.375-0.279}{\sqrt{\frac{(0.279)(0.721)}{120}}} = 2.35$

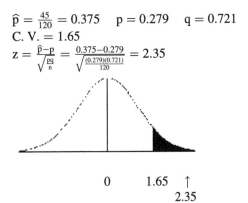

0   1.65 ↑
              2.35

Reject the null hypothesis. There is enough evidence to conclude that the proportion of female physicians at the university health system is higher than 27.9%.

9.

H_0: $p = 0.63$ (claim)

H_1: $p \neq 0.63$

$\hat{p} = \frac{85}{143} = 0.5944$ $p = 0.63$ $q = 0.37$

C. V. $= \pm 1.96$

$z = \frac{\hat{p}-p}{\sqrt{\frac{pq}{n}}} = \frac{0.5944-0.63}{\sqrt{\frac{(0.63)(0.37)}{143}}} = -0.88$

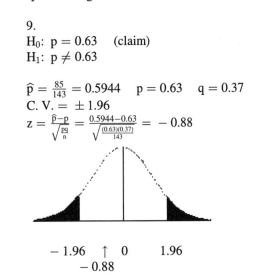

-1.96 ↑ 0   1.96
   -0.88

Do not reject the null hypothesis. There is not enough evidence to reject the claim that the percentage is the same.

10.

H_0: $p = 0.17$ (claim)

H_1: $p \neq 0.17$

$\hat{p} = \frac{22}{90} = 0.2444$ $p = 0.17$ $q = 0.83$

C. V. $= \pm 1.96$

10. continued

$$z = \frac{\hat{p}-p}{\sqrt{\frac{pq}{n}}} = \frac{0.2444-0.17}{\sqrt{\frac{(0.17)(0.83)}{90}}} = 1.88$$

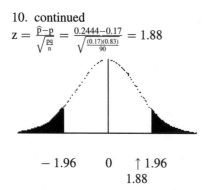

$-1.96 \qquad 0 \qquad \uparrow 1.96$
$\qquad\qquad\qquad 1.88$

Do not reject the null hypothesis. There is not enough evidence to reject the claim that the percentage is the same.

11.
H_0: $p = 0.54$
H_1: $p \neq 0.54$ (claim)

$\hat{p} = \frac{14}{30} = 0.4667$ $\qquad p = 0.54$ $\qquad q = 0.46$
C. V. $= \pm 1.96$
$z = \frac{\hat{p}-p}{\sqrt{\frac{pq}{n}}} = \frac{0.4667-0.54}{\sqrt{\frac{(0.54)(0.46)}{30}}} = -0.81$

$-1.96 \quad \uparrow \quad 0 \qquad 1.96$
$\qquad -0.81$

Do not reject the null hypothesis. There is not enough evidence to reject the claim that 54% of fatal car/truck accidents are caused by driver error.

12.
H_0: $p = 0.14$ (claim)
H_1: $p \neq 0.14$

$\hat{p} = \frac{10}{100} = 0.10$ $\qquad p = 0.14$ $\qquad q = 0.86$
$z = \frac{\hat{p}-p}{\sqrt{\frac{pq}{n}}} = \frac{0.10-0.14}{\sqrt{\frac{(0.14)(0.86)}{100}}} = -1.15$
Area $= 0.3749$
P-value $= 2(0.5 - 0.3749) = 0.2502$
Do not reject the null hypothesis. There is not enough evidence to reject the claim that 14% of men use exercise to relieve stress. The results cannot be generalized to all adults since only men were surveyed.

13.
H_0: $p = 0.54$ (claim)
H_1: $p \neq 0.54$

$\hat{p} = \frac{36}{60} = 0.6$ $\qquad p = 0.54$ $\qquad q = 0.46$
$z = \frac{\hat{p}-p}{\sqrt{\frac{pq}{n}}} = \frac{0.6-0.54}{\sqrt{\frac{(0.54)(0.46)}{60}}} = 0.93$
Area $= 0.3238$
P-value $= 2(0.5 - 0.3238) = 0.3524$
Do not reject the null hypothesis. There is not enough evidence to reject the claim that 54% of kids had a snack after school. Yes, a healthy snack should be made available for children to eat after school.

14.
H_0: $p = 0.517$ (claim)
H_1: $p \neq 0.517$

$\hat{p} = \frac{115}{200} = 0.575$ $\qquad p = 0.517$ $\qquad q = 0.483$
$z = \frac{\hat{p}-p}{\sqrt{\frac{pq}{n}}} = \frac{0.575-0.517}{\sqrt{\frac{(0.517)(0.483)}{200}}} = 1.64$
Area $= 0.4495$
P-value $= 2(0.5 - 0.4495) = 0.101$
Do not reject the null hypothesis. There is not enough evidence to reject the claim that 51.7% of homes in America were heated by natural gas. The evidence supports the claim. The conclusion could be different if the sample is taken in an area where natural gas is not commonly used to heat homes.

15.
H_0: $p = 0.18$ (claim)
H_1: $p \neq 0.18$

$\hat{p} = \frac{50}{300} = 0.1667$ $\qquad p = 0.18$ $\qquad q = 0.82$
$z = \frac{\hat{p}-p}{\sqrt{\frac{pq}{n}}} = \frac{0.1667-0.18}{\sqrt{\frac{(0.18)(0.82)}{300}}} = -0.60$
Area $= 0.2257$
P-value $= 2(0.5 - 0.2257) = 0.5486$
Since P-value > 0.05, do not reject the null hypothesis. There is not enough evidence to reject the claim that 18% of all high school students smoke at least a pack of cigarettes a day.

16.
H_0: $p \geq 0.83$
H_1: $p < 0.83$ (claim)

$\hat{p} = \frac{40}{50} = 0.8$ $\qquad p = 0.83$ $\qquad q = 0.17$
C. V. $= -1.75$

16. continued

$$z = \frac{\hat{p}-p}{\sqrt{\frac{pq}{n}}} = \frac{0.8-0.83}{\sqrt{\frac{(0.83)(0.17)}{50}}} = -0.56$$

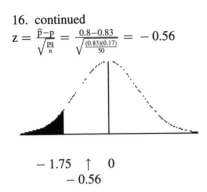

$$\begin{array}{ccc} -1.75 & \uparrow & 0 \\ & -0.56 & \end{array}$$

Do not reject the null hypothesis. There is not enough evidence to support the claim that the percentage is less than 83%.

17.
H_0: $p = 0.67$
H_1: $p \neq 0.67$ (claim)

$\hat{p} = \frac{82}{100} = 0.82$ $p = 0.67$ $q = 0.33$
C. V. $= \pm 1.96$
$$z = \frac{\hat{p}-p}{\sqrt{\frac{pq}{n}}} = \frac{0.82-0.67}{\sqrt{\frac{(0.67)(0.33)}{100}}} = 3.19$$

$$\begin{array}{cccc} -1.96 & 0 & 1.96 & \uparrow \\ & & & 3.19 \end{array}$$

Reject the null hypothesis. There is enough evidence to support the claim that the percentage is not 67%.

18.
H_0: $p \geq 0.6$
H_1: $p < 0.6$ (claim)

$\hat{p} = \frac{26}{50} = 0.52$ $p = 0.6$ $q = 0.4$
C. V. $= -1.65$
$$z = \frac{\hat{p}-p}{\sqrt{\frac{pq}{n}}} = \frac{0.52-0.6}{\sqrt{\frac{(0.6)(0.4)}{50}}} = -1.15$$

$$\begin{array}{ccc} -1.65 & \uparrow & 0 \\ & -1.15 & \end{array}$$

18. continued
Do not reject the null hypothesis. There is not enough evidence to support the claim that the percentage of paid assistantships is below 60%.

19.
H_0: $p \geq 0.576$
H_1: $p < 0.576$ (claim)

$\hat{p} = \frac{17}{36} = 0.472$ $p = 0.576$ $q = 0.424$
C. V. $= -1.65$
$$z = \frac{\hat{p}-p}{\sqrt{\frac{pq}{n}}} = \frac{0.472-0.576}{\sqrt{\frac{(0.576)(0.424)}{36}}} = -1.26$$

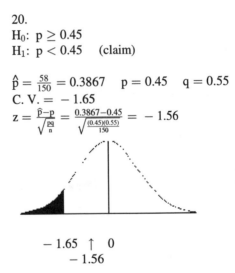

$$\begin{array}{ccc} -1.65 & \uparrow & 0 \\ & -1.26 & \end{array}$$

Do not reject the null hypothesis. There is not enough evidence to support the claim that the percentage of injuries during practice is below 57.6%.

20.
H_0: $p \geq 0.45$
H_1: $p < 0.45$ (claim)

$\hat{p} = \frac{58}{150} = 0.3867$ $p = 0.45$ $q = 0.55$
C. V. $= -1.65$
$$z = \frac{\hat{p}-p}{\sqrt{\frac{pq}{n}}} = \frac{0.3867-0.45}{\sqrt{\frac{(0.45)(0.55)}{150}}} = -1.56$$

$$\begin{array}{ccc} -1.65 & \uparrow & 0 \\ & -1.56 & \end{array}$$

Do not reject the null hypothesis. There is not enough evidence to support the claim that the proportion is below 45%.

21.
This represents a binomial distribution with $p = 0.50$ and $n = 9$. The P-value is
$2 \cdot P(X \leq 3) = 2(0.254) = 0.508$.

21. continued

Since P-value > 0.10, the conclusion that the coin is not balanced is probably false.

22.

This represents a binomial distribution with $p = 0.20$ and $n = 15$. The P-value is $2 \cdot P(X > 5) = 2(0.061) = 0.122$, which is greater than $\alpha = 0.10$. There is not enough evidence to conclude that the proportions have changed.

23.

$$z = \frac{X - \mu}{\sigma}$$

$$z = \frac{X - np}{\sqrt{npq}} \text{ since } \mu = np \text{ and } \sigma = \sqrt{npq}$$

$$z = \frac{\frac{X}{n} - \frac{np}{n}}{\frac{1}{n}\sqrt{npq}}$$

$$z = \frac{\frac{X}{n} - \frac{np}{n}}{\sqrt{\frac{npq}{n^2}}}$$

$$z = \frac{\widehat{p} - p}{\sqrt{\frac{pq}{n}}} \text{ since } \widehat{p} = \frac{X}{n}$$

EXERCISE SET 8-6

1.

a. H_0: $\sigma^2 \leq 225$
   H_1: $\sigma^2 > 225$

C. V. $= 27.587$ d. f. $= 17$

0   27.587

b. H_0: $\sigma^2 \geq 225$
   H_1: $\sigma^2 < 225$

C. V. $= 14.042$ d. f. $= 22$

0 14.042

1. continued

c. H_0: $\sigma^2 = 225$
   H_1: $\sigma^2 \neq 225$

C. V. $= 5.629, 26.119$ d. f. $= 14$

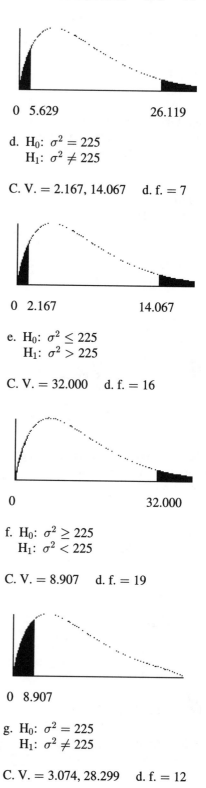

0 5.629   26.119

d. H_0: $\sigma^2 = 225$
   H_1: $\sigma^2 \neq 225$

C. V. $= 2.167, 14.067$ d. f. $= 7$

0 2.167   14.067

e. H_0: $\sigma^2 \leq 225$
   H_1: $\sigma^2 > 225$

C. V. $= 32.000$ d. f. $= 16$

0   32.000

f. H_0: $\sigma^2 \geq 225$
   H_1: $\sigma^2 < 225$

C. V. $= 8.907$ d. f. $= 19$

0 8.907

g. H_0: $\sigma^2 = 225$
   H_1: $\sigma^2 \neq 225$

C. V. $= 3.074, 28.299$ d. f. $= 12$

1g. continued

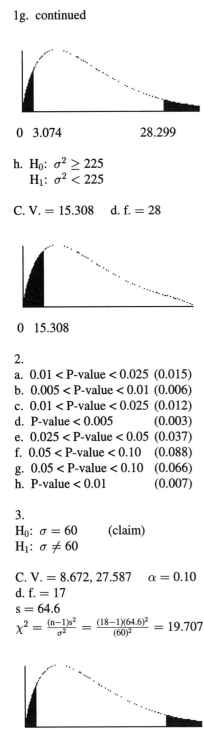

0   3.074   28.299

h. H_0: $\sigma^2 \geq 225$
    H_1: $\sigma^2 < 225$

C. V. = 15.308   d. f. = 28

0   15.308

2.
a. $0.01 < \text{P-value} < 0.025$ (0.015)
b. $0.005 < \text{P-value} < 0.01$ (0.006)
c. $0.01 < \text{P-value} < 0.025$ (0.012)
d. $\text{P-value} < 0.005$ (0.003)
e. $0.025 < \text{P-value} < 0.05$ (0.037)
f. $0.05 < \text{P-value} < 0.10$ (0.088)
g. $0.05 < \text{P-value} < 0.10$ (0.066)
h. $\text{P-value} < 0.01$ (0.007)

3.
H_0: $\sigma = 60$ (claim)
H_1: $\sigma \neq 60$

C. V. = 8.672, 27.587 $\alpha = 0.10$
d. f. = 17
s = 64.6
$\chi^2 = \frac{(n-1)s^2}{\sigma^2} = \frac{(18-1)(64.6)^2}{(60)^2} = 19.707$

0   8.672   ↑   27.587
                  19.707

Do not reject the null hypothesis. There is
not enough evidence to reject the claim that
the standard deviation is 60.

4.
H_0: $\sigma^2 \leq 140$
H_1: $\sigma^2 > 140$ (claim)

C. V. = 26.217 $\alpha = 0.01$ d. f. = 12

$\chi^2 = \frac{(n-1)s^2}{\sigma^2} = \frac{(13-1)(146)}{140} = 12.514$

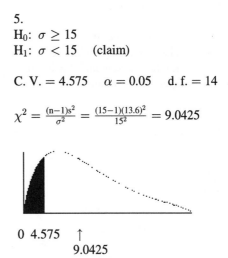

0   ↑   26.217
              12.514

Do not reject the null hypothesis. There is
not enough evidence to support the claim
that the variance is greater than 140.
Weather conditions can affect the number of
forest fires.

5.
H_0: $\sigma \geq 15$
H_1: $\sigma < 15$ (claim)

C. V. = 4.575 $\alpha = 0.05$ d. f. = 14

$\chi^2 = \frac{(n-1)s^2}{\sigma^2} = \frac{(15-1)(13.6)^2}{15^2} = 9.0425$

0 4.575   ↑
           9.0425

Do not reject the null hypothesis. There is
not enough evidence to support the claim
that the standard deviation is less than 15.

6.
H_0: $\sigma \geq 10$
H_1: $\sigma < 10$ (claim)

C. V. = 8.672 $\alpha = 0.05$ d. f. = 17

$\chi^2 = \frac{(n-1)s^2}{\sigma^2} = \frac{(18-1)(72.222)}{10} = 12.278$

6. continued

0 8.672 ↑
        12.278

Do not reject the null hypothesis. There is
not enough evidence to support the claim
that the standard deviation of the weights is
less than 10 pounds.

7.
H_0: $\sigma \leq 1.2$ (claim)
H_1: $\sigma > 1.2$

$\alpha = 0.01$ d. f. = 14
$\chi^2 = \frac{(n-1)s^2}{\sigma^2} = \frac{(15-1)(1.8)^2}{(1.2)^2} = 31.5$
P-value < 0.005   (0.0047)

Since P-value < 0.01, reject the null
hypothesis. There is enough evidence to
reject the claim that the standard deviation is
less than or equal to 1.2 minutes.

8.
H_0: $\sigma \leq 0.03$ (claim)
H_1: $\sigma > 0.03$

s = 0.043
$\alpha = 0.05$ d. f. = 7
$\chi^2 = \frac{(n-1)s^2}{\sigma^2} = \frac{(7)(0.043)^2}{0.03^2} = 14.381$
0.025 < P-value < 0.05   (0.045)

Since P-value < 0.05, reject the null
hypothesis. There is enough evidence to
reject the claim that the standard deviation is
less than or equal to 0.03 ounce.

9.
H_0: $\sigma \leq 20$
H_1: $\sigma > 20$ (claim)

s = 35.11
C. V. = 36.191 $\alpha = 0.01$ d. f. = 19
$\chi^2 = \frac{(n-1)s^2}{\sigma^2} = \frac{(20-1)(35.11)^2}{20^2} = 58.55$

9. continued

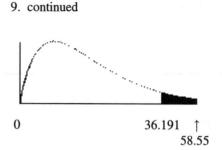

0   36.191   ↑
                                      58.55

Reject the null hypothesis. There is enough
evidence to support the claim that the
standard deviation is more than 20 calories.

10.
H_0: $\sigma \geq 10$
H_1: $\sigma < 10$ (claim)

s = 5.407
C. V. = 2.204 $\alpha = 0.10$ d. f. = 6
$\chi^2 = \frac{(n-1)s^2}{\sigma^2} = \frac{(7-1)(5.407)^2}{20^2} = 1.754$

0 ↑ 2.204
  1.754

Reject the null hypothesis. There is enough
evidence to support the claim that the
standard deviation is less than 10°.

11.
H_0: $\sigma \geq 35$
H_1: $\sigma < 35$ (claim)

C. V. = 3.940 $\alpha = 0.05$ d. f. = 10
$\chi^2 = \frac{(n-1)s^2}{\sigma^2} = \frac{(11-1)(32)^2}{35^2} = 8.3592$

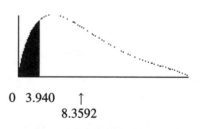

0 3.940   ↑
           8.3592

Do not reject the null hypothesis. There is
not enough evidence to support the claim
that the standard deviation is less than 35.

12.
H_0: $\sigma \leq 8$
H_1: $\sigma > 8$ (claim)

C. V. = 55.758 $\quad \alpha = 0.05 \quad$ d. f. = 49
$\chi^2 = \frac{(n-1)s^2}{\sigma^2} = \frac{(50-1)(10.5)^2}{8^2} = 84.41$

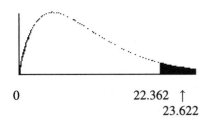

0 $\qquad\qquad$ 55.758 $\uparrow$
$\qquad\qquad\qquad\qquad$ 84.41

Reject the null hypothesis. There is enough evidence to support the claim that the standard deviation is more than 8.

13.
H_0: $\sigma^2 \leq 25$
H_1: $\sigma^2 > 25$ (claim)

C. V. = 22.362 $\quad \alpha = 0.05 \quad$ d. f. = 13
$\chi^2 = \frac{(n-1)s^2}{\sigma^2} = \frac{(14-1)(6.74)^2}{25} = 23.622$

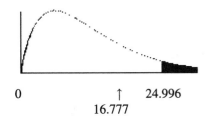

0 $\qquad\qquad$ 22.362 $\uparrow$
$\qquad\qquad\qquad\qquad$ 23.622

Reject the null hypothesis. There is enough evidence to support the claim that the variance is greater than 25.

14.
H_0: $\sigma \leq 4$
H_1: $\sigma > 4$ (claim)

C. V. = 24.996 $\quad \alpha = 0.05 \quad$ d. f. = 15
$\chi^2 = \frac{(n-1)s^2}{\sigma^2} = \frac{(16-1)(4.2303)^2}{4^2} = 16.777$

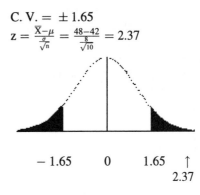

0 $\qquad\qquad$ $\uparrow$ $\quad$ 24.996
$\qquad\qquad$ 16.777

14. continued
Do not reject the null hypothesis. There is not enough evidence to support the claim that the standard deviation exceeds 4.

EXERCISE SET 8-7

1.
H_0: $\mu = 1800$ (claim)
H_1: $\mu \neq 1800$

C. V. = ± 1.96
$z = \frac{\overline{X} - \mu}{\frac{\sigma}{\sqrt{n}}} = \frac{1830 - 1800}{\frac{200}{\sqrt{10}}} = 0.47$

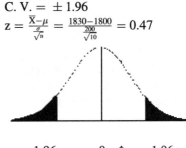

$-1.96 \qquad 0 \uparrow \qquad 1.96$
$\qquad\qquad 0.47$

The 95% confidence interval of the mean is:
$\overline{X} - z_{\frac{\alpha}{2}} \frac{\sigma}{\sqrt{n}} < \mu < \overline{X} + z_{\frac{\alpha}{2}} \frac{\sigma}{\sqrt{n}}$

$1830 - 1.96 \left(\frac{200}{\sqrt{10}}\right) < \mu < $
$\qquad\qquad\qquad 1830 + 1.96 \left(\frac{200}{\sqrt{10}}\right)$

$1706.04 < \mu < 1953.96$

Do not reject. There is not enough evidence to reject the claim that the mean is $1800. The hypothesized mean is within the interval, thus we can be 95% confident that the average sales will be between $1706.94 and $1953.96.

2.
H_0: $\mu = 42$ (claim)
H_1: $\mu \neq 42$

C. V. = ± 1.65
$z = \frac{\overline{X} - \mu}{\frac{\sigma}{\sqrt{n}}} = \frac{48 - 42}{\frac{8}{\sqrt{10}}} = 2.37$

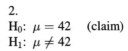

$-1.65 \qquad 0 \qquad 1.65 \quad \uparrow$
$\qquad\qquad\qquad\qquad 2.37$

2. continued

The 90% confidence interval of the mean is:

$$\overline{X} - z_{\frac{\alpha}{2}}\frac{\sigma}{\sqrt{n}} < \mu < \overline{X} + z_{\frac{\alpha}{2}}\frac{\sigma}{\sqrt{n}}$$

$$48 - 1.65 \cdot \frac{8}{\sqrt{10}} < \mu < 48 + 1.65 \cdot \frac{8}{\sqrt{10}}$$

$$43.83 < \mu < 52.17$$

The decision is to reject the null hypothesis at $\alpha = 0.10$ since $2.37 > 1.65$ and the 90% confidence interval of the mean does not contain the hypothesized mean of 42.

There is agreement between the z-test and the confidence interval. The conclusion then is that there is enough evidence to reject the claim that the mean time is still the same.

3.

H_0: $\mu = 86$ (claim)

H_1: $\mu \neq 86$

C. V. $= \pm 2.58$

$$z = \frac{\overline{X} - \mu}{\frac{\sigma}{\sqrt{n}}} = \frac{84 - 86}{\frac{6}{\sqrt{15}}} = -1.29$$

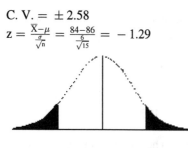

$$-2.58 \quad \uparrow \quad 0 \quad 2.58$$
$$-1.29$$

$$\overline{X} - z_{\frac{\alpha}{2}}\frac{\sigma}{\sqrt{n}} < \mu < \overline{X} + z_{\frac{\alpha}{2}}\frac{\sigma}{\sqrt{n}}$$

$$84 - 2.58 \cdot \frac{6}{\sqrt{15}} < \mu < 84 + 1.58 \cdot \frac{6}{\sqrt{15}}$$

$$80.00 < \mu < 88.00$$

The decision is do not reject the null hypothesis since $-1.29 > -2.58$ and the 99% confidence interval contains the hypothesized mean. There is not enough evidence to reject the claim that the monthly maintenance is $86.

4.

H_0: $\mu = 47$

H_1: $\mu \neq 47$ (claim)

C. V. $= \pm 1.65$

4. continued

$$z = \frac{\overline{X} - \mu}{\frac{\sigma}{\sqrt{n}}} = \frac{42 - 47}{\frac{7}{\sqrt{10}}} = -2.26$$

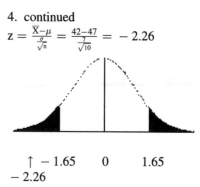

$$\uparrow -1.65 \quad 0 \quad 1.65$$
$$-2.26$$

The 90% confidence interval of the mean is:

$$\overline{X} - z_{\frac{\alpha}{2}}\frac{\sigma}{\sqrt{n}} < \mu < \overline{X} + z_{\frac{\alpha}{2}}\frac{\sigma}{\sqrt{n}}$$

$$42 - 1.65 \cdot \frac{7}{\sqrt{10}} < \mu < 42 + 1.65 \cdot \frac{7}{\sqrt{10}}$$

$$38.35 < \mu < 45.65$$

The decision is to reject the null hypothesis since $-2.26 < -1.65$ and the confidence interval does not contain the hypothesized mean of 47. There is enough evidence to support the claim that the mean has changed.

5.

H_0: $\mu = 22$

H_1: $\mu \neq 22$ (claim)

C. V. $= \pm 2.58$

$$z = \frac{\overline{X} - \mu}{\frac{\sigma}{\sqrt{n}}} = \frac{20.8 - 22}{\frac{4}{\sqrt{60}}} = -2.32$$

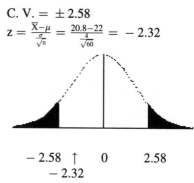

$$-2.58 \quad \uparrow \quad 0 \quad 2.58$$
$$-2.32$$

The 99% confidence interval of the mean is:

$$\overline{X} - z_{\frac{\alpha}{2}}\frac{\sigma}{\sqrt{n}} < \mu < \overline{X} + z_{\frac{\alpha}{2}}\frac{\sigma}{\sqrt{n}}$$

$$20.8 - 2.58 \cdot \frac{4}{\sqrt{60}} < \mu < 20.8 + 2.58 \cdot \frac{4}{\sqrt{60}}$$

$$19.47 < \mu < 22.13$$

5. continued

The decision is do not reject the null hypothesis since $-2.32 > -2.58$ and the 99% confidence interval does contain the hypothesized mean of 22. The conclusion is that there is not enough evidence to support the claim that the average studying time has changed.

6.
H_0: $\mu = 10.8$ (claim)
H_1: $\mu \neq 10.8$

C. V. $= \pm 2.33$
$z = \frac{\overline{X}-\mu}{\frac{\sigma}{\sqrt{n}}} = \frac{12.2-10.8}{\frac{3}{\sqrt{36}}} = 2.80$

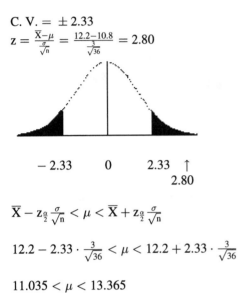

$$-2.33 \qquad 0 \qquad 2.33 \uparrow$$
$$2.80$$

$$\overline{X} - z_{\frac{\alpha}{2}}\frac{\sigma}{\sqrt{n}} < \mu < \overline{X} + z_{\frac{\alpha}{2}}\frac{\sigma}{\sqrt{n}}$$

$$12.2 - 2.33 \cdot \frac{3}{\sqrt{36}} < \mu < 12.2 + 2.33 \cdot \frac{3}{\sqrt{36}}$$

$$11.035 < \mu < 13.365$$

The decision is to reject the null hypothesis since $2.80 > 2.33$ and the confidence interval does not contain the hypothesized mean 10.8. The conclusion is that there is enough evidence to reject the claim that the average time a person spends reading a newspaper is 10.8 minutes.

REVIEW EXERCISES - CHAPTER 8

1.
H_0: $\mu = 98°$ (claim)
H_1: $\mu \neq 98°$

C. V. $= \pm 1.96$
$z = \frac{\overline{X}-\mu}{\frac{s}{\sqrt{n}}} = \frac{95.8-98}{\frac{7.71}{\sqrt{50}}} = -2.02$

1. continued

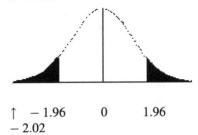

$$\uparrow \quad -1.96 \qquad 0 \qquad 1.96$$
$$-2.02$$

Reject the null hypothesis. There is enough evidence to reject the claim that the average high temperature is 98°.

2.
H_0: $\mu = 500$ (claim)
H_1: $\mu \neq 500$

C. V. $= \pm 1.96$
$z = \frac{\overline{X}-\mu}{\frac{s}{\sqrt{n}}} = \frac{506-500}{\frac{10.3}{\sqrt{40}}} = 3.684$

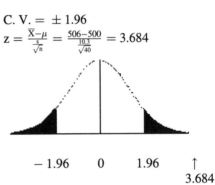

$$-1.96 \qquad 0 \qquad 1.96 \qquad \uparrow$$
$$3.684$$

Reject the null hypothesis. There is enough evidence to reject the claim that the average number of shares traded daily is 500 million. I would disagree with the broker's claim.

3.
H_0: $\mu \leq \$40,000$
H_1: $\mu > \$40,000$ (claim)

C. V. $= 1.65$
$z = \frac{\overline{X}-\mu}{\frac{\sigma}{\sqrt{n}}} = \frac{\$41,000-\$40,000}{\frac{\$3000}{\sqrt{36}}} = 2.00$

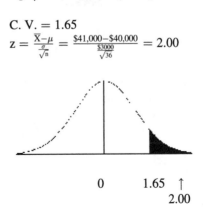

$$0 \qquad 1.65 \uparrow$$
$$2.00$$

3. continued

Reject the null hypothesis. There is enough
evidence to support the claim that the
average salary is more than $40,000.

4.
H_0: $\mu \leq \$150,000$
H_1: $\mu > \$150,000$ (claim)

C. V. = 1.895   d. f. = 7
$t = \frac{\overline{X} - \mu}{\frac{s}{\sqrt{n}}} = \frac{155,500 - 150,000}{\frac{15,000}{\sqrt{8}}} = 1.04$

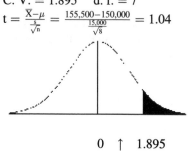

0 ↑ 1.895
1.04

Do not reject the null hypothesis. There is
not enough evidence to support the claim
that the average salary is more than
$150,000.

5.
H_0: $\mu \leq 67$
H_1: $\mu > 67$ (claim)

C. V. = 1.383   d. f. = 9
$t = \frac{\overline{X} - \mu}{\frac{s}{\sqrt{n}}} = \frac{69.6 - 67.0}{\frac{1.1}{\sqrt{10}}} = 7.47$

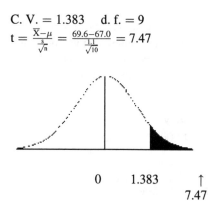

0   1.383   ↑
7.47

Reject the null hypothesis. There is enough
evidence to support the claim that 1995 was
warmer than average.

6.
H_0: $\mu \geq 32$ (claim)
H_1: $\mu < 32$

d. f. = 17
$t = \frac{\overline{X} - \mu}{\frac{s}{\sqrt{n}}} = \frac{31.3 - 32}{\frac{2.8}{\sqrt{18}}} = -1.061$

6. continued

$0.10 < \text{P-value} < 0.25$
Do not reject the null hypothesis. There is
not enough evidence to reject the claim that
the average age is 32 years.

7.
H_0: $\mu = 6$
H_1: $\mu \neq 6$ (claim)

C. V. = ± 2.821 $\overline{X} = 8.42$ $s = 4.17$
$t = \frac{\overline{X} - \mu}{\frac{s}{\sqrt{n}}} = \frac{8.42 - 6}{\frac{4.17}{\sqrt{10}}} = 1.835$

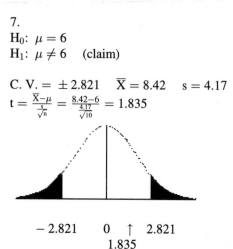

− 2.821   0 ↑ 2.821
1.835

Do not reject the null hypothesis. There is
not enough evidence to support the claim
that the average attendance has changed.

8.
H_0: $p \leq 0.585$
H_1: $p > 0.585$ (claim)

C. V. = 1.65
$\hat{p} = \frac{622}{1000} = 0.622$ $p = 0.585$ $q = 0.415$
$z = \frac{\hat{p} - p}{\sqrt{\frac{pq}{n}}} = \frac{0.622 - 0.585}{\sqrt{\frac{(0.585)(0.415)}{1000}}} = 2.37$

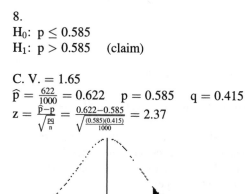

0   1.65 ↑
2.37

Reject the null hypothesis. There is enough
evidence to support the claim that the
percentage of women working is more than
58.5%.

9.
H_0: $p \leq 0.602$
H_1: $p > 0.602$ (claim)

C. V. = 1.65
$\hat{p} = 0.65$ $p = 0.602$ $q = 0.398$

9. continued

$$z = \frac{\hat{p}-p}{\sqrt{\frac{pq}{n}}} = \frac{0.65-0.602}{\sqrt{\frac{(0.602)(0.398)}{400}}} = 1.96$$

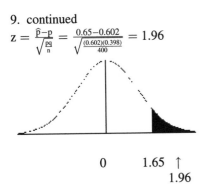

0   1.65 ↑
              1.96

Reject the null hypothesis. There is enough evidence to support the claim that the percentage of drug offenders is higher than 60.2%.

10.
H_0: $p = 0.41$ (claim)
H_1: $p \neq 0.41$

C. V. $= \pm 2.33$
$\hat{p} = \frac{15}{30} = 0.5$ $p = 0.41$ $q = 0.59$
$$z = \frac{\hat{p}-p}{\sqrt{\frac{pq}{n}}} = \frac{0.5-0.41}{\sqrt{\frac{(0.41)(0.59)}{30}}} = 1.002$$

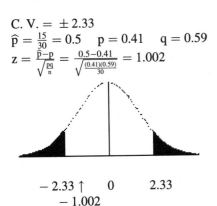

-2.33 ↑   0   2.33
   -1.002

Do not reject the null hypothesis. There is not enough evidence to reject the claim that 41% of tennis fans are female.

11.
H_0: $p = 0.65$ (claim)
H_1: $p \neq 0.65$

$\hat{p} = \frac{57}{80} = 0.7125$ $p = 0.65$ $q = 0.35$

$$z = \frac{\hat{p}-p}{\sqrt{\frac{pq}{n}}} = \frac{0.7125-0.65}{\sqrt{\frac{(0.65)(0.35)}{80}}} = 1.17$$
Area $= 0.3790$
P-value $= 2(0.5 - 0.3790) = 0.242$
Since P-value > 0.05, do not reject the null hypothesis. There is not enough evidence to reject the claim that 65% of the teenagers own their own radios.

12.
H_0: $\mu = 225$ (claim)
H_1: $\mu \neq 225$

$$z = \frac{\overline{X}-\mu}{\frac{s}{\sqrt{50}}} = \frac{230-225}{\frac{15}{\sqrt{50}}} = 2.36$$

Area $= 0.4909$
P-value $= 2(0.5 - 0.4909) = 0.0182$
Since $0.0182 > 0.01$ the decision is do not reject the null hypothesis. The conclusion is that there is not enough evidence to reject the claim that the mean is 225 pounds.

13.
H_0: $\mu \geq 10$
H_1: $\mu < 10$ (claim)

$$z = \frac{\overline{X}-\mu}{\frac{\sigma}{\sqrt{n}}} = \frac{9.25-10}{\frac{2}{\sqrt{35}}} = -2.22$$

Area $= 0.4868$
P-value $= 0.5 - 0.4699 = 0.0132$
Since $0.0132 < 0.05$, reject the null hypothesis. The conclusion is that there is enough evidence to support the claim that the average time is less than 10 minutes.

14.
H_0: $\sigma = 3.4$ (claim)
H_1: $\sigma \neq 3.4$

C. V. $= 11.689, 38.076$ d. f. $= 23$
$$\chi^2 = \frac{(n-1)s^2}{\sigma^2} = \frac{(24-1)(4.2)^2}{(3.4)^2} = 35.1$$

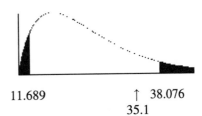

11.689   ↑ 38.076
                   35.1

Do not reject the null hypothesis. There is not enough evidence to reject the claim that the standard deviation is 3.4 minutes.

15.
H_0: $\sigma \geq 4.3$ (claim)
H_1: $\sigma < 4.3$

d. f. $= 19$
$$\chi^2 = \frac{(n-1)s^2}{\sigma^2} = \frac{(20-1)(2.6)^2}{(4.3^2)} = 6.95$$

15. continued

0.005 < P-value < 0.01   (0.006)
Since P-value < 0.05, reject the null hypothesis. There is enough evidence to reject the claim that the standard deviation is greater than or equal to 4.3 miles per gallon.

16.

H_0: $\sigma = \$95$ (claim)
H_1: $\sigma \neq \$95$

s = 89.3
C. V. = 6.408, 33.409   d. f. = 17
$\chi^2 = \frac{(n-1)s^2}{\sigma^2} = \frac{(18-1)(89.3)^2}{95^2} = 15.0212$

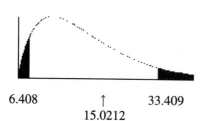

6.408   ↑   33.409
                  15.0212

Do not reject the null hypothesis. There is not enough evidence to reject the claim that the standard deviation of rental rates is $95.

17.

H_0: $\sigma = 18$ (claim)
H_1: $\sigma \neq 18$

C. V. = 11.143 and 0.484   d. f. = 4

$\chi^2 = \frac{(n-1)s^2}{\sigma^2} = \frac{(5-1)(21)^2}{18^2} = 5.44$

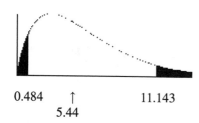

0.484   ↑   11.143
        5.44

Do not reject the null hypothesis. There is not enough evidence to reject the claim that the standard deviation is 18 minutes.

18.

H_0: $\mu = 35$ (claim)
H_1: $\mu \neq 35$

C. V. = ±1.65

18. continued

$z = \frac{\overline{X}-\mu}{\frac{s}{\sqrt{n}}} = \frac{33.5-35}{\frac{3}{\sqrt{36}}} = -3.00$

The 90% confidence interval of the mean is:

$$\overline{X} - z_{\frac{\alpha}{2}}\frac{\sigma}{\sqrt{n}} < \mu < \overline{X} + z_{\frac{\alpha}{2}}\frac{\sigma}{\sqrt{n}}$$

$$33.5 - 1.65 \cdot \frac{3}{\sqrt{36}} < \mu < 33.5 + 1.65 \cdot \frac{3}{\sqrt{36}}$$

$$32.675 < \mu < 34.325$$

The decision is to reject the null hypothesis since $-3.00 < -1.65$ and the 90% confidence interval does not contain the hypothesized mean of 35. The conclusion is that there is enough evidence to reject the claim that the mean is 35 pounds.

19.

H_0: $\mu = 4$
H_1: $\mu \neq 4$ (claim)

C. V. = ±2.58
$z = \frac{\overline{X}-\mu}{\frac{s}{\sqrt{n}}} = \frac{4.2-4}{\frac{0.6}{\sqrt{20}}} = 1.49$

The 99% confidence interval of the mean is:

$$\overline{X} - z_{\frac{\alpha}{2}}\frac{\sigma}{\sqrt{n}} < \mu < \overline{X} + z_{\frac{\alpha}{2}}\frac{\sigma}{\sqrt{n}}$$

$$4.2 - 2.58 \cdot \frac{0.6}{\sqrt{20}} < \mu < 4.2 + 2.58 \cdot \frac{0.6}{\sqrt{20}}$$
$$3.85 < \mu < 4.55$$

The decision is do not reject the null hypothesis since 1.49 < 2.58 and the confidence interval does contain the hypothesized mean of 4. There is not enough evidence to support the claim that the growth has changed.

CHAPTER 8 QUIZ

1. True
2. True
3. False, the critical value separates the critical region from the noncritical region.
4. True
5. False, it can be one-tailed or two-tailed.
6. b
7. d
8. c
9. b
10. Type I

146

11. β

12. Statistical hypothesis

13. Right

14. $n - 1$

15. H_0: $\mu = 28.6$ (claim)
H_1: $\mu \neq 28.6$
C. V. $= \pm 1.96$
$z = 2.14$
Reject the null hypothesis. There is enough evidence to reject the claim that the average age is 28.6.

16. H_0: $\mu = \$6,500$ (claim)
H_1: $\mu \neq \$6,500$
C. V. $= \pm 1.96$
$z = 5.27$
Reject the null hypothesis. There is enough evidence to reject the agent's claim.

17. H_0: $\mu \leq 8$
H_1: $\mu > 8$ (claim)
C. V. $= 1.65$
$z = 6.00$
Reject the null hypothesis. There is enough evidence to support the claim that the average number of sticks is greater than 8.

18. H_0: $\mu = 500$ (claim)
H_1: $\mu \neq 500$
C. V. $= \pm 3.707$
$t = -0.571$
Do not reject the null hypothesis. There is not enough evidence to reject the claim that the average is 500.

19. H_0: $\mu \geq 67$
H_1: $\mu < 67$ (claim)
$t = -3.1568$
P-value < 0.005 (0.003)
Since P-value < 0.05, reject the null hypothesis. There is enough evidence to support the claim that the average height is less than 67 inches.

20. H_0: $\mu \geq 12.4$
H_1: $\mu < 12.4$ (claim)
C. V. $= -1.345$
$t = -2.324$
Reject the null hypothesis. There is enough evidence to support the claim that the average is less than what the company claimed.

21. H_0: $\mu \leq 63.5$
H_1: $\mu > 63.5$ (claim)
$t = 0.47075$
P-value > 0.25 (0.322)
Since P-value > 0.05, do not reject the null hypothesis. There is not enough evidence to support the claim that the average is greater than 63.5.

22. H_0: $\mu = 26$ (claim)
H_1: $\mu \neq 26$
C. V. $= \pm 2.492$
$t = -1.5$
Do not reject the null hypothesis. There is not enough evidence to reject the claim that the average age is 26.

23. H_0: $p = 0.39$ (claim)
H_1: $p \neq 0.39$
C. V. $= \pm 1.96$
$z = -0.62$
Do not reject the null hypothesis. There is not enough evidence to reject the claim that 39% took supplements. The study supports the results of the previous study.

24. H_0: $p \geq 0.55$ (claim)
H_1: $p < 0.55$
C. V. $= -1.28$
$z = -0.899$
Do not reject the null hypothesis. There is not enough evidence to reject the survey's claim.

25. H_0: $p = 0.35$ (claim)
H_1: $p \neq 0.35$
C. V. $= \pm 2.33$
$z = 0.666$
Do not reject the null hypothesis. There is not enough evidence to reject the claim that the proportion is 35%.

26. H_0: $p = 0.75$ (claim)
H_1: $p \neq 0.75$
C. V. $= \pm 2.58$
$z = 2.6833$
Reject the null hypothesis. there is enough evidence to reject the claim.

27. The area corresponding to $z = 2.14$ is 0.4838.
P-value $= 2(0.5 - 0.4838) = 0.0324$

28. The area corresponding to $z = 5.27$ is greater than 0.4999.
Thus, P-value $\leq 2(0.5 - 0.4999) \leq 0.0002$.
(Note: Calculators give 0.0001)

29. H_0: $\sigma \leq 6$
H_1: $\sigma > 6$ (claim)
C. V. $= 36.415$
$\chi^2 = 54$
Reject the null hypothesis. There is enough evidence to support the claim that the standard deviation is more than 6 pages.

30. H_0: $\sigma = 8$ (claim)
H_1: $\sigma \neq 8$
C. V. $= 27.991, 79.490$
$\chi^2 = 33.2$
Do not reject the null hypothesis. There is not enough evidence to reject the claim that $\sigma = 8$.

31. H_0: $\sigma \geq 2.3$
H_1: $\sigma < 2.3$ (claim)
C. V. $= 10.117$
$\chi^2 = 13$
Do not reject the null hypothesis. There is not enough evidence to support the claim that the standard deviation is less than 2.3.

32. H_0: $\sigma = 9$ (claim)
H_1: $\sigma \neq 9$
$\chi^2 = 13.4$
P-value > 0.20 (0.291)
Since P-value > 0.05, do not reject the null hypothesis. There is not enough evidence to reject the claim that $\sigma = 9$.

33. $28.9 < \mu < 31.2$; no

34. $\$6562.81 < \mu < \$6,637.19$; no

Chapter 9 - Testing the Difference Between
Two Means, Two Variances, and Two Proportions

Note: Graphs are not to scale and are
intended to convey a general idea.
Answers may vary due to rounding, TI-83's,
or computer programs.

EXERCISE SET 9-2

1.

Testing a single mean involves comparing a
sample mean to a specific value such as
$\mu = 100$; whereas testing the difference
between means means comparing the means
of two samples such as $\mu_1 = \mu_2$.

2.

When both samples are greater than or equal
to 30 the distribution will be approximately
normal. The mean of the differences will be
equal to zero. The standard deviation of the
differences will be $\sqrt{\frac{\sigma_1^2}{n_1} + \frac{\sigma_2^2}{n_2}}$.

3.

The populations must be independent of
each other and they must be normally
distributed. s_1 and s_2 can be used in place of
σ_1 and σ_2 when σ_1 and σ_2 are unknown and
both samples are each greater than or equal
to 30.

4.

$H_0: \mu_1 = \mu_2$ or $H_0: \mu_1 - \mu_2 = 0$

5.

$H_0: \mu_1 = \mu_2$ (claim)
$H_1: \mu_1 \neq \mu_2$

C. V. $= \pm 2.58$

$\overline{X}_1 = 662.6111$ $\overline{X}_2 = 758.875$
$s_1 = 449.8703$ $s_2 = 474.1258$

$z = \frac{(\overline{X}_1-\overline{X}_2)-(\mu_1-\mu_2)}{\sqrt{\frac{\sigma_1^2}{n_1} + \frac{\sigma_2^2}{n_2}}} = \frac{(662.6111-758.875)-0}{\sqrt{\frac{449.8703^2}{36} + \frac{474.1258^2}{36}}} =$

$z = -0.88$
(TI83 answer is $z = -0.856$)

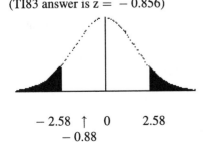

-2.58 ↑ 0 2.58
-0.88

5. continued
Do not reject the null hypothesis. There is
not enough evidence to reject the claim that
the average lengths of the rivers is the same.

6.
$H_0: \mu_1 = \mu_2$
$H_1: \mu_1 \neq \mu_2$ (claim)

C. V. $= \pm 1.65$

$z = \frac{(2-1.7)-0}{\sqrt{\frac{0.6^2}{120} + \frac{0.7^2}{34}}} = 2.274$

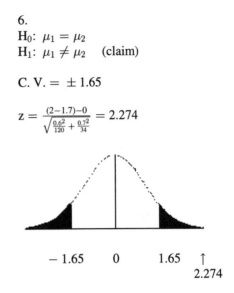

-1.65 0 1.65 ↑
              2.274

Reject the null hypothesis. There is enough
evidence to support the claim that there is a
difference in coping skills.

7.
$H_0: \mu_1 \leq \mu_2$
$H_1: \mu_1 > \mu_2$ (claim)

C. V. $= 1.65$

$z = \frac{(\overline{X}_1-\overline{X}_2)-(\mu_1-\mu_2)}{\sqrt{\frac{s_1^2}{n_1} + \frac{s_2^2}{n_2}}} = \frac{(90-88)-0}{\sqrt{\frac{5^2}{100} + \frac{6^2}{100}}} = 2.56$

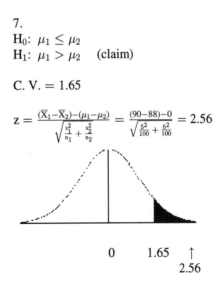

0 1.65 ↑
            2.56

Reject the null hypothesis. There is enough
evidence to support the claim that pulse rates
of smokers are higher than the pulse rates of
non-smokers.

8.
$\overline{D} = 126.2 - 123.5 = 2.7$

8. continued

$$(\overline{X}_1 - \overline{X}_2) - z_{\frac{\alpha}{2}}\sqrt{\frac{\sigma_1^2}{n_1} + \frac{\sigma_2^2}{n_2}} < \mu_1 - \mu_2 <$$
$$(\overline{X}_1 - \overline{X}_2) + z_{\frac{\alpha}{2}}\sqrt{\frac{\sigma_1^2}{n_1} + \frac{\sigma_2^2}{n_2}}$$

$$2.7 - 1.96\sqrt{\frac{98}{60} + \frac{120}{50}} < \mu_1 - \mu_2 <$$
$$2.7 + 1.96\sqrt{\frac{98}{60} + \frac{120}{50}}$$

$2.7 - 3.9363 < \mu_1 - \mu_2 < 2.7 + 3.9363$
$-1.2363 < \mu_1 - \mu_2 < 6.6363$

Yes, the interval supports the claim since 0 is contained in the interval.

9.
H_0: $\mu_1 \leq \mu_2$
H_1: $\mu_1 > \mu_2$ (claim)

C. V. = 2.05

$$z = \frac{(\overline{X}_1 - \overline{X}_2) - (\mu_1 - \mu_2)}{\sqrt{\frac{s_1^2}{n_1} + \frac{s_2^2}{n_2}}} = \frac{(61.2 - 59.4) - 0}{\sqrt{\frac{7.9^2}{84} + \frac{7.9^2}{34}}} = 1.12$$

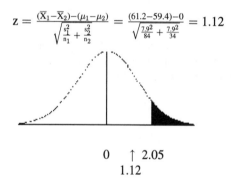

0   ↑ 2.05
      1.12

Do not reject the null hypothesis. There is not enough evidence to support the claim that noise levels in the corridors are higher than in the clinics.

10.
H_0: $\mu_1 = \mu_2$ (claim)
H_1: $\mu_1 \neq \mu_2$

C. V. = ±2.58

$$z = \frac{(93430 - 98043) - 0}{\sqrt{\frac{5602^2}{35} + \frac{4731^2}{40}}} = -3.82$$

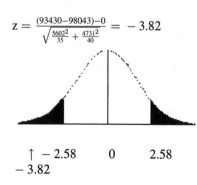

↑ −2.58   0   2.58
−3.82

10. continued
Reject the null hypothesis. There is enough evidence to reject the claim that the average costs are the same.

11.
H_0: $\mu_1 \geq \mu_2$
H_1: $\mu_1 < \mu_2$ (claim)

C. V. = −1.65

$$z = \frac{(\overline{X}_1 - \overline{X}_2) - (\mu_1 - \mu_2)}{\sqrt{\frac{s_1^2}{n_1} + \frac{s_2^2}{n_2}}} = \frac{(3.16 - 3.28) - 0}{\sqrt{\frac{0.52^2}{103} + \frac{0.46^2}{225}}} = -2.01$$

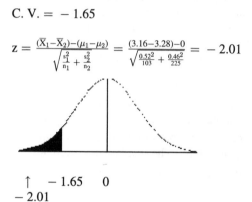

↑   −1.65   0
−2.01

Reject the null hypothesis. There is enough evidence to support the claim that stayers have a higher GPA than leavers.

12.
H_0: $\mu_1 \leq \mu_2$
H_1: $\mu_1 > \mu_2$ (claim)

C. V. = 1.65
$\overline{X}_1 = 21.4$ $\overline{X}_2 = 20.8$
$s_1 = 3$ $s_2 = 3$

$$z = \frac{(21.4 - 20.8) - 0}{\sqrt{\frac{3^2}{1000} + \frac{3^2}{500}}} = 3.65$$

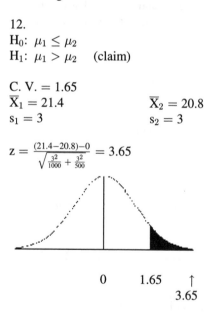

0   1.65   ↑
            3.65

Reject the null hypothesis. There is enough evidence to support the claim that ACT scores for Ohio students are below the national average.

13.
H_0: $\mu_1 \leq \mu_2$
H_1: $\mu_1 > \mu_2$ (claim)

13. continued

C. V. = 2.33

$\overline{X}_1 = \$9224$ $\overline{X}_2 = \$8497.5$

$s_1 = 3829.826$ $s_2 = 2745.293$

$$z = \frac{(\overline{X}_1 - \overline{X}_2) - (\mu_1 - \mu_2)}{\sqrt{\frac{s_1^2}{n_1} + \frac{s_2^2}{n_2}}}$$

$$z = \frac{(9224 - 8497.5) - 0}{\sqrt{\frac{3829.826^2}{50} + \frac{2745.293^2}{50}}} = 1.09$$

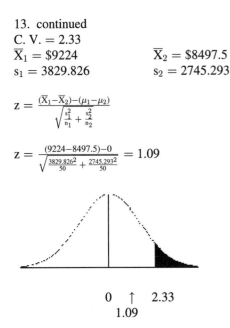

0   ↑   2.33
   1.09

Do not reject the null hypothesis. There is not enough evidence to support the claim that colleges spent more money on men's sports than women's.

14.

H_0: $\mu_1 = \mu_2$

H_1: $\mu_1 \neq \mu_2$ (claim)

$$z = \frac{(837 - 753) - 0}{\sqrt{\frac{30^2}{35} + \frac{40^2}{40}}} = 10.36$$

Area > 0.4999

P-value = 2(0.5 − 0.4999) < 0.0002

Reject the null hypothesis. There is enough evidence to support the claim that there is a difference in the average miles traveled for each of the two taxi companies.

15.

H_0: $\mu_1 = \mu_2$

H_1: $\mu_1 \neq \mu_2$ (claim)

$$z = \frac{(\overline{X}_1 - \overline{X}_2) - (\mu_1 - \mu_2)}{\sqrt{\frac{s_1^2}{n_1} + \frac{s_2^2}{n_2}}} = \frac{(3.05 - 2.96) - 0}{\sqrt{\frac{0.75^2}{103} + \frac{0.75^2}{225}}}$$

z = 1.01

Area = 0.3438

P-value = 2(0.5 − 0.3438) = 0.3124

Do not reject the null hypothesis. There is not enough evidence to support the claim that there is a difference in scores.

16.

Residents	Commuters
$\overline{X}_1 = 22.12$	$\overline{X}_2 = 22.76$
$s_1 = 3.68$	$s_2 = 4.70$
$n_1 = 50$	$n_2 = 50$

H_0: $\mu_1 = \mu_2$ (claim)

H_1: $\mu_1 \neq \mu_2$

$$z = \frac{(22.12 - 22.76) - 0}{\sqrt{\frac{3.68^2}{50} + \frac{4.70^2}{50}}} = -0.76$$

Area = 0.2764

P-value = 2(0.5 − 0.2764) = 0.4472

Do not reject the null hypothesis. There is not enough evidence to reject the claim that there is no difference in the ages.

17.

$\overline{D} = 83.6 - 79.2 = 4.4$

$$(\overline{X}_1 - \overline{X}_2) - z_{\frac{\alpha}{2}}\sqrt{\frac{\sigma_1^2}{n_1} + \frac{\sigma_2^2}{n_2}} < \mu_1 - \mu_2 <$$
$$(\overline{X}_1 - \overline{X}_2) + z_{\frac{\alpha}{2}}\sqrt{\frac{\sigma_1^2}{n_1} + \frac{\sigma_2^2}{n_2}}$$

$$4.4 - (1.65)\sqrt{\frac{4.3^2}{36} + \frac{3.8^2}{36}} < \mu_1 - \mu_2 <$$
$$4.4 + (1.65)\sqrt{\frac{4.3^2}{36} + \frac{3.8^2}{36}}$$

$2.8 < \mu_1 - \mu_2 < 6.0$

18.

H_0: $\mu_1 \leq \mu_2$

H_1: $\mu_1 > \mu_2$ (claim)

C. V. = 1.65

$$z = \frac{(9205 - 6618) - 0}{\sqrt{\frac{1928^2}{35} + \frac{1928^2}{35}}} = 5.61$$

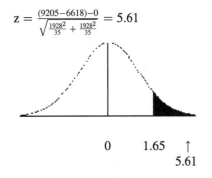

0   1.65   ↑
              5.61

Reject the null hypothesis. There is enough evidence to support the claim that average credit card debt has increased. One possible reason could be that the price of the merchandise purchased has increased.

19.

$$\overline{D} = 28.6 - 32.9 = -4.3$$

$$(\overline{X}_1 - \overline{X}_2) - z_{\frac{\alpha}{2}}\sqrt{\frac{\sigma_1^2}{n_1} + \frac{\sigma_2^2}{n_2}} < \mu_1 - \mu_2 <$$
$$(\overline{X}_1 - \overline{X}_2) + z_{\frac{\alpha}{2}}\sqrt{\frac{\sigma_1^2}{n_1} + \frac{\sigma_2^2}{n_2}}$$

$$-4.3 - (2.58)\sqrt{\frac{5.1^2}{30} + \frac{4.4^2}{40}} < \mu_1 - \mu_2 <$$

$$-4.3 + (2.58)\sqrt{\frac{5.2^2}{30} + \frac{4.4^2}{40}}$$

$$-7.3 < \mu_1 - \mu_2 < -1.3$$

20.

$$\overline{D} = 9.2 - 8.8 = 0.4$$

$$0.4 - (1.96)\sqrt{\frac{0.3^2}{27} + \frac{0.1^2}{30}} < \mu_1 - \mu_2 <$$

$$0.4 + (1.96)\sqrt{\frac{0.3^2}{27} + \frac{0.1^2}{30}}$$

$$0.281 < \mu_1 - \mu_2 < 0.519$$
or $0.3 < \mu_1 - \mu_2 < 0.5$

21.

H_0: $\mu_1 - \mu_2 \leq 8$ (claim)
H_1: $\mu_1 - \mu_2 > 8$

C. V. = 1.65

$$z = \frac{(\overline{X}_1 - \overline{X}_2) - K}{\sqrt{\frac{s_1^2}{n_1} + \frac{s_2^2}{n_2}}} = \frac{(110 - 104) - 8}{\sqrt{\frac{15^2}{60} + \frac{15^2}{60}}} = -0.73$$

$\uparrow$ 0   1.65
-0.73

Do not reject the null hypothesis. There is
not enough evidence to reject the claim that
private school students have exam scores
that are at most 8 points higher than public
school students.

EXERCISE SET 9-3

1.
It should be the larger of the two variances.

2.
The critical region is on the right side
because the F test value is always greater
than or equal to 1, since the larger variance
is always placed in the numerator.

3.
One d.f. is used for the variance associated
with the numerator and one is used for the
variance associated with the denominator.

4.
The characteristics of the F-distribution are:
1. The values of F cannot be negative.
2. The distribution is positively skewed.
3. The mean value of F is approximately
equal to one.
d. The F distribution is a family of curves
based upon the degrees of freedom.

5.
a. d. f. N = 15, d. f. D = 22; C. V. = 3.36
b. d. f. N = 24, d. f. D = 13; C. V. = 3.59
c. d. f. N = 45, d. f. D = 29; C. V. = 2.03
d. d. f. N = 20, d. f. D = 16; C. V. = 2.28
e. d. f. N = 10, d. f. D = 10; C. V. = 2.98

6.
Note: Specific P-values are in parentheses.
a. 0.025 < P-value < 0.05 (0.033)
b. 0.05 < P-value < 0.10   (0.072)
c. P-value = 0.05
d. 0.005 < P-value < 0.01 (0.006)
e. P-value = 0.05
f. P > 0.10   (0.112)
g. 0.05 < P-value < 0.10   (0.068)
h. 0.01 < P-value < 0.02   (0.015)

7.
H_0: $\sigma_1^2 = \sigma_2^2$
H_1: $\sigma_1^2 \neq \sigma_2^2$ (claim)

C. V. = 2.53 $\alpha = \frac{0.10}{2}$
d. f. N = 14   d. f. D = 14
$F = \frac{s_1^2}{s_2^2} = \frac{13.12^2}{6.17^2} = 4.52$

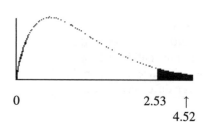

0   2.53 $\uparrow$
                          4.52

7. continued
Reject the null hypothesis. There is enough evidence to support the claim that there is a difference in the variances of the best seller lists for fiction and non-fiction.

8.
H_0: $\sigma_1 \geq \sigma_2$

H_1: $\sigma_1 < \sigma_2$ (claim)

C. V. = 2.04 $\alpha = 0.05$
d. f. N = 15   d. f. D = 28

$F = \frac{3.5^2}{2.7^2} = 1.68$

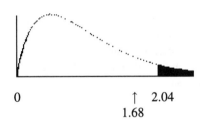

0   ↑ 2.04
                    1.68

Do not reject the null hypothesis. There is not enough evidence to support the claim that the standard deviation of the ages of cats is smaller than the standard deviation of the ages of dogs.

9.
H_0: $\sigma_1^2 = \sigma_2^2$

H_1: $\sigma_1^2 \neq \sigma_2^2$ (claim)

$s_1 = 25.97$ $s_2 = 72.74$
C. V. = 2.86 $\alpha = \frac{0.05}{2}$
d. f. N = 15   d. f. D = 15

$F = \frac{s_1^2}{s_2^2} = \frac{72.74^2}{25.97^2} = 7.85$

0   2.86 ↑
                          7.85

Reject the null hypothesis. There is enough evidence to support the claim that the

9. continued
variances of the values of tax exempt properties are different. Since both data sets vary greatly from normality, the results are suspect.

10.
H_0: $\sigma_1 = \sigma_2$

H_1: $\sigma_1 \neq \sigma_2$ (claim)

C. V. = 2.51 $\alpha = \frac{0.05}{2}$
d. f. N = 23   d. f. D = 19
$F = \frac{(7.5)^2}{(4.1)^2} = 3.346$

0   2.51 ↑
                          3.346

Reject the null hypothesis. There is enough evidence to support the claim that there is a difference in the standard deviations.

11.
H_0: $\sigma_1^2 = \sigma_2^2$
H_1: $\sigma_1^2 \neq \sigma_2^2$ (claim)

$s_1 = 33.99$ $s_2 = 33.99$
C. V. = 4.99 $\alpha = \frac{0.05}{2}$
d. f. N = 7   d. f. D = 7
$F = \frac{s_1^2}{s_2^2} = \frac{(33.99)^2}{(33.99)^2} = 1$

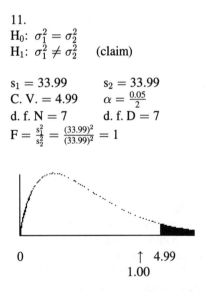

0   ↑ 4.99
                    1.00

Do not reject the null hypothesis. There is not enough evidence to support the claim that the variance in the number of calories differs between the two brands.

12.
H_0: $\sigma_1^2 = \sigma_2^2$
H_1: $\sigma_1^2 \neq \sigma_2$ (claim)

12. continued

$s_1 = 1.79$ $\qquad s_2 = 1.305$

C. V. $= 3.53$ $\qquad \alpha = \frac{0.05}{2}$

d. f. N $= 11$ $\qquad$ d. f. D $= 11$

$F = \frac{(1.79)^2}{(1.305)^2} = 1.88$

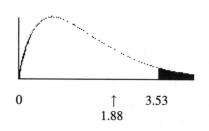

0 $\qquad\qquad\uparrow\qquad$ 3.53
$\qquad\qquad$ 1.88

Do not reject the null hypothesis. There is not enough evidence to support the claim that the variances in the number of vehicles are different.

13.

H_0: $\sigma_1 = \sigma_2$

H_1: $\sigma_1 \neq \sigma_2$ $\quad$ (claim)

$s_1 = 6.8$ $\qquad s_2 = 3.2$

$n_1 = 25$ $\qquad n_2 = 25$

C. V. $= 2.27$ $\qquad \alpha = \frac{0.05}{2}$

d. f. N $= 24$ $\qquad$ d. f. D $= 24$

$F = \frac{s_1^2}{s_2^2} = \frac{(6.8)^2}{(3.2)^2} = 4.52$

0 $\qquad\qquad\qquad$ 2.27 $\quad\uparrow$
$\qquad\qquad\qquad\qquad\qquad$ 4.52

Reject the null hypothesis. There is enough evidence to support the claim that the standard deviations are different. One reason is that there are many more people who play the slot machines than people who play roulette. This could possibly account for the larger standard deviation in the ages of the players.

14.

H_0: $\sigma_1^2 = \sigma_2^2$

H_1: $\sigma_1^2 \neq \sigma_2^2$ $\quad$ (claim)

14. continued

Chocolate: $s = 6.4985$

Non-chocolate: $s = 11.2006$

C. V. $= 2.75$ $\qquad \alpha = \frac{0.10}{2}$

d. f. N $= 10$ $\qquad$ d. f. D $= 12$

$F = \frac{11.2006^2}{6.4985^2} = 2.9707$

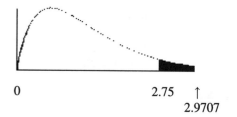

0 $\qquad\qquad\qquad\qquad$ 2.75 $\quad\uparrow$
$\qquad\qquad\qquad\qquad\qquad\qquad$ 2.9707

Reject the null hypothesis. There is enough evidence to support the claim that the variances in carbohydrate grams of chocolate candy and non-chocolate candy are not the same.

15.

H_0: $\sigma_1^2 = \sigma_2^2$

H_1: $\sigma_1^2 \neq \sigma_2^2$ $\quad$ (claim)

Research: $s_1 = 5501.118$

Primary Care: $s_2 = 5238.809$

C. V. $= 4.03$ $\qquad \alpha = \frac{0.05}{2}$

d. f. N $= 9$ $\qquad$ d. f. D $= 9$

$F = \frac{s_1^2}{s_2^2} = \frac{(5501.118)^2}{(5238.809)^2} = 1.1026$

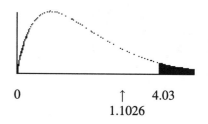

0 $\qquad\qquad\qquad\uparrow\qquad$ 4.03
$\qquad\qquad\qquad$ 1.1026

Do not reject the null hypothesis. There is not enough evidence to support the claim that there is a difference between the variances in tuition costs.

16.

H_0: $\sigma_1^2 \geq \sigma_2^2$

H_1: $\sigma_1^2 < \sigma_2^2$ $\quad$ (claim)

$s_1 = 98.2$ $\qquad\qquad s_2 = 118.4$

16. continued
C. V. = 3.15 $\quad \alpha = 0.01$
d. f. N = 19 $\quad$ d. f. D = 19
$F = \frac{(118.4)^2}{(98.2)^2} = 1.45$

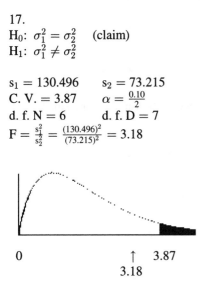

0 $\qquad \uparrow \quad$ 3.15
$\qquad$ 1.45

Do not reject the null hypothesis. There is not enough evidence to support the claim that the variance of the areas in Indiana is less than the variance of the areas in Iowa.

17.
H_0: $\sigma_1^2 = \sigma_2^2$ $\quad$ (claim)
H_1: $\sigma_1^2 \neq \sigma_2^2$

$s_1 = 130.496 \qquad s_2 = 73.215$
C. V. = 3.87 $\qquad \alpha = \frac{0.10}{2}$
d. f. N = 6 $\qquad$ d. f. D = 7
$F = \frac{s_1^2}{s_2^2} = \frac{(130.496)^2}{(73.215)^2} = 3.18$

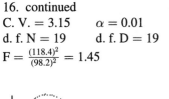

0 $\qquad \uparrow \quad$ 3.87
$\qquad$ 3.18

Do not reject the null hypothesis. There is not enough evidence to reject the claim that the variances of the heights are equal.

18.
H_0: $\sigma_1^2 \leq \sigma_2^2$
H_1: $\sigma_1^2 > \sigma_2^2$ $\quad$ (claim)

$\alpha = 0.05$ $\quad$ d. f. N = 29 $\quad$ d. f. D = 29
$F = \frac{8324}{2862} = 2.91$

Since P-value < 0.005 (0.003), reject the null hypothesis. There is enough evidence to support the claim that the variation in the salaries of the elementary school teachers is greater than the variation in salaries of the secondary teachers.

19.

Men	Women
$s_1^2 = 2.363$	$s_2^2 = 0.444$
$n_1 = 15$	$n_2 = 15$

H_0: $\sigma_1^2 = \sigma_2^2$ $\quad$ (claim)
H_1: $\sigma_1^2 \neq \sigma_2$

$\alpha = 0.05$ $\qquad$ P-value = 0.004
d. f. N = 14 $\qquad$ d. f. D = 14
$F = \frac{s_1^2}{s_2^2} = \frac{2.363}{0.444} = 5.32$

Since P-value < 0.01, reject the null hypothesis. There is enough evidence to reject the claim that the variances in weights are equal.

20.

Hard Body	Soft Body
$s_1^2 = 6.007$	$s_2^2 = 22.667$
$n_1 = 17$	$n_2 = 6$

H_0: $\sigma_1^2 = \sigma_2^2$
H_1: $\sigma_1^2 \neq \sigma_2$ $\quad$ (claim)

C. V. = 3.50 $\qquad \alpha = \frac{0.05}{2}$
d. f. N = 5 $\qquad$ d. f. D = 16
$F = \frac{22.667}{6.007} = 3.773$

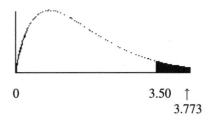

0 $\qquad$ 3.50 $\uparrow$
$\qquad$ 3.773

Reject the null hypothesis. There is enough evidence to support the claim that there is a difference in the variances.

EXERCISE SET 9-4

1.
H_0: $\sigma_1^2 = \sigma_2^2$
H_1: $\sigma_1^2 \neq \sigma_2^2$
d. f. N = 9 $\quad$ d. f. D = 9 $\quad \alpha = \frac{0.05}{2}$
$F = \frac{3256^2}{2341^2} = 1.93$ $\quad$ C. V. = 4.03
Do not reject. The variances are equal.

H_0: $\mu_1 = \mu_2$
H_1: $\mu_1 \neq \mu_2$ $\quad$ (claim)

1. continued

C. V. $= \pm 2.101$ d. f. $= 18$

$$t = \frac{(\overline{X}_1 - \overline{X}_2) - (\mu_1 - \mu_2)}{\sqrt{\frac{(n_1-1)s_1^2 + (n_2-1)s_2^2}{n_1 + n_2 - 2}}\sqrt{\frac{1}{n_1} + \frac{1}{n_2}}}$$

$$t = \frac{(83{,}256 - 88{,}354) - 0}{\sqrt{\frac{9(3256)^2 + 9(2341)^2}{18}}\sqrt{\frac{1}{10} + \frac{1}{10}}}$$

$$t = -4.02$$

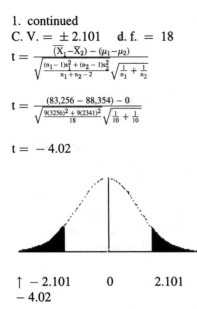

$\uparrow -2.101$ 0 2.101
-4.02

Reject the null hypothesis. There is enough evidence to support the claim that there is a significant difference in the values of the homes based upon the appraisers' values.

Confidence Interval:

$$-5098 - 2.101\left(\sqrt{\frac{9(3256)^2 + 9(2341)^2}{18}}\right.$$

$$\left.\sqrt{\frac{1}{10} + \frac{1}{10}}\right) < \mu_1 - \mu_2 <$$

$$-5098 + 2.101\left(\sqrt{\frac{9(3256)^2 + 9(2341)^2}{18}}\right.$$

$$\left.\sqrt{\frac{1}{10} + \frac{1}{10}}\right) =$$

$$-5098 - 2.101(1268.14) < \mu_1 - \mu_2 <$$
$$-5098 + 2.101(1268.14)$$

$$-\$7762 < \mu_1 - \mu_2 < -\$2434$$

2.

H_0: $\sigma_1^2 = \sigma_2^2$
H_1: $\sigma_1^2 \neq \sigma_2^2$
d. f. N $= 15$ d. f. D $= 19$ $\alpha = \frac{0.05}{2}$
$F = \frac{300^2}{250^2} = 1.44$ C. V. $= 2.62$
Do not reject. The variances are equal.

H_0: $\mu_1 \leq \mu_2$
H_1: $\mu_1 > \mu_2$ (claim)

C. V. $= 1.65$ d. f. $= 34$

$$t = \frac{(23{,}800 - 23{,}750) - 0}{\sqrt{\frac{(16-1)300^2 + (20-1)250^2}{16 + 20 - 2}}\sqrt{\frac{1}{16} + \frac{1}{20}}}$$

2. continued

$$t = \frac{50}{\sqrt{74632.35}\sqrt{0.1125}} = 0.55$$

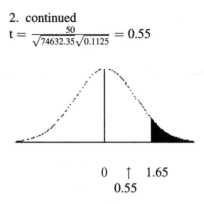

0 $\uparrow$ 1.65
0.55

Do not reject the null hypothesis. There is not enough evidence to support the claim that male nurses earn more than female nurses.

3.

H_0: $\sigma_1^2 = \sigma_2^2$
H_1: $\sigma_1^2 \neq \sigma_2^2$

d. f. N $= 14$ d. f. D $= 14$ $\alpha = \frac{0.05}{2}$
$F = \frac{20{,}000^2}{20{,}000^2} = 1$ C. V. $= 3.05$
Do not reject. The variances are equal.

H_0: $\mu_1 = \mu_2$
H_1: $\mu_1 \neq \mu_2$ (claim)

C. V. $= \pm 2.048$
d. f. $= 14 + 14 - 2 = 28$

$$t = \frac{(\overline{X}_1 - \overline{X}_2) - (\mu_1 - \mu_2)}{\sqrt{\frac{(n_1-1)s_1^2 + (n_2-1)s_2^2}{n_1 + n_2 - 2}}\sqrt{\frac{1}{n_1} + \frac{1}{n_2}}}$$

$$t = \frac{(501{,}580 - 513{,}360) - 0}{\sqrt{\frac{14(20{,}000^2) + 14(20{,}000^2)}{15 + 15 - 2}}\sqrt{\frac{1}{15} + \frac{1}{15}}}$$

$$t = -1.61$$

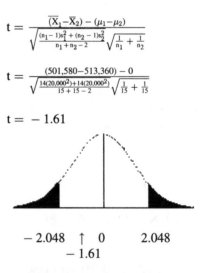

-2.048 $\uparrow$ 0 2.048
-1.61

Do not reject the null hypothesis. There is not enough evidence to reject the claim that there is no difference between the means.

4.

$H_0: \sigma_1^2 = \sigma_2^2$
$H_1: \sigma_1^2 \neq \sigma_2^2$
$\overline{X}_1 = 39.67 \qquad s_1 = 18.37$
$\overline{X}_2 = 28.83 \qquad s_2 = 17.13$
d. f. N = 5   d. f. D = 5 $\alpha = 0.01$
$F = \frac{18.37^2}{17.13^2} = 1.15 \qquad$ C. V. = 7.15
Do not reject. The variances are equal.

$H_0: \mu_1 \leq \mu_2$
$H_1: \mu_1 > \mu_2$ (claim)

C. V. = 2.764   d. f. = 10

$t = \dfrac{(39.67 - 28.82) - 0}{\sqrt{\frac{(6-1)(18.37)^2 + (6-1)(17.13)^2}{6 + 6 - 2}}\sqrt{\frac{1}{6} + \frac{1}{6}}}$

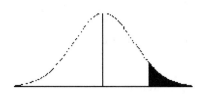

$t = 1.057$

0   ↑   2.764
      1.057

Do not reject the null hypothesis. There is not enough evidence to support the claim that the average number of students attending cyber schools in Allegheny County is greater than those who attend cyber schools outside Allegheny County. One reason why caution should be used is that cyber charter schools are a relatively new concept.

5.

$H_0: \sigma_1^2 = \sigma_2^2$
$H_1: \sigma_1^2 \neq \sigma_2^2$
$\overline{X}_1 = 37.167 \qquad \overline{X}_2 = 25$
$s_1 = 13.2878 \qquad s_2 = 15.7734$
d. f. N = 5   d. f. D = 5 $\alpha = 0.01$
$F = \frac{15.7734^2}{13.2878^2} = 1.41 \qquad$ C. V. = 14.94
Do not reject. The variances are equal.

$H_0: \mu_1 \leq \mu_2$
$H_1: \mu_1 > \mu_2$ (claim)

C. V. = 2.764   d. f. = 10

5. continued

$t = \dfrac{(\overline{X}_1 - \overline{X}_2) - (\mu_1 - \mu_2)}{\sqrt{\frac{(n_1 - 1)s_1^2 + (n_2 - 1)s_2^2}{n_1 + n_2 - 2}}\sqrt{\frac{1}{n_1} + \frac{1}{n_2}}}$

$t = \dfrac{(37.167 - 25) - 0}{\sqrt{\frac{5(13.2878)^2 + 5(15.7734)^2}{6 + 6 - 2}}\sqrt{\frac{1}{6} + \frac{1}{6}}} = 1.45$

↑   2.764
1.45

Do not reject the null hypothesis. There is not enough evidence to support the claim that the average number of family day care homes is greater than the average number of day care centers.

6.

$H_0: \sigma_1^2 = \sigma_2^2$
$H_1: \sigma_1^2 \neq \sigma_2^2$
$\overline{X}_1 = 63,356.2 \qquad \overline{X}_2 = 35,386.8$
$s_1 = 2808.31385 \quad s_2 = 2631.03947$
d. f. N = 4   d. f. D = 4 $\alpha = 0.10$
$F = \frac{2808.31385^2}{2631.03947^2} = 1.14 \qquad$ C. V. = 6.39
Do not reject. The variances are equal.

$H_0: \mu_1 \leq \mu_2$
$H_1: \mu_1 > \mu_2$ (claim)

C. V. = 1.397   d. f. = 8

$t = \dfrac{(63,356.2 - 35,386.8) - 0}{\sqrt{\frac{4(2808.31385)^2 + 4(2631.03947)^2}{5 + 5 - 2}}\sqrt{\frac{1}{5} + \frac{1}{5}}}$

$= 16.252$

0   1.397   ↑
          16.252

Reject the null hypothesis. There is enough evidence to support the claim that more juveniles are reported missing than adults.

7.

H_0: $\sigma_1^2 = \sigma_2^2$

H_1: $\sigma_1^2 \neq \sigma_2^2$

d. f. N = 9   d. f. D = 13 $\alpha = 0.02$

$F = \frac{5.6^2}{4.3^2} = 1.7$ C. V. = 4.19

Do not reject. The variances are equal.

H_0: $\mu_1 = \mu_2$

H_1: $\mu_1 \neq \mu_2$ (claim)

C. V. = ±2.508   d. f. = 22

$$t = \frac{(\overline{X}_1 - \overline{X}_2) - (\mu_1 - \mu_2)}{\sqrt{\frac{(n_1 - 1)s_1^2 + (n_2 - 1)s_2^2}{n_1 + n_2 - 2}}\sqrt{\frac{1}{n_1} + \frac{1}{n_2}}}$$

$$t = \frac{(21 - 27) - 0}{\sqrt{\frac{9(5.6)^2 + 13(4.3)^2}{10 + 14 - 2}}\sqrt{\frac{1}{10} + \frac{1}{14}}} = -2.97$$

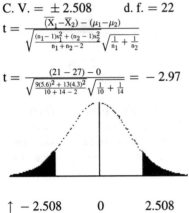

↑ − 2.508   0   2.508

− 2.97

Reject the null hypothesis. There is enough evidence to support the claim that there is a difference in the average times of the two groups.

Confidence Interval:

− 6 − 2.508(2.02) < $\mu_1 - \mu_2$ <

− 6 + 2.508(2.02)

− 11.1 < $\mu_1 - \mu_2$ < − 0.93

8.

H_0: $\sigma_1^2 = \sigma_2^2$

H_1: $\sigma_1^2 \neq \sigma_2^2$

d. f. N = 19   d. f. D = 17 $\alpha = \frac{0.01}{2}$

$F = \frac{3.5}{2.2} = 1.59$ C. V. = 3.79

Do not reject. The variances are equal.

H_0: $\mu_1 = \mu_2$

H_1: $\mu_1 \neq \mu_2$ (claim)

C. V. = ±2.58

d. f. = 18 + 20 − 2 = 36

$$t = \frac{(2.5 - 3.8) - 0}{\sqrt{\frac{17(2.2) + 19(3.5)}{18 + 20 - 2}}\sqrt{\frac{1}{18} + \frac{1}{20}}} = -2.355$$

8. continued

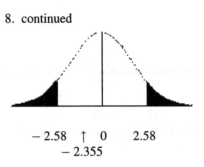

− 2.58   ↑   0   2.58

− 2.355

Do not reject the null hypothesis. There is not enough evidence to support the claim that there is a difference between the average number of volunteer hours.

9.

H_0: $\sigma_1^2 = \sigma_2^2$

H_1: $\sigma_1^2 \neq \sigma_2^2$

d. f. N = 24   d. f. D = 24 $\alpha = 0.10$

$F = \frac{3.20^2}{2.57^2} = 1.55$ C.V. = 1.98

Do not reject. The variances are equal.

H_0: $\mu_1 \leq \mu_2$

H_1: $\mu_1 > \mu_2$ (claim)

C.V. = 1.282   df = 48

$$t = \frac{(\overline{X}_1 - \overline{X}_2) - (\mu_1 - \mu_2)}{\sqrt{\frac{(n_1 - 1)s_1^2 + (n_2 - 1)s_2^2}{n_1 + n_2 - 2}}\sqrt{\frac{1}{n_1} + \frac{1}{n_2}}}$$

$$t = \frac{(19.63 - 10.25) - 0}{\sqrt{\frac{24(3.2)^2 + 24(2.57)^2}{25 + 25 - 2}}\sqrt{\frac{1}{25} + \frac{1}{25}}}$$

$t = 11.427$

Reject the null hypothesis. There is enough evidence to support the claim that the average cost of a movie ticket in London is greater than the average cost of a ticket in New York City. One reason for the difference could be the rate of exchange of the money.

10.

H_0: $\sigma_1^2 = \sigma_2^2$

H_1: $\sigma_1^2 \neq \sigma_2^2$

d. f. N = 15   d. f. D = 15 $\alpha = 0.01$

$F = \frac{0.6^2}{0.6^2} = 1$ P-value > 0.20 (1.00)

Do not reject since P-value > 0.01. The variances are equal.

H_0: $\mu_1 = \mu_2$ (claim)

H_1: $\mu_1 \neq \mu_2$

10. continued
d. f. $= 30$

$$t = \frac{(2.3 - 1.9) - 0}{\sqrt{\frac{15(0.6)^2 + 15(0.6)^2}{30}}\sqrt{\frac{1}{16} + \frac{1}{16}}} = 1.89$$

$0.05 <$ P-value < 0.10 (0.069)
Since P-value > 0.01, do not reject the null
hypothesis. There is not enough evidence to
reject the claim that the mean hospital stay is
the same.

Confidence Interval:
$0.4 - 2.58(0.2121) < \mu_1 - \mu_2 <$
$\qquad\qquad 0.4 + 2.58(0.2121)$
$-0.15 < \mu_1 - \mu_2 < 0.95$
(Note: TI83 confidence interval is
$-0.18 < \mu_1 - \mu_2 < 0.98$)

11.

White Mice	Brown Mice
$\overline{X}_1 = 17$	$\overline{X}_2 = 16.67$
$s_1 = 4.56$	$s_2 = 5.05$
$n_1 = 6$	$n_2 = 6$

$H_0: \sigma_1^2 = \sigma_2^2$
$H_1: \sigma_1^2 \neq \sigma_2^2$
d. f. N $= 5$ d. f. D $= 5$ $\alpha = \frac{0.05}{2}$
$F = \frac{5.05^2}{4.56^2} = 1.23$ C. V. $= 7.15$
Do not reject. The variances are equal.

$H_0: \mu_1 = \mu_2$
$H_1: \mu_1 \neq \mu_2$ (claim)

C. V. $= \pm 2.228$ d. f. $= 10$

$$t = \frac{(17 - 16.67) - 0}{\sqrt{\frac{5(4.56)^2 + 5(5.05)^2}{6+6-2}}\sqrt{\frac{1}{6} + \frac{1}{6}}} = 0.119$$

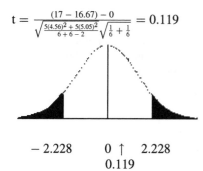

-2.228 $0 \uparrow$ 2.228
$\qquad\quad 0.119$

Do not reject the null hypothesis. There is
not enough evidence to support the claim
that the color of the mice made a difference.

11. continued
Confidence Interval:
$0.33 - 2.228(2.78) < \mu_1 - \mu_2 <$
$\qquad\qquad 0.33 + 2.228(2.78)$
$-5.9 < \mu_1 - \mu_2 < 6.5$

12.
Research: $\overline{X}_1 = 596.2353$ $s_1 = 163.2362$
Primary Care: $\overline{X}_2 = 481.5$ $s_2 = 179.3957$

F test:
d. f. N $= 16 - 1 = 15$
d. f. D $= 17 - 1 = 16$
C. V. $= 2.35$
$F = \frac{179.3957^2}{163.2362^2} = 1.21$
Do not reject. The variances are equal.

Confidence Interval:
$$t_{\frac{\alpha}{2}}\sqrt{\frac{(n_1-1)s_1^2 + (n_2-1)s_2^2}{n_1 + n_2 - 2}}\sqrt{\frac{1}{n_1} + \frac{1}{n_2}} =$$

$$1.645\sqrt{\frac{(17-1)(163.2362)^2 + (16-1)(179.3957)^2}{17 + 16 - 2}}\sqrt{\frac{1}{17} + \frac{1}{16}}$$

$= 98.1202$

$(596.2353 - 481.5) - 98.1202 < \mu_1 - \mu_2$
$\qquad\qquad < (596.2353 - 481.5) + 98.1202$

$114.7353 - 98.1202 < \mu_1 - \mu_2$
$\qquad\qquad < 114.7353 + 98.1202$
$16.62 < \mu_1 - \mu_2 < 212.86$
(Note: TI83 confidence interval is
$13.6 < \mu_1 - \mu_2 < 215.9$)

13.
Private: $\overline{X} = \$16{,}147.5$ $s = 4023.7$
Public: $\overline{X} = \$9039.9$ $s = 3325.5$

F test:
d. f. N $= 6 - 1 = 5$
d. f. D $= 7 - 1 = 6$
C. V. $= 5.99$
$F = \frac{4023.7^2}{3325.5^2} = 1.46$
Do not reject. The variances are equal.

Confidence Interval:

$$t_{\frac{\alpha}{2}}\sqrt{\frac{(n_1-1)s_1^2 + (n_2-1)s_2^2}{n_1 + n_2 - 2}}\sqrt{\frac{1}{n_1} + \frac{1}{n_2}} =$$

$$2.201\sqrt{\frac{5(4023.7)^2 + 6(3325.5)^2}{6+7-2}}\sqrt{\frac{1}{6} + \frac{1}{7}}$$

$= 4481.04$

13. continued

$16{,}147.5 - 9039.9 = 7107.6$

$7107.6 - 4481.04 < \mu_1 - \mu_2 <$
$\qquad 7107.6 + 4481.04$

$\$2626.60 < \mu_1 - \mu_2 < \$11{,}588.64$

EXERCISE SET 9-5

1.
a. Dependent
b. Dependent
c. Independent
d. Dependent
e. Independent

2.

Before	After	D	D²
2	1	1	1
3	4	-1	1
6	3	3	9
7	8	-1	1
4	3	1	1
5	3	2	4
3	1	2	4
1	0	1	1
0	1	-1	1
0	0	0	0
		$\sum D = 7$	$\sum D^2 = 23$

H_0: $\mu_D \leq 0$
H_1: $\mu_D > 0$ (claim)

C. V. $= 1.833$ $\qquad$ d. f. $= 9$

$\overline{D} = \frac{\sum D}{n} = \frac{7}{10} = 0.7$

$s_D = \sqrt{\frac{\sum D^2 - \frac{(\sum D)^2}{n}}{n-1}} = \sqrt{\frac{23 - \frac{7^2}{10}}{9}} = 1.42$

$t = \frac{\overline{D} - \mu_D}{\frac{s_D}{\sqrt{n}}} = \frac{0.7 - 0}{\frac{1.42}{\sqrt{10}}} = 1.56$

$\qquad\qquad 0 \quad \uparrow 1.833$
$\qquad\qquad\qquad 1.56$

Do not reject the null hypothesis. There is not enough evidence to support the claim

2. continued
that the workers missed fewer days after completing the program.

3.

Before	After	D	D²
9	9	0	0
12	17	-5	25
6	9	-3	9
15	20	-5	25
3	2	1	1
18	21	-3	9
10	15	-5	25
13	22	-9	81
7	6	1	1
		$\sum D = -28$	$\sum D^2 = 176$

H_0: $\mu_D \geq 0$
H_1: $\mu_D < 0$ (claim)

C. V. $= -1.397$ $\qquad$ d. f. $= 8$

$\overline{D} = \frac{\sum D}{n} = -3.11$

$s_D = \sqrt{\frac{\sum D^2 - \frac{(\sum D)^2}{n}}{n-1}} = \sqrt{\frac{176 - \frac{(-28)^2}{9}}{8}} = 3.33$

$t = \frac{-3.11 - 0}{\frac{3.33}{\sqrt{9}}} = -2.8$

$\uparrow -1.397 \qquad 0$
-2.8

Reject the null hypothesis. There is enough evidence to support the claim that the seminar increased the number of hours students studied.

4.

Before	After	D	D²
12	13	-1	1
11	12	-1	1
14	10	4	16
9	9	0	0
8	8	0	0
6	8	-2	4
8	7	1	1
5	6	-1	1
4	5	-1	1
7	5	2	4
		$\sum D = 1$	$\sum D^2 = 29$

4. continued

H_0: $\mu_D = 0$
H_1: $\mu_D \neq 0$ (claim)

C. V. $= \pm 2.262$ d. f. $= 9$
$\overline{D} = \frac{1}{10} = 0.1$
$s_D = \sqrt{\frac{29 - \frac{(1)^2}{10}}{9}} = 1.79$

$t = \frac{0.1 - 0}{\frac{1.79}{\sqrt{10}}} = 0.176$

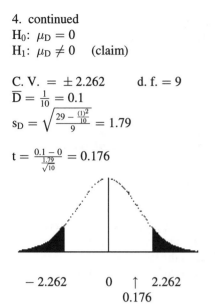

-2.262 0 $\uparrow$ 2.262
                        0.176

Do not reject the null hypothesis. There is
not enough evidence to support the claim
that there was a change in attitude.

Confidence Interval:
$0.1 - 2.262\left(\frac{1.79}{\sqrt{10}}\right) < \mu_D <$
                $0.1 + 2.262\left(\frac{1.79}{\sqrt{10}}\right)$
$-1.18 < \mu_D < 1.38$

5.

F - S	S - Th	D	D ^{2}
4	8	-4	16
7	5.5	1.5	2.25
10.5	7.5	3	9
12	8	4	16
11	7	4	16
9	6	3	9
6	6	0	0
9	8	1	1
		$\sum D = 12.5$	$\sum D^2 = 69.25$

H_0: $\mu_D = 0$
H_1: $\mu_D \neq 0$ (claim)

C. V. $= \pm 2.365$ d. f. $= 7$
$\overline{D} = \frac{\sum D}{n} = \frac{12.5}{8} = 1.5625$
$s_D = \sqrt{\frac{\sum D^2 - \frac{(\sum D)^2}{n}}{n - 1}}$

$= \sqrt{\frac{69.25 - \frac{(12.5)^2}{8}}{7}} = 2.665$

$t = \frac{1.5625 - 0}{\frac{2.665}{\sqrt{8}}} = 1.6583$

5. continued

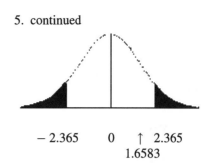

-2.365 0 $\uparrow$ 2.365
                        1.6583

Do not reject the null hypothesis. There is
not enough evidence to support the claim
that there is a difference in the mean number
of hours slept.

6.

Year 1	Year 2	D	D ^{2}
61	62	-1	1
26	40	-14	196
9	10	-1	1
16	23	-7	49
61	38	23	529
71	118	-47	2209
14	18	-4	16
86	67	19	361
17	21	-4	16
24	20	4	16
		$\sum D = -32$	$\sum D^2 = 3394$

H_0: $\mu_D = 0$
H_1: $\mu_D \neq 0$ (claim)

C. V. $= \pm 2.262$ d. f. $= 9$

$\overline{D} = -3.2$
$s_D = 19.124$

$t = \frac{-3.2 - 0}{\frac{19.124}{\sqrt{10}}} = -0.53$

-2.262 $\uparrow$ 0 2.262
        -0.53

Do not reject the null hypothesis. There is
not enough evidence to support the claim
that there is a difference. No significant
difference exists.

7.

Before	After	D	D^2
12	9	3	9
9	6	3	9
0	1	-1	1
5	3	2	4
4	2	2	4
3	3	0	0
		$\sum D = 9$	$\sum D^2 = 27$

H_0: $\mu_D \leq 0$
H_1: $\mu_D > 0$ (claim)

C. V. = 2.571   d. f. = 5

$\overline{D} = \frac{\sum D}{n} = \frac{9}{6} = 1.5$

$s_D = \sqrt{\frac{\sum D^2 - \frac{(\sum D)^2}{n}}{n-1}} = \sqrt{\frac{27 - \frac{9^2}{6}}{5}} = 1.64$

$t = \frac{1.5 - 0}{\frac{1.64}{\sqrt{6}}} = 2.24$

0   ↑ 2.571
    2.24

Do not reject the null hypothesis. There is not enough evidence to support the claim that the errors have been reduced.

8.

Year 1	Year 2	D	D^2
108	138	-30	900
36	28	8	64
65	67	-2	4
108	181	-73	5329
87	97	-10	100
94	126	-32	1024
10	18	-8	64
40	67	-27	729
		$\sum D = -174$	$\sum D^2 = 8214$

H_0: $\mu_D = 0$
H_1: $\mu_D \neq 0$ (claim)

C. V. = ± 2.365   d. f. = 7

$\overline{D} = -21.75$
$s_D = 25.155$

8. continued

$t = \frac{-21.75 - 0}{\frac{25.155}{\sqrt{8}}} = -2.45$

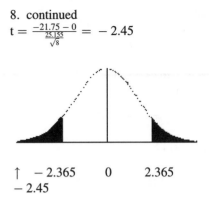

↑ − 2.365   0   2.365
− 2.45

Reject the null hypothesis. There is enough evidence to support the claim that there is a difference in the legal costs. There may have been more law suits in Year 2.

9.

A	B	D	D^2
87	83	4	16
92	95	-3	9
78	79	-1	1
83	83	0	0
88	86	2	4
90	93	-3	9
84	80	4	16
93	86	7	49
		$\sum D = 10$	$\sum D^2 = 104$

H_0: $\mu_D = 0$
H_1: $\mu_D \neq 0$ (claim)

d. f. = 7

$\overline{D} = \frac{\sum D}{n} = \frac{10}{8} = 1.25$

$s_D = \sqrt{\frac{\sum D^2 - \frac{(\sum D)^2}{n}}{n-1}} = \sqrt{\frac{104 - \frac{10^2}{8}}{7}} = 3.62$

$t = \frac{1.25 - 0}{\frac{3.62}{\sqrt{8}}} = 0.978$

0.20 < P-value < 0.50 (0.361) Do not reject the null hypothesis since P-value > 0.01. There is not enough evidence to support the claim that there is a difference in the pulse rates.

Confidence Interval:
$1.25 - 3.499\left(\frac{3.62}{\sqrt{8}}\right) < \mu_D <$
$\qquad 1.25 + 3.499\left(\frac{3.62}{\sqrt{8}}\right)$
$- 3.23 < \mu_D < 5.73$

10.

1994	1999	D	D^2
184	161	23	529
414	382	32	1024
22	22	0	0
99	109	-10	100
116	120	-4	16
49	52	-3	9
24	28	-4	16
50	50	0	0
282	297	-15	225
25	40	-15	225
141	148	-7	49
45	56	-11	121
12	20	-8	64
37	38	-1	1
9	9	0	0
17	19	-2	4

$$\sum D = -25 \quad \sum D^2 = 2383$$

H_0: $\mu_D = 0$
H_1: $\mu_D \neq 0$ (claim)

P-value > 0.50 (0.624)   d. f. = 15

$\overline{D} = -1.5625$
$s_D = 12.5$

$t = \dfrac{-1.5625 - 0}{\frac{12.5}{\sqrt{16}}} = -0.5$

Since P-value > 0.05, do not reject the null hypothesis. There is not enough evidence to support the claim that the average of the assessed values has changed.

11.
Using the previous problem, $\overline{D} = -1.5625$ whereas the mean of the 1994 values is 95.375 and the mean of the 1999 values is 96.9375; hence,
$\overline{D} = 95.375 - 96.9375 = -1.5625$

EXERCISE SET 9-6

1A.
Use $\hat{p} = \dfrac{x}{n}$ and $\hat{q} = 1 - \hat{p}$

a. $\hat{p} = \frac{34}{48}$ $\hat{q} = \frac{14}{48}$

b. $\hat{p} = \frac{28}{75}$ $\hat{q} = \frac{47}{75}$

c. $\hat{p} = \frac{50}{100}$ $\hat{q} = \frac{50}{100}$

d. $\hat{p} = \frac{6}{24}$ $\hat{q} = \frac{18}{24}$

e. $\hat{p} = \frac{12}{144}$ $\hat{q} = \frac{132}{144}$

1B.
a. x = 0.16(100) = 16
b. x = 0.08(50) = 4
c. x = 0.06(800) = 48
d. x = 0.52(200) = 104
e. x = 0.20(150) = 30

2.
For each part, use the formulas $\overline{p} = \dfrac{X_1 + X_2}{n_1 + n_2}$ and $\overline{q} = 1 - \overline{p}$

a. $\overline{p} = \frac{60 + 40}{100 + 100} = 0.5$
$\overline{q} = 1 - 0.5 = 0.5$

b. $\overline{p} = \frac{22 + 18}{50 + 30} = 0.5$
$\overline{q} = 1 - 0.5 = 0.5$

c. $\overline{p} = \frac{18 + 20}{60 + 80} = 0.27$
$\overline{q} = 1 - 0.27 = 0.73$

d. $\overline{p} = \frac{5 + 12}{32 + 48} = 0.2125$
$\overline{q} = 1 - 0.2125 = 0.7875$

e. $\overline{p} = \frac{12 + 15}{75 + 50} = 0.216$
$\overline{q} = 1 - 0.216 = 0.784$

3.
$\hat{p}_1 = \dfrac{X_1}{n_1} = \dfrac{80}{150} = 0.533 \quad \hat{p}_2 = \dfrac{30}{100} = 0.3$

$\overline{p} = \dfrac{X_1 + X_2}{n_1 + n_2} = \dfrac{80 + 30}{150 + 100} = \dfrac{110}{250} = 0.44$

$\overline{q} = 1 - \overline{p} = 1 - 0.44 = 0.56$

H_0: $p_1 = p_2$
H_1: $p_1 \neq p_2$ (claim)

C. V. = ± 1.96

$z = \dfrac{(\hat{p}_1 - \hat{p}_2) - (p_1 - p_2)}{\sqrt{(\overline{p})(\overline{q})\left(\frac{1}{n_1} + \frac{1}{n_2}\right)}} = \dfrac{(0.533 - 0.3) - 0}{\sqrt{(0.44)(0.56)\left(\frac{1}{150} + \frac{1}{100}\right)}}$

$z = 3.64$

$-1.96 \qquad 0 \qquad 1.96 \quad \uparrow$
$\qquad\qquad\qquad\qquad\qquad 3.64$

3. continued

Reject the null hypothesis. There is enough evidence to support the claim that there is a significant difference in the proportions.

4.

$$\hat{p}_1 = \frac{X_1}{n_1} = \frac{180}{300} = 0.6 \quad \hat{p}_2 = \frac{200}{250} = 0.8$$

$$\bar{p} = \frac{X_1 + X_2}{n_1 + n_2} = \frac{180 + 200}{300 + 250} = 0.691$$

$$\bar{q} = 1 - \bar{p} = 1 - 0.691 = 0.309$$

H_0: $p_1 = p_2$
H_1: $p_1 \neq p_2$ (claim)

C. V. $= \pm 2.58$

$$z = \frac{(\hat{p}_1 - \hat{p}_2) - (p_1 - p_2)}{\sqrt{(\bar{p})(\bar{q})\left(\frac{1}{n_1} + \frac{1}{n_2}\right)}} = \frac{(0.6 - 0.8) - 0}{\sqrt{(0.691)(0.309)\left(\frac{1}{300} + \frac{1}{250}\right)}}$$

$$z = -5.054$$

↑ -2.58 0   2.58
-5.054

Reject the null hypothesis. There is enough evidence to support the claim that the proportion of students receiving aid has changed.

5.

$$\hat{p}_1 = \frac{X_1}{n_1} = \frac{112}{150} = 0.7467 \quad \hat{p}_2 = \frac{150}{200} = 0.75$$

$$\bar{p} = \frac{X_1 + X_2}{n_1 + n_2} = \frac{112 + 150}{150 + 200} = 0.749$$

$$\bar{q} = 1 - \bar{p} = 1 - 0.749 = 0.251$$

H_0: $p_1 = p_2$
H_1: $p_1 \neq p_2$ (claim)

C. V. $= \pm 1.96$

$$z = \frac{(\hat{p}_1 - \hat{p}_2) - (p_1 - p_2)}{\sqrt{(\bar{p})(\bar{q})\left(\frac{1}{n_1} + \frac{1}{n_2}\right)}} = \frac{(0.7467 - 0.75) - 0}{\sqrt{(0.749)(0.251)\left(\frac{1}{150} + \frac{1}{200}\right)}}$$

$$z = -0.07$$

5. continued

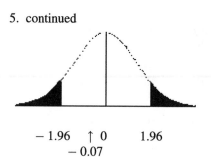

-1.96 ↑   0   1.96
-0.07

Do not reject the null hypothesis. There is not enough evidence to support the claim that the proportions are different.

6.

$$\hat{p}_1 = \frac{10}{73} = 0.14 \quad \hat{p}_2 = \frac{16}{80} = 0.20$$

$$\bar{p} = \frac{10 + 16}{73 + 80} = 0.17$$

$$\bar{q} = 1 - 0.17 = 0.83$$

H_0: $p_1 = p_2$
H_1: $p_1 \neq p_2$ (claim)

C. V. $= \pm 1.96$

$$z = \frac{(0.14 - 0.20) - 0}{\sqrt{(0.17)(0.83)\left(\frac{1}{73} + \frac{1}{80}\right)}} = -0.99$$

-1.96 ↑   0   1.96
-0.99

Do not reject the null hypothesis. There is not enough evidence to support the claim that there is a difference in the proportions.

$$(\hat{p}_1 - \hat{p}_2) - z_{\frac{\alpha}{2}}\sqrt{\frac{\hat{p}_1 \hat{q}_1}{n_1} + \frac{\hat{p}_2 \hat{q}_2}{n_2}} < p_1 - p_2 <$$
$$(\hat{p}_1 - \hat{p}_2) + z_{\frac{\alpha}{2}}\sqrt{\frac{\hat{p}_1 \hat{q}_1}{n_1} + \frac{\hat{p}_2 \hat{q}_2}{n_2}}$$

$$(0.14 - 0.2) - 1.96\sqrt{\frac{0.14(0.86)}{73} + \frac{0.2(0.8)}{80}} <$$

$$p_1 - p_2 < (0.14 - 0.2) + 1.96\sqrt{\frac{0.14(0.86)}{73} + \frac{0.2(0.8)}{80}}$$

$$-0.06 - 0.12 < p_1 - p_2 < -0.06 + 0.12$$

6. continued

$-0.18 < p_1 - p_2 < 0.06$

7.

$\hat{p}_1 = 0.83 \qquad \hat{p}_2 = 0.75$

$X_1 = 0.83(100) = 83$

$X_2 = 0.75(100) = 75$

$\bar{p} = \frac{83 + 75}{100 + 100} = 0.79 \qquad \bar{q} = 1 - 0.79 = 0.21$

H_0: $p_1 = p_2$ (claim)

H_1: $p_1 \neq p_2$

C. V. $= \pm 1.96 \qquad \alpha = 0.05$

$z = \frac{(\hat{p}_1 - \hat{p}_2) - (p_1 - p_2)}{\sqrt{(\bar{p})(\bar{q})(\frac{1}{n_1} + \frac{1}{n_2})}} = \frac{(0.83 - 0.75) - 0}{\sqrt{(0.79)(0.21)(\frac{1}{100} + \frac{1}{100})}}$

$z = 1.39$

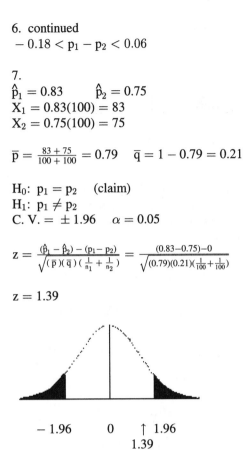

$-1.96 \qquad 0 \qquad \uparrow 1.96$
$\qquad\qquad\qquad\qquad 1.39$

Do not reject the null hypothesis. There is not enough evidence to reject the claim that the proportions are equal.

$(\hat{p}_1 - \hat{p}_2) - z_{\frac{\alpha}{2}} \sqrt{\frac{\hat{p}_1 \hat{q}_1}{n_1} + \frac{\hat{p}_2 \hat{q}_2}{n_2}} < p_1 - p_2 <$

$\qquad (\hat{p}_1 - \hat{p}_2) + z_{\frac{\alpha}{2}} \sqrt{\frac{\hat{p}_1 \hat{q}_1}{n_1} + \frac{\hat{p}_2 \hat{q}_2}{n_2}}$

$0.08 - 1.96 \sqrt{\frac{0.83(0.17)}{100} + \frac{0.75(0.25)}{100}} < p_1 - p_2$

$\qquad < 0.08 + 1.96 \sqrt{\frac{0.83(0.17)}{100} + \frac{0.75(0.25)}{100}}$

$-0.032 < p_1 - p_2 < 0.192$

8.

$\hat{p}_1 = \frac{44}{50} = 0.88 \qquad \hat{p}_2 = \frac{48}{50} = 0.96$

$\bar{p} = \frac{X_1 + X_2}{n_1 + n_2} = \frac{44 + 48}{50 + 50} = 0.92$

$\bar{q} = 1 - 0.92 = 0.08$

H_0: $p_1 = p_2$

H_1: $p_1 \neq p_2$ (claim)

8. continued

C. V. $= \pm 1.65$

$z = \frac{(0.88 - 0.96) - 0}{\sqrt{(0.92)(0.08)(\frac{1}{50} + \frac{1}{50})}} = -1.47$

$-1.65 \quad \uparrow \quad 0 \qquad 1.65$
$\qquad\quad -1.47$

Do not reject the null hypothesis. There is not enough evidence to support the claim that the proportions are different. A researcher might want to find out why people feel that they have less leisure time now as opposed to 10 years ago. Are they working more? Raising a family? etc.

9.

$\hat{p}_1 = 0.55 \qquad \hat{p}_2 = 0.45$

$X_1 = 0.55(80) = 44 \quad X_2 = 0.45(90) = 40.5$

$\bar{p} = \frac{X_1 + X_2}{n_1 + n_2} = \frac{44 + 40.5}{80 + 90} = 0.497$

$\bar{q} = 1 - \bar{p} = 1 - 0.497 = 0.503$

H_0: $p_1 = p_2$

H_1: $p_1 \neq p_2$ (claim)

C. V. $= \pm 2.58 \qquad \alpha = 0.01$

$z = \frac{(\hat{p}_1 - \hat{p}_2) - (p_1 - p_2)}{\sqrt{(\bar{p})(\bar{q})(\frac{1}{n_1} + \frac{1}{n_2})}} = \frac{(0.55 - 0.45) - 0}{\sqrt{(0.497)(0.503)(\frac{1}{80} + \frac{1}{90})}}$

$z = 1.302$

$-2.58 \qquad 0 \quad \uparrow \quad 2.58$
$\qquad\qquad\qquad 1.302$

Do not reject the null hypothesis. There is not enough evidence to support the claim that the proportions are different.

9. continued

$$(\hat{p}_1 - \hat{p}_2) - z_{\frac{\alpha}{2}}\sqrt{\frac{\hat{p}_1\hat{q}_1}{n_1} + \frac{\hat{p}_2\hat{q}_2}{n_2}} < p_1 - p_2 <$$

$$(\hat{p}_1 - \hat{p}_2) + z_{\frac{\alpha}{2}}\sqrt{\frac{\hat{p}_1\hat{q}_1}{n_1} + \frac{\hat{p}_2\hat{q}_2}{n_2}}$$

$$0.1 - 2.58\sqrt{\frac{0.55(0.45)}{80} + \frac{0.45(0.55)}{90}} < p_1 - p_2$$

$$< 0.1 + 2.58\sqrt{\frac{0.55(0.45)}{80} + \frac{0.45(0.55)}{90}}$$

$$-0.097 < p_1 - p_2 < 0.297$$

10.
$$\hat{p}_1 = \frac{X_1}{n_1} = \frac{130}{200} = 0.65$$
$$\hat{p}_2 = \frac{X_2}{n_2} = \frac{63}{300} = 0.21$$

$$\bar{p} = \frac{X_1 + X_2}{n_1 + n_2} = \frac{130 + 63}{200 + 300} = 0.386$$

$$\bar{q} = 1 - \bar{p} = 1 - 0.386 = 0.614$$

H_0: $p_1 \le p_2$
H_1: $p_1 > p_2$ (claim)

$$z = \frac{(0.65 - 0.21) - 0}{\sqrt{(0.386)(0.614)(\frac{1}{200} + \frac{1}{300})}} = 9.90$$

P-value < 0001
Since P-value < 0.01, reject the null
hypothesis. There is enough evidence to
support the claim that men are more safety-
conscious than women.

11.
$$\hat{p}_1 = \frac{26}{75} = 0.3467 \qquad \hat{p}_2 = \frac{26}{60} = 0.4333$$

$$\bar{p} = \frac{X_1 + X_2}{n_1 + n_2} = \frac{26 + 26}{75 + 60} = 0.3852$$

$$\bar{q} = 1 - \bar{p} = 1 - 0.3852 = 0.6148$$

H_0: $p_1 = p_2$
H_1: $p_1 \ne p_2$ (claim)

C. V. = ± 1.96 $\alpha = 0.05$
$$z = \frac{(\hat{p}_1 - \hat{p}_2) - (p_1 - p_2)}{\sqrt{(\bar{p})(\bar{q})(\frac{1}{n_1} + \frac{1}{n_2})}} = \frac{(0.3467 - 0.4333) - 0}{\sqrt{(0.3852)(0.6148)(\frac{1}{75} + \frac{1}{60})}}$$

$z = -1.027$ or -1.03

11. continued

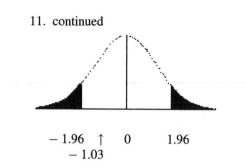

-1.96 ↑ 0   1.96
     -1.03

Do not reject the null hypothesis. There is
not enough evidence to support the claim
that the proportin of dog owners has
changed.

$$(\hat{p}_1 - \hat{p}_2) - z_{\frac{\alpha}{2}}\sqrt{\frac{\hat{p}_1\hat{q}_1}{n_1} + \frac{\hat{p}_2\hat{q}_2}{n_2}} < p_1 - p_2 <$$

$$(\hat{p}_1 - \hat{p}_2) + z_{\frac{\alpha}{2}}\sqrt{\frac{\hat{p}_1\hat{q}_1}{n_1} + \frac{\hat{p}_2\hat{q}_2}{n_2}}$$

$$-0.0866 - 1.96\sqrt{\frac{0.3467(0.6533)}{75} + \frac{0.4333(0.5667)}{60}}$$
$$< p_1 - p_2 <$$

$$-0.0866 + 1.96\sqrt{\frac{0.3467(0.6533)}{75} + \frac{0.4333(0.5667)}{60}}$$

$$-0.252 < p_1 - p_2 < 0.079$$

Yes, the confidence interval contains 0.
This is another way to conclude that there is
no difference in the proportions.

12.
$$\hat{p}_1 = 0.30 \qquad \hat{p}_2 = 0.24$$

$$X_1 = 0.30(100) = 30$$
$$X_2 = 0.24(100) = 24$$

$$\bar{p} = \frac{30 + 24}{100 + 100} = 0.27$$
$$\bar{q} = 1 - \bar{p} = 1 - 0.27 = 0.73$$

H_0: $p_1 = p_2$
H_1: $p_1 \ne p_2$ (claim)

$$z = \frac{(0.30 - 0.24) - 0}{\sqrt{(0.27)(0.73)(\frac{1}{100} + \frac{1}{100})}} = 0.96$$

P-value = 0.337
Since P-value > 0.02, do not reject the null
hypothesis. There is not enough evidence to
support the claim that the proportions are
different.

13.
$\hat{p}_1 = \frac{X_1}{n_1} = \frac{50}{200} = 0.25$

$\hat{p}_2 = \frac{X_2}{n_2} = \frac{93}{300} = 0.31$

$\bar{p} = \frac{X_1 + X_2}{n_1 + n_2} = \frac{50 + 93}{200 + 300} = 0.286$

$\bar{q} = 1 - \bar{p} = 1 - 0.286 = 0.714$

H_0: $p_1 = p_2$
H_1: $p_1 \neq p_2$ (claim)

C. V. $= \pm 2.58$ $\alpha = 0.01$
$z = \frac{(\hat{p}_1 - \hat{p}_2) - (p_1 - p_2)}{\sqrt{(\bar{p})(\bar{q})(\frac{1}{n_1} + \frac{1}{n_2})}} = \frac{(0.25 - 0.31) - 0}{\sqrt{(0.286)(0.714)(\frac{1}{200} + \frac{1}{300})}}$

$z = -1.45$

$-2.58 \quad \uparrow \quad 0 \qquad 2.58$
$\qquad\quad -1.45$

Do not reject the null hypothesis. There is not enough evidence to support the claim that the proportions are different.

$(\hat{p}_1 - \hat{p}_2) - z_{\frac{\alpha}{2}} \sqrt{\frac{\hat{p}_1 \hat{q}_1}{n_1} + \frac{\hat{p}_2 \hat{q}_2}{n_2}} < p_1 - p_2 <$

$\qquad (\hat{p}_1 - \hat{p}_2) + z_{\frac{\alpha}{2}} \sqrt{\frac{\hat{p}_1 \hat{q}_1}{n_1} + \frac{\hat{p}_2 \hat{q}_2}{n_2}}$

$-0.06 - 2.58 \sqrt{\frac{0.25(0.75)}{200} + \frac{0.31(0.69)}{300}} <$

$p_1 - p_2 < -0.06 + 2.58 \sqrt{\frac{0.25(0.75)}{200} + \frac{0.31(0.69)}{300}}$

$-0.165 < p_1 - p_2 < 0.045$

14.
$\hat{p}_1 = \frac{8}{50} = 0.16$ $\hat{p}_2 = \frac{20}{75} = 0.267$

$\bar{p} = \frac{8 + 20}{50 + 75} = 0.224$

$\bar{q} = 1 - \bar{p} = 0.776$

14. continued
H_0: $p_1 \geq p_2$
H_1: $p_1 < p_2$ (claim)

$z = \frac{(0.16 - 0.267) - 0}{\sqrt{(0.224)(0.776)(\frac{1}{50} + \frac{1}{75})}} = -1.41$

P-value $= 0.0793$
Since P-value > 0.05, do not reject the null hypothesis. There is not enough evidence to support the claim that the proportion of college freshmen who have their own cars is higher than the proportion of high school seniors who have their own cars.

15.
$\alpha = 0.01$
$\hat{p}_1 = 0.8$ $\qquad \hat{q}_1 = 0.2$
$\hat{p}_2 = 0.6$ $\qquad \hat{q}_2 = 0.4$

$\hat{p}_1 - \hat{p}_2 = 0.8 - 0.6 = 0.2$

$(\hat{p}_1 - \hat{p}_2) - z_{\frac{\alpha}{2}} \sqrt{\frac{\hat{p}_1 \hat{q}_1}{n_1} + \frac{\hat{p}_2 \hat{q}_2}{n_2}} < p_1 - p_2 <$

$\qquad (\hat{p}_1 - \hat{p}_2) + z_{\frac{\alpha}{2}} \sqrt{\frac{\hat{p}_1 \hat{q}_1}{n_1} + \frac{\hat{p}_2 \hat{q}_2}{n_2}}$

$0.2 - 2.58 \sqrt{\frac{(0.8)(0.2)}{150} + \frac{(0.6)(0.4)}{200}} < p_1 - p_2 <$

$\qquad 0.2 + 2.58 \sqrt{\frac{(0.8)(0.2)}{150} + \frac{(0.6)(0.4)}{200}}$

$0.077 < p_1 - p_2 < 0.323$

16.
$\hat{p}_1 = \frac{X_1}{n_1} = \frac{622}{1000} = 0.622$
$\hat{p}_2 = \frac{594}{1000} = 0.594$

$\bar{p} = \frac{X_1 + X_2}{n_1 + n_2} = \frac{622 + 594}{1000 + 1000} = 0.608$

$\bar{q} = 1 - \bar{p} = 1 - 0.608 = 0.392$

H_0: $p_1 \leq p_2$
H_1: $p_1 > p_2$ (claim)

C. V. $= 1.65$

$z = \frac{(\hat{p}_1 - \hat{p}_2) - (p_1 - p_2)}{\sqrt{(\bar{p})(\bar{q})(\frac{1}{n_1} + \frac{1}{n_2})}} = \frac{(0.622 - 0.594) - 0}{\sqrt{(0.608)(0.392)(\frac{1}{1000} + \frac{1}{1000})}}$

$z = 1.28$

16. continued

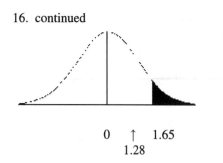

$$0 \quad \uparrow \quad 1.65$$
$$1.28$$

Do not reject the null hypothesis. There is not enough evidence to support the claim that the proportion of women working in Miami County is higher than in Greene County.

17.

$$\hat{p}_1 = \frac{X_1}{n_1} = \frac{43}{100} = 0.43 \quad \hat{p}_2 = \frac{58}{100} = 0.58$$

$$\bar{p} = \frac{X_1 + X_2}{n_1 + n_2} = \frac{43 + 58}{100 + 100} = 0.505$$

$$\bar{q} = 1 - \bar{p} = 1 - 0.505 = 0.495$$

H_0: $p_1 = p_2$
H_1: $p_1 \neq p_2$ (claim)

C. V. $= \pm 1.96$

$$z = \frac{(\hat{p}_1 - \hat{p}_2) - (p_1 - p_2)}{\sqrt{(\bar{p})(\bar{q})\left(\frac{1}{n_1} + \frac{1}{n_2}\right)}} = \frac{(0.43 - 0.58) - 0}{\sqrt{(0.505)(0.495)\left(\frac{1}{100} + \frac{1}{100}\right)}}$$

$$z = -2.12$$

$$\uparrow \quad -1.96 \qquad 0 \qquad 1.96$$
$$-2.12$$

Reject the null hypothesis. There is enough evidence to support the claim that the proportions are different.

18.
$$\hat{p}_1 = 0.4 \qquad \hat{q}_1 = 0.6$$

$$\hat{p}_2 = 0.56 \qquad \hat{q}_2 = 0.44$$

$$\hat{p}_1 - \hat{p}_2 = 0.4 - 0.56 = -0.16$$

18. continued

$$(\hat{p}_1 - \hat{p}_2) - z_{\frac{\alpha}{2}}\sqrt{\frac{\hat{p}_1\hat{q}_1}{n_1} + \frac{\hat{p}_2\hat{q}_2}{n_2}} < p_1 - p_2 <$$

$$(\hat{p}_1 - \hat{p}_2) + z_{\frac{\alpha}{2}}\sqrt{\frac{\hat{p}_1\hat{q}_1}{n_1} + \frac{\hat{p}_2\hat{q}_2}{n_2}}$$

$$-0.16 - 1.96\sqrt{\frac{(0.4)(0.6)}{200} + \frac{(0.56)(0.44)}{100}} < p_1 - p_2 <$$
$$-0.16 + 1.96\sqrt{\frac{(0.4)(0.6)}{200} + \frac{(0.56)(0.44)}{100}}$$

$$-0.279 < p_1 - p_2 < -0.041$$

19.
$$\hat{p}_1 = 0.2875 \qquad \hat{q}_1 = 0.7125$$
$$\hat{p}_2 = 0.2857 \qquad \hat{q}_2 = 0.7143$$

$$\hat{p}_1 - \hat{p}_2 = 0.0018$$

$$(\hat{p}_1 - \hat{p}_2) - z_{\frac{\alpha}{2}}\sqrt{\frac{\hat{p}_1\hat{q}_1}{n_1} + \frac{\hat{p}_2\hat{q}_2}{n_2}} < p_1 - p_2 <$$

$$(\hat{p}_1 - \hat{p}_2) + z_{\frac{\alpha}{2}}\sqrt{\frac{\hat{p}_1\hat{q}_1}{n_1} + \frac{\hat{p}_2\hat{q}_2}{n_2}}$$

$$0.0018 - 1.96\sqrt{\frac{(0.2875)(0.7125)}{400} + \frac{(0.2857)(0.7143)}{350}} < p_1 - p_2$$

$$< 0.0018 + 1.96\sqrt{\frac{(0.2875)(0.7125)}{400} + \frac{(0.2857)(0.7143)}{350}}$$

$$-0.0631 < p_1 - p_2 < 0.0667$$

It does agree with the *Almanac* statistics stating a difference of -0.042 since -0.042 is contained in the interval.

20.
No, because p_1 could equal p_3.

REVIEW EXERCISES - CHAPTER 9

1.
H_0: $\mu_1 \leq \mu_2$
H_1: $\mu_1 > \mu_2$ (claim)

$CV = 2.33 \qquad \alpha = 0.01$
$\bar{X}_1 = 120.1 \qquad \bar{X}_2 = 117.8$
$s_1 = 16.722 \qquad s_2 = 16.053$

$$z = \frac{(\bar{X}_1 - \bar{X}_2) - (\mu_1 - \mu_2)}{\sqrt{\frac{s_1^2}{n_1} + \frac{s_2^2}{n_2}}} = \frac{(120.1 - 117.8) - 0}{\sqrt{\frac{16.722^2}{36} + \frac{16.053^2}{35}}}$$

$$z = 0.587 \text{ or } 0.59$$

1. continued

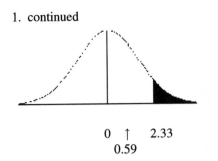

$$0 \quad \uparrow \quad 2.33$$
$$0.59$$

Do not reject the null hypothesis. There is not enough evidence to support the claim that single people do more pleasure driving than married people.

2.
H_0: $\sigma_1^2 = \sigma_2^2$
H_1: $\sigma_1^2 \neq \sigma_2^2$ (claim)

C. V. = 2.86 $\alpha = 0.05$
d. f. N = 17   d. f. D = 15

$F = \frac{s_1^2}{s_2^2} = \frac{585}{261} = 2.24$

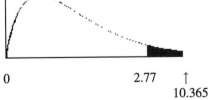

$$0 \qquad \uparrow \; 2.86$$
$$2.24$$

Do not reject the null hypothesis. There is not enough evidence to support the claim that the variances are different.

3.
H_0: $\sigma_1 = \sigma_2$
H_1: $\sigma_1 \neq \sigma_2$ (claim)

C. V. = 2.77 $\alpha = 0.10$
d. f. N = 23   d. f. D = 10

$F = \frac{13.2^2}{4.1^2} = 10.365$

$$0 \qquad\qquad 2.77 \quad \uparrow$$
$$10.365$$

3. continued
Reject the null hypothesis. There is enough evidence to support the claim that there is a difference in standard deviations.

4.
H_0: $\sigma_1^2 = \sigma_2^2$
H_1: $\sigma_1^2 \neq \sigma_2^2$ (claim)

C. V. = 1.98 $\alpha = 0.10$
d. f. N = 24   d. f. D = 24

$F = \frac{4.85^2}{2.25^2} = 2.16$

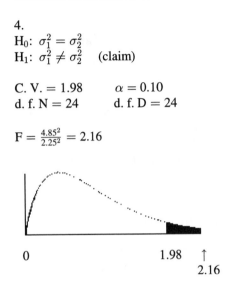

$$0 \qquad\qquad 1.98 \quad \uparrow$$
$$2.16$$

Reject the null hypothesis. There is enough evidence to support the claim that there is a significant difference between the variances of the heights for the two leagues.

5.
H_0: $\sigma_1^2 \leq \sigma_2^2$
H_1: $\sigma_1^2 > \sigma_2^2$ (claim)

$\alpha = 0.05$
d. f. N = 9   d. f. D = 9
$F = \frac{s_1^2}{s_2^2} = \frac{6.3^2}{2.8^2} = 5.06$

The P-value for the F test is $0.01 <$ P-value < 0.025 (0.012). Since P-value < 0.05, reject the null hypothesis. There is enough evidence to support the claim that the variance of the number of speeding tickets on Route 19 is greater than the variance of the number of speeding tickets issued on Route 22.

6.
H_0: $\sigma_1 = \sigma_2$
H_1: $\sigma_1 \neq \sigma_2$ (claim)

C. V. = 2.76 $\alpha = 0.01$
d. f. N = 29   d. f. D = 29

$F = \frac{4.9^2}{2.5^2} = 3.84$

6. continued

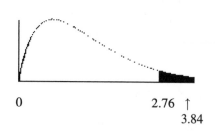

0   2.76 ↑
             3.84

Reject the null hypothesis. There is enough evidence to support the claim that there is a difference in the standard deviations in the number of absentees of the two schools.

7.

H_0: $\sigma_1^2 \leq \sigma_2^2$
H_1: $\sigma_1^2 > \sigma_2^2$ (claim)

C. V. = 1.47 $\alpha = 0.10$
d. f. N = 64   d. f. D = 41

$F = \frac{s_1^2}{s_2^2} = \frac{3.2^2}{2.1^2} = 2.32$

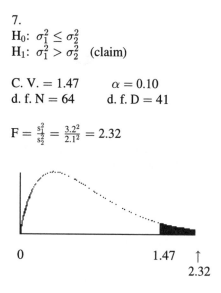

0   1.47 ↑
           2.32

Reject the null hypothesis. There is enough evidence to support the claim that the variation in the number of days factory workers miss per year due to illness is greater than the variation in the number of days hospital workers miss per year.

8.

H_0: $\sigma_1^2 = \sigma_2^2$ (claim)
H_1: $\sigma_1^2 \neq \sigma_2^2$
C. V. = 3.47 $F = \frac{(0.05)^2}{(0.03)^2} = 2.78$
Do not reject. The variances are equal.

H_0: $\mu_1 = \mu_2$
H_1: $\mu_1 \neq \mu_2$

C. V. = ± 2.58 d. f. = 37

$t = \frac{(0.73 - 0.91) - 0}{\sqrt{\frac{14(0.05)^2 + 23(0.03)^2}{15 + 24 - 2}}\sqrt{\frac{1}{15} + \frac{1}{24}}} = -14.09$

8. continued

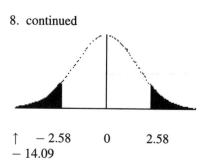

↑ -2.58 0   2.58
-14.09

Reject the null hypothesis. There is enough evidence to support the claim that there is a difference in the prices of soups.

9.
H_0: $\sigma_1^2 = \sigma_2^2$
H_1: $\sigma_1^2 \neq \sigma_2^2$

$\overline{X}_1 = 72.9$ $\overline{X}_2 = 70.8$
$s_1 = 5.5$ $s_2 = 5.8$
CV = 1.98 $\alpha = 0.01$
dfN = 24   dfD = 24
$F = \frac{5.8^2}{5.5^2} = 1.11$

Do not reject H_0. The variances are equal.

H_0: $\mu_1 \leq \mu_2$
H_1: $\mu_1 > \mu_2$ (claim)

C. V. = 1.28   d. f. = 48 $\alpha = 0.10$

$t = \frac{(\overline{X}_1 - \overline{X}_2) - (\mu_1 - \mu_2)}{\sqrt{\frac{(n_1 - 1)s_1^2 + (n_2 - 1)s_2^2}{n_1 + n_2 - 2}}\sqrt{\frac{1}{n_1} + \frac{1}{n_2}}}$

$t = \frac{(72.9 - 70.8) - 0}{\sqrt{\frac{24(5.5)^2 + 24(5.8)^2}{25 + 25 - 2}}\sqrt{\frac{1}{25} + \frac{1}{25}}} = 1.31$

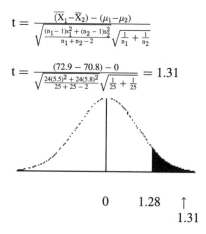

0   1.28 ↑
          1.31

Reject the null hypothesis. There is enough evidence to support the claim that it is warmer in Birmingham.

10.
H_0: $\sigma_1^2 = \sigma_2^2$
H_1: $\sigma_1^2 \neq \sigma_2^2$

10. continued

C. V. $= 2.87$ $\quad$ F $= \frac{3256^2}{1432^2} = 5.17$

Reject. The variances are unequal.

H_0: $\mu_1 = \mu_2$
H_1: $\mu_1 \neq \mu_2$ $\quad$ (claim)

C. V. $= \pm 2.624$ $\qquad$ d. f. $= 14$

$t = \frac{(\overline{X}_1 - \overline{X}_2) - (\mu_1 - \mu_2)}{\sqrt{\frac{s_1^2}{n_1} + \frac{s_2^2}{n_2}}} = \frac{(35,270 - 29,512) - 0}{\sqrt{\frac{3256^2}{15} + \frac{1432^2}{15}}}$

$t = 6.54$

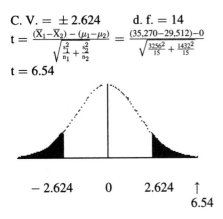

$-2.624 \qquad 0 \qquad 2.624 \qquad \uparrow$
$\qquad\qquad\qquad\qquad\qquad\qquad 6.54$

Reject the null hypothesis. There is enough evidence to support the claim that there is a difference in the teachers' salaries.

98% Confidence Interval:
$3,494.80 < \mu_1 - \mu_2 < 8,021.20$

11.
H_0: $\sigma_1^2 = \sigma_2^2$
H_1: $\sigma_1^2 \neq \sigma_2^2$
$\overline{X}_1 = 150.8333$ $\quad$ $s_1 = 173.1432$
$\overline{X}_2 = 254$ $\qquad$ $s_2 = 183.4748$
$\alpha = 0.05$
dfN $= 15$ $\quad$ dfD $= 11$
F $= \frac{183.47^2}{173.14^2} = 1.12$ (TI83 gives 0.89)
Do not reject H_0 since P-value > 0.10. The variances are equal.

H_0: $\mu_1 = \mu_2$
H_1: $\mu_1 \neq \mu_2$ $\quad$ (claim)

$\alpha = 0.05$ $\quad$ P-value $= 0.4348$

$t = \frac{(150.8333 - 254) - 0}{\sqrt{\frac{5(173.1432)^2 + 2(183.4748)^2}{7}} \sqrt{\frac{1}{6} + \frac{1}{3}}} = -0.828$

Do not reject the null hypothesis since P-value > 0.10. There is not enough evidence to support the claim that the means are different. A cafeteria manager would want to know the results in order to make a decision on which beverage to serve.

12.

Pre-Test	Post-Test	D	D^2
83	88	-5	25
76	82	-6	36
92	100	-8	64
64	72	-8	64
82	81	1	1
68	75	-7	49
70	79	-9	81
71	68	3	9
72	81	-9	81
63	70	-7	49
		$\sum D = -55$	$\sum D^2 = 459$

H_0: $\mu_D \geq 0$
H_1: $\mu_D < 0$ $\quad$ (claim)

C. V. $= -2.821$ $\qquad$ d. f. $= 9$

$\overline{D} = \frac{\sum D}{n} = -5.5$

$s_D = \sqrt{\frac{\sum D^2 - \frac{(\sum D)^2}{n}}{n-1}} = \sqrt{\frac{459 - \frac{(-55)^2}{10}}{9}}$

$s_D = 4.17$

$t = \frac{\overline{D} - \mu_D}{\frac{s_D}{\sqrt{n}}} = \frac{-5.5 - 0}{\frac{4.17}{\sqrt{10}}} = -4.17$

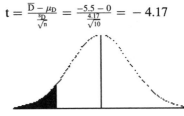

$\uparrow \quad -2.821 \qquad 0$
-4.17

Reject the null hypothesis. There is enough evidence to support the claim that the tutoring sessions helped to improve the students' vocabulary.

13.

Before	After	D	D^2
6	10	-4	16
8	12	-4	16
10	9	1	1
9	12	-3	9
5	8	-3	9
12	13	-1	1
9	8	1	1
7	10	-3	9
		$\sum D = -16$	$\sum D^2 = 62$

H_0: $\mu_D \geq 0$
H_1: $\mu_D < 0$ $\quad$ (claim)

C. V. $= -1.895$ $\quad$ d. f. $= 7$ $\quad$ $\alpha = 0.05$

$\overline{D} = \frac{\sum D}{n} = \frac{-16}{8} = -2$

13. continued

$$s_D = \sqrt{\frac{62 - \frac{(-16)^2}{8}}{7}} = 2.07$$

$$t = \frac{-2 - 0}{\frac{2.07}{\sqrt{8}}} = -2.73$$

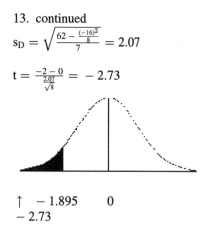

$\uparrow \quad -1.895 \qquad 0$
-2.73

Reject the null hypothesis. There is enough evidence to support the claim that the music has increased production.

14.

$$\hat{p}_1 = \frac{207}{365} = 0.567 \quad \hat{p}_2 = \frac{166}{365} = 0.455$$

$$\bar{p} = \frac{207 + 166}{365 + 365} = 0.511$$

$$\bar{q} = 1 - 0.51 = 0.489$$

H_0: $p_1 = p_2$
H_1: $p_1 \neq p_2$ (claim)

C. V. $= \pm 2.33$

$$z = \frac{(0.567 - 0.455) - 0}{\sqrt{(0.511)(0.489)(\frac{1}{365} + \frac{1}{365})}} = 3.03$$

$-2.33 \qquad 0 \qquad 2.33 \quad \uparrow$
3.03

Reject the null hypothesis. There is enough evidence to support the claim that the proportions are different.

For the 98% confidence interval:

$$(\hat{p}_1 - \hat{p}_2) - z_{\frac{\alpha}{2}}\sqrt{\frac{\hat{p}_1\hat{q}_1}{n_1} + \frac{\hat{p}_2\hat{q}_2}{n_2}} < p_1 - p_2 <$$
$$(\hat{p}_1 - \hat{p}_2) + z_{\frac{\alpha}{2}}\sqrt{\frac{\hat{p}_1\hat{q}_1}{n_1} + \frac{\hat{p}_2\hat{q}_2}{n_2}}$$

$\hat{p}_1 = 0.567 \qquad \hat{q}_1 = 0.433$

14. continued

$\hat{p}_2 = 0.455 \qquad \hat{q}_2 = 0.545$

$$(0.567 - 0.455) - 2.33\sqrt{\frac{(0.567)(0.433)}{365} + \frac{(0.455)(0.545)}{365}}$$

$$< p_1 - p_2 < (0.567 - 0.455) + 2.33\sqrt{\frac{(0.567)(0.433)}{365} + \frac{(0.455)(0.545)}{365}}$$

$$0.112 - 0.086 < p_1 - p_2 < 0.112 + 0.086$$

$$0.026 < p_1 - p_2 < 0.198$$

15.

$$\hat{p}_1 = \frac{18}{120} = 0.15 \qquad \hat{p}_2 = \frac{5}{100} = 0.05$$

$$\bar{p} = \frac{18 + 5}{120 + 100} = 0.1045$$

$$\bar{q} = 1 - 0.1045 = 0.8955$$

H_0: $p_1 = p_2$ (claim)
H_1: $p_1 \neq p_2$

C. V. $= \pm 1.96 \qquad \alpha = 0.05$

$$z = \frac{(0.15 - 0.05) - 0}{\sqrt{(0.1045)(0.8955)(\frac{1}{120} + \frac{1}{100})}} = 2.41$$

$-1.96 \qquad 0 \qquad 1.96 \quad \uparrow$
2.41

Reject the null hypothesis. There is enough evidence to support the claim that the proportion has changed.

For the 95% confidence interval:
$\hat{p}_1 = 0.15 \qquad \hat{q}_1 = 0.85$
$\hat{p}_2 = 0.05 \qquad \hat{q}_2 = 0.95$

$$(0.15 - 0.05) - 1.96\sqrt{\frac{(0.15)(0.85)}{120} + \frac{(0.05)(0.95)}{100}}$$

$$< p_1 - p_2 < (0.15 - 0.05) + 1.96\sqrt{\frac{(0.15)(0.85)}{120} + \frac{(0.05)(0.95)}{100}}$$

$$0.10 - 1.96(0.0392) < p_1 - p_2 <$$

$$0.10 + 1.96(0.0392)$$

$$0.023 < p_1 - p_2 < 0.177$$

Chapter 9 - Testing the Difference Between
Two Means, Two Variances, and Two Proportions

CHAPTER 9 QUIZ

1. False, there are different formulas for independent and dependent samples.
2. False, the samples are independent.
3. True
4. False, they can be right, left, or two tailed.
5. d
6. a
7. c
8. b
9. $\mu_1 = \mu_2$
10. Pooled
11. Normal
12. Negative
13. $\frac{s_1^2}{s_2^2}$

14. H_0: $\mu_1 = \mu_2$
   H_1: $\mu_1 \neq \mu_2$ (claim)
   C. V. $= \pm 2.58$ $z = -3.69$
   Reject the null hypothesis. There is enough evidence to support the claim that there is a difference in the cholesterol levels of the two groups.
   99% Confidence Interval:
   $-10.2 < \mu_1 - \mu_2 < -1.8$

15. H_0: $\mu_1 \leq \mu_2$
   H_1: $\mu_1 > \mu_2$ (claim)
   C. V. $= 1.28$ $z = 1.60$
   Reject the null hypothesis. There is enough evidence to support the claim that average rental fees for the eastern apartments is greater than the average rental fees for the western apartments.

16. H_0: $\sigma_1^2 = \sigma_2^2$
   H_1: $\sigma_1^2 \neq \sigma_1^2$ (claim)
   F $= 1.637$ P-value > 0.20 (0.357)
   Do not reject the null hypothesis since P-value > 0.05. There is not enough evidence to support the claim that the variances are different.

17. H_0: $\sigma_1^2 = \sigma_2^2$
   H_1: $\sigma_1^2 \neq \sigma_2^2$ (claim)
   C. V. $= 1.90$ F $= 1.296$
   Do not reject the null hypothesis. There is not enough evidence to support the claim that the variances are different.

18. H_0: $\sigma_1 = \sigma_2$ (claim)
   H_1 $\sigma_1 \neq \sigma_2$
   C. V. $= 3.53$ F $= 1.13$
   Do not reject the null hypothesis. There is not enough evidence to reject the claim that the standard deviations of the number of hours of television viewing are the same.

19. H_0: $\sigma_1^2 = \sigma_2^2$
   H_1 $\sigma_1^2 \neq \sigma_2^2$ (claim)
   C. V. $= 3.01$ F $= 1.94$
   Do not reject the null hypothesis. There is not enough evidence to support the claim that the variances are different.

20. H_0: $\sigma_1^2 \leq \sigma_2^2$
   H_1 $\sigma_1^2 > \sigma_2^2$ (claim)
   C. V. $= 5.05$ F $= 1.08$
   Do not reject the null hypothesis. There is not enough evidence to support the claim that the variance of the number of murders committed on the East Coast is greater than the variance of the number of murders committed on the West Coast. One factor that could influence the results is the populations of the cities that were selected.

21. H_0: $\sigma_1 = \sigma_2$
   H_1 $\sigma_1 \neq \sigma_2$ (claim)
   C. V. $= 2.46$ F $= 1.65$
   Do not reject the null hypothesis. There is not enough evidence to support the claim that the standard deviations are different.

22. H_0: $\sigma_1^2 = \sigma_2^2$
   H_1 $\sigma_1^2 \neq \sigma_2^2$
   C. V. $= 5.05$ F $= 1.23$
   Do not reject. The variances are equal.

   H_0: $\mu_1 = \mu_2$
   H_1: $\mu_1 \neq \mu_2$ (claim)
   C. V. $= \pm 2.779$ $t = 10.922$
   Reject the null hypothesis. There is enough evidence to support the claim that the average prices are different.

   99% Confidence Interval:
   $0.298 < \mu_1 - \mu_2 < 0.502$

23. H_0: $\sigma_1^2 = \sigma_2^2$
   H_1 $\sigma_1^2 \neq \sigma_2^2$
   C. V. $= 9.6$ F $= 5.71$
   Do not reject. The variances are equal.

23. continued
H_0: $\mu_1 \geq \mu_2$
H_1: $\mu_1 < \mu_2$ (claim)
C. V. $= -1.860$ $t = -4.05$
Reject the null hypothesis. There is enough
evidence to support the claim that accidents
have increased.

24. H_0: $\sigma_1^2 = \sigma_2^2$
H_1 $\sigma_1^2 \neq \sigma_2^2$
C. V. $= 4.02$ $F = 6.155$
Reject. The variances are unequal.

H_0: $\mu_1 = \mu_2$
H_1: $\mu_1 \neq \mu_2$ (claim)
C. V. $= \pm 2.718$ $t = 9.807$
Reject the null hypothesis. There is enough
evidence to support the claim that the
salaries are different.

98% Confidence Interval:
$\$6653 < \mu_1 - \mu_2 < \$11,757$

25. H_0: $\sigma_1^2 = \sigma_2^2$
H_1 $\sigma_1^2 \neq \sigma_2^2$
$F = 23.08$ P-value < 0.05
Reject. The variances are unequal.

H_0: $\mu_1 \leq \mu_2$
H_1: $\mu_1 > \mu_2$ (claim)
$t = 0.874$ $0.10 < $ P-value < 0.25 (0.198)
Do not reject the null hypothesis since P-
value > 0.05. There is not enough evidence
to support the claim that incomes of city
residents is greater than incomes of rural
residents.

26. H_0: $\mu_1 \geq \mu_2$
H_1: $\mu_1 < \mu_2$ (claim)
$\overline{D} = -6.5$ $s_D = 4.93$
C. V. $= -2.821$ $t = -4.172$
Reject the null hypothesis. There is enough
evidence to support the claim that the
sessions improved math skills.

27. H_0: $\mu_1 \geq \mu_2$
H_1: $\mu_1 < \mu_2$ (claim)
$\overline{D} = -0.8$ $s_D = 1.48$
C. V. $= -1.833$ $t = -1.714$
Do not reject the null hypothesis. There is
not enough evidence to support the claim
that egg production increased.

28. H_0: $p_1 = p_2$
H_1: $p_1 \neq p_2$ (claim)
C. V. $= \pm 1.65$ $z = -0.69$
Do not reject the null hypothesis. There is
not enough evidence to support the claim
that the proportions are different.

90% Confidence Interval:
$-0.105 < p_1 - p_2 < 0.045$

29. H_0: $p_1 = p_2$ (claim)
H_1: $p_1 \neq p_2$
C. V. $= \pm 1.96$ $z = 0.544$
Do not reject the null hypothesis. There is
not enough evidence to support the claim
that the proportions have changed.

95% Confidence Interval:
$-0.026 < p_1 - p_2 < 0.0460$

Yes, the confidence interval contains 0;
hence, the null hypothesis is not rejected.

Note: Graphs are not to scale and are intended to convey a general idea.

Answers may vary due to rounding, TI-83's, or computer programs.

EXERCISE SET 10-2

1.
Two variables are related when there exists a discernible pattern between them.

2.
Relationships are measured by the correlation coefficient, r. When r is near $+1$, there is a strong positive linear relationship between the variables. When r is near -1, there is a strong negative linear relationship. When r is near zero, there is no linear relationship between the variables.

3.
r, ρ (rho)

4.
The range of r is from -1 to $+1$.

5.
A positive relationship means that as x increases, y also increases.
A negative relationship means that as x increases, y decreases.

6.
Answers will vary.

7.
Answers will vary.

8.
The diagram is called a scatter plot. It shows the nature of the relationship.

9.
Pearson's Product Moment Correlation Coefficient.

10.
t test

11.
There are many other possibilities, such as chance, relationship to a third variable, etc.

12.

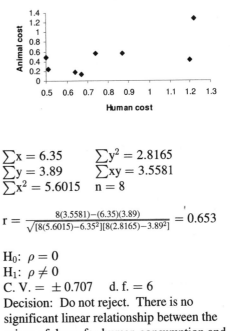

Human vs. Animal Cost

$\sum x = 6.35 \qquad \sum y^2 = 2.8165$
$\sum y = 3.89 \qquad \sum xy = 3.5581$
$\sum x^2 = 5.6015 \qquad n = 8$

$$r = \frac{8(3.5581)-(6.35)(3.89)}{\sqrt{[8(5.6015)-6.35^2][8(2.8165)-3.89^2]}} = 0.653$$

H_0: $\rho = 0$
H_1: $\rho \neq 0$
C. V. $= \pm 0.707$ \qquad d. f. $= 6$
Decision: Do not reject. There is no significant linear relationship between the prices of drugs for human consumption and the prices of the same drugs for animal consumption.

13.

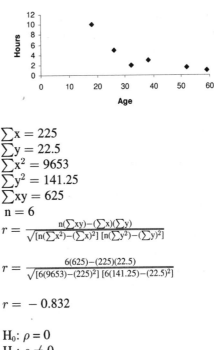

Age vs. Exercise

$\sum x = 225$
$\sum y = 22.5$
$\sum x^2 = 9653$
$\sum y^2 = 141.25$
$\sum xy = 625$
$n = 6$

$$r = \frac{n(\sum xy)-(\sum x)(\sum y)}{\sqrt{[n(\sum x^2)-(\sum x)^2][n(\sum y^2)-(\sum y)^2]}}$$

$$r = \frac{6(625)-(225)(22.5)}{\sqrt{[6(9653)-(225)^2][6(141.25)-(22.5)^2]}}$$

$$r = -0.832$$

H_0: $\rho = 0$
H_1: $\rho \neq 0$
C. V. $= \pm 0.811$ \qquad d. f. $= 4$

13. continued
Decision: Reject. There is a significant
linear relationship between a person's age
and the number of hours a person exercises.

14.

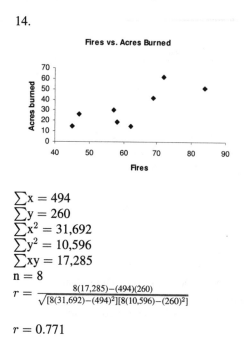

Fires vs. Acres Burned

$\sum x = 494$
$\sum y = 260$
$\sum x^2 = 31{,}692$
$\sum y^2 = 10{,}596$
$\sum xy = 17{,}285$
$n = 8$
$$r = \frac{8(17{,}285) - (494)(260)}{\sqrt{[8(31{,}692) - (494)^2][8(10{,}596) - (260)^2]}}$$

$r = 0.771$

H_0: $\rho = 0$
H_1: $\rho \neq 0$
C. V. $= \pm 0.707$ d. f. $= 6$
Decision: Reject. There is a significant
linear relationship between the number of
forest fires and the number of acres burned.

15.

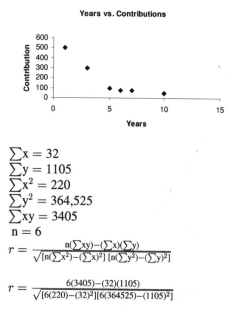

Years vs. Contributions

$\sum x = 32$
$\sum y = 1105$
$\sum x^2 = 220$
$\sum y^2 = 364{,}525$
$\sum xy = 3405$
$n = 6$
$$r = \frac{n(\sum xy) - (\sum x)(\sum y)}{\sqrt{[n(\sum x^2) - (\sum x)^2]\,[n(\sum y^2) - (\sum y)^2]}}$$

$$r = \frac{6(3405) - (32)(1105)}{\sqrt{[6(220) - (32)^2][6(364525) - (1105)^2]}}$$

15. continued
$r = -0.883$

H_0: $\rho = 0$
H_1: $\rho \neq 0$
C. V. $= \pm 0.811$ d. f. $= 4$
Decision: Reject. There is a significant
linear relationship between the number of
years a person has been out of school and his
or her contribution.

16.

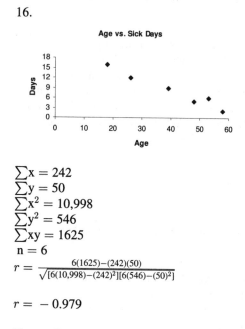

Age vs. Sick Days

$\sum x = 242$
$\sum y = 50$
$\sum x^2 = 10{,}998$
$\sum y^2 = 546$
$\sum xy = 1625$
$n = 6$
$$r = \frac{6(1625) - (242)(50)}{\sqrt{[6(10{,}998) - (242)^2][6(546) - (50)^2]}}$$

$r = -0.979$

H_0: $\rho = 0$
H_1: $\rho \neq 0$
C. V. $= \pm 0.811$ d. f. $= 4$
Decision: Reject. There is a significant
linear relationship between a person's age
and the number of sick days that person
takes each year.

17.

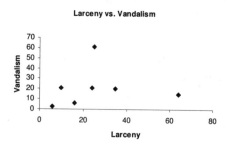

Larceny vs. Vandalism

$\sum x = 180$
$\sum y = 147$
$\sum x^2 = 6914$

176

17. continued

$\sum y^2 = 5273$

$\sum xy = 4013$

$n = 7$

$r = \frac{n(\sum xy) - (\sum x)(\sum y)}{\sqrt{[n(\sum x^2) - (\sum x)^2][n(\sum y^2) - (\sum y)^2]}}$

$r = \frac{7(4013) - (180)(147)}{\sqrt{[7(6914) - (180)^2][7(5273) - (147)^2]}}$

$r = 0.104$

H_0: $\rho = 0$

H_1: $\rho \neq 0$

C. V. $= \pm 0.754$ d. f. $= 5$

Decision: Do not reject. There is no significant linear relationship between the number of larceny crimes and the number of vandalism crimes committed on college campuses in southwestern Pennsylvania.

18.

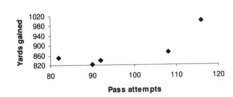

Pass Attempts vs. Yards Gained

$\sum x = 488$

$\sum y = 4387$

$\sum x^2 = 48,408$

$\sum y^2 = 3,869,581$

$\sum xy = 431,440$

$n = 5$

$r = \frac{5(431,440) - (488)(4387)}{\sqrt{[5(48,408) - (488)^2][5(3,869,581) - (4387)^2]}}$

$r = 0.819$

H_0: $\rho = 0$

H_1: $\rho \neq 0$

C. V. $= \pm 0.878$ d. f. $= 3$

Decision: Do not reject. There is no significant linear relationship between the number of pass attempts by a quarterback and the number of yards gained on these plays.

19.

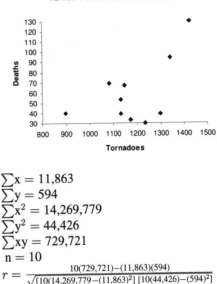

Numbers of Tornadoes vs. Deaths

$\sum x = 11,863$

$\sum y = 594$

$\sum x^2 = 14,269,779$

$\sum y^2 = 44,426$

$\sum xy = 729,721$

$n = 10$

$r = \frac{10(729,721) - (11,863)(594)}{\sqrt{[10(14,269,779) - (11,863)^2][10(44,426) - (594)^2]}}$

$r = 0.580$

H_0: $\rho = 0$

H_1: $\rho \neq 0$

C. V. $= \pm 0.632$ d. f. $= 8$

Decision: Do not reject. There is no significant linear relationship between the number of tornadoes per year and the number of deaths per year from these tornadoes.

20.

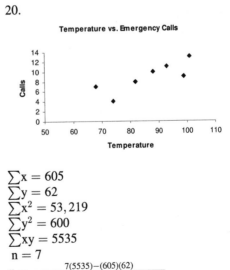

Temperature vs. Emergency Calls

$\sum x = 605$

$\sum y = 62$

$\sum x^2 = 53,219$

$\sum y^2 = 600$

$\sum xy = 5535$

$n = 7$

$r = \frac{7(5535) - (605)(62)}{\sqrt{[7(53219) - (605)^2][7(600) - (62)^2]}}$

$r = 0.811$

20. continued

H_0: $\rho = 0$

H_1: $\rho \neq 0$

C. V. $= \pm 0.754$ d. f. $= 5$

Decision: Reject. There is a significant linear relationship between the temperature and the number of emergency calls received.

21.

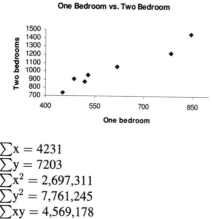

Age Relationship

$\sum$x $= 1862$

$\sum$y $= 3222$

$\sum$x^2 $= 1,026,026$

$\sum$y^2 $= 3,009,596$

$\sum$xy $= 1,754,975$

n $= 6$

$$r = \frac{n(\sum xy) - (\sum x)(\sum y)}{\sqrt{[n(\sum x^2) - (\sum x)^2]\,[n(\sum y^2) - (\sum y)^2]}}$$

$$r = \frac{6(1,754,975) - (1862)(3222)}{\sqrt{[6(1,026,026) - 1862^2][6(3,009,596) - 3222^2]}}$$

$r = 0.997$

H_0: $\rho = 0$

H_1: $\rho \neq 0$

C. V. $= \pm 0.811$ d. f. $= 4$

Decision: Reject. There is a significant linear relationship between the under 5 age group and the 65 and over age group.

22.

One Bedroom vs. Two Bedroom

$\sum$x $= 4231$

$\sum$y $= 7203$

$\sum$x^2 $= 2,697,311$

$\sum$y^2 $= 7,761,245$

$\sum$xy $= 4,569,178$

n $= 7$

22. continued

$$r = \frac{7(4,569,178) - (4231)(7203)}{\sqrt{[7(2,697,311) - (4231)^2][7(7,761,245) - (7203)^2]}}$$

$r = 0.974$

H_0: $\rho = 0$

H_1: $\rho \neq 0$

C. V. $= \pm 0.754$ d. f. $= 5$

Decision: Reject. There is a significant linear relationship between monthly rents for one bedroom and two bedroom apartments.

23.

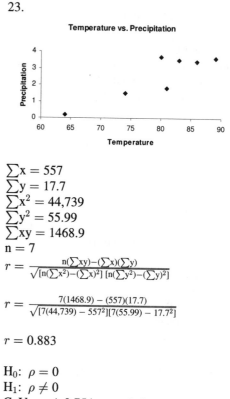

Temperature vs. Precipitation

$\sum$x $= 557$

$\sum$y $= 17.7$

$\sum$x^2 $= 44,739$

$\sum$y^2 $= 55.99$

$\sum$xy $= 1468.9$

n $= 7$

$$r = \frac{n(\sum xy) - (\sum x)(\sum y)}{\sqrt{[n(\sum x^2) - (\sum x)^2]\,[n(\sum y^2) - (\sum y)^2]}}$$

$$r = \frac{7(1468.9) - (557)(17.7)}{\sqrt{[7(44,739) - 557^2][7(55.99) - 17.7^2]}}$$

$r = 0.883$

H_0: $\rho = 0$

H_1: $\rho \neq 0$

C. V. $= \pm 0.754$ d. f. $= 5$

Decision: Reject. There is a significant linear relationship between the average daily temperature and the average monthly precipitation.

24.

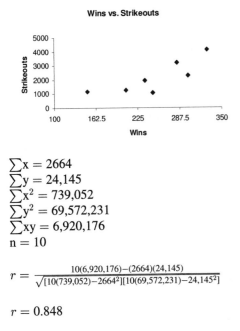

$\sum x = 2664$
$\sum y = 24{,}145$
$\sum x^2 = 739{,}052$
$\sum y^2 = 69{,}572{,}231$
$\sum xy = 6{,}920{,}176$
$n = 10$

$$r = \frac{10(6{,}920{,}176)-(2664)(24{,}145)}{\sqrt{[10(739{,}052)-2664^2][10(69{,}572{,}231)-24{,}145^2]}}$$

$r = 0.848$

H_0: $\rho = 0$
H_1: $\rho \neq 0$
C. V. $= \pm 0.632$ d. f. $= 8$

Decision: Reject. There is a significant linear relationship between the number of career wins and the number of strikeouts for Hall of Fame pitchers.

25.

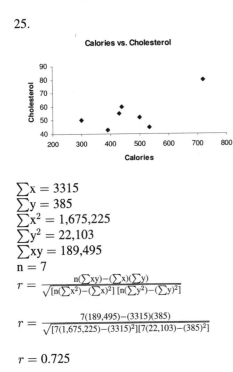

$\sum x = 3315$
$\sum y = 385$
$\sum x^2 = 1{,}675{,}225$
$\sum y^2 = 22{,}103$
$\sum xy = 189{,}495$
$n = 7$
$$r = \frac{n(\sum xy)-(\sum x)(\sum y)}{\sqrt{[n(\sum x^2)-(\sum x)^2]\,[n(\sum y^2)-(\sum y)^2]}}$$

$$r = \frac{7(189{,}495)-(3315)(385)}{\sqrt{[7(1{,}675{,}225)-(3315)^2][7(22{,}103)-(385)^2]}}$$

$r = 0.725$

25. continued
H_0: $\rho = 0$
H_1: $\rho \neq 0$
C. V. $= \pm 0.754$ d. f. $= 5$
Decision: Do not reject. There is a no significant linear relationship between the number of calories and the cholesterol content of fast-food chicken sandwiches.

26.

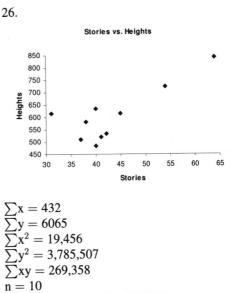

$\sum x = 432$
$\sum y = 6065$
$\sum x^2 = 19{,}456$
$\sum y^2 = 3{,}785{,}507$
$\sum xy = 269{,}358$
$n = 10$
$$r = \frac{10(269{,}358)-(432)(6065)}{\sqrt{[10(19{,}456)-(432)^2][10(3{,}785{,}507)-(6065)^2]}}$$

$r = 0.797$

H_0: $\rho = 0$
H_1: $\rho \neq 0$
C. V. $= \pm 0.632$ d. f. $= 8$
Decision: Reject. There is a significant linear relationship between the heights of buildings and the number of stories these buildings contain.

27.

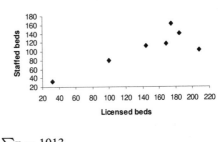

$\sum x = 1013$
$\sum y = 748$
$\sum x^2 = 168{,}435$
$\sum y^2 = 90{,}626$

27. continued

$\sum xy = 120,953$

n = 7

$r = \dfrac{7(120,953)-(1013)(748)}{\sqrt{[7(168,435)-(1013)^2][7(90,626)-(748)^2]}}$

$r = 0.831$

H_0: $\rho = 0$
H_1: $\rho \neq 0$
C. V. $= \pm 0.754$ d. f. $= 5$
Decision: Reject. There is a significant linear relationship between the number of licensed beds in a hospital and the number of staffed beds.

28.

$\bar{x} = 144.714$
$\bar{y} = 106.857$
$\sum(x - \bar{x})(y - \bar{y}) = 12,706.715$
$s_x = 60.332$
$s_y = 42.223$
$r = \dfrac{(12,706.715)}{(7-1)(60.332)(42.223)} = 0.831$

29.

$r = \dfrac{n(\sum xy)-(\sum x)(\sum y)}{\sqrt{[n(\sum x^2)-(\sum x)^2][n(\sum y^2)-(\sum y)^2]}}$

$r = \dfrac{5(125)-(15)(35)}{\sqrt{[5(55)-(15)^2][5(285)-(35)^2]}} = 1$

$r = \dfrac{5(125)-(35)(15)}{\sqrt{[5(285)-(35)^2][5(55)-(15)^2]}} = 1$

The value of r does not change when the values for x and y are interchanged.

30.

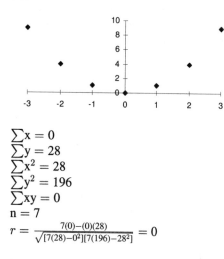

$\sum x = 0$
$\sum y = 28$
$\sum x^2 = 28$
$\sum y^2 = 196$
$\sum xy = 0$
n = 7
$r = \dfrac{7(0)-(0)(28)}{\sqrt{[7(28)-0^2][7(196)-28^2]}} = 0$

The relationship is non-linear, as shown in the scatter plot.

EXERCISE 10-3

1.
Draw the scatter plot and test the significance of the correlation coefficient.

2. The assumptions are:

1. For any specific value of the independent variable x, the value of the dependent variable y must be normally distributed about the regression line.

2. The standard deviation of each of the dependent variables must be the same for each value of the independent variable.

3.
$y' = a + bx$

4.
b, a

5.
It is the line that is drawn through the points on the scatter plot such that the sum of the squares of the vertical distances each point is from the line is at a minimum.

6.
r would equal $+1$ or -1

7.
When r is positive, b will be positive. When r is negative, b will be negative.

8.
They would be clustered closer to the line.

9.
The closer r is to $+1$ or -1, the more accurate the predicted value will be.

10.
If the value of r is not significant, no regression should be done. Any regression line is meaningless.

11.
When r is not significant, the mean of the y values should be used to predict y.

12.
Since r is not significant, no regression should be done.

13.

$$a = \frac{(\sum y)(\sum x^2) - (\sum x)(\sum xy)}{n(\sum x^2) - (\sum x)^2}$$

$$a = \frac{(22.5)(9653) - (225)(625)}{6(9653) - (225)^2} = 10.499$$

$$b = \frac{n(\sum xy) - (\sum x)(\sum y)}{n(\sum x^2) - (\sum x)^2}$$

$$b = \frac{6(625) - (225)(22.5)}{6(9653) - (225)^2} = -0.18$$

$y' = a + bx$
$y' = 10.499 - 0.18x$
$y' = 10.499 - 0.18(35) = 4.199$ hours or
4.2 hours

14.

$$a = \frac{(260)(31,692) - (494)(17,285)}{8(31,692) - (494)^2}$$

$$a = \frac{-298,870}{9500} = -31.46$$

$$b = \frac{8(17,285) - (494)(260)}{8(31,692) - (494)^2} = \frac{9840}{9500}$$

$b = 1.036$

$y' = -31.46 + 1.036x$
$y' = -31.46 + 1.036(60) = 30.7$ acres

15.

$$a = \frac{(\sum y)(\sum x^2) - (\sum x)(\sum xy)}{n(\sum x^2) - (\sum x)^2}$$

$$a = \frac{(1105)(220) - (32)(3405)}{6(220) - (32)^2}$$

$$a = \frac{243100 - 108960}{1320 - 1024} = \frac{134140}{296} = 453.176$$

$$b = \frac{n(\sum xy) - (\sum x)(\sum y)}{n(\sum x^2) - (\sum x)^2}$$

$$b = \frac{6(3405) - (32)(1105)}{6(220) - (32)^2} = \frac{20430 - 35360}{296}$$

$$b = \frac{-14930}{296} = -50.439$$

$y' = a + bx$
$y' = 453.176 - 50.439x$
$y' = 453.176 - 50.439(4) = \$251.42$

16.

$$a = \frac{(50)(10998) - (242)(1625)}{6(10998) - (242)^2}$$

$$a = \frac{549900 - 393250}{7424} = \frac{156650}{7424} = 21.1$$

$$b = \frac{6(1625) - (242)(50)}{7424} = \frac{9750 - 12100}{7424}$$

16. continued

$$b = \frac{-2350}{7424} = -0.317$$

$y' = 21.1 - 0.317x$
$y' = 21.1 - 0.317(47) = 6.201 \approx 6$ days

17.
Since r is not significant, no regression should be done.

18.
Since r is not significant, no regression should be done.

19.
Since r is not significant, no regression should be done.

20.

$$a = \frac{(62)(53219) - (605)(5535)}{7(53219) - (605)^2} = -7.544$$

$$b = \frac{7(5535) - (605)(62)}{7(53219) - (605)^2} = 0.190$$

$y' = -7.554 + 0.190x$
$y' = -7.554 + 0.190(80) = 7.656 \approx 8$ calls

21.

$$a = \frac{(\sum y)(\sum x^2) - (\sum x)(\sum xy)}{n(\sum x^2) - (\sum x)^2}$$

$$a = \frac{(3222)(1026026) - (1862)(1754975)}{6(1026026) - (1862)^2}$$

$a = 14.165$

$$b = \frac{n(\sum xy) - (\sum x)(\sum y)}{n(\sum x^2) - (\sum x)^2}$$

$$b = \frac{6(1754975) - (1862)(3222)}{6(1026026) - (1862)^2} = 1.685$$

$y' = a + bx$
$y' = 14.165 + 1.685x$
$y' = 14.165 + 1.685(200) = 351$ under 5.

22.

$$a = \frac{(7203)(2697311) - (4231)(4569178)}{7(2697311) - (4231)^2} = 98.528$$

$$b = \frac{7(4569178) - (4231)(7203)}{7(2697311) - (4231)^2} = 1.539$$

$y' = a + bx$
$y' = 98.528 + 1.539x$
$y' = 98.528 + 1.539(700) = \$1175.83$ rent
for a two-bedroom apartment.

23.
$$a = \frac{(\sum y)(\sum x^2) - (\sum x)(\sum xy)}{n(\sum x^2) - (\sum x)^2}$$

$$a = \frac{(17.7)(44739) - (557)(1468.9)}{7(44739) - (557)^2} = -8.994$$

$$b = \frac{n(\sum xy) - (\sum x)(\sum y)}{n(\sum x^2) - (\sum x)^2}$$

$$b = \frac{7(1468.9) - (557)(17.7)}{7(44739) - (557)^2} = 0.1448$$

$y' = a + bx$
$y' = -8.994 + 0.1448x$
$y' = -8.994 + 0.1448(70) = 1.1$ inches

24.
$$a = \frac{(24145)(739052) - (2664)(6920176)}{10(739052) - (2664)^2}$$
$a = -2012.568$

$$b = \frac{10(6920176) - (2664)(24145)}{10(739052) - (2664)^2} = 16.618$$

$y' = a + bx$
$y' = -2012.568 + 16.618x$
$y' = -2012.568 + 16.618(260)$
$y' = 2308$ strikeouts

25.
Since r is not significant, no regression should be done.

26.
$$a = \frac{(6065)(19,456) - (432)(269,358)}{10(19,456) - (432)^2}$$
$a = 206.399$

$$b = \frac{10(269,358) - (432)(6065)}{10(19,456) - (432)^2} = 9.262$$

$y' = 206.399 + 9.262x$
$y' = 206.399 + 9.262(44)$
$y' = 613.9$ feet

27.
$$a = \frac{(\sum y)(\sum x^2) - (\sum x)(\sum xy)}{n(\sum x^2) - (\sum x)^2}$$

$$a = \frac{(748)(168,435) - (1013)(120,953)}{7(168,435) - (1013)^2}$$
$a = 22.659$

$$b = \frac{n(\sum xy) - (\sum x)(\sum y)}{n(\sum x^2) - (\sum x)^2}$$

$$b = \frac{7(120,953) - (1013)(748)}{7(168,435) - (1013)^2} = 0.582$$

$y' = a + bx$
$y' = 22.659 + 0.582x$

27. continued
$y' = 22.659 + 0.582(44) = 48.267$ staffed beds

28.

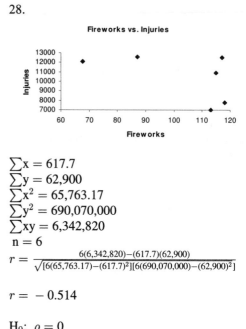

$\sum x = 617.7$
$\sum y = 62,900$
$\sum x^2 = 65,763.17$
$\sum y^2 = 690,070,000$
$\sum xy = 6,342,820$
$n = 6$
$$r = \frac{6(6,342,820) - (617.7)(62,900)}{\sqrt{[6(65,763.17) - (617.7)^2][6(690,070,000) - (62,900)^2]}}$$

$r = -0.514$

$H_0: \rho = 0$
$H_1: \rho \neq 0$

C. V. $= \pm 0.811$ d. f. $= 4$
Decision: Do not reject. There is no significant relationship between the number of fireworks in use and the number of related injuries. No regression should be done.

29.

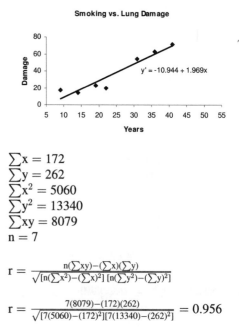

$\sum x = 172$
$\sum y = 262$
$\sum x^2 = 5060$
$\sum y^2 = 13340$
$\sum xy = 8079$
$n = 7$

$$r = \frac{n(\sum xy) - (\sum x)(\sum y)}{\sqrt{[n(\sum x^2) - (\sum x)^2][n(\sum y^2) - (\sum y)^2]}}$$

$$r = \frac{7(8079) - (172)(262)}{\sqrt{[7(5060) - (172)^2][7(13340) - (262)^2]}} = 0.956$$

29. continued

H_0: $\rho = 0$
H_1: $\rho \neq 0$
C. V. $= \pm 0.754$ d. f. $= 5$

Decision: Reject
There is a significant relationship between
the number of years a person smokes and the
amount of lung damage.

$$a = \frac{(\sum y)(\sum x^2)-(\sum x)(\sum xy)}{n(\sum x^2)-(\sum x)^2}$$

$$a = \frac{(262)(5060)-(172)(8079)}{7(5060)-(172)^2} = -10.944$$

$$b = \frac{n(\sum xy)-(\sum x)(\sum y)}{n(\sum x^2)-(\sum x)^2}$$

$$b = \frac{7(8079)-(172)(262)}{7(5060)-(172)^2} = 1.969$$

$y' = a + bx$
$y' = -10.944 + 1.969x$
$y' = -10.944 + 1.969(30) = 48.126\%$

30.

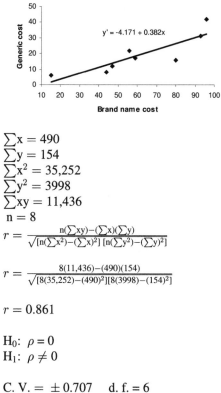

Brand Name Cost vs. Generic Cost

$\sum x = 490$
$\sum y = 154$
$\sum x^2 = 35,252$
$\sum y^2 = 3998$
$\sum xy = 11,436$
$n = 8$

$$r = \frac{n(\sum xy)-(\sum x)(\sum y)}{\sqrt{[n(\sum x^2)-(\sum x)^2]\,[n(\sum y^2)-(\sum y)^2]}}$$

$$r = \frac{8(11,436)-(490)(154)}{\sqrt{[8(35,252)-(490)^2][8(3998)-(154)^2]}}$$

$r = 0.861$

H_0: $\rho = 0$
H_1: $\rho \neq 0$

C. V. $= \pm 0.707$ d. f. $= 6$
Decision: Reject. There is a significant
linear relationship between brand name drug
cost and generic equivalent drug cost.

30. continued

$$a = \frac{(\sum y)(\sum x^2)-(\sum x)(\sum xy)}{n(\sum x^2)-(\sum x)^2}$$

$$a = \frac{(154)(35,252)-(490)(11,436)}{8(35,252)-(490)^2} = -4.171$$

$$b = \frac{n(\sum xy)-(\sum x)(\sum y)}{n(\sum x^2)-(\sum x)^2}$$

$$b = \frac{8(11,436)-(490)(154)}{8(35,252)-(490)^2} = 0.382$$

$y' = a + bx$
$y' = -4.171 + 0.382x$

31.

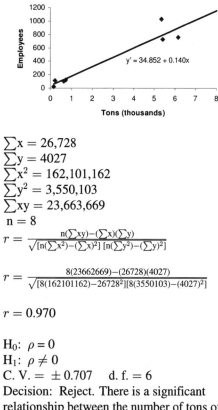

Tons of Coal vs. Number of Employees

$y' = 34.852 + 0.140x$

$\sum x = 26,728$
$\sum y = 4027$
$\sum x^2 = 162,101,162$
$\sum y^2 = 3,550,103$
$\sum xy = 23,663,669$
$n = 8$

$$r = \frac{n(\sum xy)-(\sum x)(\sum y)}{\sqrt{[n(\sum x^2)-(\sum x)^2]\,[n(\sum y^2)-(\sum y)^2]}}$$

$$r = \frac{8(23662669)-(26728)(4027)}{\sqrt{[8(162101162)-26728^2][8(3550103)-(4027)^2]}}$$

$r = 0.970$

H_0: $\rho = 0$
H_1: $\rho \neq 0$
C. V. $= \pm 0.707$ d. f. $= 6$
Decision: Reject. There is a significant
relationship between the number of tons of
coal produced and the number of employees.

$$a = \frac{(\sum y)(\sum x^2)-(\sum x)(\sum xy)}{n(\sum x^2)-(\sum x)^2}$$

$$a = \frac{(4027)(162101162)-(26728)(23663669)}{8(162101162)-(26728)^2}$$

$a = 34.852$

$$b = \frac{n(\sum xy)-(\sum x)(\sum y)}{n(\sum x^2)-(\sum x)^2}$$

31. continued

$$b = \frac{8(23663669)-(26728)(4027)}{8(162101162)-(26728)^2} = 0.140$$

$$y' = a + bx$$
$$y' = 34.852 + 0.140x$$
$$y' = 34.852 + 0.140(500) = 104.9$$

32.

Viewers for Two Years

$$y' = -3.668 + 1.281x$$

$$\sum x = 188.85$$
$$\sum y = 205.3$$
$$\sum x^2 = 3659.7025$$
$$\sum y^2 = 4432.31$$
$$\sum xy = 3996.6$$
$$n = 10$$

$$r = \frac{10(3996.6)-(188.85)(205.3)}{\sqrt{[10(3659.7025)-(188.85)^2][10(4432.31)-(205.3)^2]}}$$

$$r = 0.839$$

H_0: $\rho = 0$
H_1: $\rho \neq 0$
C. V. $= \pm 0.632$ d. f. $= 8$
Decision: Reject. There is a significant linear relationship between the number of viewers of last year's show and the number of viewers of the same shows this year.

$$a = \frac{(205.3)(3659.7025)-(188.85)(3996.6)}{10(3659.7025)-(188.85)^2} = -3.668$$

$$b = \frac{10(3996.6)-(188.85)(205.3)}{10(3659.7025)-(188.85)^2} = 1.281$$

$$y' = -3.668 + 1.281x$$

33.

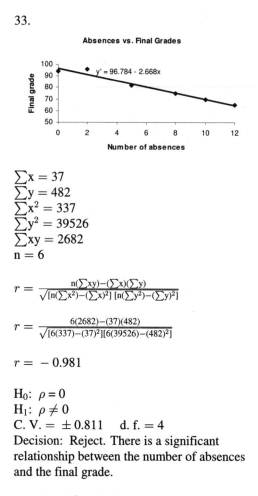

Absences vs. Final Grades

$$y' = 96.784 - 2.668x$$

$$\sum x = 37$$
$$\sum y = 482$$
$$\sum x^2 = 337$$
$$\sum y^2 = 39526$$
$$\sum xy = 2682$$
$$n = 6$$

$$r = \frac{n(\sum xy)-(\sum x)(\sum y)}{\sqrt{[n(\sum x^2)-(\sum x)^2][n(\sum y^2)-(\sum y)^2]}}$$

$$r = \frac{6(2682)-(37)(482)}{\sqrt{[6(337)-(37)^2][6(39526)-(482)^2]}}$$

$$r = -0.981$$

H_0: $\rho = 0$
H_1: $\rho \neq 0$
C. V. $= \pm 0.811$ d. f. $= 4$
Decision: Reject. There is a significant relationship between the number of absences and the final grade.

$$a = \frac{(\sum y)(\sum x^2)-(\sum x)(\sum xy)}{n(\sum x^2)-(\sum x)^2}$$

$$a = \frac{(482)(337)-(37)(2682)}{6(337)-(37)^2} = 96.784$$

$$b = \frac{n(\sum xy)-(\sum x)(\sum y)}{n(\sum x^2)-(\sum x)^2}$$

$$b = \frac{6(2682)-(37)(482)}{6(337)-(37)^2} = -2.668$$

$$y' = a + bx$$
$$y' = 96.784 - 2.668x$$

34.

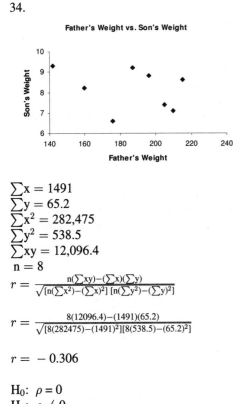

Father's Weight vs. Son's Weight

$\sum x = 1491$
$\sum y = 65.2$
$\sum x^2 = 282,475$
$\sum y^2 = 538.5$
$\sum xy = 12,096.4$
n = 8

$$r = \frac{n(\sum xy)-(\sum x)(\sum y)}{\sqrt{[n(\sum x^2)-(\sum x)^2][n(\sum y^2)-(\sum y)^2]}}$$

$$r = \frac{8(12096.4)-(1491)(65.2)}{\sqrt{[8(282475)-(1491)^2][8(538.5)-(65.2)^2]}}$$

$r = -0.306$

H_0: $\rho = 0$
H_1: $\rho \neq 0$
t = -0.787; $0.20 < $ P-value < 0.50 (0.462)
Decision: Do not reject since P-value > 0.05.
There is no significant relationship between
the weights of the fathers and sons. Since r
is not significant, no regression analysis
should be done.

35.

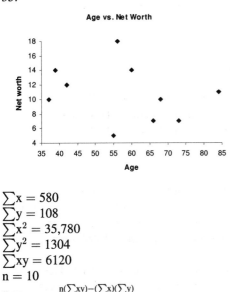

Age vs. Net Worth

$\sum x = 580$
$\sum y = 108$
$\sum x^2 = 35,780$
$\sum y^2 = 1304$
$\sum xy = 6120$
n = 10

$$r = \frac{n(\sum xy)-(\sum x)(\sum y)}{\sqrt{[n(\sum x^2)-(\sum x)^2][n(\sum y^2)-(\sum y)^2]}}$$

35. continued
$$r = \frac{10(6120)-(580)(108)}{\sqrt{10(35,780)-580^2][10(1304)-108^2]}}$$

$r = -0.265$
H_0: $\rho = 0$
H_1: $\rho \neq 0$
P-value > 0.05 (0.459)
Decision: Do not reject since P-value >
0.05. There is no significant linear
relationship between the ages of billionaires
and their net worth. Since r is not
significant, no regression should be done.

36.
For Exercise 13:
$\bar{x} = 37.5$
$\bar{y} = 3.75$
$y' = 10.499 - 0.18x$
$y' = 10.499 - 0.18(37.5)$
$y' = 10.499 - 6.75$
$y' = 3.749$ or 3.75
$\bar{y} = y'$

For Exercise 15:
$\bar{x} = 5.333$
$\bar{y} = 184.167$ (or 184)
$y' = 453.176 - 50.439x$
$y' = 453.176 - 50.439(5.333)$
$y' = 184.185$ or 184
$\bar{y} = y'$

For Exercise 21:
$\bar{x} = 310.333$
$\bar{y} = 537$
$y' = 14.165 + 1.685x$
$y' = 14.165 + 1.685(310.333)$
$y' = 537.08$ or 537
$\bar{y} = y'$

In all cases $\bar{y} = y'$, hence the regression line
will always pass through the point $(\bar{x}, \bar{y})$.
Slight differences occur between $\bar{y}$ and y'
due to rounding.

37.
For Exercise 15:
$\bar{x} = 5.3333$
$\bar{y} = 184.1667$
b = -50.439
$a = \bar{y} - b\bar{x}$
$a = 184.1667 - (-50.439)(5.3333)$
$a = 184.1667 + 269.0063$
$a = 453.173$ (differs due to rounding)

37. continued

For Exercise 16:

$\bar{x} = 40.33$

$\bar{y} = 8.33$

$b = -0.317$

$a = \bar{y} - b\bar{x}$

$a = 8.33 - (-0.317)(40.33)$

$a = 8.33 + 12.78$

$a = 21.11$ or 21.1

38.

For Exercise 18:

$b = 4.2094$

$s_x = 13.9571$

$s_y = 64.1623$

$r = \frac{bs_x}{s_y} = \frac{4.2097(13.9571)}{71.7356} = 0.819$

For Exercise 20:

$b = 0.190$

$s_x = 12.448$

$s_y = 2.911$

$r = \frac{0.190(12.448)}{2.911} = 0.812$

(differs due to rounding)

EXERCISE SET 10-4

1.
Explained variation is the variation due to the relationship and is computed by $\sum(y' - \bar{y})^2$.

2.
Unexplained variation is the variation due to chance and is computed by $\sum(y - y')^2$.

3.
Total variation is the sum of the squares of the vertical distances of the points from the mean. It is computed by $\sum(y - \bar{y})^2$.

4.
The coefficient of determination is a measure of variation of the dependent variable that is explained by the regression line and the independent variable.

5.
It is found by squaring r.

6.
It is the percent of the variation in y that is not due to the variation in x.

7.
The coefficient of non-determination is $1 - r^2$.

8.
For $r = 0.81$, $r^2 = 0.6561$ and $1 - r^2 = 0.3439$. Thus 65.61% of the variation of y is due to the variation of x, and 34.39% of the variation of y is due to chance.

9.
For $r = 0.70$, $r^2 = 0.49$ and $1 - r^2 = 0.51$. Thus 49% of the variation of y is due to the variation of x, and 51% of the variation of y is due to chance.

10.
For $r = 0.45$, $r^2 = 0.2025$ and $1 - r^2 = 0.7975$. Thus 20.25% of the variation of y is due to the variation of x, and 79.75% of the variation of y is due to chance.

11.
For $r = 0.37$, $r^2 = 0.1369$ and $1 - r^2 = 0.8631$. Thus 13.69% of the variation of y is due to the variation of x, and 86.31% of the variation of y is due to chance.

12.
For $r = 0.15$, $r^2 = 0.0225$ and $1 - r^2 = 0.9775$. Thus 2.25% of the variation of y is due to the variation of x, and 97.75% of the variation of y is due to chance.

13.
For $r = 0.05$, $r^2 = 0.0025$ and $1 - r^2 = 0.9975$. Thus 0.25% of the variation of y is due to the variation of x, and 99.75% of the variation of y is due to chance.

14.
The standard error of estimate is the standard deviation of the observed y values about the predicted y' values. It can be used when one is using the t distribution.

Note: For Exercises $15 - 18$, values for a and b are rounded to 3 decimal places according to the textbook's rounding rule for intercept and slope of the regression equation. Where these answers differ from the text, additional decimal places are included to show consistency with text answers.

15.

$$S_{est} = \sqrt{\frac{\sum y^2 - a\sum y - b\sum xy}{n-2}}$$

$$S_{est} = \sqrt{\frac{141.25 - 10.499(22.5) - (-0.180)(625)}{6-2}}$$

$$S_{est} = \sqrt{4.38065} = 2.093$$

Using $a = 10.4988$ and $b = -0.17997$,
$S_{est} = 2.09214304$ or 2.092

16.

$$S_{est} = \sqrt{\frac{10,596 - (-31.46)(260) - (1.036)(17,285)}{8-2}}$$

$$S_{est} = \sqrt{144.723333} = 12.03$$

Using $a = -31.46$ and $b = 1.035789$,
$S_{est} = 12.0553$ or 12.06

17.

$$S_{est} = \sqrt{\frac{\sum y^2 - a\sum y - b\sum xy}{n-2}} =$$

$$S_{est} = \sqrt{\frac{364525 - (453.176)(1105) - (-50.439)(3405)}{6-2}}$$

$$S_{est} = 94.22$$

18.

$$S_{est} = \sqrt{\frac{546 - 21.100(50) - (-0.317)(1625)}{6-2}}$$

$$S_{est} = \sqrt{1.53125} = 1.237$$

Using $a = 21.1005$ and $b = -0.31654$,
$S_{est} = 1.15677$ or 1.157

19.
$y' = 10.499 - 0.18x$
$y' = 10.499 - 0.18(20)$
$y' = 6.899$

$$y' - t_{\frac{\alpha}{2}} \cdot S_{est}\sqrt{1 + \frac{1}{n} + \frac{n(x-\overline{X})}{n\sum x^2 - (\sum x)^2}} < y <$$

$$y' + t_{\frac{\alpha}{2}} \cdot S_{est}\sqrt{1 + \frac{1}{n} + \frac{n(x-\overline{X})^2}{n\sum x^2 - (\sum x)^2}}$$

19. continued
$$6.899 - (2.132)(2.09)\sqrt{1 + \frac{1}{6} + \frac{6(20-37.5)^2}{6(9653) - 225^2}}$$

$$< y < 6.899 +$$
$$(2.132)(2.09)\sqrt{1 + \frac{1}{6} + \frac{6(20-37.5)^2}{6(9653) - 225^2}}$$

$$6.899 - (2.132)(2.09)(1.191) < y <$$

$$6.899 + (2.132)(2.09)(1.91)$$

$$1.59 < y < 12.21$$

20.
$y' = -31.46 + 1.036x$
$y' = -31.46 + 1.036(60)$
$y' = 30.7$

$$30.7 - (2.447)(12.06)\sqrt{1 + \frac{1}{8} + \frac{8(60-61.75)^2}{8(31,692) - (494)^2}}$$

$$< y <$$

$$30.7 + (2.447)(12.06)\sqrt{1 + \frac{1}{8} + \frac{8(60-31.75)^2}{8(31,692) - (494)^2}}$$

$$30.7 - (2.447)(12.06)(1.062) < y <$$

$$30.7 + (2.447)(12.06)(1.062)$$

$$-0.64 < y < 62.04 \text{ or } 0 < y < 62$$

21.
$y' = 453.176 - 50.439x$
$y' = 453.176 - 50.439(4)$
$y' = 251.42$
$$y' - t_{\frac{\alpha}{2}} \cdot S_{est}\sqrt{1 + \frac{1}{n} + \frac{n(x-\overline{X})^2}{n\sum x^2 - (\sum x)^2}} < y <$$

$$y' + t_{\frac{\alpha}{2}} \cdot S_{est}\sqrt{1 + \frac{1}{n} + \frac{n(x-\overline{X})^2}{n\sum x^2 - (\sum x)^2}}$$

$$251.42 - 2.132(94.22)\sqrt{1 + \frac{1}{6} + \frac{6(4-5.33)^2}{6(220) - 32^2}}$$

$$< y < 251.42 + 2.132(94.22)\sqrt{1 + \frac{1}{6} + \frac{6(4-5.33)^2}{6(220) - 32^2}}$$

$$251.42 - (2.132)(94.22)(1.1) < y <$$
$$251.42 + (2.132)(94.22)(1.1)$$
$$\$30.46 < y < \$472.38$$

22.
$y' = 21.1 - 0.317x$
$y' = 21.1 - 0.317(47)$
$y' = 6.201$

22. continued

$$6.201 - (3.747)(1.157)\sqrt{1 + \frac{1}{6} + \frac{6(47-40.333)^2}{6(10998)-(242)^2}}$$

$$< y < 6.201 + (3.747)(1.157)\sqrt{1 + \frac{1}{6} + \frac{6(47-40.333)^2}{6(10998)-(242)^2}}$$

$$6.201 - (3.747)(1.157)(1.0966) < y <$$

$$6.201 - (3.747)(1.157)(1.0966)$$

$$1.44675 < y < 10.95525 \text{ or } 1 < y < 11$$

REVIEW EXERCISES - CHAPTER 10

1.

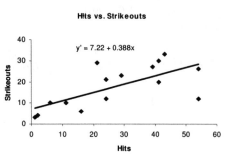

Hits vs. Strikeouts

$y' = 7.22 + 0.388x$

$\sum x = 406$
$\sum y = 266$
$\sum x^2 = 15,416$
$\sum y^2 = 6154$
$\sum xy = 8919$
$n = 15$

$$r = \frac{n(\sum xy)-(\sum x)(\sum y)}{\sqrt{[n(\sum x^2)-(\sum x)^2][n(\sum y^2)-(\sum y)^2]}}$$

$$r = \frac{15(8919)-(406)(266)}{\sqrt{[15(15416)-(406)^2][15(6154)-(266)^2]}}$$

$$r = 0.682$$

$H_0: \rho = 0$
$H_1: \rho \neq 0$
C. V. $= \pm 0.641$ d. f. $= 13$

Decision: Reject. There is a significant linear relationship between the number of hits and the number of strikeouts.

$$a = \frac{(\sum y)(\sum x^2)-(\sum x)(\sum xy)}{n(\sum x^2)-(\sum x)^2}$$

$$a = \frac{(266)(15416)-(406)(8919)}{15(15416)-(406)^2} = 7.222$$

$$b = \frac{n(\sum xy)-(\sum x)(\sum y)}{n(\sum x^2)-(\sum x)^2}$$

1. continued

$$b = \frac{15(8919)-(406)(266)}{15(15416)-(406)^2} = 0.388$$

$y' = a + bx$
$y' = 7.222 + 0.388x$
$y' = 7.222 + 0.388(30) = 18.86 \text{ or } 18.9$
strikeouts

2.

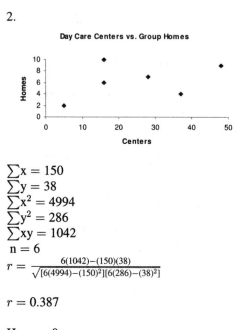

Day Care Centers vs. Group Homes

$\sum x = 150$
$\sum y = 38$
$\sum x^2 = 4994$
$\sum y^2 = 286$
$\sum xy = 1042$
$n = 6$

$$r = \frac{6(1042)-(150)(38)}{\sqrt{[6(4994)-(150)^2][6(286)-(38)^2]}}$$

$$r = 0.387$$

$H_0: \rho = 0$
$H_1: \rho \neq 0$
C. V. $= \pm 0.917$ d. f. $= 4$

Decision: Do not reject. There is no significant relationship between the number of day care centers and the number of group day care homes. No regression should be done.

3.

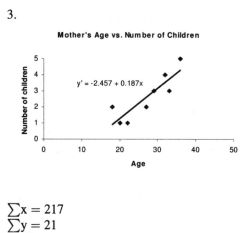

Mother's Age vs. Number of Children

$y' = -2.457 + 0.187x$

$\sum x = 217$
$\sum y = 21$
$\sum x^2 = 6187$

188

3. continued

$\sum y^2 = 69$

$\sum xy = 626$

$n = 8$

$r = \dfrac{n(\sum xy) - (\sum x)(\sum y)}{\sqrt{[n(\sum x^2) - (\sum x)^2]\,[n(\sum y^2) - (\sum y)^2]}}$

$r = \dfrac{8(626) - (217)(21)}{\sqrt{[8(6187) - (217)^2][8(69) - (21)^2]}}$

$r = 0.873$

$H_0:\ \rho = 0$

$H_1:\ \rho \neq 0$

C. V. $= \pm 0.834$ d. f. $= 6$

Decision: Reject. There is a significant relationship between the mother's age and the number of children she has.

$a = \dfrac{(\sum y)(\sum x^2) - (\sum x)(\sum xy)}{n(\sum x^2) - (\sum x)^2}$

$a = \dfrac{(21)(6187) - (217)(626)}{8(6187) - (217)^2} = -2.457$

$b = \dfrac{n(\sum xy) - (\sum x)(\sum y)}{n(\sum x^2) - (\sum x)^2}$

$b = \dfrac{8(626) - (217)(21)}{8(6187) - (217)^2} = 0.187$

$y' = a + bx$

$y' = -2.457 + 0.187x$

$y' = -2.457 + 0.187(34) = 3.9$

4.

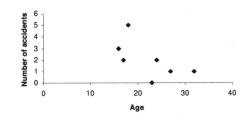

Driver's Age vs. Number of Accidents

$\sum x = 157$

$\sum y = 14$

$\sum x^2 = 3727$

$\sum y^2 = 44$

$\sum xy = 279$

$n = 7$

$r = \dfrac{7(279) - (157)(14)}{\sqrt{[7(3727) - (157)^2][7(44) - (14)^2]}}$

$r = -0.610$

4. continued

$H_0:\ \rho = 0$

$H_1:\ \rho \neq 0$

C. V. $= \pm 0.875$ d. f. $= 5$

Decision: Do not reject. There is not a significant relationship between age and the number of accidents a person has. No regression analysis should be done since the null hypothesis has not been rejected.

5.

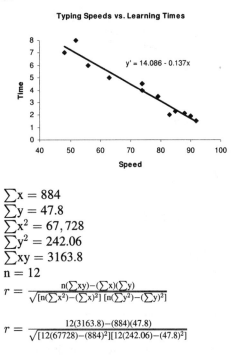

Typing Speeds vs. Learning Times

y' = 14.086 - 0.137x

$\sum x = 884$

$\sum y = 47.8$

$\sum x^2 = 67,728$

$\sum y^2 = 242.06$

$\sum xy = 3163.8$

$n = 12$

$r = \dfrac{n(\sum xy) - (\sum x)(\sum y)}{\sqrt{[n(\sum x^2) - (\sum x)^2]\,[n(\sum y^2) - (\sum y)^2]}}$

$r = \dfrac{12(3163.8) - (884)(47.8)}{\sqrt{[12(67728) - (884)^2][12(242.06) - (47.8)^2]}}$

$r = -0.974$

$H_0:\ \rho = 0$

$H_1:\ \rho \neq 0$

C. V. $= \pm 0.708$ d. f. $= 10$

Decision: Reject. There is a significant relationship between speed and time.

$a = \dfrac{(\sum y)(\sum x^2) - (\sum x)(\sum xy)}{n(\sum x^2) - (\sum x)^2}$

$a = \dfrac{(47.8)(67728) - (884)(3163.8)}{12(67728) - (884)^2}$

$a = 14.086$

$b = \dfrac{n(\sum xy) - (\sum x)(\sum y)}{n(\sum x^2) - (\sum x)^2}$

$b = \dfrac{12(3163.8) - (884)(47.8)}{12(67728) - (884)^2}$

5. continued
b = − 0.137

$y' = a + bx$
$y' = 14.086 − 0.137x$
$y' = 14.086 − 0.137(72) = 4.222$

6.

Grams vs. Blood Pressure

$y' = 64.936 + 2.662x$

$\sum x = 66.7$
$\sum y = 762$
$\sum x^2 = 535.99$
$\sum y^2 = 64,868$
$\sum xy = 5758.2$
$n = 9$
$r = \dfrac{9(5758.2)−(66.7)(762)}{\sqrt{[9(535.99)−(66.7)^2][9(64868)−(762)^2]}}$

$r = 0.916$

H_0: $\rho = 0$
H_1: $\rho \neq 0$
C. V. = ± 0.798   d. f. = 7

Decision: Reject. There is a significant relationship between grams and pressure.

$a = \dfrac{(762)(535.99)−(66.7)(5758.2)}{9(535.99)−66.7^2} = 64.936$

$b = \dfrac{9(5758.2)−(66.7)(762)}{9(535.99)−66.7^2} = 2.662$

$y' = 64.936 + 2.662x$
$y' = 64.936 + 2.662(8) = 86.232$

7.

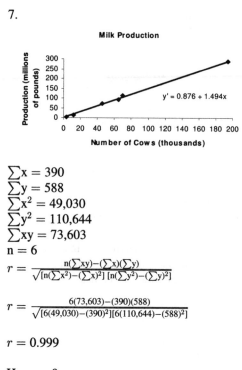

Milk Production

$y' = 0.876 + 1.494x$

$\sum x = 390$
$\sum y = 588$
$\sum x^2 = 49,030$
$\sum y^2 = 110,644$
$\sum xy = 73,603$
$n = 6$
$r = \dfrac{n(\sum xy)−(\sum x)(\sum y)}{\sqrt{[n(\sum x^2)−(\sum x)^2]\,[n(\sum y^2)−(\sum y)^2]}}$

$r = \dfrac{6(73,603)−(390)(588)}{\sqrt{[6(49,030)−(390)^2][6(110,644)−(588)^2]}}$

$r = 0.999$

H_0: $\rho = 0$
H_1: $\rho \neq 0$
C. V. ± 0.917   d. f. = 4

Decision: Reject. There is a significant relationship between the number of cows and the number of pounds of milk produced in the counties located in southwestern Pennsylvania.

$a = \dfrac{(\sum y)(\sum x^2)−(\sum x)(\sum xy)}{n(\sum x^2)−(\sum x)^2}$

$a = \dfrac{(588)(49,030)−(390)(73,603)}{6(49,030)−(390)^2}$

$a = 0.876$

$b = \dfrac{n(\sum xy)−(\sum x)(\sum y)}{n(\sum x^2)−(\sum x)^2}$

$b = \dfrac{6(73,603)−(390)(588)}{6(49030)−(390)^2}$

$b = 1.494$

$y' = a + bx$
$y' = 1.494 + 0.876x$

8.
(For calculation purposes only, since no regression should be done.)

$S_{est} = \sqrt{\dfrac{\sum y^2 − a\sum y − b\sum xy}{n−2}}$

8. continued

$$S_{est} = \sqrt{\frac{44-(5.816)(14)-(-0.1701)(279)}{7-2}} = 1.417$$

$$S_{est} = \sqrt{\frac{10.0339}{5}} = \sqrt{2.00678} = 1.417$$

9.

$$S_{est} = \sqrt{\frac{\sum y^2 - a\sum y - b\sum xy}{n-2}}$$

$$S_{est} = \sqrt{\frac{242.06 - 14.086(47.8) + 0.137(3163.8)}{12-2}}$$

$$S_{est} = \sqrt{\frac{2.1898}{10}} = \sqrt{0.21898} = 0.468$$

(Note: TI-83 calculator answer is 0.513)

10.

$$S_{est} = \sqrt{\frac{\sum y^2 - a\sum y - b\sum xy}{n-2}}$$

$$S_{est} = \sqrt{\frac{64,868 - (64.936)(762) - (2.662)(5758.2)}{9-2}}$$

$$S_{est} = \sqrt{\frac{64,868 - 49,481.232 - 15,328.328}{7}}$$

$$S_{est} = \sqrt{\frac{58.44}{7}} = \sqrt{8.349} = 2.89$$

(Note: TI-83 calculator answer is 2.845)

11.
(For calculation purposes only, since no regression should be done.)

$y' = 14.086 - 0.137x$
$y' = 14.086 - 0.137(72) = 4.222$

$$y' - t_{\frac{\alpha}{2}} \cdot S_{est}\sqrt{1 + \frac{1}{n} + \frac{n(x-\overline{X})^2}{n\sum x^2 - (\sum x)^2}} < y <$$

$$y' + t_{\frac{\alpha}{2}} \cdot S_{est}\sqrt{1 + \frac{1}{n} + \frac{n(x-\overline{X})^2}{n\sum x^2 - (\sum x)^2}}$$

$$4.222 - 1.812(0.468)\sqrt{1 + \frac{1}{12} + \frac{12(72-73.667)^2}{12(67,728)-884^2}}$$
$$< y < 4.222 + 1.812(0.468)\sqrt{1 + \frac{1}{12} + \frac{12(72-73.667)^2}{12(67,728)-884^2}}$$

$4.222 - 1.812(0.468)(1.041) < y <$
$\qquad 4.222 + 1.812(0.468)(1.041)$
$3.34 < y < 5.10$

12.
$y' = 64.936 + 2.662x$
$y' = 64.936 + 2.662(8) = 86.232$

12. continued

$$86.232 - 2.365(2.89)\sqrt{1 + \frac{1}{9} + \frac{9(8-7.411)^2}{9(535.99)-66.7^2}}$$

$$< y < 86.232 + 2.365(2.89)\sqrt{1 + \frac{1}{9} + \frac{9(8-7.411)^2}{9(535.99)-66.7^2}}$$

$86.232 - 2.365(2.89)(1.058) < y <$
$\qquad 86.232 + 2.365(2.89)(1.058)$

$79.1 < y < 93.4$ or $79 < y < 93$

CHAPTER 10 QUIZ

1. False, the y variable would decrease.
2. True
3. True
4. False, the relationship may be affected by another variable, or by chance.
5. False, a relationship may be caused by chance.
6. False, there are several independent variables and one dependent variable.
7. a
8. a
9. d
10. c
11. b
12. Scatter plot
13. Independent
14. $-1, +1$
15. b
16. Line of best fit
17. $+1, -1$

18.

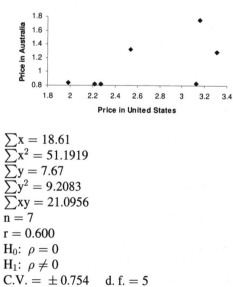

Price Comparison of Drugs

$\sum x = 18.61$
$\sum x^2 = 51.1919$
$\sum y = 7.67$
$\sum y^2 = 9.2083$
$\sum xy = 21.0956$
$n = 7$
$r = 0.600$
$H_0: \rho = 0$
$H_1: \rho \neq 0$
C.V. $= \pm 0.754$ d. f. $= 5$

18. continued

Do not reject. There is no significant linear relationship between the price of the same drugs in the United States and in Australia. No regression should be done.

19.

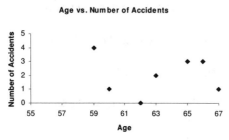

$$\sum x = 442$$
$$\sum x^2 = 27,964$$
$$\sum y = 14$$
$$\sum y^2 = 40$$
$$\sum xy = 882$$
$$n = 7$$
$$r = -0.078$$
$$H_0: \rho = 0$$
$$H_1: \rho \neq 0$$
C. V. $= \pm 0.754$ d. f. $= 5$
Decision: Do not reject. There is not a significant relationship between age and number of accidents. No regression should be done.

20.

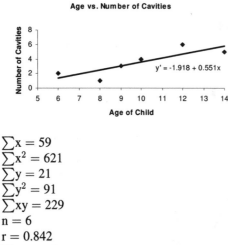

$$\sum x = 59$$
$$\sum x^2 = 621$$
$$\sum y = 21$$
$$\sum y^2 = 91$$
$$\sum xy = 229$$
$$n = 6$$
$$r = 0.842$$
$$H_0: \rho = 0$$
$$H_1: \rho \neq 0$$
C. V. $= \pm 0.811$ d. f. $= 4$
Decision: Reject. There is a significant linear relationship between age and number of cavities.

20. continued

$$a = -1.918 \qquad b = 0.551$$
$$y' = -1.918 + 0.551x$$
When x $= 11$: $y' = -1.918 + 0.551(11)$
$$y' = 4.14 \text{ or } 4 \text{ cavities}$$

21.

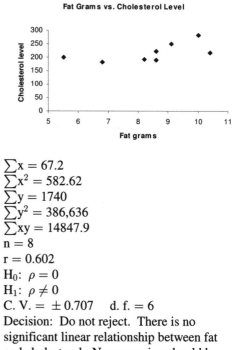

$$\sum x = 67.2$$
$$\sum x^2 = 582.62$$
$$\sum y = 1740$$
$$\sum y^2 = 386,636$$
$$\sum xy = 14847.9$$
$$n = 8$$
$$r = 0.602$$
$$H_0: \rho = 0$$
$$H_1: \rho \neq 0$$
C. V. $= \pm 0.707$ d. f. $= 6$
Decision: Do not reject. There is no significant linear relationship between fat and cholesterol. No regression should be done.

22.
$$S_{est} = \sqrt{\frac{91 - (-1.918)(21) - 0.551(229)}{6 - 2}}$$
$$S_{est} = 1.129*$$

23.
(For calculation purposes only, since no regression should be done.)

$$S_{est} = \sqrt{\frac{386,636 - 110.12(1740) - 12.784(14,847.9)}{8 - 2}}$$
$$S_{est} = 29.47*$$

24.
$$y' = -1.918 + 0.551(7) = 1.939 \text{ or } 2$$

$$2 - 2.132(1.129)\sqrt{1 + \frac{1}{6} + \frac{6(11 - 9.833)^2}{6(621) - 59^2}} < y$$

$$< 2 + 2.132(1.129)\sqrt{1 + \frac{1}{6} + \frac{6(11 - 9.833)^2}{6(621) - 59^2}}$$

24. continued
$$2 - 2.132(1.129)(1.095) < y < 2 +$$
$$2.132(1.129)(1.095)$$

$$-0.6 < y < 4.6 \text{ or } 0 < y < 5*$$

25.
Since no regression should be done, the average of the y' values is used: 217.5

Note: Graphs are not to scale and are intended to convey a general idea.

Answers may vary due to rounding, TI-83's, or computer programs.

EXERCISE SET 11-2

1.
The variance test compares a sample variance to a hypothesized population variance, while the goodness of fit test compares a distribution obtained from a sample with a hypothesized distribution.

2.
The degrees of freedom is the number of categories minus one.

3.
The expected values are computed based on what the null hypothesis states about the distribution.

4.
The categories should be combined with other categories.

5.
H_0: The ages of automobiles are equally distributed over the three categories. (claim)
H_1: The ages of automobiles are not equally distributed over the three categories.
C. V. = 5.991   d. f. = 2 $\alpha = 0.05$
$E = \frac{30}{3} = 10$
$\chi^2 = \sum \frac{(O-E)^2}{E} = \frac{(8-10)^2}{10} + \frac{(10-10)^2}{10} +$

$\frac{(12-10)^2}{10} = 0.8$

Alternate Solution:

O	E	O − E	$(O-E)^2$	$\frac{(O-E)^2}{E}$
8	10	-2	4	0.4
10	10	0	0	0
12	10	2	4	0.4
				0.8

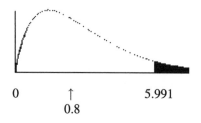

0   ↑   5.991
          0.8

5. continued
Do not reject the null hypothesis. There is not enough evidence to reject the claim that the average age of automobiles is equally distributed over the three categories. Tire manufacturers need to make enough tires to fit automobiles of all ages.

6.
H_0: The methods used by workers to combat midday drowsiness are equally distributed among the five categories. (claim)
H_1: The methods are not equally distributed among the five categories.
C. V. = 7.779   d. f. = 4 $\alpha = 0.10$
$E = \frac{60}{5} = 12$

$\chi^2 = \frac{(21-12)^2}{12} + \frac{(16-12)^2}{12}$

$+ \frac{(10-12)^2}{12} + \frac{(8-12)^2}{12} + \frac{(5-12)^2}{12}$

$\chi^2 = 13.833$

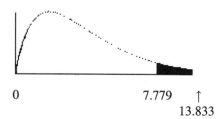

0   7.779   ↑
                            13.833

Reject the null hypothesis. There is enough evidence to reject the claim that the methods used are equally distributed over the categories. An employer could plan ways to help workers. For example, the employer could install a beverage machine in the workplace.

7.
H_0: The proportions are distributed as follows: 28.1% purchased a small car, 47.8% purchased a mid-sized car, 7% purchased a large car, and 17.1% purchased a luxury car.
H_1: The distribution is not the same as stated in the null hypothesis. (claim)
C. V. = 7.815   d. f. = 3 $\alpha = 0.05$

$\chi^2 = \sum \frac{(O-E)^2}{E} = \frac{(25-28.1)^2}{28.1} + \frac{(50-47.8)^2}{47.8}$

$+ \frac{(10-7)^2}{7} + \frac{(15-17.1)^2}{17.1} = 1.9869$

194

7. continued
Alternate Solution:

O	E	O − E	$(O − E)^2$	$\frac{(O−E)^2}{E}$
25	28.1	-3.1	9.61	0.3420
50	47.8	2.2	4.84	0.1013
10	7	3	9	1.2857
15	17.1	-2.1	4.41	0.2579
				1.9869

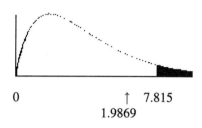

0   ↑ 7.815
              1.9869

Do not reject the null hypothesis. There is not enough evidence to support the claim that the proportions are different.

8.
H_0: The proportions are distributed as follows: 68% of families have two parents present, 23% have only a mother present, 5% have only a father present, and 4% have no parent present.
H_1: The distribution is not the same as stated in the null hypothesis. (claim)
C. V. = 7.815   d. f. = 3 $\alpha = 0.05$

$$\chi^2 = \sum \frac{(O−E)^2}{E} = \frac{(120−136)^2}{136} + \frac{(40−46)^2}{46}$$

$$+ \frac{(30−10)^2}{10} + \frac{(10−8)^2}{8} = 43.165$$

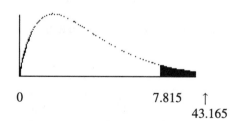

0   7.815   ↑
                                43.165

Reject the null hypothesis. There is enough evidence to support the claim that the proportions are different.

9.
H_0: The proportions are distributed as follows: safe - 35%, not safe - 52%, no opinion - 13%.

9. continued
H_1: The distribution is not the same as stated in the null hypothesis. (claim)
C. V. = 9.210   d. f. = 2 $\alpha = 0.01$

$$\chi^2 = \frac{(40−42)^2}{42} + \frac{(60−62.4)^2}{62.4} + \frac{(20−15.6)^2}{15.6}$$

$$\chi^2 = 1.4286$$

Alternate Solution:

O	E	O − E	$(O − E)^2$	$\frac{(O−E)^2}{E}$
40	42	-2	4	0.09524
60	62.4	-2.4	5.76	0.09231
20	15.6	4.4	19.36	1.24103
				1.42858

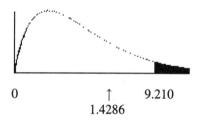

0   ↑   9.210
                  1.4286

Do not reject the null hypothesis. There is not enough evidence to support the claim that the proportions are different.

10.
H_0: The proportions are distributed as follows: should continue - 56%, should not continue - 40%, no opinion - 4%.
H_1: The distribution is not the same as stated in the null hypothesis. (claim)
C. V. = 5.991 $\alpha = 0.05$ d. f. = 2

$$\chi^2 = \frac{(126−112)^2}{112} + \frac{(65−80)^2}{80} + \frac{(9−8)^2}{8}$$

$$\chi^2 = 4.6875$$

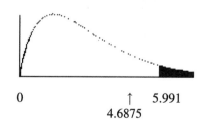

0   ↑   5.991
                  4.6875

Do not reject the null hypothesis. There is not enough evidence to support the claim that the proportions are different.

11.

H_0: The distribution of loans is as follows: 21% - mortgages, 39% - autos, 20% - credit card, 12% - real estate, and 8% - miscellaneous. (claim)

H_1: The distribution is not the same as stated in the null hypothesis.

C. V. $= 9.488$ d. f. $= 4$ $\alpha = 0.05$

$\chi^2 = \frac{(25-21)^2}{21} + \frac{(44-39)^2}{39} + \frac{(19-20)^2}{20} +$

$\frac{(8-12)^2}{12} + \frac{(4-8)^2}{8} = 4.7862$

Alternate Solution:

O	E	O − E	(O − E)²	$\frac{(O-E)^2}{E}$
25	21	4	16	0.7619
44	39	5	25	0.6410
19	20	-1	1	0.05
8	12	-4	16	1.3333
4	8	-4	16	2.0000
				4.7862

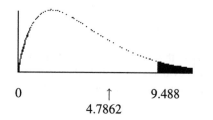

0   ↑   9.488
          4.7862

Do not reject the null hypothesis. There is not enough evidence to reject the claim that the distribution is the same.

12.

H_0: The proportions are as follows: transportation - 33%, industry - 30%, residential - 20%, and commercial - 17%. (claim)

H_1: The distribution is not the same as stated in the null hypothesis.

C. V. $= 7.815$ d. f. $= 3$ $\alpha = 0.05$

$\chi^2 = \frac{(108-99)^2}{99} + \frac{(93-90)^2}{90} + \frac{(51-60)^2}{60} + \frac{(48-51)^2}{51}$

$\chi^2 = 2.4447$

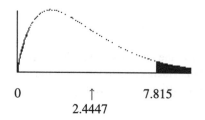

0   ↑   7.815
          2.4447

12. continued

Do not reject the null hypothesis. There is not enough evidence to reject the claim that the proportions are as stated.

13.

H_0: The methods of payment for purchases are distributed as follows: 53% use cash, 30% use checks, 16% use credit cards, and 1% have no preference. (claim)

H_1: The distribution is not the same as stated in the null hypothesis.

C. V. $= 11.345$ d. f. $= 3$ $\alpha = 0.01$

$\chi^2 = \frac{(400-424)^2}{424} + \frac{(210-240)^2}{240} + \frac{(170-128)^2}{128}$

$+ \frac{(20-8)^2}{8} = 36.8897$

Alternate Solution:

O	E	O − E	(O − E)²	$\frac{(O-E)^2}{E}$
400	424	-24	576	1.35849
210	240	-30	900	3.7500
170	128	42	1764	13.78125
20	8	12	144	18.0000
				36.88974

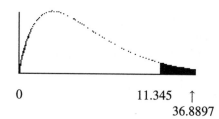

0   11.345   ↑
                          36.8897

Reject the null hypothesis. There is enough evidence to reject the claim that the distribution is the same as reported in the survey.

14.

H_0: The distribution is as follows: violent offenses - 12.6%, property offenses - 8.5%, drug offenses - 60.2%, weapons offenses - 8.2%, immigration offenses - 4.9%, and other offenses - 5.6%. (claim)

H_1: The distribution is not the same as stated in the null hypothesis.

C. V. $= 11.071$ d. f. $= 5$ $\alpha = 0.05$

$\chi^2 = \frac{(64-63)^2}{63} + \frac{(40-42.5)^2}{42.5} + \frac{(326-301)^2}{301} +$

$\frac{(42-41)^2}{41} + \frac{(25-24.5)^2}{24.5} + \frac{(3-28)^2}{28} = 24.58$

14. continued

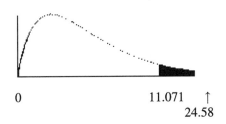

0   11.071   ↑
                      24.58

Reject the null hypothesis. There is enough evidence to reject the claim that the proportions are as stated.

15.
H_0: The distribution is as follows: violent offenses - 29.5%, property offenses - 29%, drug offenses - 30.2%, weapons offenses - 10.6%, other offenses - 0.7%. (claim)
H_1: The distribution is not the same as stated in the null hypothesis.
C. V. = 9.488   d. f. = 4 $\alpha = 0.05$

$$\chi^2 = \sum \frac{(O-E)^2}{E} = \frac{(298-295)^2}{295} + \frac{(275-290)^2}{290}$$

$$+ \frac{(344-302)^2}{302} + \frac{(80-106)^2}{106} + \frac{(3-7)^2}{7}$$

$$\chi^2 = 15.3106 \text{ or } 15.31$$

Alternate Solution:

O	E	O − E	$(O-E)^2$	$\frac{(O-E)^2}{E}$
298	295	3	9	0.0305
275	290	-15	225	0.7759
344	302	42	1764	5.8411
80	106	-26	676	6.3774
3	7	-4	16	2.2857
				15.3106

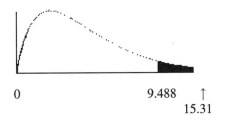

0   9.488   ↑
                     15.31

Reject the null hypothesis. There is enough evidence to reject the claim that the proportions are as stated.

16.
H_0: The number of people who do not have health insurance is equally distributed over the three educational categories.
H_1: The number of people who do not have health insurance is not equally distributed over the three categories. (claim)
$\alpha = 0.05$ d. f. = 2
$0.01 < \text{P-value} < 0.025$
$E = \frac{60}{3} = 20$

$$\chi^2 = \frac{(29-20)^2}{20} + \frac{(20-20)^2}{20} + \frac{(11-20)^2}{20}$$

$$\chi^2 = 8.1$$

Reject the null hypothesis since $0.01 < \text{P-value} < 0.05$. There is enough evidence to support the claim that the number of people who don't have health insurance is not equally distributed over the three educational categories. Perhaps those with more education have better jobs that provide employee health insurance.

17.
H_0: The distribution of the ways people pay for their prescriptions is as follows: 60% used personal funds, 25% used insurance, and 15% used Medicare. (claim)
H_1: The distribution is not the same as stated in the null hypothesis.
$\alpha = 0.05$ d. f. = 2
P-value > 0.05

$$\chi^2 = \sum \frac{(O-E)^2}{E} = \frac{(32-30)^2}{30} + \frac{(10-12.5)^2}{12.5} +$$

$$\frac{(8-7.5)^2}{7.5} = 0.667$$

Alternate Solution:

O	E	O − E	$(O-E)^2$	$\frac{(O-E)^2}{E}$
32	30	2	4	0.133
10	12.5	-2.5	6.25	0.5
8	7.5	0.5	0.25	0.033
				0.666*

*differs due to rounding

Do not reject the null hypothesis since P-value > 0.05. There is not enough evidence to reject the claim that the distribution is the same as stated in the null hypothesis. An implication of the results is that the majority of people are using their own money to pay

17. continued
for medications. A less expensive medication could help people financially.

18.
H_0: The coins are balanced and randomly tossed. (claim)
H_1: The distribution is not the same as stated in the null hypothesis.
C. V. = 7.815   d. f. = 3
$E(0) = 0.125(72) = 9$
$E(1) = 0.375(72) = 27$
$E(2) = 0.375(72) = 27$
$E(3) = 0.125(72) = 9$
(use the binomial distribution with n = 3 and p = 0.05)

$$\chi^2 = \frac{(3-9)^2}{9} + \frac{(10-27)^2}{27} + \frac{(17-27)^2}{27} +$$

$$\frac{(42-9)^2}{9} = 139.4$$

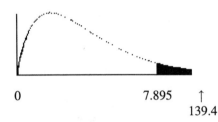

0	7.895 ↑
	139.4

Reject the null hypothesis. There is enough evidence to reject the claim that the coins are balanced and randomly tossed.

19.
Answers will vary.

EXERCISE SET 11-3

1.
The independence test and the goodness of fit test both use the same formula for computing the test-value; however, the independence test uses a contingency table whereas the goodness of fit test does not.

2.
d. f. = (rows − 1)(columns − 1)

3.
H_0: The variables are independent or not related.
H_1: The variables are dependent or related.

4.
Contingency table.

5.
The expected values are computed as (row total · column total) ÷ grand total.

6.
The test of independence is used to determine whether two variables selected from a single sample are related. The test of homogeneity of proportions is used to determine whether proportions are equal.

7.
H_0: $p_1 = p_2 = p_3 = \cdots = p_n$
H_1: At least one proportion is different from the others.

8.
H_0: The consumption of supplements is independent of jogging status. (claim)
H_1: The consumption of supplements is dependent upon the jogging status of the individuals.
C. V. = 5.991   d. f. = 2 $\alpha = 0.05$

Consumption of Supplements

	Daily	Weekly	As needed
Joggers	34(26.991)	52(60.729)	23(21.281)
Non-joggers	18(25.010)	65(56.271)	18(19.719)

$$\chi^2 = \sum \frac{(O-E)^2}{E} = \frac{(34-26.991)^2}{26.991} + \frac{(52-60.729)^2}{60.729} +$$

$$\frac{(23-21.281)^2}{21.281} + \frac{(18-25.010)^2}{25.010} + \frac{(65-56.271)^2}{56.271}$$

$$+ \frac{(18-19.719)^2}{19.719}$$

$$\chi^2 = 6.682$$

0	5.991 ↑
	6.682

Reject the null hypothesis. There is enough evidence to reject the claim that the consumption of supplements is independent of the jogging status of an individual. Supplement manufacturers can use the information to design their advertisements.

9.

H_0: Type of pet owned is independent of annual household income.

H_1: Type of pet owned is dependent on annual household income. (claim)

C. V. = 21.026   d. f. = 12 $\alpha = 0.05$

$E = \dfrac{\text{(row sum)(column sum)}}{\text{grand total}}$

$E_{1,1} = \dfrac{(534)(1003)}{4004} = 133.7667$

$E_{1,2} = \dfrac{(534)(1000)}{4004} = 133.3666$

$E_{1,3} = \dfrac{(534)(1000)}{4004} = 133.3666$

$E_{1,4} = \dfrac{(534)(1001)}{4004} = 133.5$

$E_{2,1} = \dfrac{(800)(1003)}{4004} = 200.3996$

$E_{2,2} = \dfrac{(800)(1000)}{4004} = 199.8002$

$E_{2,3} = \dfrac{(800)(1000)}{4004} = 199.8002$

$E_{2,4} = \dfrac{(800)(1001)}{4004} = 200.0$

$E_{3,1} = \dfrac{(869)(1003)}{4004} = 208.6661$

$E_{3,2} = \dfrac{(833)(1000)}{4004} = 208.0420$

$E_{3,3} = \dfrac{(833)(1000)}{4004} = 208.0420$

$E_{3,4} = \dfrac{(833)(1001)}{4004} = 208.25$

$E_{4,1} = \dfrac{(968)(1003)}{4004} = 242.2835$

$E_{4,2} = \dfrac{(968)(1000)}{4004} = 241.7582$

$E_{4,3} = \dfrac{(968)(1000)}{4004} = 241.7582$

$E_{4,4} = \dfrac{(968)(1001)}{4004} = 242.0$

Type of Pet

Income	Dog	Cat
< $12,500	127(133.7667)	139(133.3666)
$12,500 - $24,999	191(199.8002)	197(199.8002)
$25,000 - $39,999	216(217.6841)	215(217.0330)
$40,000 - $59,999	215(208.6661)	212(208.0420)
$60,000 & over	254(242.4835)	237(241.7582)

9. continued

Income	Bird	Horse
< $12,500	173(133.3666)	95(133.5)
$12,500 - $24,999	209(199.8002)	203(200.0)
$25,000 -$39,999	220(217.0330)	218(217.25)
$40,000 - $59,999	175(208.0420)	231(208.25)
$60,000 & over	223(241.7582)	254(242.0)

$\chi^2 = \sum \dfrac{(O-E)^2}{E} = \dfrac{(127-133.7667)^2}{133.7667} + \dfrac{(139-133.3666)^2}{133.3666}$

$+ \dfrac{(173-133.3666)^2}{133.3666} + \dfrac{(95-133.5)^2}{133.5} + \dfrac{(191-199.8002)^2}{199.8002}$

$+ \dfrac{(197-199.8002)^2}{199.8002} + \dfrac{(209-199.8002)^2}{199.8002} + \dfrac{(203-200.0)^2}{200}$

$+ \dfrac{(216-217.6841)^2}{217.6841} + \dfrac{(215-217.0330)^2}{217.0330} + \dfrac{(220-217.0330)^2}{217.0330}$

$+ \dfrac{(218-217.25))^2}{217.25} + \dfrac{(215-208.6661)^2}{208.6661} + \dfrac{(212-208.0420)^2}{208.0420}$

$+ \dfrac{(175-208.0420)^2}{208.0420} + \dfrac{(231-208.25)^2}{208.25} + \dfrac{(254-242.4835)^2}{242.4835}$

$+ \dfrac{(237-241.7582)^2}{241.7582} + \dfrac{(223-241.7582)^2}{241.7582} + \dfrac{(254-242.0)^2}{242}$

$\chi^2 = 35.177$

0   21.026   ↑
                                  35.177

Reject the null hypothesis. There is enough evidence to support the claim that the type of pet is dependent upon the income of the owner.

10.

H_0: The rank of women personnel is independent of the military branch of service.

H_1: The rank of women personnel is dependent upon the military branch of service. (claim)

C. V. = 7.815   d. f. = 3 $\alpha = 0.05$

Rank

Branch	Officers	Enlisted
Army	10,791(11,463.0612)	62,491(61,818.9388)
Navy	7816(7909.7344)	42,750(42,656.2656)
Marine Corps	932(1635.7254)	9525(8821.2746)
Air Force	11,819(10,349.4790)	54,344(55,813.5210)

10. continued

$$\chi^2 = \frac{(10791-11463.0612)^2}{11463.0612} + \frac{(62491-61818.9388)^2}{61818/9388}$$

$$+ \frac{(7816-7909.7344)^2}{7909.7344} + \frac{(42750-42656.2656)^2}{42656.2656}$$

$$+ \frac{(932-1635.7254)^2}{1635.7254} + \frac{(9525-8821.2746)^2}{8821.2746}$$

$$+ \frac{(11819-10349.4790)^2}{10349.4790} + \frac{(54344-55813.5210)^2}{55813.5210}$$

$$\chi^2 = 654.2719$$

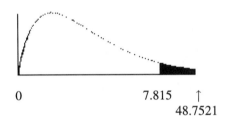

0   7.815   ↑
                   654.2719

Reject the null hypothesis. There is enough evidence to support the claim that rank is dependent upon the military branch of service.

11.

H_0: The composition of the House of Representatives is independent of the state.
H_1: The composition of the House of Representatives is dependent upon the state. (claim)

C. V. = 7.815   d. f. = 3 $\alpha = 0.05$

$$E = \frac{\text{(row sum)(column sum)}}{\text{grand total}}$$

$$E_{1,1} = \frac{(203)(320)}{542} = 119.8524$$

$$E_{1,2} = \frac{(203)(222)}{542} = 83.1476$$

$$E_{2,1} = \frac{(98)(320)}{542} = 57.8598$$

$$E_{2,2} = \frac{(98)(222)}{542} = 40.1402$$

$$E_{3,1} = \frac{(100)(320)}{542} = 59.0406$$

$$E_{3,2} = \frac{(100)(222)}{542} 40.9594$$

$$E_{4,1} = \frac{(141)(320)}{542} = 83.2472$$

$$E_{4,2} = \frac{(141)(222)}{542} = 57.7528$$

11. continued

State	Democrats	Republicans
PA	100(119.8524)	103(83.1476)
OH	39(57.8598)	59(40.1402)
WV	75(59.0406)	25(40.9594)
MD	106(83.2472)	35(57.7528)

$$\chi^2 = \sum\frac{(O-E)^2}{E} = \frac{(100-119.8524)^2}{119.8524} + \frac{(103-83.1476)^2}{83.1476}$$

$$+ \frac{(39-57.8598)^2}{57.8598} + \frac{(59-40.1402)^2}{40.1402} + \frac{(75-59.0406)^2}{59.0406}$$

$$+ \frac{(25-40.9594)^2}{40.9594} + \frac{(106-83.2472)^2}{83.2472} + \frac{(35-57.7528)^2}{57.7528}$$

$$\chi^2 = 48.7521$$

0   7.815   ↑
                   48.7521

Reject the null hypothesis. There is enough evidence to support the claim that the composition of the legislature is dependent upon the state.

12.

H_0: The size of the population (by age) is independent of the state.
H_1: The size of the population (by age) is dependent upon the state. (claim)

C. V. = 11.071   d. f. = 5 $\alpha = 0.05$

State	Under 5	5 - 17	18 - 24
PA	721(753.9308)	2140(2190.0631)	1025(1078.5184)
OH	740(707.0692)	2104(2053.9369)	1065(1011.4816)

State	25 - 44	45 - 64	65 +
PA	3515(3547.2417)	2702(2677.7185)	1899(1754.5275)
OH	3359(3326.7583)	2487(2511.2815)	1501(1645.4725)

$$\chi^2 = \frac{(721-753.9308)^2}{753.9308} + \frac{(2140-2190.0631)^2}{2190.0631}$$

$$+ \frac{(1025-1078.5184)^2}{1078.5184} + \frac{(3515-3547.2417)^2}{3547.2417}$$

$$+ \frac{(2702-2677.7185)^2}{2677.7185} + \frac{(1899-1754.5275)^2}{1754.5275}$$

$$+ \frac{(740-707.0692)^2}{707.0692} + \frac{(2104-2053.9369)^2}{2053.9369}$$

$$+ \frac{(1065-1011.4816)^2}{1011.4816} + \frac{(3359-3326.7583)^2}{3326.7583}$$

12. continued

$$+ \frac{(2487-2511.2815)^2}{2511.2815} + \frac{(1501-1645.4725)^2}{1645.4725}$$

$$\chi^2 = 36.4656$$

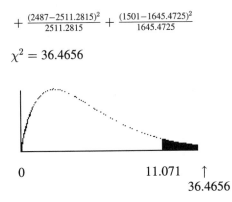

0   11.071   ↑
                      36.4656

Reject the null hypothesis. There is enough evidence to support the claim that the size of the population (by age) is dependent upon the state.

13.

H_0: The number of ads people think they've seen or heard in the media is independent of the gender of the individual.

H_1: The number of ads people think they've seen or heard in the media is dependent upon the gender of the individual. (claim)

C. V. = 13.277   d. f. = 4 $\alpha = 0.01$

$$E_{1,1} = \frac{(300)(95)}{510} = 55.882$$

$$E_{1,2} = \frac{(300)(110)}{510} = 64.706$$

$$E_{1,3} = \frac{(300)(144)}{510} = 84.706$$

$$E_{1,4} = \frac{(300)(84)}{510} = 49.412$$

$$E_{1,5} = \frac{(300)(77)}{510} = 45.294$$

$$E_{2,1} = \frac{(210)(95)}{510} = 39.118$$

$$E_{2,2} = \frac{(210)(110)}{510} = 45.294$$

$$E_{2,3} = \frac{(210)(144)}{510} = 59.294$$

$$E_{2,4} = \frac{(210)(84)}{510} = 34.588$$

$$E_{2,5} = \frac{(210)(77)}{510} = 31.706$$

Gender	1 - 30	31 - 50	51 - 100
Men	45(55.882)	60(64.706)	90(84.706)
Women	50(39.118)	50(45.294)	54(59.294)
Total	95	110	144

13. continued

Gender	101 - 300	301 or more	Total
Men	54(49.412)	51(45.294)	300
Women	30(34.588)	26(31.706)	210
Total	84	77	510

$$\chi^2 = \sum \frac{(O-E)^2}{E} = \frac{(45-55.882)^2}{55.882} + \frac{(60-64.706)^2}{64.706}$$

$$+ \frac{(90-84.706)^2}{84.706} + \frac{(54-49.412)^2}{49.412} + \frac{(51-45.294)^2}{45.294}$$

$$+ \frac{(50-39.118)^2}{39.118} + \frac{(50-45.294)^2}{45.294} + \frac{(54-59.294)^2}{59.294}$$

$$+ \frac{(30-34.588)^2}{34.588} + \frac{(26-31.706)^2}{31.706} = 9.562$$

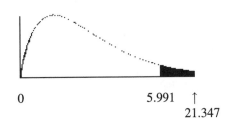

0   ↑   13.277
            9.562

Do not reject the null hypothesis. There is not enough evidence to support the claim that the number of ads people think they've seen or heard is related to the gender of the individual.

14.

H_0: The way people obtain information is independent of their educational background. (claim)

H_1: The way people obtain information is dependent on their educational background.

C. V. = 5.991   d. f. = 2

$$\chi^2 = \frac{(159-139.5)^2}{139.5} + \frac{(90-99)^2}{99} + \frac{(51-61.5)^2}{61.5}$$

$$+ \frac{(27-46.5)^2}{46.5} + \frac{(42-33)^2}{33} + \frac{(31-20.5)^2}{20.5}$$

$$\chi^2 = 21.347$$

	TV	Paper	Other	Total
High School	159(139.5)	90(99)	51(61.5)	300
College	27(46.5)	42(33)	31(20.5)	100
Total	186	132	82	400

0   5.991   ↑
                       21.347

14. continued
Reject the null hypothesis. There is enough evidence to reject the claim that the way people obtain information is independent of their educational background.

15.
H_0: The type of practice of an attorney is independent of the gender of the attorney. (claim)
H_1: The type of practice of an attorney is dependent upon the gender of the attorney.
C. V. = 5.991   d. f. = 2 $\alpha = 0.05$

$$E_{1,1} = \frac{(176)(140)}{240} = 102.667$$

$$E_{1,2} = \frac{(34)(140)}{240} = 19.833$$

$$E_{1,3} = \frac{(30)(140)}{240} = 17.5$$

$$E_{2,1} = \frac{(176)(100)}{240} = 73.333$$

$$E_{2,2} = \frac{(34)(100)}{240} = 14.167$$

$$E_{2,3} = \frac{(30)(100)}{240} = 12.5$$

Gender	Private Practice	Law Firm
Male	112(102.667)	16(19.833)
Female	64(73.333)	18(14.167)

Gender	Government
Male	12(17.5)
Female	18(12.5)

$$\chi^2 = \sum \frac{(O-E)^2}{E} = \frac{(112-102.667)^2}{102.667} + \frac{(16-19.833)^2}{19.833}$$

$$+ \frac{(12-17.5)^2}{17.5} + \frac{(64-73.333)^2}{73.333} + \frac{(18-14.167)^2}{14.167}$$

$$+ \frac{(18-12.5)^2}{12.5} = 7.963$$

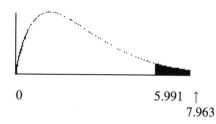

0   5.991 ↑
                            7.963

Reject the null hypothesis. There is enough evidence to reject the claim that the type of practice is independent of the gender of the attorney.

16.
H_0: The number of speeders is independent of the state where the drivers reside.
H_1: The number of speeders is dependent upon the state where the driver resides. (claim)

C. V. = 3.841   d. f. = 1 $\alpha = 0.05$

	Ohio	Michigan
66 mph or more	18(22.7647)	25(20.2353)
65 mph or less	27(22.2353)	15(19.7647)

$$\chi^2 = \frac{(18-22.7647)^2}{22.7647} + \frac{(25-20.2353)^2}{20.2353}$$

$$+ \frac{(27-22.2353)^2}{22.2353} + \frac{(15-19.7647)^2}{19.7647} = 4.289$$

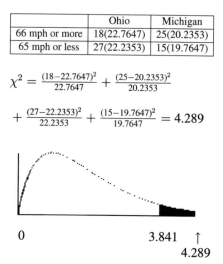

0   3.841 ↑
                            4.289

Reject the null hypothesis. There is enough evidence to support the claim that the number of speeders is dependent upon the state where the driver resides.

17.
H_0: The type of video rented by a person is independent of the person's age.
H_1: The type of video a person rents is dependent on the person's age. (claim)
C. V. = 13.362   d. f. = 8 $\alpha = 0.10$

Age	Doc.	Comedy	Mystery
12-20	14(6.588)	9(13.433)	8(10.979)
21-29	15(8.075)	14(16.467)	9(13.458)
30-38	9(14.663)	21(29.9)	39(24.438)
39-47	7(9.775)	22(19.933)	17(16.292)
48 +	6(11.9)	38(24.267)	12(19.833)

$$\chi^2 = \frac{(14-6.588)^2}{6.588} + \frac{(9-13.433)^2}{13.433} + \frac{(8-10.979)^2}{10.979}$$

$$+ \frac{(15-8.075)^2}{8.075} + \frac{(14-16.467)^2}{16.467} + \frac{(9-13.458)^2}{13.458}$$

$$+ \frac{(9-14.663)^2}{14.663} + \frac{(21-29.9)^2}{29.9} + \frac{(39-24.438)^2}{24.438}$$

$$+ \frac{(7-9.775)^2}{9.775} + \frac{(22-19.933)^2}{19.933} + \frac{(17-16.292)^2}{16.292}$$

$$+ \frac{(6-11.9)^2}{11.9} + \frac{(38-24.267)^2}{24.267} + \frac{(12-19.833)^2}{19.833}$$

17. continued

$\chi^2 = 46.733$

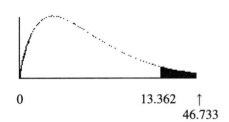

0   13.362   ↑
                     46.733

Reject the null hypothesis. There is enough evidence to support the claim that the type of movie selected is related to the age of the customer.

18.
H_0: The time a person decides what to prepare for dinner is independent of the gender of the preparer. (claim)
H_1: The time a person decides what to prepare for dinner is dependent on the gender of the preparer.
C. V. = 5.991   d. f. = 2

Gender	Afternoon	Morning	Day Before
Male	20(20.057)	9(11.7)	10(7.243)
Female	16(15.943)	12(9.3)	3(5.757)

$\chi^2 = \frac{(20-20.057)^2}{20.057} + \frac{(9-11.7)^2}{11.7} + \frac{(10-7.243)^2}{7.243}$

$+ \frac{(16-15.943)^2}{15.943} + \frac{(12-9.3)^2}{9.3} + \frac{(3-5.757)^2}{5.757}$

$\chi^2 = 3.78$

0   ↑   5.991
                    3.78

Do not reject the null hypothesis. There is not enough evidence to reject the claim that the time is independent of the gender of the preparer. In summary, the timing of the decision of what to prepare for dinner is not related to the gender of the cook!

19.
H_0: The type of snack purchased is independent of the gender of the consumer. (claim)
H_1: The type of snack purchased is dependent upon the gender of the consumer.
C. V. = 4.605   d. f. = 2

Gender	Hot Dog	Peanuts	Popcorn	Total
Male	12(13.265)	21(15.388)	19(23.347)	52
Female	13(11.735)	8(13.612)	25(20.653)	46
Total	25	29	44	98

$\chi^2 = \sum \frac{(O-E)^2}{E} = \frac{(12-13.265)^2}{13.265} + \frac{(21-15.388)^2}{15.388}$

$+ \frac{(19-23.347)^2}{23.347} + \frac{(13-11.735)^2}{11.735} + \frac{(8-13.612)^2}{13.612}$

$+ \frac{(25-20.653)^2}{20.653} = 6.342$

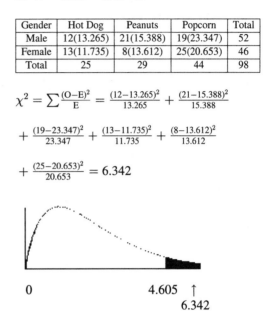

0   4.605   ↑
                            6.342

Reject the null hypothesis. There is enough evidence to reject the claim that the type of snack chosen is independent of the gender of the individual.

20.
H_0: The drug is not effective.
H_1: The drug is effective. (claim)
$\alpha = 0.10$ d. f. = 1

	Effective	Not effective	Total
Drug	32(25.408)	9(15.592)	41
Placebo	12(18.592)	18(11.408)	30
Total	44	27	71

$\chi^2 = \frac{(32-25.408)^2}{25.408} + \frac{(9-15.592)^2}{15.592} +$

$\frac{(12-18.592)^2}{18.592} + \frac{(18-11.408)^2}{11.408} = 10.643$

P-value < 0.005 (0.001)
Reject the null hypothesis since P-value < 0.10. There is enough evidence to support the claim that the drug is effective.

21.
H_0: The type of book purchased by the individual is independent of the gender of the individual. (claim)
H_1: The type of book purchased by the individual is dependent on the gender of the individual.
$\alpha = 0.05$ d. f. $= 2$

Gender	Mystery	Romance	Self-help	Total
Male	243(214.121)	201(198.260)	191(222.618)	635
Female	135(163.879)	149(151.740)	202(170.382)	486
Total	378	350	393	1121

$\chi^2 = \sum \frac{(O-E)^2}{E} = \frac{(243-214.121)^2}{214.121} + \frac{(201-198.260)^2}{198.260}$

$+ \frac{(191-222.618)^2}{222.618} + \frac{(135-163.879)^2}{163.879}$

$+ \frac{(149-151.740)^2}{151.740} + \frac{(202-170.382)^2}{170.382} = 19.429$

P-value < 0.005 (0.00006)
Reject the null hypothesis since P-value < 0.05. There is enough evidence to reject the claim that the type of book purchased is independent of gender.

22.
H_0: $p_1 = p_2 = p_3$ (claim)
H_1: At least one proportion is different.
C. V. $= 9.210$ d. f. $= 2$

$E(\text{will donate}) = \frac{50(63)}{150} = 21$

$E(\text{will not donate}) = \frac{50(87)}{150} = 29$

	A	B	C
will donate	28(21)	14(21)	21(21)
won't donate	22(29)	36(29)	29(29)

$\chi^2 = \frac{(28-21)^2}{21} + \frac{(14-21)^2}{21} + \frac{(21-21)^2}{21} +$

$\frac{(22-29)^2}{29} + \frac{(36-29)^2}{29} + \frac{(29-29)^2}{29} = 8.046$

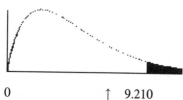

0   ↑ 9.210
                  8.046

22. continued
Do not reject the null hypothesis. There is not enough evidence to reject the claim that the proportions are equal.

23.
H_0: $p_1 = p_2 = p_3 = p_4$ (claim)
H_1: At least one proportion is different.

C. V. $= 7.815$ d. f. $= 3$

$E(\text{passed}) = \frac{120(167)}{120} = 41.75$

$E(\text{failed}) = \frac{120(313)}{120} = 78.25$

	Southside	West End	East Hills	Jefferson
Passed	49(41.75)	38(41.75)	46(41.75)	34(41.75)
Failed	71(78.25)	82(78.25)	74(78.25)	86(78.25)

$\chi^2 = \frac{(49-41.75)^2}{41.75} + \frac{(38-41.75)^2}{41.75} + \frac{(46-41.75)^2}{41.75}$

$+ \frac{(34-41.75)^2}{41.75} + \frac{(71-78.25)^2}{78.25} + \frac{(82-78.25)^2}{78.25}$

$+ \frac{(74-78.25)^2}{78.25} + \frac{(86-78.25)^2}{78.25} = 5.317$

0   ↑ 7.851
                  5.317

Do not reject the null hypothesis. There is not enough evidence to reject the claim that the proportions are equal.

24.
H_0: $p_1 = p_2 = p_3$ (claim)
H_1: At least one proportion is different.
C. V. $= 9.210$ d. f. $= 2$

$E(\text{yes}) = \frac{92(133)}{276} = 44.33$

$E(\text{no}) = \frac{92(143)}{276} = 47.67$

	Mall A	Mall B	Mall C
Yes	52(44.33)	45(44.33)	36(44.33)
No	40(47.67)	47(47.67)	56(47.67)

$\chi^2 = \frac{(52-44.33)^2}{44.33} + \frac{(45-44.33)^2}{44.33} + \frac{(36-44.33)^2}{44.33}$

$\frac{(40-47.67)^2}{47.67} + \frac{(47-47.67)^2}{47.67} + \frac{(56-47.67)^2}{47.67}$

24. continued

$\chi^2 = 5.602$

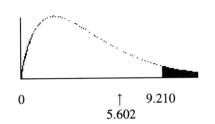

0   ↑   9.210
        5.602

Do not reject the null hypothesis. There is not enough evidence to reject the claim that the proportions are equal.

25.

H_0: $p_1 = p_2 = p_3 = p_4$ (claim)
H_1: At least one proportion is different.
C. V. $= 7.815$ d. f. $= 3$

	Services	Manufacturing	Government	Other
10 years ago	33(30.6)	13(15)	11(11.4)	3(3)
Now	18(20.4)	12(10)	8(7.6)	2(2)
Total	51	25	19	5

$$\chi^2 = \frac{(33-30.6)^2}{30.6} + \frac{(13-15)^2}{15} + \frac{(11-11.4)^2}{11.4} +$$

$$\frac{(3-3)^2}{3} + \frac{(18-20.4)^2}{20.4} + \frac{(12-10)^2}{10} + \frac{(8-7.6)^2}{7.6}$$

$$+ \frac{(2-2)^2}{2} = 1.172$$

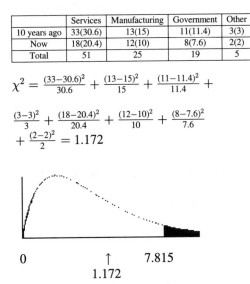

0   ↑   7.815
        1.172

Do not reject the null hypothesis. There is not enough evidence to reject the claim that the proportions are the same. Since the survey was done in Pennsylvania, it is doubtful that it can be generalized to the population of the United States.

26.

H_0: $p_1 = p_2 = p_3$ (claim)
H_1: At least one proportion is different.
C. V. $= 4.605$ d. f. $= 2$

$$E(\text{mother works}) = \frac{60(118)}{180} = 39.33$$

$$E(\text{mother doesn't work}) = \frac{60(62)}{180} = 20.67$$

26. continued

	Elem.	Middle	High
work	29(39.33)	38(39.33)	51(39.33)
no work	31(20.67)	22(20.67)	9(20.67)

$$\chi^2 = \frac{(29-39.33)^2}{39.33} + \frac{(38-39.33)^2}{39.33} + \frac{(51-39.33)^2}{39.33}$$

$$+ \frac{(31-20.67)^2}{20.67} + \frac{(22-20.67)^2}{20.67} + \frac{(9-20.67)^2}{20.67}$$

$$\chi^2 = 18.06$$

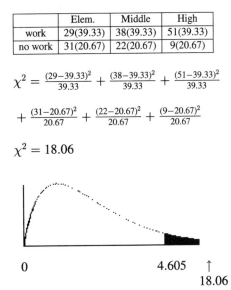

0   4.605   ↑
                            18.06

Reject the null hypothesis. There is enough evidence to reject the claim that the proportions are equal.

27.

H_0: $p_1 = p_2 = p_3 = p_4$ (claim)
H_1: At least one proportion is different.
C. V. $= 6.251$ d. f. $= 3$

$$E(\text{yes}) = \frac{(100)(132)}{400} = 33$$

$$E(\text{no}) = \frac{(100)(268)}{400} = 67$$

	North	South	East	West
Yes	43(33)	39(33)	22(33)	28(33)
No	57(67)	61(67)	78(67)	72(67)

$$\chi^2 = \frac{(43-33)^2}{33} + \frac{(39-33)^2}{33} + \frac{(22-33)^2}{33} +$$

$$\frac{(28-33)^2}{33} + \frac{(57-67)^2}{67} + \frac{(61-67)^2}{67} + \frac{(78-67)^2}{67}$$

$$+ \frac{(72-67)^2}{67} = 12.755$$

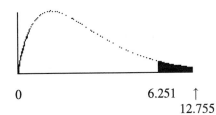

0   6.251   ↑
                            12.755

27. continued
Reject the null hypothesis. There is enough evidence to reject the claim that the proportions are the same.

28.
H_0: $p_1 = p_2 = p_3 = p_4$ (claim)
H_1: At least one proportion is different.
C. V. = 7.815   d. f. = 3

$E(\text{present}) = \frac{239(75)}{300} = 59.75$

$E(\text{not present}) = \frac{61(75)}{300} = 15.25$

	A	B	C	D
Present	66(59.75)	60(59.75)	57(59.75)	56(59.75)
Not present	9(15.25)	15(15.25)	18(15.25)	19(15.25)

$\chi^2 = \frac{(66-59.75)^2}{59.75} + \frac{(60-59.75)^2}{59.75} + \frac{(57-59.75)^2}{59.75}$

$+ \frac{(56-59.75)^2}{59.75} + \frac{(9-15.25)^2}{15.25} + \frac{(15-15.25)^2}{15.25} +$

$\frac{(18-15.25)^2}{15.25} + \frac{(19-15.25)^2}{15.25} = 5.0$

Do not reject the null hypothesis. There is not enough evidence to reject the claim that the proportions are the same.

29.
H_0: $p_1 = p_2 = p_3 = p_4$ (claim)
H_1: At least one proportion is different.
$\alpha = 0.05$ d. f. = 3

$E(\text{on bars}) = \frac{30(62)}{120} = 15.5$

$E(\text{not on bars}) = \frac{30(58)}{120} = 14.5$

	N	S	E	W
on	15(15.5)	18(15.5)	13(15.5)	16(15.5)
off	15(14.5)	12(14.5)	17(14.5)	14(14.5)

$\chi^2 = \frac{(15-15.5)^2}{15.5} + \frac{(18-15.5)^2}{15.5} + \frac{(13-15.5)^2}{15.5} +$

$\frac{(16-15.5)^2}{15.5} + \frac{(15-14.5)^2}{14.5} + \frac{(12-14.5)^2}{14.5} +$

29. continued

$\frac{(17-14.5)^2}{14.5} + \frac{(14-14.5)^2}{14.5} = 1.734$

P-value > 0.10 (0.629)
Do not reject the null hypothesis. There is not enough evidence to reject the claim that the proportions are the same.

30.
H_0: $p_1 = p_2 = p_3 = p_4$ (claim)
H_1: At least one proportion is different.
$\alpha = 0.10$ d. f. = 3

$E(\text{will travel}) = \frac{125(184)}{500} = 46$

$E(\text{will not travel}) = \frac{125(316)}{500} = 79$

	A	B	C	D
will	37(46)	52(46)	46(46)	49(46)
will not	88(79)	73(79)	79(79)	76(79)

$\chi^2 = \frac{(37-46)^2}{46} + \frac{(52-46)^2}{46} + \frac{(46-46)^2}{46} +$

$\frac{(49-46)^2}{46} + \frac{(88-79)^2}{79} + \frac{(73-79)^2}{79} +$

$\frac{(79-79)^2}{79} + \frac{(76-79)^2}{79} = 4.334$

P-value > 0.10 (0.228)
Do not reject the null hypothesis since P-value > 0.10. There is not enough evidence to reject the claim that the proportions are the same.

31.
H_0: $p_1 = p_2 = p_3$ (claim)
H_1: At least one proportion is different.
C. V. = 4.605   d. f. = 2

$E(\text{list}) = \frac{96(219)}{288} = 73$

$E(\text{no list}) = \frac{96(69)}{288} = 23$

	A	B	C
list	77(73)	74(73)	68(73)
no list	19(23)	22((23)	28(23)

$\chi^2 = \frac{(77-73)^2}{73} + \frac{(74-73)^2}{73} + \frac{(68-73)^2}{73}$

$+ \frac{(19-23)^2}{23} + \frac{(22-23)^2}{23} + \frac{(28-23)^2}{23}$

$\chi^2 = 2.401$

31. continued

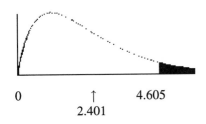

$$0 \qquad \overset{\uparrow}{\underset{2.401}{}} \qquad 4.605$$

Do not reject the null hypothesis. There is not enough evidence to reject the claim that the proportions are the same.

32.

			Total
	12(9.61)	15(17.39)	27
	9(11.39)	23(20.61)	32
Total	21	38	59

$$\chi^2 = \frac{(12-9.61)^2}{9.61} + \frac{(15-17.39)^2}{17.39}$$

$$+ \frac{(9-11.39)^2}{11.39} + \frac{(23-20.61)^2}{20.61} = 1.70$$

$$\chi^2 = \frac{59(12 \cdot 23 - 15 \cdot 9)^2}{(12+15)(12+9)(9+23)(15+23)}$$

$$= \frac{1172979}{689472} = 1.70$$

Alternate Method:

$$\chi^2 = \frac{n(ad-bc)^2}{(a+b)(a+c)(c+d)(b+d)}$$

$$\chi^2 = \frac{59(12 \cdot 23 - 15 \cdot 9)^2}{(12+15)(12+9)(9+23)(15+23)} = 1.70$$

Both answers are the same.

33.
$$\chi^2 = \frac{(|O-E|-0.5)^2}{E} = \frac{(|12-9.6|-0.5)^2}{9.6}$$

$$+ \frac{(|15-17.4|-0.5)^2}{17.4} + \frac{(|9-11.4|-0.5)^2}{11.4}$$

$$+ \frac{(|23-20.6|-0.5)^2}{20.6}$$

$$= \frac{3.61}{9.6} + \frac{3.61}{17.4} + \frac{3.61}{11.4} + \frac{3.61}{20.6}$$

$$= 0.376 + 0.207 + 0.317 + 0.175 = 1.075$$

34.
For 8:
$$\chi^2 = 6.789$$
$$n = 34 + 57 + 21 + 15 + 63 + 20 = 210$$

34. continued
$$C = \sqrt{\frac{\chi^2}{\chi^2+n}} = \sqrt{\frac{6.789}{6.789 + 210}} = 0.177$$

For 20:
$$\chi^2 = 10.643$$
$$n = 32 + 9 + 12 + 18 = 71$$

$$C = \sqrt{\frac{10.643}{10.643 + 71}} = 0.361$$

EXERCISE SET 11-4

1.
The analysis of variance using the F-test can be used to compare 3 or more means.

2.
a. Comparing two means at a time ignores all other means.
b. The probability of type I error is actually larger than α when multiple t-tests are used.
c. The more sample means, the more t-tests are needed.

3.
The populations from which the samples were obtained must be normally distributed. The samples must be independent of each other. The variances of the populations must be equal.

4.
The between-group variance estimates the population variance using the means. The within-group variance estimates the population variance using all the data values.

5.
$$F = \frac{s_B^2}{s_W^2}$$

6.
H_0: $\mu_1 = \mu_2 = ... = \mu_n$
H_1: At least one mean is different from the others.

7.
One.

8.
H_0: $\mu_1 = \mu_2 = \mu_3$
H_1: At least one mean is different from the others. (claim)
C. V. = 3.52 $\alpha = 0.05$

8. continued

d. f. N = 2   d. f. D = 19

$\bar{X}_1 = 165.714$ $\bar{X}_2 = 245.714$ $\bar{X}_3 = 237.5$

$s_1^2 = 5695.238$ $s_2^2 = 3928.571$ $s_3^2 = 7335.714$

$\bar{X}_{GM} = \frac{4780}{22} = 217.273$

$s_B^2 = \frac{\sum n_i (\bar{X}_i - \bar{X}_{GM})^2}{k-1} =$

$\frac{7(165.714 - 217.273)^2 + 7(245.714 - 217.273)^2 + 8(237.5 - 217.273)^2}{2}$

$= 13,771.799$

$s_W^2 = \frac{\sum (n_i - 1)s_i^2}{\sum (n_i - 1)}$

$= \frac{6(5695.238) + 6(3928.571) + 7(7335.714)}{6 + 6 + 7} = 5741.729$

$F = \frac{s_B^2}{s_W^2} = \frac{13771.799}{5741.729} = 2.3985$

Do not reject the null hypothesis. There is not enough evidence to support the claim that at least one mean is different.

9.

H_0: $\mu_1 = \mu_2 = \mu_3$

H_1: At least one mean is different from the others. (claim)

C. V. = 3.47 $\alpha = 0.05$

d. f. N. = 2   d. f. D. = 21

$\bar{X}_{GM} = 4.554$ $s_B^2 = 9.82113$ $s_W^2 = 4.93225$

$F = \frac{9.82113}{4.93225} = 1.9912$

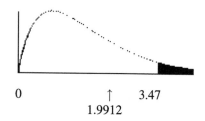

0   ↑   3.47
                    1.9912

Do not reject the null hypothesis. There is not enough evidence to support the claim that at least one mean is different from the others.

10.

H_0: $\mu_1 = \mu_2 = \mu_3 = \mu_4$ (claim)

H_1: At least one mean is different from the others.

C. V. = 2.30 $\alpha = 0.10$

d. f. N = 3   d. f. D = 27

$\bar{X}_1 = 3689$ $s_1^2 = 904,361.667$

$\bar{X}_2 = 5183.143$ $s_2^2 = 2,387,825.81$

$\bar{X}_3 = 5889.125$ $s_3^2 = 6,446,701.554$

$\bar{X}_4 = 4671.222$ $s_4^2 = 4,951,768.194$

$\bar{X}_{GM} = \frac{\sum X}{n} = \frac{151259}{31} = 4879.323$

$s_B^2 = \frac{\sum n_i (\bar{X}_i - \bar{X}_{GM})^2}{k-1} =$

$\frac{7(3689 - 4879.323)^2 + 7(5183.143 - 4879.323)^2}{4-1}$

$+ \frac{8(5889.125 - 4879.323)^2 + 9(4671.222 - 4879.323)^2}{4-1}$

$= 6,370,527.64$

$s_W^2 = \frac{\sum (n_i - 1)s_i^2}{\sum (n_i - 1)}$

$= \frac{6(904361.667) + 6(2387825.81)}{6 + 6 + 7 + 8}$

$+ \frac{7(6446701.554) + 8(4951768.194)}{6 + 6 + 7 + 8}$

$= 3,870,154.86$

$F = \frac{6370527.64}{3870154.86} = 1.646$

Do not reject the null hypothesis. There is not enough evidence to reject the claim that the means are the same.

11.

H_0: $\mu_1 = \mu_2 = \mu_3$

H_1: At least one mean is different from the others. (claim)

C. V. = 3.98 $\alpha = 0.05$

d. f. N = 2   d. f. D = 11

$\bar{X}_{GM} = \frac{52414}{14} = 3743.857$

$s_B^2 = 3,633,540.88$

$s_W^2 = 1,330,350$

$F = \frac{3633540.88}{1330350} = 2.7313$

11. continued

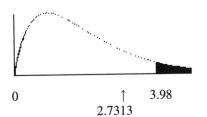

0   ↑   3.98

2.7313

Do not reject the null hypothesis. There is not enough evidence to support the claim that at least one mean is different from the others.

12.

H_0: $\mu_1 = \mu_2 = \mu_3$
H_1: At least one mean is different from the others. (claim)
$\alpha = 0.05$
d. f. N = 2   d. f. D = 11

$$\bar{X}_{GM} = \frac{\sum X}{n} = \frac{99}{14} = 7.07$$

$$s_B^2 = \frac{101.095}{2} = 50.548$$

$$s_W^2 = \frac{71.833}{11} = 6.530$$

$$F = \frac{s_B^2}{s_W^2} = \frac{50.548}{6.530} = 7.74$$

P-value = 0.00797
Reject since P-value < 0.05.

There is enough evidence to support the claim that at least one mean is different from the others.

13.

H_0: $\mu_1 = \mu_2 = \mu_3$
H_1: At least one mean is different. (claim)

k = 3   N = 18   d.f.N. = 2   d.f.D. = 15
CV = 3.68

$\bar{X}_1 = 7$ $s_1^2 = 1.37$
$\bar{X}_2 = 8.12$ $s_2^2 = 0.64$
$\bar{X}_3 = 5.23$ $s_3^2 = 2.66$

$\bar{X}_{GM} = 6.7833$

$$s_B^2 = \frac{6(7-6.78)^2}{2} + \frac{6(8.12-6.78)^2}{2}$$

$$+ \frac{6(5.23-6.78)^2}{2} = 12.7$$

13. continued

$$s_W^2 = \frac{5(1.37)+5(0.64)+5(2.66)}{5+5+5}$$

$$s_W^2 = \frac{23.35}{15} = 1.56$$

$$F = \frac{12.7}{1.56} = 8.14$$

0   3.68   ↑

                  8.14

Reject the null hypothesis. There is enough evidence to support the claim that at least one mean is different.

14.

H_0: $\mu_1 = \mu_2 = \mu_3$
H_1: At least one mean is different from the others. (claim)

C. V. = 5.93 $\alpha = 0.01$
d. f. N = 2   d. f. D = 19

$\bar{X}_1 = 234$ $s_1^2 = 7106.333$
$\bar{X}_2 = 223$ $s_2^2 = 15842.667$
$\bar{X}_3 = 193.625$ $s_3^2 = 7222.554$

$$\bar{X}_{GM} = \frac{\sum X}{N} = \frac{4748}{22} = 215.818$$

$$s_B^2 = \frac{\sum n_i (\bar{X}_i - \bar{X}_{GM})^2}{k-1}$$

$$= \frac{7(234-215.818)^2 + 7(223-215.818)^2}{3-1}$$

$$+ \frac{8(193.625-215.818)^2}{3-1} = 3307.699$$

$$s_W^2 = \frac{\sum (n_i - 1)s_i^2}{\sum (n_i - 1)}$$

$$= \frac{6(7106.333) + 6(15842.667) + 7(7222.554)}{6 + 6 + 7}$$

$$s_W^2 = 9907.994$$

$$F = \frac{s_B^2}{s_W^2} = \frac{3307.699}{9907.994} = 0.3338$$

14. continued

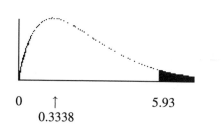

0   ↑   5.93
    0.3338

Do not reject the null hypothesis. There is not enough evidence to support the claim that at least one of the means is different from the others.

15.

H_0: $\mu_1 = \mu_2 = \mu_3$ (claim)
H_1: At least one mean is different from the others.

C. V. = 4.10 $\alpha = 0.10$
d. f. N = 2   d. f. D = 10

$\overline{X}_1 = 35.4$ $s_1^2 = 351.8$
$\overline{X}_2 = 68.75$ $s_2^2 = 338.25$
$\overline{X}_3 = 44.25$ $s_3^2 = 277.583$

$\overline{X}_{GM} = \frac{629}{13} = 48.385$

$s_B^2 = \frac{\sum n_i (\overline{X}_i - \overline{X}_{GM})^2}{k-1}$

$s_B^2 = \frac{5(35.4-48.385)^2}{2} + \frac{4(68.75-48.385)^2}{2}$

$+ \frac{4(44.25-48.385)^2}{2} = 1285.188$

$s_W^2 = \frac{\sum (n_i - 1)s_i^2}{\sum (n_i - 1)}$

$= \frac{4(351.8) + 3(338.25) + 3(277.583)}{4 + 3 + 3}$

$= 325.47$

$F = \frac{s_B^2}{s_W^2} = \frac{1285.188}{325.47} = 3.9487$

Do not reject the null hypothesis. There is not enough evidence to reject the claim that the means are the same.

16.

H_0: $\mu_1 = \mu_2 = \mu_3$
H_1: At least one mean is different from the others. (claim)

16. continued
C. V. = 4.10 $\alpha = 0.05$
d. f. N = 2   d. f. D = 10

$\overline{X}_1 = 6091.4$ $s_1^2 = 667,494.3$

$\overline{X}_2 = 6519.75$ $s_2^2 = 425,494.25$

$\overline{X}_3 = 6831.5$ $s_3^2 = 1,881,561.667$

$X_{GM} = \frac{\sum X}{N} = 6450.923$

$s_B^2 = \frac{\sum n_i (\overline{X}_i - \overline{X}_{GM})^2}{k-1}$

$s_B^2 = \frac{5(6091.4-6450.923)^2 + 4(6519.75-6450.923)^2}{3-1}$

$+ \frac{4(6831.5-6450.923)^2}{3-1} = 622,293.987$

$s_W^2 = \frac{\sum (n_i - 1)s_i^2}{\sum (n_i - 1)}$

$= \frac{4(667494.3) + 3(425494.25) + 3(1881561.667)}{4 + 3 + 3}$

$= 959114.495$

$F = \frac{s_B^2}{s_W^2} = \frac{622293.987}{959114.495} = 0.6488$

0   ↑   4.10
    0.6488

Do not reject the null hypothesis. There is not enough evidence to support the claim that at least one mean is different from the others.

17.

H_0: $\mu_1 = \mu_2 = \mu_3$
H_1: At least one mean is different from the others. (claim)
$\alpha = 0.10$
d. f. N = 2   d. f. D = 19

$\overline{X}_1 = 233.33$ $s_1 = 28.225$
$\overline{X}_2 = 203.125$ $s_2 = 39.364$
$\overline{X}_3 = 155.625$ $s_3 = 28.213$

$\overline{X}_{GM} = 194.091$

17. continued

$$s_B^2 = \frac{21,729.735}{2} = 10,864.8675$$

$$s_W^2 = \frac{20,402.083}{19} = 1073.794$$

$$F = \frac{s_B^2}{s_W^2} = \frac{10,864.8675}{1073.794} = 10.12$$

P-value = 0.00102
Reject since P-value < 0.10.
The is enough evidence to support the claim that at least one mean is different from the others.

18.

$H_0: \mu_1 = \mu_2 = \mu_3$
$H_1:$ At least one mean is different from the others. (claim)
C. V. = 3.81 $\alpha = 0.05$
d. f. N = 2   d. f. D = 12

$\overline{X}_1 = 60.6$ $s_1 = 2.074$
$\overline{X}_2 = 54.4$ $s_2 = 2.302$
$\overline{X}_3 = 52.8$ $s_3 = 2.588$

$\overline{X}_{GM} = 55.93$

$$s_B^2 = \frac{169.7335}{2} = 84.867$$

$$s_W^2 = \frac{65.193696}{12} = 5.433$$

$$F = \frac{s_B^2}{s_W^2} = \frac{84.867}{5.433} = 15.62$$

Reject the null hypothesis. There is enough evidence to support the claim that at least one mean is different from the others.

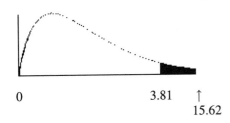

0   3.81   ↑
                                   15.62

19.

$H_0: \mu_1 = \mu_2 = \mu_3 = \mu_4$
$H_1:$ At least one mean is different. (claim)
C. V. = 5.29 $\alpha = 0.01$
d. f. N = 3   d. f. D = 16

$$\overline{X}_{GM} = \frac{42}{20} = 2.1$$

19. continued

$$s_B^2 = \frac{10.2}{3} = 3.4$$

$$s_W^2 = \frac{85.6193}{16} = 5.35$$

$$F = \frac{3.4}{5.35} = 0.636$$

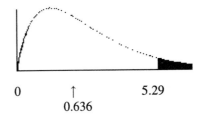

0   ↑   5.29
              0.636

Do not reject the null hypothesis. There is not enough evidence to support the claim that at least one mean is different. Students may have had discipline problems. Parents may not like the regular school district, etc.

REVIEW EXERCISES - CHAPTER 11

1.
$H_0:$ The number of sales is equally distributed over five regions. (claim)
$H_1:$ The null hypothesis is not true.

C. V. = 9.488   d. f. = 4
$E = \frac{1328}{5} = 265.6$

$$\chi^2 = \sum \frac{(O-E)^2}{E} = \frac{(236-265.6)^2}{265.6}$$

$$+ \frac{(324-265.6)^2}{265.6} + \frac{(182-265.6)^2}{265.6}$$

$$+ \frac{(221-265.6)^2}{265.6} + \frac{(365-265.6)^2}{265.6} = 87.14$$

Alternate Solution:

1. continued

O	E	O − E	(O − E)²	$\frac{(O-E)^2}{E}$
236	265.6	-29.6	876.18	3.299
324	265.6	58.4	3410.56	12.841
182	265.6	-83.6	6988.96	26.314
221	265.6	-44.6	1989.16	7.489
365	265.6	99.4	9880.36	37.200
				87.143

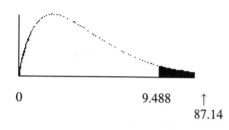

0   9.488   ↑
                     87.14

Reject the null hypothesis. There is enough evidence to reject the claim that the number of items sold in each region is the same.

2.

H_0: The ad produced the same number of responses in each county. (claim)

H_1: The null hypothesis is not true.

C. V. = 11.345   d. f. = 3

$$E = \frac{298}{4} = 74.5$$

$$\chi^2 = \frac{(87-74.5)^2}{74.5} + \frac{(62-74.5)^2}{74.5}$$

$$+ \frac{(56-74.5)^2}{74.5} + \frac{(93-74.5)^2}{74.5} = 13.38$$

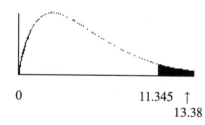

0   11.345 ↑
                   13.38

Reject the null hypothesis. There is enough evidence to reject the claim that the ad produced the same number of responses in each county.

3.

H_0: The gender of the individual is not related to whether or not a person would use the labels.

H_1: The gender is related to use of the labels. (claim)

3. continued

C. V. = 4.605   d. f. = 2

Gender	Yes	No	Undecided
Men	114(120.968)	30(22.258)	6(6.774)
Women	136(129.032)	16(23.742)	8(7.226)

$$\chi^2 = \frac{(114-120.968)^2}{120.968} + \frac{(30-22.258)^2}{22.258} + \frac{(6-6.774)^2}{6.774}$$

$$+ \frac{(136-129.032)^2}{129.032} + \frac{(16-23.742)^2}{23.742} + \frac{(8-7.226)^2}{7.226}$$

$$\chi^2 = 6.16$$

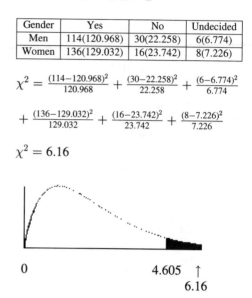

0   4.605 ↑
                  6.16

Reject the null hypothesis. There is enough evidence to support the claim that opinion is dependent on gender.

4.

H_0: The condiment preference is independent of the sex of the purchaser. (claim)

H_1: The condiment preference is dependent on the sex of the purchaser.

C. V. = 4.605   d. f. = 2

	Relish	Catsup	Mustard
Men	15(19.11)	18(15.29)	10(8.60)
Women	25(20.89)	14(16.71)	8(9.60)

$$\chi^2 = \sum \frac{(O-E)^2}{E} = \frac{(15-19.11)^2}{19.11} + \frac{(18-15.29)^2}{15.29}$$

$$+ \frac{(10-8.60)^2}{8.60} + \frac{(25-20.89)^2}{20.89} + \frac{(14-16.71)^2}{16.71}$$

$$+ \frac{(8-9.40)^2}{9.40} = 3.050$$

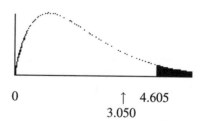

0   ↑ 4.605
        3.050

4. continued
Do not reject the null hypothesis. There is not enough evidence to reject the claim that the condiment chosen is independent of the gender of the individual.

5.
H_0: The type of investment is independent of the age of the investor.
H_1: The type of investment is dependent upon the age of the investor. (claim)
C. V. = 9.488   d. f. = 4

Age	Large	Small	Inter.
45	20(28.18)	10(15.45)	10(15.45)
65	42(33.82)	24(18.55)	24(18.55)

Age	CD	Bond
45	15(9.55)	45(31.36)
65	6(11.45)	24(37.64)

$$\chi^2 = \frac{(20-28.18)^2}{28.18} + \frac{(10-15.45)^2}{15.45} + \frac{(10-15.45)^2}{15.45}$$

$$+ \frac{(15-9.55)^2}{9.55} + \frac{(45-31.36)^2}{31.36} + \frac{(42-33.82)^2}{33.82} +$$

$$\frac{(24-18.55)^2}{18.55} + \frac{(24-18.55)^2}{18.55} + \frac{(6-11.45)^2}{11.45} +$$

$$\frac{(24-37.64)^2}{37.64} = 28.0$$

0   9.488   ↑
                    28.0

Reject the null hypothesis. There is enough evidence to support the claim that the type of investment is dependent on age.

6.
H_0: The type of pet a person purchases is independent of the gender of the purchaser.
H_1: The type of pet a person purchases is dependent upon the gender of the purchaser. (claim)
C. V. = 4.605   d. f. = 2 $\alpha = 0.10$

	Dog	Cat	Bird	Total
Males	32(37.5)	27(21.136)	16(16.364)	75
Females	23(17.5)	4(9.864)	8(7.636)	35
Total	55	31	24	90

6. continued
$$\chi^2 = \sum \frac{(O-E)^2}{E} = \frac{(32-37.5)^2}{37.5} + \frac{(27-21.136)^2}{21.136}$$

$$+ \frac{(16-16.364)^2}{16.364} + \frac{(23-17.5)^2}{17.5} + \frac{(4-9.864)^2}{9.864}$$

$$+ \frac{(8-7.636)^2}{7.636} = 7.674$$

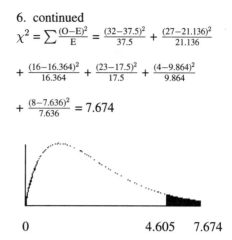

0   4.605   7.674

Reject the null hypothesis. There is enough evidence to support the claim that the type of pet purchased is related to the gender of the purchaser.

7.
H_0: $p_1 = p_2 = p_3$ (claim)
H_1: At least one proportion is different.
$\alpha = 0.01$ d. f. = 2
C. V. = 9.210

$$E(\text{work}) = \frac{80(114)}{240} = 38$$

$$E(\text{don't work}) = \frac{80(126)}{240} = 42$$

	16	17	18
work	45(38)	31(38)	38(38)
don't work	35(42)	49(42)	42(42)

$$\chi^2 = \frac{(45-38)^2}{38} + \frac{(31-38)^2}{38} + \frac{(38-38)^2}{38}$$

$$+ \frac{(35-42)^2}{42} + \frac{(49-42)^2}{42} + \frac{(42-42)^2}{42} = 4.912$$

Do not reject the null hypothesis. There is not enough evidence to reject the claim that the proportions are the same.

8.
H_0: $p_1 = p_2 = p_3 = p_4$ (claim)
H_1: At least one proportion is different.
C. V. = 7.851   d. f. = 3

$$E(\text{male}) = \frac{100(219)}{400} = 54.75$$

$$E(\text{female}) = \frac{100(181)}{400} = 45.25$$

213

8. continued

	May	June	July	Aug
Male	51(54.75)	47(54.75)	58(54.75)	63(54.75)
Female	49(45.25)	53(45.25)	42(45.25)	37(45.25)

$$\chi^2 = \frac{(51-54.75)^2}{54.75} + \frac{(47-54.75)^2}{54.75} + \frac{(58-54.75)^2}{54.75}$$

$$+ \frac{(63-54.75)^2}{54.75} + \frac{(49-45.25)^2}{45.25} + \frac{(53-45.25)^2}{45.25} +$$

$$\frac{(42-45.25)^2}{45.25} + \frac{(37-45.25)^2}{45.25} = 6.17$$

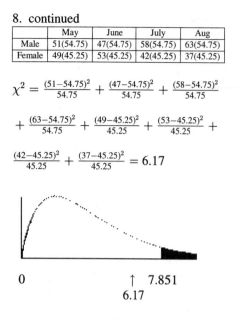

0   ↑ 7.851
                   6.17

Do not reject the null hypothesis. There is not enough evidence to reject the claim that the proportions are the same.

9.

H_0: $p_1 = p_2 = p_3 = p_4$
H_1: At least one proportion is different.
C. V. = 6.251   d. f. = 3

$$E(yes) = \frac{50(58)}{200} = 14.5$$

$$E(no) = \frac{50(142)}{200} = 35.5$$

	A	B	C	D
Yes	12(14.5)	15(14.5)	10(14.5)	21(14.5)
No	38(35.5)	35(35.5)	40(35.5)	29(35.5)

$$\chi^2 = \frac{(12-14.5)^2}{14.5} + \frac{(15-14.5)^2}{14.5} + \frac{(10-14.5)^2}{14.5} +$$

$$\frac{(21-14.5)^2}{14.5} + \frac{(38-35.5)^2}{35.5} + \frac{(35-35.5)^2}{35.5} +$$

$$+ \frac{(40-35.5)^2}{35.5} + \frac{(29-35.5)^2}{35.5} = 6.70$$

0   6.251 ↑
                         6.70

9. continued

Reject the null hypothesis. There is enough evidence to reject the claim that the proportions are the same.

10.

H_0: $p_1 = p_2 = p_3$ (claim)
H_1: At least one proportion is different.
C. V. = 9.210   d. f. = 2

$$E(yes) = \frac{200(186)}{600} = 62$$

$$E(no) = \frac{200(414)}{600} = 138$$

	#1	#2	#3
Yes	87(62)	56(62)	43(62)
No	113(138)	144(138)	157(138)

$$\chi^2 = \frac{(87-62)^2}{62} + \frac{(56-62)^2}{62} + \frac{(43-62)^2}{62}$$

$$+ \frac{(113-138)^2}{138} + \frac{(144-138)^2}{138} + \frac{(157-138)^2}{138}$$

$$\chi^2 = 23.89$$

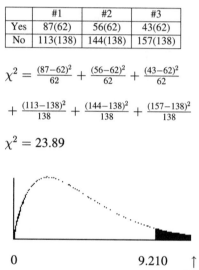

0   9.210   ↑
                          23.89

Reject the null hypothesis. There is enough evidence to reject the claim that the proportions are the same.

11.

H_0: $\mu_1 = \mu_2 = \mu_3$ (claim)
H_1: At least one mean is different from the others.
C. V. = 6.01 $\alpha = 0.01$
d. f. N = 2   d. f. D = 18

$\bar{X}_1 = 197.57$ $s_1^2 = 373.62$

$\bar{X}_2 = 295.57$ $s_2^2 = 6639.29$

$\bar{X}_3 = 103.14$ $s_3^2 = 181.48$

$\bar{X}_{GM} = \frac{4174}{21} = 198.76$

11. continued

$$s_B^2 = \frac{\sum n_i (\overline{X}_i - \overline{X}_{GM})^2}{k-1}$$

$$= \frac{7(197.57 - 198.76)^2 + 7(295.57 - 198.76)^2}{3-1}$$

$$+ \frac{7(103.14 - 198.76)^2}{3-1} = 64808.72$$

$$s_W^2 = \frac{\sum (n_i - 1)s_i^2}{\sum (n_i - 1)}$$

$$= \frac{6(373.62) + 6(6639.29) + 6(181.48)}{6 + 6 + 6} = 2398.13$$

$$F = \frac{s_B^2}{s_W^2} = \frac{64808.72}{2398.13} = 27.02$$

0   6.01   ↑
                                 27.02

Reject. At least one mean is different from the others.

12.

H_0: $\mu_1 = \mu_2 = \mu_3$
H_1: At least one mean is different from the others. (claim)
C. V. = 3.81 $\alpha = 0.05$
d. f.N = 2   d. f. D = 13

$\overline{X}_1 = 106.286$ $s_1 = 73.234$
$\overline{X}_2 = 97.0$ $s_2 = 22.804$
$\overline{X}_3 = 73.0$ $s_3 = 12.910$

$$\overline{X}_{GM} = \frac{1521}{16} = 95.06$$

$$s_B^2 = \frac{\sum n_i (\overline{X}_i - \overline{X}_{GM})^2}{k-1}$$

$$= \frac{7(106.286 - 95.06)^2}{2} + \frac{5(97 - 95.06)^2}{2}$$

$$+ \frac{4(73 - 95.06)^2}{2} = 1423.8$$

$$s_W^2 = \frac{\sum (n_i - 1)s_i^2}{\sum (n_i - 1)}$$

$$= \frac{6(73.234)^2 + 4(22.804)^2 + 3(12.910)^2}{6 + 4 + 3}$$

$$= 2673.8$$

12. continued

$$F = \frac{s_B^2}{s_W^2} = \frac{1423.8}{2673.8} = 0.533$$

Do not reject the null hypothesis. There is not enough evidence to support the claim that at least one mean is different from the others.

13.

H_0: $\mu_1 = \mu_2 = \mu_3 = \mu_4$ (claim)
H_1: At least one mean is different from the others.
C. V. = 3.86 $\alpha = 0.05$
d. f. N = 3   d. f. D = 9

$\overline{X}_1 = 7$ $s_1 = 0.816$

$\overline{X}_2 = 6.333$ $s_2 = 0.578$

$\overline{X}_3 = 11.667$ $s_3 = 0.577$

$\overline{X}_4 = 7.333$ $s_4 = 1.528$

$\overline{X}_{GM} = 8$

$$s_B^2 = \frac{\sum n_i (\overline{X}_i - \overline{X}_{GM})^2}{k-1}$$

$$s_B^2 = \frac{4(7-8)^2}{3} + \frac{3(6.333-8)^2}{3} + \frac{3(11.667-8)^2}{3}$$

$$+ \frac{3(7.333-8)^2}{3} = \frac{54.01}{3} = 18.0$$

$$s_W^2 = \frac{\sum (n_i - 1)s_i^2}{\sum (n_i - 1)}$$

$$s_W^2 = \frac{3(0.816)^2 + 2(0.578)^2 + 2(0.577)^2 + 2(1.528)^2}{3 + 2 + 2 + 2}$$

$$s_W^2 = 0.889$$

$$F = \frac{s_B^2}{s_W^2} = \frac{18.0}{0.889} = 20.25$$

Reject. At least one mean is different from the others.

14.

H_0: $\mu_1 = \mu_2 = \mu_3$
H_1: At least one mean is different from the others. (claim)

C. V. = 3.89 $\alpha = 0.05$
d. f. N = 2   d. f. D = 12

14. continued

$\bar{X}_1 = 26 \qquad \bar{X}_2 = 10.429 \qquad \bar{X}_3 = 17.5$

$s_1^2 = 50 \qquad s_2^2 = 34.95 \qquad s_3^2 = 83$

$\bar{X}_{GM} = \frac{\sum X}{N} = \frac{247}{15} = 16.467$

$s_B^2 = \frac{\sum n_i(\bar{X}_i - \bar{X}_{GM})^2}{k-1}$

$= \frac{4(26-16.467)^2 + 7(10.429-16.467)^2}{3-1}$

$+ \frac{4(17.5-16.467)^2}{3-1} = 311.5$

$s_W^2 = \frac{\sum(n_i-1)s_i^2}{\sum(n_i-1)}$

$= \frac{3(50) + 6(34.95) + 3(83)}{3 + 6 + 3} = 50.726$

$F = \frac{s_B^2}{s_W^2} = \frac{311.5}{50.726} = 6.141$

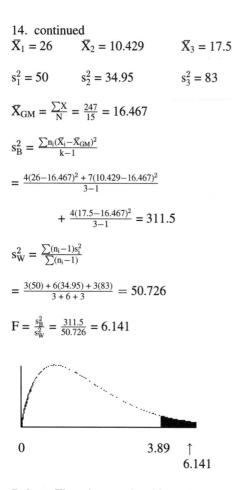

0   3.89   ↑

              6.141

Reject. There is enough evidence to support the claim that at least one mean is different from the others.

15.
H_0: $\mu_1 = \mu_2 = \mu_3$
H_1: At least one mean is different.
C. V. = 3.89 $\qquad \alpha = 0.05$
d. f. N = 2 $\qquad$ d. f. D = 12

$F = \frac{4300.8}{65.9} = 65.263$

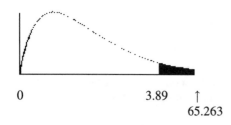

0   3.89   ↑

              65.263

Reject. At least one mean is different from the others.

16.
H_0: $\mu_1 = \mu_2 = \mu_3$
H_1: At least one mean is different from the others.
C. V. = 3.89 $\qquad \alpha = 0.05$
d. f. N = 2 $\qquad$ d. f. D = 12

$\bar{X}_1 = 74 \qquad \bar{X}_2 = 65.8 \qquad \bar{X}_3 = 90.6$
$s_1^2 = 368 \qquad s_2^2 = 258.7 \qquad s_3^2 = 25.3$

$\bar{X}_{GM} = \frac{\sum X}{n} = \frac{1152}{15} = 76.8$

$s_B^2 = \frac{\sum n_i(\bar{X}_i - \bar{X}_{GM})^2}{k-1} = \frac{5(74-76.8)^2 + 5(65.8-76.8)^2}{3-1}$

$+ \frac{5(90.6-76.8)^2}{3-1} = 798.2$

$s_W^2 = \frac{\sum(n_i-1)s_i^2}{\sum(n_i-1)}$

$= \frac{4(368) + 4(258.7) + 4(25.3)}{4 + 4 + 4} = 217.333$

$F = \frac{s_B^2}{s_W^2} = \frac{798.2}{217.333} = 3.673$

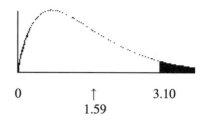

0   ↑   3.89

         3.673

Do not reject the null hypothesis. There is not enough evidence to conclude that there is a difference in the means.

17.
H_0: $\mu_1 = \mu_2 = \mu_3 = \mu_4$
H_1: At least one mean is different from the others.
C. V. = 3.10 $\qquad \alpha = 0.05$
d. f. N = 3 $\qquad$ d. f. D = 20

$F = \frac{20.264}{12.7585} = 1.59$

0   ↑   3.10

         1.59

17. continued
Do not reject the null hypothesis. There is
not enough evidence to conclude that there
is a difference in the means.

18.
H_0: $\mu_1 = \mu_2 = \mu_3$
H_1: At least one mean is different from the
others. (claim)
C. V. = 6.36 $\alpha = 0.01$
d. f. N = 2   d. f. D = 15
$F = \frac{25.287}{9.353} = 2.704$

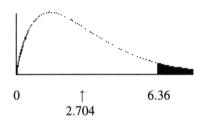

0   ↑   6.36
          2.704

Do not reject. Ther is not enough evidence
to support the claim that at least one mean is
different from the others.

CHAPTER 11 QUIZ

1. False, it is one-tailed right.
2. True
3. False, there is little agreement between
observed and expected frequencies.
4. False, there could be a significant
difference between only some of the means.
5. False, degrees of freedom are used to
find the critical value.
6. False, the null hypothesis should not be
rejected.
7. c
8. b
9. d
10. d
11. a
12. a
13. 6
14. Independent
15. Right
16. At least five
17. ANOVA

18. H_0: The number of advertisements is
equally distributed over five geographic
regions.
H_1: The number of advertisements is not
equally distributed over five regions.

18. continued
C. V. = 9.488   d. f. = 4   E = 240.4
$\chi^2 = \sum \frac{(O-E)^2}{E} = 45.4$
Reject the null hypothesis. There is enough
evidence to reject the claim that the number
of advertisements is equally distributed.

19. H_0: The ads produced the same number
of responses. (claim)
H_1: The ads produced different numbers of
responses.
C. V. = 13.277   d. f. = 4   E = 64.6
$\chi^2 = \sum \frac{(O-E)^2}{E} = 12.6$
Do not reject the null hypothesis. There is
not enough evidence to reject the claim that
the ads produced the same number of
responses.

20. H_0: 48% of the customers order
hamburgers, 33% order chicken, 19% order
salad. (claim)
H_1: The distribution is not the same as
stated in the null hypothesis.
C. V. = 5.991   d. f. = 2
$\chi^2 = 4.6$
Do not reject the null hypothesis. There is
not enough evidence to reject the manager's
claim.

21. H_0: Each gift was purchased with the
same frequency.   (claim)
H_1: The gifts were not purchased with the
same frequency.
C. V. = 9.21   d. f. = 2
$\chi^2 = 73.1$
Reject the null hypothesis. There is enough
evidence to reject the claim that the gifts
were purchased with the same frequency.

22. H_0: The type of novel purchased is
independent of the gender of the purchaser.
(claim)
H_1: The type of novel purchased is
dependent on the gender of the purchaser.
C. V. = 5.991   d. f. = 2
$\chi^2 = 132.9$
Reject the null hypothesis. There is enough
evidence to reject the claim that the novel
purchased is independent of the gender of
the purchaser.

23. H_0: The type of pizza ordered is
independent of the age of the purchaser.

23. continued
H_1: The type of pizza ordered is dependent on the age of the purchaser. (claim)
C. V. = 14.684   d. f. = 9
$\chi^2 = 107.3$
Reject the null hypothesis. There is enough evidence to support the claim that the type of pizza ordered is related to the age of the purchaser.

24. H_0: The color of the pennant purchased is independent of the gender of the purchaser. (claim)
H_1: The color of the pennant purchased is dependent on the gender of the purchaser.
C. V. = 4.605   d. f. = 2
$\chi^2 = 5.6$
Reject the null hypothesis. There is enough evidence to reject the claim that the color of the pennant purchased is independent of the gender of the purchaser.

25. H_0: $\mu_1 = \mu_2 = \mu_3$ (claim)
H_1: At least one mean is different from the others.
C. V. = 3.55
$s_B^2 = 785.333$ $s_W^2 = 6607.238$
$F = \frac{785.333}{6607.238} = 0.119$
Do not reject. There is not enough evidence to say there is a difference in the means.

26. H_0: $\mu_1 = \mu_2 = \mu_3 = \mu_4$ (claim)
H_1: At least one mean is different from the others.
C. V. = 3.10
$s_B^2 = 42.37$ $s_W^2 = 10.125$
$F = \frac{42.37}{10.125} = 4.185$
Reject H_0. At least one mean is different from the others.

27. H_0: $\mu_1 = \mu_2 = \mu_3$
H_1: At least one mean is different from the others. (claim)
C. V. = 6.36 $\alpha = 0.01$
$s_B^2 = 4.936$ $s_W^2 = 6.975$
$F = 0.71$
Do not reject H_0. There is not enough evidence to show there is a difference in the means.

28. H_0: $\mu_1 = \mu_2 = \mu_3$
H_1: At least one mean is different from the others. (claim)
C. V. = 3.63 $\alpha = 0.05$

28. continued
$s_B^2 = 13.379$ $s_W^2 = 271.486$
$F = 0.049$
Do not reject H_0. There is not enough evidence to say there is a difference in the means.

29. H_0: $\mu_1 = \mu_2 = \mu_3$
H_1: At least one mean is different from the others. (claim)
C. V. = 3.89 $\alpha = 0.05$
$s_B^2 = 3913.87$ $s_W^2 = 78.767$
$F = 49.689$
Reject H_0. At least one mean is different from the others.

A-1

A-1. $9! = 9 \cdot 8 \cdot 7 \cdot 6 \cdot 5 \cdot 4 \cdot 3 \cdot 2 \cdot 1 = 362,880$

A-2. $7! = 7 \cdot 6 \cdot 5 \cdot 4 \cdot 3 \cdot 2 \cdot 1 = 5040$

A-3. $5! = 5 \cdot 4 \cdot 3 \cdot 2 \cdot 1 = 120$

A-4. $0! = 1$

A-5. $1! = 1$

A-6. $3! = 3 \cdot 2 \cdot 1 = 6$

A-7. $\frac{12!}{9!} = \frac{12 \cdot 11 \cdot 10 \cdot 9!}{9!} = 1320$

A-8. $\frac{10!}{2!} = \frac{10 \cdot 9 \cdot 8 \cdot 7 \cdot 6 \cdot 5 \cdot 4 \cdot 3 \cdot 2!}{2!}$

$= 1,814,400$

A-9. $\frac{5!}{3!} = \frac{5 \cdot 4 \cdot 3!}{3!} = 20$

A-10. $\frac{11!}{7!} = \frac{11 \cdot 10 \cdot 9 \cdot 8 \cdot 7!}{7!} = 7920$

A-11. $\frac{9!}{(4!)(5!)} = \frac{9 \cdot 8 \cdot 7 \cdot 6 \cdot 5!}{4 \cdot 3 \cdot 2 \cdot 1 \cdot 5!} = 126$

A-12. $\frac{10!}{(7!)(3!)} = \frac{10 \cdot 9 \cdot 8 \cdot 7!}{3 \cdot 2 \cdot 1 \cdot 7!} = 120$

A-13. $\frac{8!}{4!4!} = \frac{8 \cdot 7 \cdot 6 \cdot 5 \cdot 4!}{4 \cdot 3 \cdot 2 \cdot 1 \cdot 4!} = 70$

A-14. $\frac{15!}{12!3!} = \frac{15 \cdot 14 \cdot 13 \cdot 12!}{3 \cdot 2 \cdot 1 \cdot 12!} = 455$

A-15. $\frac{10!}{(10!)(0!)} = \frac{10!}{10! \cdot 1} = 1$

A-16. $\frac{5!}{3!2!1!} = \frac{5 \cdot 4 \cdot 3!}{3! \cdot 2 \cdot 1 \cdot 1} = 10$

A-17. $\frac{8!}{3!3!2!} = \frac{8 \cdot 7 \cdot 6 \cdot 5 \cdot 4 \cdot 3!}{3! \cdot 3 \cdot 2 \cdot 1 \cdot 2 \cdot 1} = 560$

A-18. $\frac{11!}{7!2!2!} = \frac{11 \cdot 10 \cdot 9 \cdot 8 \cdot 7!}{7! \cdot 2 \cdot 1 \cdot 2 \cdot 1} = 1980$

A-19. $\frac{10!}{3!2!5!} = \frac{10 \cdot 9 \cdot 8 \cdot 7 \cdot 6 \cdot 5!}{3 \cdot 2 \cdot 1 \cdot 2 \cdot 1 \cdot 5!} = 2520$

A-20. $\frac{6!}{2!2!2!} = \frac{6 \cdot 5 \cdot 4 \cdot 3 \cdot 2!}{2 \cdot 1 \cdot 2 \cdot 1 \cdot 2!} = 90$

A-2

A-21.

X	X^2	$X - \overline{X}$	$(X - \overline{X})^2$
9	81	-3.1	9.61
17	289	4.9	24.01
32	1024	19.9	396.01
16	256	3.9	15.21
8	64	-4.1	16.81
2	4	-10.1	102.01
9	81	-3.1	9.61
7	49	-5.1	26.01
3	9	-9.1	82.81
18	324	5.9	34.81
121	2181		716.9

$\sum X = 121 \quad \overline{X} = \frac{121}{10} = 12.1 \quad \sum X^2 = 2181$

$(\sum X)^2 = 121^2 = 14641 \quad \sum (X-\overline{X})^2 = 716.9$

A-22.

X	X^2	$X - \overline{X}$	$(X - \overline{X})^2$
4	16	-3	9
12	144	5	25
9	81	2	4
13	169	6	36
0	0	-7	49
6	36	-1	1
2	4	-5	25
10	100	3	9
56	550		158

$\sum X = 56 \quad \overline{X} = \frac{56}{8} = 7 \quad \sum X^2 = 550$

$(\sum X)^2 = 56^2 = 3136 \quad \sum (X-\overline{X})^2 = 158$

A-23.

X	X^2	$X - \overline{X}$	$(X - \overline{X})^2$
5	25	-1.4	1.96
12	144	5.6	31.36
8	64	1.6	2.56
3	9	-3.4	11.56
4	16	-2.4	5.76
32	258		53.20

$\sum X = 32 \quad \overline{X} = \frac{32}{5} = 6.4 \quad \sum X^2 = 258$

$(\sum X)^2 = 32^2 = 1024 \quad \sum (X-\overline{X})^2 = 53.2$

A-24.

X	X^2	$X - \overline{X}$	$(X - \overline{X})^2$
6	36	-12.75	163.5625
2	4	-16.75	280.5625
18	324	-0.75	0.5625
30	900	11.25	126.5625
31	961	12.25	150.0625
42	1764	23.25	540.5625
16	256	-2.75	7.5625
5	25	-13.75	189.0625
150	4270		1457.5000

$\sum X = 150$ $\overline{X} = \frac{150}{8} = 18.75$ $\sum X^2 = 4270$

$(\sum X)^2 = 150^2 = 22500$ $\sum(X-\overline{X})^2 = 1457.5$

A-25.

X	X^2	$X - \overline{X}$	$(X - \overline{X})^2$
80	6400	14.4	207.36
76	5776	10.4	108.16
42	1764	-23.6	556.96
53	2809	-12.6	158.76
77	5929	11.4	129.96
328	22678		1161.20

$\sum X = 328$ $\overline{X} = \frac{328}{5} = 65.6$ $\sum X^2 = 22678$

$(\sum X)^2 = 328^2 = 107584$ $\sum(X-\overline{X})^2 = 1161.2$

A-26.

X	X^2	$X - \overline{X}$	$(X - \overline{X})^2$
123	15129	-15.17	230.1289
132	17424	-6.17	38.0689
216	46656	77.83	6057.5089
98	9604	-40.17	1613.6289
146	21316	7.83	61.3089
114	12996	-24.17	584.1889
829	123125		8584.8334

$\sum X = 829$ $\overline{X} = \frac{829}{6} = 138.17$

$\sum X^2 = 123125$ $(\sum X)^2 = 829^2 = 687241$

$\sum(X-\overline{X})^2 = 8584.8334$

A-27.

X	X^2	$X - \overline{X}$	$(X - \overline{X})^2$
53	2809	-16.3	265.69
72	5184	2.7	7.29
81	6561	11.7	136.89
42	1764	-27.3	745.29
63	3969	-6.3	39.69
71	5041	1.7	2.89
73	5329	3.7	13.69
85	7225	15.7	246.49
98	9604	28.7	823.69
55	3025	-14.3	204.49
693	50511		2486.10

$\sum X = 693$ $\overline{X} = \frac{693}{10} = 69.3$ $\sum X^2 = 50511$

$(\sum X)^2 = 693^2 = 480249$ $\sum(X-\overline{X})^2 = 2486.1$

A-28.

X	X^2	$X - \overline{X}$	$(X - \overline{X})^2$
43	1849	-38.8	1505.44
32	1024	-49.8	2480.04
116	13456	34.2	1169.64
98	9604	16.2	262.44
120	14400	38.2	1459.24
409	40333		6876.80

$\sum X = 409$ $\overline{X} = \frac{409}{5} = 81.8$ $\sum X^2 = 40333$

$(\sum X)^2 = 409^2 = 167281$ $\sum(X-\overline{X})^2 = 6876.8$

A-29.

X	X^2	$X - \overline{X}$	$(X - \overline{X})^2$
12	144	-41	1681
52	2704	-1	1
36	1296	-17	289
81	6561	28	784
63	3969	10	100
74	5476	21	441
318	20150		3296

$\sum X = 318$ $\overline{X} = \frac{318}{6} = 53$ $\sum X^2 = 20150$

$(\sum X)^2 = 318^2 = 101124$ $\sum(X-\overline{X})^2 = 3296$

A-30.

X	X^2	$X - \overline{X}$	$(X - \overline{X})^2$
− 9	81	− 5.67	32.1489
− 12	144	− 8.67	75.1689
18	324	21.33	454.9689
0	0	3.33	11.0889
− 2	4	1.33	1.7689
− 15	225	− 11.67	136.1889
− 20	778		711.3334

$\overline{X} = \frac{-20}{6} = -3.33$ $(\sum X)^2 = -20^2 = 400$

A-3

A-31.

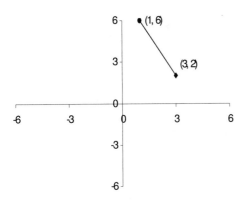

A-32.

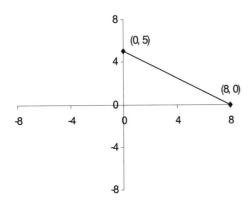

A-33.

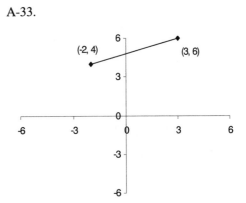

A-34.

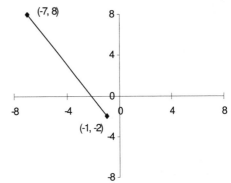

A-35.

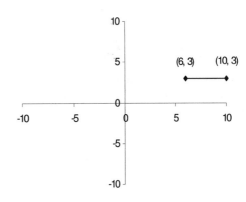

A-36.

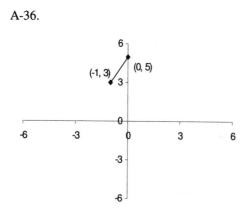

Two points are: (0, 5) and (-1, 3).

A-37.

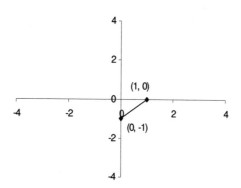

Two points are: (1, 0) and (0, -1).

A-38.

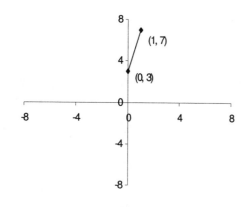

Two points are: (1, 7) and (0, 3).

A-39

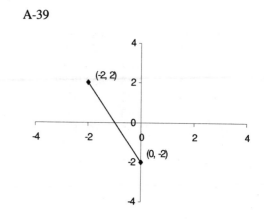

Two points are: (-2, 2) and (0, -2).

A-40.

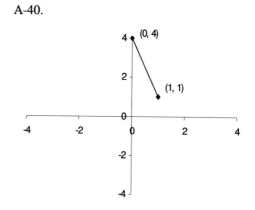

Two points are: (1, 1) and (0, 4)

Notes

Notes

Notes

Notes